STUDENTS TO MARS!

The Mars Society's
International Design Competition
for High School Students 2022-2023

Foreword by Nicole Willett, M.S.
Director of Education

Students to Mars!
The Mars Society's International Design Competition for High School Students 2022-2023

Polaris Books
1100 Johnson Road
Suite 18257
Golden, CO 80402
www.polarisbooks.org

Copyright © 2024 by The Mars Society
© All rights reserved. No part of this book may be used or reproduced in any manner whatsoever without written permission from the publisher except in the case of brief quotations embodied in critical articles or reviews.

Paperback ISBN: 979-8-9902823-3-9
eBook ISBN: 979-8-9902823-4-6

Layout and cover by Marie Stirk
Cover art by Pat Rawlings, NASA

TABLE OF CONTENTS

Foreword v
Introduction 1
Team I: Valles Marineris Exploration Mission 7
Ares-1: Student Designed Mars Mission 61
N.E.W. E.R.A. 101
Polemos 165
The Niger Vallis Mission 199
Group A Mars Mission 211
M.A.R.T.I.A.N. Mission 259
Moses I 311
Exploring the Red Planet 349
Mission to Mars 2023 383

FOREWORD

A HUMAN MISSION to Mars has long been the central goal of The Mars Society, under the leadership of Dr. Robert Zubrin. His vision and passion have inspired millions, including myself. In 1988, as a high school student, I came across an article titled "Human Mission to Mars" in *National Geographic*. Shortly after, I discovered Dr. Zubrin's work, and from that moment on, I became a dedicated advocate of Mars exploration. Since 2012, I have served as the Director of Education for The Mars Society, a role that has allowed me to channel my passion for teaching and space exploration. My background as a secondary school educator and adjunct professor of astronomy fueled this journey, and now, I am proud to dedicate myself full-time as the Director of Education Programs for The Mars Society.

The Humans to Mars Engineering Design Contest is an exceptional educational experience, integrating various scientific disciplines into one cohesive STEM challenge for students. Beyond mastering STEM subjects, students also learn leadership, teamwork, and the importance of compromise—skills that will serve them well into adulthood. The students who have participated in this contest have consistently excelled. Their creativity, critical thinking, and determination have been nothing short of remarkable, and it has been an incredible privilege to witness their growth as an educator.

The importance of educating students about a human mission to Mars is vast and far-reaching. This is not only real science but a field with practical applications across numerous areas of research and development, including engineering, physics, astronomy, geology, astrobiology, and many more. Whether or not we are directly involved, a human mission to Mars is on the horizon. It is crucial for students and educators to recognize the significance of this mission as we take steps toward becoming a multiplanetary species.

We aim to ensure that students are at the forefront of innovation, not left wondering what they could have achieved had they been given the opportunity to participate in such a remarkable project. Much like the Apollo missions to the Moon, a mission to Mars has the potential to inspire hundreds of thousands of students to pursue careers in STEM fields. By engaging in this project, students can explore subjects that ignite their curiosity, conduct meaningful research, and participate in debates that challenge their thinking on how they would design and implement a human mission to Mars.

Critical thinking is essential, particularly in a project fraught with complex challenges. Collaboration, whether among students or professional scientists and engineers, is key to the success of any mission of this magnitude. In an era where students are often placed in front of screens, this hands-on project—developed by me in partnership with the Mars Society—offers an exciting alternative. It combines engaging activities with technology use for research, shifting the focus from passive learning to active participation.

A human mission to Mars will showcase to the world the resilience and adaptability of humankind. With determination and ingenuity, we can achieve this ambitious goal. And when children witness the first human setting foot on Mars, the sense of wonder and possibility they will feel is immeasurable. This inspiration will not only propel students into STEM fields but will also have a lasting impact across many other areas of research.

The journey to Mars represents not only the next great leap in space exploration but also an unparalleled opportunity to inspire and educate the next generation. As educators, scientists, and dreamers, it is our responsibility to ensure that students are part of this monumental endeavor. By teaching them about a human mission to Mars, we are giving them the tools to think critically, collaborate, and innovate—skills that are essential not only for space exploration but for the future of humanity.

The Mars Society's work, particularly through initiatives like the Humans to Mars Engineering Design Contest, allows students to immerse themselves in the challenges and wonders of space travel. It is through this engagement that we hope to foster the curiosity, resilience, and determination that will propel them—and us—toward a future where Mars is within our reach.

As we look to the horizon and the promise of Mars, I am confident that the students of today will become the pioneers of tomorrow. Together, we will continue to push the boundaries of what is possible, ensuring that the legacy of human exploration lives on, not only in the red dust of Mars but in the minds and hearts of those who dare to dream.

Join us for next year's contest or implement the project into your classrooms this school year. Contact Nicole Willett, Director of Education Programs for more information.

NICOLE WILLETT is the Director of Education Programs for The Mars Society and has been the driving force behind its educational initiatives since 2012. With a Bachelor of Science in Biology and a Master of Science in Astronomy, Nicole has been a passionate advocate for human exploration of Mars since she first read the November 1988 *National Geographic* article titled *Mission to Mars*. Shortly after, she discovered Dr. Robert Zubrin's Mars Direct concept, which solidified her commitment to Mars advocacy.

Nicole plays a key role in promoting science and space education. She maintains The Mars Society's educational website, regularly writes for the Society's blog, *The Red Planet Pen,* and contributes articles to *Marspedia.org* and other online magazines. She has spearheaded engineering design competitions for high school students worldwide, aiming to inspire the next generation of space explorers.

In addition to her ongoing projects, Nicole is developing a comprehensive Mars curriculum for K-12 students and collaborates with educators, organizations, and students on various global initiatives to advance space and science education.

INTRODUCTION
A NEW WAY TO TEACH SCIENCE

DR. ROBERT ZUBRIN
PRESIDENT, THE MARS SOCIETY

AROUND THE WORLD, in all the best university engineering programs, students encounter at some point a class different from all the others. This is the engineering design class, within which, instead of being tested as individuals on their mastery of lectures and texts, the class is challenged to work as a team to design a complex engineering system capable of meeting a difficult set of requirements.

For example, an aerospace engineering class might be tasked to design a new high-performance, low-cost fighter aircraft, with speed, range, ceiling, maneuverability, weaponry, survivability, and producibility capabilities all exceeding specified lower limits. Typically, the class might then divide into subgroups, with each assigned to find the best solutions to critical areas, such as aerodynamics, propulsion, weaponry, structures, and cost.

Inevitability, the best solutions in each area will conflict with all the rest. For example, more powerful engines would maximize the aircraft's speed, but take away mass that could be

Introduction

used for more weapons or stronger structures, and improving anything almost always leads to higher costs. So trades need to be made to try to find a compromise that hopefully enables the best aircraft overall. It is a deeply creative process, which is sometimes intensified further by having classes from different universities all work on the same design problem, and compete their designs against each other in intercollegiate tournaments.

I graduated college with a bachelor's degree in applied mathematics, and taught secondary school science and math for several years before I went back to graduate school to become an engineer. In consequence I did not encounter an engineering design class until *after* I had been a teacher. When I did, it immediately struck me that engineering design classes could provide a terrific methodology for teaching science in high schools as well.

I didn't do anything about it for four decades, but in the summer of 2022 I made use of my position as head of the Mars Society to give the idea a try. So in April, we made a public announcement that this summer the Mars Society would offer a six-week Mars mission design class and contest, open to students anywhere in the world. We set an admission fee of $50, low enough to make it affordable to almost anyone, but high enough to keep out freeloaders.

Everything would be done by zoom, making location irrelevant, but teams were organized roughly by time zone, to facilitate intra-team collaboration. Forty students signed up, who were divided into five teams. Team 1 was from Europe and the Middle East, which its largest contingent from Poland. Team 2 was from India and East Asia. Teams 3, 5, and 6 were from western, eastern, and central time zone North America respectively. (Team 4 didn't work out, so its members were divided among the rest.).

The class began with two weeks of lectures from twelve different experts specializing in various aspects of Mars mission design, ranging from astrobiology and geology to life support and nuclear engineering. This was to provide background knowledge. However, we made no attempt to coordinate the messages delivered by each expert into a party line. Some of the viewpoints, and suggested readings offered by the lecturers were frankly contradictory. But that is how it is in the real world. It was up to the students to sort out what made the most sense.

Then with this background knowledge in hand, the design teams went to work. The problem they were given was to design a human Mars mission with the greatest possible scientific return assuming a transportation system capable of delivering up to 30 metric tons and a crew of up to six people to the surface of Mars. It was up to the teams to determine their landing site, the science objectives, the crew size, skills, and equipment, and duration of the stay, with up to 18 months allowable. Then they had to design their exploration plan and all their equipment accordingly.

As with any good design problem, these requirements contradicted each other. For example, to first order, a larger crew with the longest possible stay time on Mars maximizes the mission exploration capability. But the consumables and accommodations required to support them take away mass that could be used for more extensive equipment, for example pressurized rovers or piloted helicopters that could greatly expand the crew's effective exploratory range.

The design challenge specifically excluded consideration of the interplanetary exploration system. The latter is NASA's obsession, to the exclusion of the mission's scientific purpose. That is why the space agency's human Mars mission designs—which involve 30-day surface stays directed to the scientifically least interesting areas—are completely absurd. But there is no point going to Mars unless you can do something useful when you get there. The purpose of the mission needs to come first, with mission and systems designs following.

Introduction

The students took to this challenge with gusto, spending three weeks working hard in their teams, with minimal guidance from coaches assigned to each team, to develop and write up their designs.

Then came the time for the shootout, which occurred over three days. On the first day, each team had 30 minutes to present their designs to a panel of expert judges. That is how college engineering design contests are ordinarily done. But then we through in a spin. The teams were given 30 minutes each on the second day to rip apart the designs of their competitors. Then we had a third day in which each team had a chance to defend its design against the attacks from the rest.

This latter procedure is not customary in university engineering design contests. But it approximates how things happen in the real world. In the real world, when you propose a design solution for a NASA mission or technology need, you have competitors out there who try to tear you down. (Believe me on this. I know.) The process of attack and defense in our contest was a bit more civilized than that which occurs between competitors in the cutthroat free market, because in our contest adversarial critics had to make their attacks openly, rather than behind their targets' backs. But still, the resulting intellectual dust-up provided scope for the kids to invoke their competitive instincts, and they loved it.

The results were amazing. All the teams delivered work that was way above high school level. You don't need to take my word for it. The entire course,[1] including videos of the expert lectures, the teams' design presentations, attacks and defenses can be viewed online. [2]

Of course, not everyone could win. The east coast American team took first prize for science, the western American team won decisively on engineering, the Asian team took the human factors design prize, and the Europeans—who thought creatively on how to reduce overall program expense by generating income—ran away with the prize on cost. While only winning one category, the Asian team also placed well on most of the others, and so won the contest overall.

I believe that what occurred in this class is worthy of broad attention. Its value goes way beyond the course's direct impact on a small group of students (and hopefully NASA Mars mission designs!) It has the potential to make educational history. The engineering design differs from conventional classes by not just asking students to master some material for a test, but to put their knowledge into action by working as a team to design some complex engineering system. By doing so, it reverses the conventional relationship of students to scientific knowledge. Instead of knowledge being a burden ("How much of this will we need to know for the test?") it becomes a tool, or even a magic sword if you will ("There must be a better way to do this. We need to find it!")

By delivering as they did, the students showed that this same creative methodology can be brought into high schools. Furthermore, they showed the value of debate. In real life, design engineering is a contact sport. So is pure science, for that matter. Consider the uproar over the recent claims made for biosignatures in the Venus atmosphere, or the 1996 Alan Hills meteorite claims, or the results of the Viking life detection experiments performed on Mars in 1976. Science is never settled. Scientists and engineers need to be able to defend their ideas. To give students a chance to learn how science really makes its way forward, they should be given a chance to mix it up themselves.

So have a look. The designs of the teams in the 2022 and 2023 contests are presented in this book. The kids had a blast, and the results were grand.

Programs like this should be implemented everywhere.

REFERENCES

1. Mars Society Concludes Its International Mission to Mars Design Class https://www.marssociety.org/news/2022/08/17/mars-society-concludes-its-international-mission-to-mars-design-class-competition-for-high-school-students/ (accessed Nov 1, 2024)
2. Videos of Mars mission design teams https://drive.google.com/file/d/1ZQM4p4MDem2G8uBxMiEYbIXkcBTDBDVN/view (accessed Nov 1, 2024)

TEAM I
VALLES MARINERIS EXPLORATION MISSION

ANTONI KLEJMAN
TEAM LEADER, ENGINEERING, SCIENCE

EMILIA ANDRES
ENGINEERING, SCIENCE

KLAUDIA WALCZAK
ENGINEERING, SCIENCE

RACHEL HWANG
LIFE SUPPORT

LEONARD KOCH
ENERGY, CREW SELECTION, BUDGET

KLEOUR APPROACH

Assuming our mission could be the only human landing on Mars in the foreseeable future, we intend to visit the site where we expect to find answers to the most relevant questions:

- Was there life on Mars?
- Is there life on Mars?
- Could we live on Mars in the future?

We have created a mission which builds on existing or upcoming technologies which have at least a Technology Readiness Level (TRL) of 5. This means there is a good chance they will be available at the proposed launch date in about 10 years.

As our mission includes extensive usage of vehicles, the core technologies are energy production, its efficient use, distribution and storage. All primary systems are designed to be interchangeable and multiuse to provide several layers of security and redundancy for mission-critical functions and prioritise the survival of the astronauts.

We propose to land a supply mission 2 years before the astronauts arrival, to automatically produce all the required water, propellant, food and materials in advance. This way we avoid the risks of the ISRU systems failing during the main mission period and endangering the life of the astronauts. We also intend to produce consumables for our scientific research on-site to reduce mission weight. The experience from the production of numerous resources will be a part of the scientific results, serving potential future missions or colonisation. Having an automated resource base in place will support future landings on Mars.

LANDING SITE SELECTION

Valles Marineris combines most features we expect from a perfect landing site:

- Unique geology (1) and landscapes—valleys, caves and land slopes;
- Possible traces of flowing water;
- Most "extreme" Mars environments, potentially harbouring traces of life;
- Exposure of the geological sandwich;
- One of the highest pressures and temperatures on Mars.
- The specific landing site needs to support the basecamp. We have chosen Candor Chasma, as it has the best combination of features:
- It is relatively flat and therefore easy and safe to land on;
- Has an abundance of water-rich regolith (2) with an average of 40% water content within the first metre of depth;
- It provides mostly uninterrupted solar irradiation for solar panels.

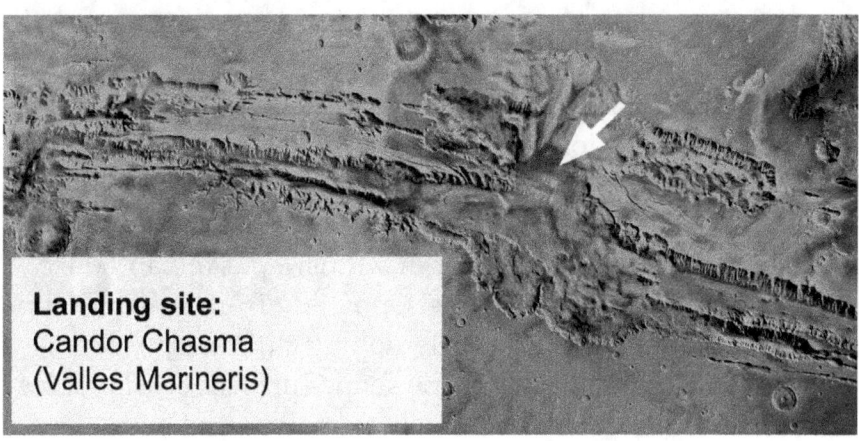

Landing site:
Candor Chasma
(Valles Marineris)

Valles Marineris (NASA/JPL-Caltech)

NASA suggested the MSL Rover Landing Site in West Candor Chasma. The geography of the landing site in VM limits automated missions and clearly requires human interaction to serve various mission objectives.

PART 1: SCIENCE

1.1 SCIENTIFIC GOALS

The mission will focus on the unique environment in VM and scientific research that cannot be performed by automated rovers. The mission itself is subject to research. The research conducted during the mission will consist of several branches to be conducted simultaneously. Every science branch has its own primary goal and distinctive secondary goals. Here we present the main scientific goals in order of priority:

Geological research
- Studying cliffsides where Recurring Slope Lineae (3) was observed
- Create seismic profiles using man-made explosions
- Potential of dry flows
- Study visible geologic layers and core samples
- Study core samples from drilling into deep layers not sterilised by radiation
- Research the history of Mars, specific conditions which influence abundance and properties
- Jagged bedrock jutting out of windswept sand and dust
- Research gully-like channels, possibly from seasonal run-off of liquid water down the sloping cliff-faces
- Observe canyon walls whose shapes present erosional features (4) present in arid or alpine regions on Earth
- Features observed on shallow slopes and plateaus, like yardangs—erosional landforms reworked by abrasion

- Cap rock / soft filling units—deposited by aeolian processes
- Accumulation of ferric material in dunes (caused by wind)
- Volatile interactions resulting in the formation of viscous flows and polygonal and chaotic terrains

Finding traces of life
- Search for proto-life fragments and complex organic molecules
- Study origins of sulphate deposits (5)
- Sample subterranean water deposits
- Sample deep drill cores

Finding water
- Search for water trapped by hygroscopic salts
- Research chemical composition and microbiology of sub-surface brines
- Water bound in hydrated minerals
- Water condensed on regolith grains' surface
- Water-atmosphere interactions
- Potential of larger subterrain water bodies
- Host rock lithologies to trace past environment
- Formation of grey crystalline hematite can be associated with igneous, sedimentary, or hydrothermal processes on Earth

Studying Martian climate
- Monitoring of seasonal differences out of the deep VM
- Water extraction possibilities from fog
- Establishing weather monitoring stations on different heights of VM
- Monitoring of the seasonal weather variability in VM
- Study of the microclimate within VM: humidity and water vapour saturation, winds, temperature, pressure, condensation

- Analysis of the geological data to research for the past climate of Mars

Monitoring the effects of Martian environment on human health
- Observe human health in reduced gravity
- Observe and compare effects different diets and physical activity
- Observe psychological effects of Mars environment
- Effects of radiation on performance and human body functions
- Effects of Mars dust on human health

Investigating food production on Mars
- Fertiliser production from Mars minerals
- Mars regolith as a soil substrate and its potential improvement
- Effect of Mars radiation on plant life
- Efficiency level of aquaponic and hydroponic systems
- Investigating silica aerogel-based passive greenhouses (6)

Finding Mars minerals and resources for future colonisation
- Ferric oxides in association with ILD
- Study rich ferric oxide-rich deposits (7°S, 67.7°W) which are associated with a piedmont glacier
- Study of the abundance, composition and layering of the sulphates
- History and physical laws of mineral deposits on Mars
- Determine the best sources for iron, aluminium and fertiliser

Studying the utilisation of in-situ materials for future colonisation
- Find out which materials meet the requirements for radiation protection

- Testing and production of Martian concrete/bricks out of local resources
- Production of the polymer-based materials for the 3D printing purposes; testing stability and effectivity of the 3D printed habitats
- Research on the possibility to synthesise multiple chemicals and metals from local sources potentially relevant to an eventual colonisation
- Find lava tubes and other geological structures for potential colonies

1.2 RESEARCH EQUIPMENT

The mission will introduce scientific equipment which previous robotic missions were unable to operate.

General principles for scientific operation on Mars

The key goal for scientific operation is maximising the time spent on EVA. The geologists will collect samples and bring them to the main lab. Our lab has sufficiently sophisticated equipment to carry out in-depth analysis of particularly interesting samples, but for most of them, there is no need to waste time on long investigations on Mars.

Biologists and medical scientists will spend most of their time in the lab, performing pre-prepared experiments and overseeing the equipment.

Seismic sensors and explosives

Robotic missions cannot perform complex tasks of seismic exploration as the explosive chemicals age quickly and will have to be produced on Mars. Mission scientists will install a number of multi-functional devices (weather monitoring stations, seismic sensors and communication relays) all over the canyon and choose as professional geologists the most interesting sites for detonations.

Drilling equipment

Robotic missions were never able to perform deep drills. This is important for the search for life, as the surface of Mars is sterilised. Also, liquid water can only exist in subterranean structures without immediate evaporation. We will use lightweight drills in order to access rocks laying as deep as 3 km under the surface.

3D printers

The 3D printers will be used to produce materials for stress tests in the Martian environment. The printers will also produce packing material for the core samples and other interesting items to be sent back to Earth.

Indoor farming (greenhouse)

Research on plant growth under a number of different scenarios to measure the effect of Mars soils, radiation and gravity will also be carried out. The harvested crops will be used as an auxiliary food source for the astronauts, providing them with variety in their diets.

1.3 BASECAMP LABORATORY

The laboratory will be equipped with highly advanced instruments intended to carry out research in many fields of science. The laboratory will be divided into several sections to prevent contamination of the living quarters. The laboratory will be well-ventilated, lit and equipped with the latest safety features. All these measures should allow us to maintain a clean and well-organised work area.

This is the list of the necessary equipment for the laboratory (7):

Lab section: Geology/Chemistry	
Primary equipment	Purposes
General geology lab equipment: rock hammers, hand lenses, mineral hardness kits, rock kits, fluorescent mineral kits, Mohs hardness testing kits, polarising microscopes, rock saws, portable spectrometers, etc. General chemistry lab equipment: test glasses, beakers, biurets, pipettes.	
Press device	Shaping regolith into a denser form
SEM-EDX and X-ray Diffraction (XRD)	Chemical analysis and crystal structure analysis of samples
Electron micro-probes and petrographic microscope	Sample analysis
Microscopes: visible, polarised, SEM	Analysing samples, screening
Spectrometers and Vibrational Spectroscopy instruments: UV-vis-IR, Raman, EDX, LIBS	Analysing samples, screening
Rock cutter	Preparing samples for microscope
Recording tools: camera, sketch pad, etc.	Surveying, recording of geological context
Thermal oven: conventional, laser beam, microwave	Sample treatment
Density measuring device, Mechanical testing devices, Thermal property analyser: laser flash (LFA), heat capacity, heat conductivity Differential Scanning Calorimeter, Viscometer	Testing material properties
Electronic tongues	Basic in-situ analysis of taste-related compounds
3D scanner	Volume analysis

Lab section: Geology/Chemistry	
Primary equipment	**Purposes**
Contained workstation (e.g. glovebox)	Working with dangerous and contamination-sensitive samples
Infra-red gas analyzers (IRGA)	Gas exchange measurements

Lab section: Biology / Medicine	
Primary equipment	**Purposes**
Biology lab equipment: microscopes, beakers, test tubes, magnifying glasses, etc.	
Environmentally controlled chambers	Research on food production and fundamental biology experiments with plants, monitoring and control of all environmental parameters
Exposure platform	Exposure of bio-molecules and organisms to the environment
Chemical fixation	Storing samples
ICP-OES	Assessments of plant biomass composition, determining on site the effects of microbial activity on the rates of elemental release from the regolith
RT-qPCR	DNA extraction or entire microarray-based gene expression protocols, from cell lysis to data analysis)
Camera and image-analysis software	Plant morphology measurements
Low-speed centrifuges	Accommodate samples of various sizes
High-speed centrifuge	Microbiology and molecular biology protocols
MinION	Nucleic acid sequencing, detecting mutations, assessing contamination, and documenting population dynamics of non-axenic cultures in BLSS, checking the correct manufacturing and insertion of engineered genetic constructs

Lab section: Biology / Medicine	
Primary equipment	**Purposes**
Nucleic acid (cDNA or RNA) sequencing	Monitoring gene expression
Automated flow cytometry devices	Quick assessments of contamination, population dynamics, growth rates etc.
RT-PCR	Documenting the expression of a moderate number of genes
DNA microarrays	Assessing the expression levels of a large number of genes simultaneously
Mass spectrometry-based platforms (MS)	Identification, characterization and quantification of macromolecules over a wide range of concentrations, in complex samples and with a high throughput
Contactless, gravity-independent systems	Reducing the generation of waste associated with pipette tip-based robots, and help miniaturise processes
Accelerated solvent extraction system	Extracting organic compounds from a mineral
Imaging techniques	Monitoring plant health and development, automation on the experiments
Plant growth units	All plant growth experiments
Biosensor arrays	Biomarker analysis

Lab section: Biology / Medicine	
Primary equipment	**Purposes**
Thermometers, accelerometers, actigraphy, pulse oximetry, ECG, ICG, seismocardiography	Monitoring of basic physiological functions
Ultrasound, X-ray techniques	Analysing bone and muscle mass
Magnetic resonance imaging (MRI)	Morphological data on cardiovascular system, brain, bone and muscle mass
Positron emission tomography (PET)	Functional mapping of cardiovascular system, brain, bone and muscle mass

1.4 EXPLORATION SITES

The rich variety of geological structures, as well as nearby sites with potential sources of usable materials (8), require the team to investigate far away from the base. While general scouting can be delegated to autonomous rovers, we see a necessity for a human specialist directly *in situ*.

Map of potential exploration sites; map based on observations from HiRISE, CTX, MOC, CRISM and CaSSIS suggestions (https://www.uahirise.org/hiwish/browse)

- Area 1: Wallrock spurs that are aligned and extend into Melas Chasma, valley network along Melas Chasma wallrock, layered deposits near Ius Mensa, ductile folds in possibly evaporite sediments, circular depression, eastern side of Melas region basin with light-toned layering, mixed sulphates along Melas Chasma wallrock, alcove,

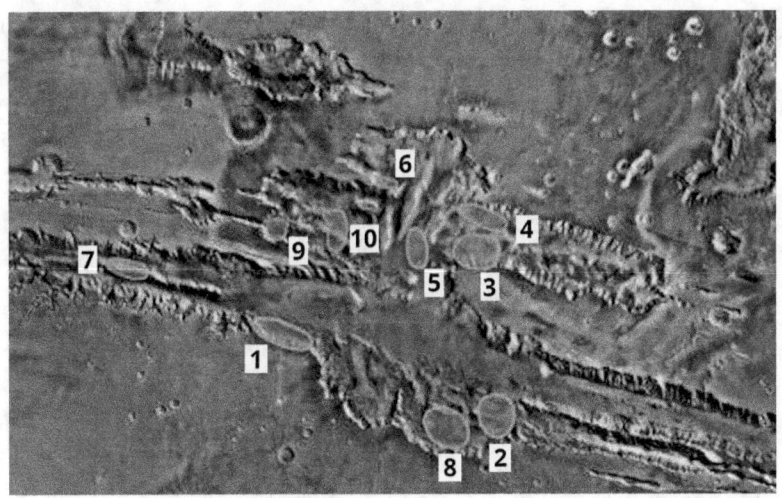

possible submarine fan in the eastern portion of small Melas Chasma basin, clinoforms, RSL, layered material and other landforms, jarosite stratigraphy, circular depression, fluvial channels along Melas Chasma wallrock, Melas Chasma valley network.

- Area 2: Light-toned stratified materials, potential clays and sulphates, possible poly-hydrated sulphate deposits, debris flow, possible phyllosilicate deposit.
- Area 3: layered sulphates, irregular depression, hematite, small chaos region, layered deposits, ellipse depression.
- Area 4: Layered deposits, multi-sulfate exposure, Chaos and cavus, small gullies, hematite site, graben.
- Area 5: Different lithology, polygonal features in layered deposits, ride-along, light-toned rock exposures on the north wall of Candor Chasma, steep slopes and bedrock, fluvial systems, diurnal change, dune change detection.
- Area 6: RSL in Ophir, contact between wall rock and light-toned deposits, possible hematite-rich terrain, sulphates, ride-along, light-toned rock exposures on southwest Ophir Chasma wall.

- Area 7: Exposures of light-toned layering along plains, RSL, light-toned material in lower west Candor Chasma wall, layered deposits, landslide deposit, hydrated mineral deposit, possible sulphates, transition between thin Ius Chasma landslides, ride-along, layered deposits, landslide material, jarosite stratigraphy, possible phyllosilicate-rich deposits, dunes near Geryon Montes, possible hydrated phase in landslide, Mariner Valley Fault line.
- Area 8: Mass wasting chutes, landslide deposit, possible ancient bedforms, exposed strata near Melas wall, possible sulphates, possible blocky deposit, RSL, light-toned stratified materials, aeolian units, dune field, gap in Melas Chasma Interior Layered Deposits, south crater, sedimentary units.
- Area 9: Investigation of anomaly, faulted layered deposits, Ceti Mersa investigation of the potential anomalous impact on the Martian surface, contact between W Candor polyhydrated cap and underlying monohydrate, fine layering, layered sedimentary rocks, contact between wallrock and light-toned layering, layers in lower southwest.
- Area 10: Low-albedo ridged material, aeolian interaction between bedrock and ripples, distinct spur and gully mesa, possible hydrated sulphate, survey layering and faulting in layered deposits, caprock with large angular clasts, especially bright materials, truncation and fold.

PART 2: ENGINEERING

2.1 GENERAL ASSUMPTIONS ON TECHNICAL DEVELOPMENT

We assume the following upcoming technologies with a high Technology Readiness Level to be available for our mission until the launch date of the early 2030s:

- 40% efficient solar panels for vehicles and 0.4 kW/kg for the base
- Temperature-resistant battery packs with an energy density of 1 kWh/kg
- Lightweight Solid Oxide Fuel Cells with a power-to-weight ratio of 2.5 kW/kg
- Ultra-strong materials for the habitat and rovers
- Miniature chemical plants for plastics and other chemicals production
- Advanced 3D printing with paraformaldehyde and carbon nanotubes
- Efficient algae photobioreactors with automatic nutrient extraction
- Autonomously inflating aerogel for insulation
- Lightweight inflatable propellant storage tanks
- AI and robotics which allow for autonomous construction of the basecamp
- Lightweight aircraft for usage on Mars

2.2 HABITAT

Design

The habitat will have the shape of a flattened hemisphere with a diameter of 16 metres and will be made of Nextel-Kevlar fabric, the same that is used in Bigelow Aerospace's inflatable ISS module. The habitat is designed to be unfolded upon arrival autonomously when being filled with locally produced water and gases. To withstand the extreme Martian conditions, the base will be composed of layers that each will have a unique task and type of filling:

- CO_2: rigidity and insulation—this will be instantly available by compression of the Martian atmosphere. Later in

the mission, the CO_2 can be replaced with oxygen as an emergency reserve.
- Silica aerogel: thermal insulation—the lightest and most efficient insulation material; inflated after the unfolding of the dome.
- Water: radiation shielding and storage.
- Nitrogen-oxygen atmosphere: living space for astronauts.

Features
- Durable
- Oxygen providing system—reverse SOFC, algae tanks
- Radiation protection using a water shell
- Thermal control system, humidity regulation
- Reutilization of packing materials as furniture

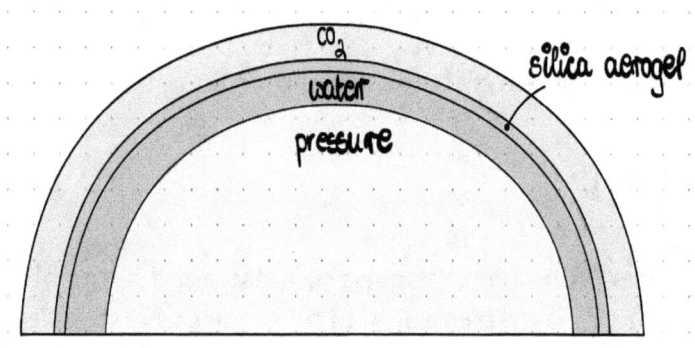

Weight estimates
- Density of Nextel-Kevlar fabric: 0.25 kg/m².
- Additional layers are needed for insulation (silica aerogel) and hermeticity (polymer/rubber), weighing up to 1.5 kg/m².
- Final density: 2 kg/m².

- Including insulation layers for the floor, the final weight estimate is 1 tonne. A 20 cm layer of water would reduce radiation inside the habitat to ~40mSv/year (9). The dome has ~200m² of usable floor space.

Basecamp interior

The living quarters will be designed with optimised spacing usage in mind and will be divided into two broad areas: personal space and shared area. The shared space will be mostly used as the dining area, a place for entertainment and group meetings if necessary. Using curtains, the crewmembers will be able to divide the shared space into different sections, depending on how many astronauts are on an EVA or other expeditions.

The living quarters will also contain specific necessities: medical equipment, entertainment devices and cooking utilities. Furthermore, there will be gaming devices and lightweight gym equipment for the astronauts.

We intend to reuse equipment packages for fully functional furniture, parallel to using inflatable furniture or the art of origami. The filler of packages like foam peanuts will be made of edible materials for additional food resources.

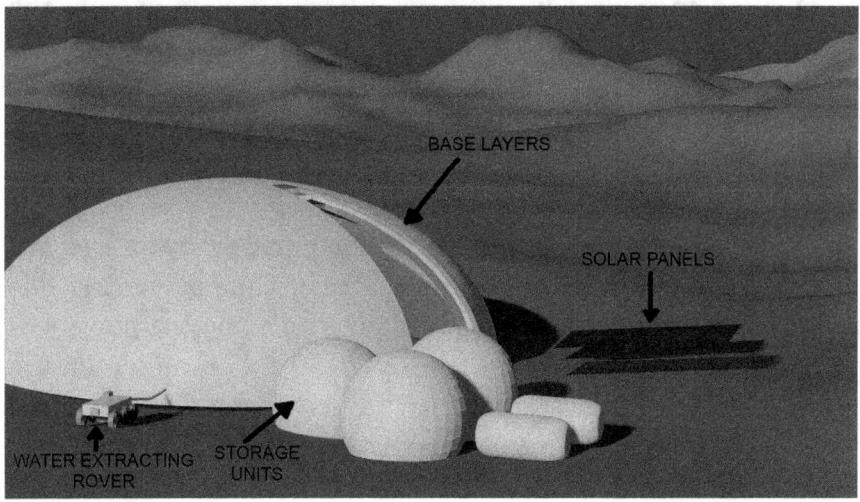

The photobioreactors and greenhouses will be integrated into the dome to add elements of Earth's natural environment for the mental well-being of the astronauts.

The spare 40 m² can be used as storage or as a bigger living area.

2.3 LIFE-SUPPORT SYSTEMS

Since oxygen and water will be produced *in situ* on Mars, the life-support system is tasked only with the removal of CO_2 produced by the astronauts and regulating air temperature. Therefore, the design can be much simpler than a life-support system on a spacecraft.

Human waste will be utilised as a biomass source in a cockroach bioreactor, turning them into easily absorbable protein in the form of surplus bugs. In addition to the bioreactor, the waste will be used as a fertiliser for different scientific experiments involving growing plants.

Water will be reused in a cascade system, from drinking water to urine to the cockroach bioreactor to the algae PBRs and greenhouses. At the end of the cycle, half of the water will be purified and recycled, with the other half coming from the water extractors, thus making the recycling equipment relatively lightweight.

2.4 SOLAR POWER

For power generation at the base, solar panels optimised for power-to-weight ratio will be used. At the time of writing this report, the best panels for use in space can achieve a power-to-weight ratio of 4.3 kW/kg (10). By 2030 this number should reach 5 kW/kg. For use in the Martian environment the panels will need to be ruggedised, reducing the power-to-weight ratio to 1 kW/kg on Earth and 0,4 kW/kg on Mars. We expect the following features to be available:

- A great power-to-weight ratio of 0.4 kW/kg, 50 W/m^2;
- Reasonably durable;
- Flexible and easily deployable by rolling out onto a flat surface.

The overall max capacity of the PV installation at the base will be 200 kW.

For power generation on vehicles, solar panels optimised for efficiency will be used. Currently, the most promising ones achieve 32% efficiency whilst weighing 1 kg/m^2 (11). By 2030 solar cells with 40% efficiency and the same weight should be available. On Mars, they would produce 234 W/m^2.

2.5 FUEL CELLS

Our mission PV energy supply is backed up with methane-oxygen Solid Oxide Fuel Cells (SOFC), which can also operate in reverse mode. NASA forecasts SOFC with 2.5 kW/kg (12). We assume 0.25 kW/kg for a future space SOFC system, including peripherals and efficiencies of above 80% for methane to power conversion.

$$CH_4 + 2O_2 \rightarrow CO_2 + 2H_2O$$

The same 10 kW SOFC units can produce the equivalent of 40kW chemical energy in form of methane or syngas from PV power, water and CO_2 with an efficiency of 85% during daytime (13). Prototypes are currently under development.

$$CO_2 + 2H_2O \rightarrow CH_4 + 2O_2 \text{ or syngas}$$

Using several identical systems for power production and fuel synthesis improves redundancy levels. Modular reverse SOFC are very reliable and can operate longer than the proposed mission period already with current technology. SOFC systems can have different tasks in different phases of the mission, e.g. propellant and syngas production before the arrival of the astronauts and power source for vehicles in later phases. In this way a reduction in the landing weight is possible. We assume 10 kW multi-purpose SOFC systems with each weighing 40 kg including insulated housing and plug-and-play connectors.

Fuel cells will be used for the following systems:

- Methane/oxygen generation in the basecamp for energy storage and vehicle propellant;
- Syngas generation for plastic production feedstock;
- Night-time power and backup for the base power supply;
- Power supply for vehicles (rovers, aeroplanes);
- Power supply for energy-intensive science equipment, such as drills.

2.5 BATTERIES

There is currently enormous technical progress in battery design. We assume that compact, temperature-resistant and lightweight batteries will be available at the mission launch date. Still, we try to limit their weight by a concept of exchangeability and multi-usage. Batteries are used for the following:

- Exoskeletons—full charge is necessary at landing to roll out the PV;
- Backup power and UPS for the base;
- Rovers and aircraft;
- EVA Suits;

- Seismic and climate sensors including communication relays.

We assume that 100 kWh of battery packs is sufficient. Power density for commercial batteries is proposed at 0.3 kWh/kg for 2030 (14).

2.6 WATER EXTRACTION

Design
Autonomous vehicles for water extraction will use microwaves to apply energy to the water directly, while the regolith won't be heated (15). By controlling the frequency, the rovers can penetrate different regolith depths. We can expect 10 GHz waves to penetrate at least 2 metres down into the surface (16). The produced water vapour will be collected with a large funnel and transported through modular pipes to the collecting equipment in the base that includes filters for eventual Martian dust. The autonomous vehicles will use AI to drive around the base and collect water.

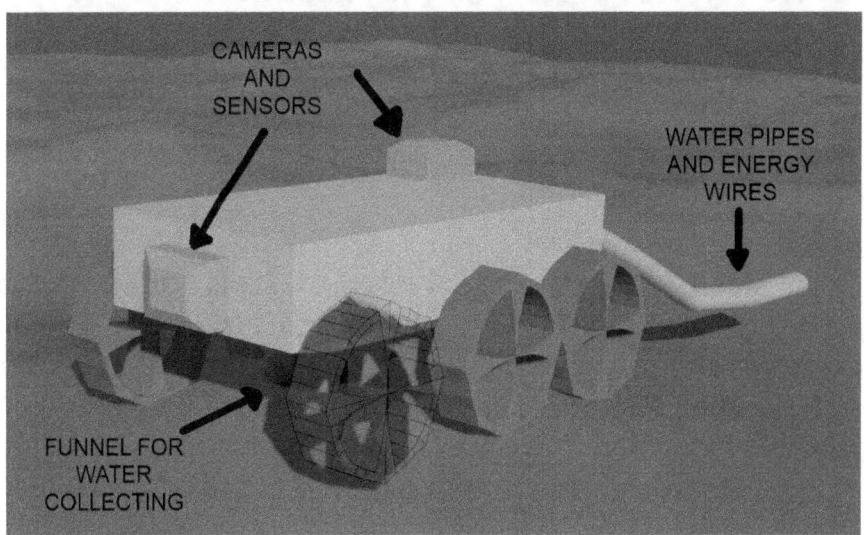

Features
- Lightweight—230 kg
- Power flows directly from the PV array via cables to the rover
- Water vapour flows directly into the basecamp with flexible pipes
- Range sufficient to collect the required amount of water

Power requirements
$Q = c*m*(100°-T)+\Delta hvap*m$ = 2,55 MJ to evaporate 1kg of water. We assume 40% water content within the first metre of soil at the landing site. We are able to extract 396 litres from 1m³ regolith with 99% efficiency (17). The equipment is designed to collect up to 1 tonne of water per day.

2.7 FOOD PRODUCTION AND STORAGE

90% of the food required will be produced upfront from resources extracted *in situ* by genetically modified algae. We will use 3 types of algae for the 3 key nutrients:

- *Chlorella Vulgaris* grown under special conditions for carbohydrates [18];
- *Spirulina* cyanobacteria for proteins [19];
- *Chlorella Vulgaris* grown using a different process for fats [20].

For each type of algae, the respective nutrient content can get as high as 80%. The algae will be grown in several redundant photobioreactors (PBRs) and harvested every week by an automated system of draining and drying. Then, the algae will be fractionated in order to extract the respective types of nutrients, which will be mixed together in specific proportions, turning them into a complete-meal powder, such as Soylent. The astronauts will have a variety of artificial flavours to choose from in order to make the powder pleasant to eat. The algae can provide some vitamins, but astronauts will take vitamin pills to supplement the algae.

The remaining 10% of the food will be brought from Earth in the form of lyophilised meals in order to conserve the mental health of the astronauts and ensure variety, although, in emergencies, it is possible to survive on Soylent as the only food source.

Additional food resources are living organisms such as fish, *Blattodea* insects and plants, which are purposefully grown for science. They could provide an adequate amount of diversity in the astronauts' diet.

The surplus algae will be the main food source for living animals. The water drained from the photobioreactor will be purified and will be used for the plant growth units.

	Item	Weight [kg]
Mass estimates	Photobioreactors	80
	Minerals for algae growing	50
	Initial dried algae	4.86
	Total	134.86
Water consumption estimates	58.1 litres of water can produce 1.428 kg of dried algae per week	
	Total mass of the algae needed for the mission is 11.7 t	
	The water consumption rate will be: Assuming that we harvest every week for 2 years	883.12 l/week

Area estimates	Total volume of the PBRs:	940 l
	Total land area of the PBRs:	4.64 m²
Energy consumption	PBRs energy consumption:	1.18 kW

2.8 CHEMICALS PRODUCTION PLANT: CH_4 AND O_2 PRODUCTION

10 kW SOFC in reverse mode can produce the equivalent of 40 kW methane/oxygen or Syngas from PV power, water and CO_2 with an efficiency of 85% (21). Oxygen is also produced along with CH_4.

$$CO_2 + 2H_2O \rightarrow CH_4 + 2O_2$$

$$CO_2 + H_2O \rightarrow CO + H_2 + \text{spare } O_2$$

For the synthesis of methane no further step is necessary, providing a great reduction of weight and complexity. SOFC modules will be interchangeable for different purposes and will also provide Syngas for other chemical processes below.

2.9 CHEMICALS PRODUCTION PLANT: EXPLOSIVES

A great candidate for a Martian explosive is a mixture of hydrogen peroxide, glycerol and water with an energy release comparable to that of TNT (22). Glycerol can be replaced with ethanol to form a mixture of similar power, although less stable (23). When the ingredients are not mixed together, they are safe for handling by humans. Both hydrogen peroxide (24) and ethanol (25) can be produced from H_2O and CO_2 efficiently and using lightweight equipment.

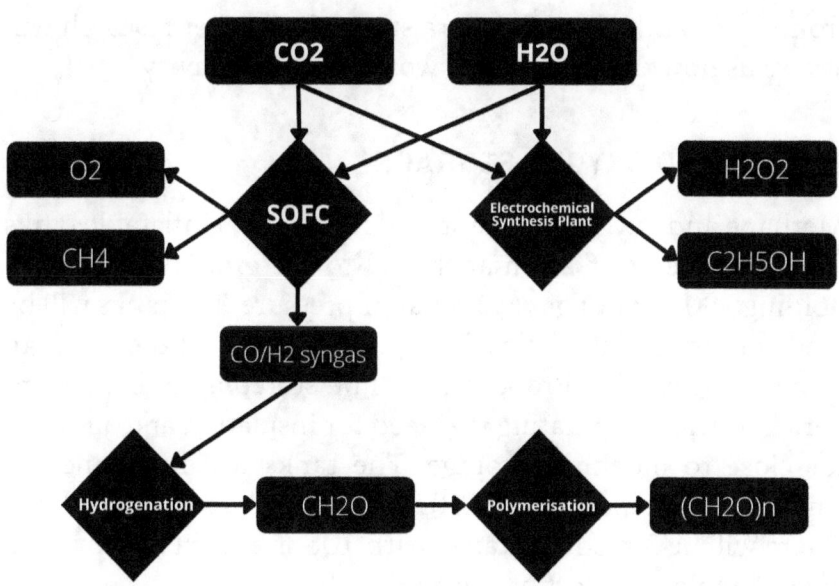

After being produced at their respective facilities, the peroxide-water mixture and ethanol are transported to the explosion site in separate insulated containers, which are then joined together via a valve system to allow for remote detonation. The production plant capacity is up to 200 kg of explosives per day.

2.10 CHEMICALS PRODUCTION PLANT: PLASTICS

Formaldehyde is produced from Syngas using efficient nickel-based catalysts (26) and polymerised to form paraformaldehyde, which is stored in granule form until the astronauts arrive, serving as a filament for 3D printing.

2.11 3D PRINTERS

We will use 3D printers for printing of spare parts, furniture, boxes for samples, drilling equipment parts, vessels for algae and chemical product storage. Carbon nanotubes will be brought from Earth and added for extra strength. Further research will assure us how this technology works in microgravity.

2.12 CH_4 AND OXYGEN STORAGE

Methane and oxygen will be stored in spherical inflatable tanks with a diameter of 25 m anchored to the ground, capable of holding ~8000m³ of gas at 1.4 bar of pressure. The tanks will be made out of Kevlar fabric with a polymer layer on the inside to ensure hermeticity. Propellant will be stored at ambient temperature, thus eliminating the need for insulation and allowing for close to indefinite storage. The tanks will be connected using flexible pipes to the ISRU plant and the rest of the base. There will be 3 methane tanks with 10t of capacity each and 6 oxygen tanks with 20t of capacity each.

2.13 EVA SUITS

Astronauts will be using mechanical counterpressure suits with a suitport to maximise mobility and reduce dust exposure to a minimum at the base and the rovers. The suits will use technologies from MIT's Biosuit (27), such as Shape Memory Alloy coils, which is expected to be ready in the near future. When entering the suit, it fits loosely, but later it contracts to form-fit the suit to the body. This allows for the suits to be interchangeable between astronauts. Features:

- Provides extremely good mobility
- Fast and easy to ingress/egress
- Massively reduces dust exposure
- Interchangeable between astronauts

2.14 EXOSKELETONS

To utilise the limited time and human resources as best as possible, teleoperation technologies must be implemented. For that, triple-purpose exoskeletons will be used. Firstly, they could be worn by an astronaut to enhance his strength, enabling them to lift 250 kg. Secondly, an exoskeleton could be remotely operated by an astronaut wearing a VR headset. Thirdly, the exoskeletons could operate semi-autonomously, guided by an advanced AI system partly supervised from Earth.

All exoskeletons will have a rescue mode—when they detect that the astronaut inside them is unconscious, they will alert the rest of the crew and return to the base autonomously.

All parameters of the exoskeletons were extrapolated from one of today's most advanced exoskeletons, the Guardian-XO (28).

2.15 ROVERS

Features
- 1000 km of range and back
- Capable of reaching 25 km/h on a 30° slope
- Able to support 3 crew members for up to 14 sols
- Contains a small laboratory for on-site sample analysis
- Drives autonomously using onboard lidars and cameras with the help of radar imagery collected by scout drones

Design
- Central fuselage, an elliptic cylinder 3 metres high, 5 metres wide and 10 metres long, made from carbon fibre and insulated with aerogel, limited from the top by a flat roof and bottom by a flat floor, 2 metres apart. The space between them and the fuselage will be used for life support systems, storage, batteries and communication equipment.

- Forward dome, made out of strong, transparent, scratch-resistant reinforced acrylic. The primary focus of its design is to allow for good visibility from the inside.
- Aft bulkhead with a semi-flat end containing 3 hatches for attaching EVA suits and exoskeletons along with an airlock for transferring samples and equipment inside.
- Wheels with inflatable Kevlar tyres 3 m in diameter. With 3 of them per side, this configuration allows the vehicle to drive over 1 metre high rocks with ease and provides good traction for climbing over large obstacles (29).
- Chassis, a lightweight rigid structure located under the outermost parts of the cabin, containing methane and oxygen fuel tanks, fuel cells and a compressor for pressurising the wheels with CO_2.
- Primary power source: Solar panels located on the roof of the rover.
- Auxiliary power source: SOFC with methane and oxygen as fuel; 10kW capacity.
- Water supply: SOFC exhaust and recycling.

There will be a passenger and a cargo variant of the rover, the latter will have an unpressurised cargo bay and no life-support systems, thus being able to carry 2 tonnes of payload.

Rover energy production and consumption
- Solar panels peak power generation: 11 kW
- Electric motor peak power consumption: 10 kW
- Lifesupport systems power consumption: 3 kW

All power for driving will be provided by solar panels.
- Total life support energy consumption for the longest mission: 750 kWh
- Methane / Oxygen stoichiometric mixture energy density: 3 kWh/kg
- Total propellant weight per mission: 500 kg

Team I: Valles Marineris Exploration Mission

Category	Crew Rover		Cargo Rover	
	Part and Weight [kg]		Part and Weight [kg]	
Structure	Main fuselage	800	Main fuselage	400
	Furniture & science equipment	500	Electric motors	100
	Electric motors	100	Wheels	40
	Wheels	40	Compressor	10
	Compressor	10	Tanks	100
	Tanks	100	Fuel cells	50
	Fuel cells	50	Solar panels	25
	Solar panels	25	Batteries	100
	Batteries	100	Communication equipment	20
	Life-support systems	50		
	Communication equipment	20		

	Crew Rover		Cargo Rover	
Category	Part and Weight [kg]		Part and Weight [kg]	
Load	Spacesuits & exoskeletons	170	Fuel	500
	Crew	250		
	Fuel	500	Cargo	2000
	Consumables	100		
Sum	Total dry mass	1795	Total dry mass	845
	Total wet mass	2815	Total wet mass	3345

2.16 AEROPLANE

Our aeroplane will be based on the RMMP-1 (Raymer Manned Mars Aeroplane-1), a robust and well-studied concept. We advise the reader to familiarise themselves with the original concept here (30). Modifications include:

- Reducing its size by 30%
- Using methane & oxygen as fuel for the rocket motors
- Exchanging batteries for solar panels and methane-oxygen SOFC
- Using a lighter, unpressurised cabin
- Updating the wing to be made out of new, lighter materials

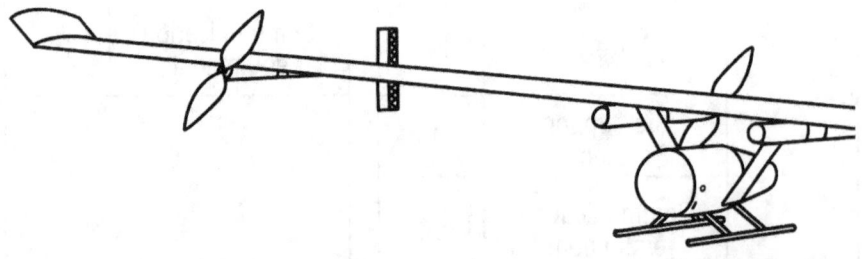

- Adapting the landing legs to accommodate landings in steep terrain
- Making the motors and propellers bigger in order to reduce fuel consumption during landing by using reverse thrust

Features
- Dry mass: 1.5 t
- Cruise speed: 300 km/h
- Range: 2000 km and back
- Payload: 500 kg
- Propellant usage: 100 kg per 2-way flight

2.17 SAMPLE GATHERING DRONE

Small drones can scout the area before the arrival of the astronauts in detail. Their task will be to go to places too difficult or dangerous to reach by manned vehicles.

The drone will include a drilling and landing system consisting of an arm located under the drone. The arm will extend, anchor to the ground and remain rigid so the drone can turn off its motors, collect samples and slowly recharge using solar cells.

2.18 DRILLING EQUIPMENT

We propose to use a modification of the Mars Mole Drilling technique (31). The system would consist of a main drilling unit, which would crush the rock in front of it, turning it into a fine powder before ejecting it at the back to be blown out of the hole by high-pressure CO_2 provided via a flexible pipe running from a power unit at the surface. Running along the pipe would also be power and data connections. The whole system could be powered either by its own solar arrays or by a SOFC module connected to fuel tanks filled with propellant from the rover.

In the upper part of the Martian crust, we could encounter loose sand or gravel layers, which would be contained using 3D printed tubing inserted along the circumference of the hole. In deeper parts, this is less of a concern, since they consist mostly of solid rock. The system is designed to be able to drill down 1000 m in a week, powered only by sunlight. Theoretically, the only limiting factors for the maximum reachable depth are the length of the piping and the internal heat of Mars. Astronauts could try to dig as deep as possible, reaching depths of 10s of kilometres. We will have 6 drilling rigs available to be set up in remote points of interest.

We also suggest looking into alternative technologies such as laser, plasma or ultrasonic drilling, which could turn out to be lighter, faster or more efficient in the near future.

2.19 COMMUNICATION WITH EARTH

For our mission we assume that a small satellite, probably using laser beams and an antenna will be available above our mission area.

The local communication will be designed to use low-energy antennas built into every rover and aeroplane. The communication will be centralised and all information will be passed through the main base, and only then transmitted to the Earth via communication satellites. The main base will be equipped with a high-energy antenna. All components will have their redundant backups built-in, in case of failures. We expect to establish several self-powered relay antennas far from the base to enhance the signal when communicating between the drones or EVAs and the main base. The self-powered relays could serve also as local weather and seismic stations, to provide us with additional monitoring of the current conditions.

2.20 REDUNDANCY CONCEPT

Solar power supply
At night or during dust storms, the base camp will be supplied with power from SOFC. For short power outages, batteries serve as UPS.

Standardised fuel cells
The SOFC are the core of our energy supply concept. They are interchangeable between the basecamp backup energy, gas processors and rovers. This offers a degree of flexibility to bring additional energy to drilling sides in shadow, or produce additional energy at night if required. The same fuel cells can produce oxygen, syngas or methane, avoiding weight for specialised processing machines.

Compressors
There are many uses for compressors in the mission, from the initial unfolding of the habitat to compressing CO_2 for fuel production or compressed CO_2 for the removal of drilling dust. These machine parts, like many others, will be interchangeable.

Standardised batteries
The batteries are always necessary when the SOFCs are too large. Using identical battery packs for exoskeletons, space suits, rovers and base camp backup will offer a degree of additional security, but it is essential to reduce weight, as not all battery devices will work simultaneously.

Oxygen supply
The primary source of oxygen will come from reverse SOFC units which produce Oxygen together with CH4. Food production will supply the remaining necessary oxygen. In emergencies, astronauts can drain oxygen from external oxygen storage tanks or their inflatable furniture.

Water supply
All water will be collected by several automated machines before the arrival of the astronauts and stored as a radiation barrier in the base camp. If this process has to stop due to technical difficulties or lack of power, the astronauts can utilise the water from the radiation barriers of the habitat.

Rovers in operation
We intend to always have 2 rovers in tandem, operating at a distance not too far away to provide emergency aid within a short period.

Communications
All communication devices will include internal backups in case of emergencies. If high-capacity satellite data transfer is not available, shortwave radios will be used for the basic communication of EVA suits, rovers and the basecamp. Relay antennas will provide basic communications between sites of seismic detectors, drilling activities, rovers and the basecamp.

Aeroplanes
In case a plane breaks down during flight or is damaged during landing far from the base camp and no second aircraft is available, the rovers will be sent out with maximum supplies for long range. The maximum range of manned flights should be limited to the maximum range for a rover return trip or a staged rover supply mission with fuel deposits.

Rescue operations
The aircraft is capable of transporting up to two passengers for fast evacuations in case a rover gets damaged or a medical emergency arises.

EVA Suit failure

Exoskeletons can be operated remotely and move incapacitated astronauts into rovers if necessary. Battery packs of suits, rovers, water collectors and exoskeletons are interchangeable. Oxygen tanks for propulsion and oxygen supply for suits will always have compatible connectors and regulators.

Habitat collapse

Rovers can serve as lifeboats in case of habitat failure.

Food supply

Besides the nutrient powder extracted from algae, additional food can be provided by agricultural experiments as well as insects eating the algae or waste biomass. Packaging materials, spacers, and housing of machines could be made from edible starch compounds to serve as last-resort emergency rations.

PART 3: HUMAN OPERATIONS

3.1 GENERAL QUALIFICATIONS

All Astronauts are expected to be able to provide first aid in emergencies. All of them will receive training in the operation and basic maintenance of the life support systems of the base and the rovers, as these are essential for the survival of the group.

All geologists receive extensive technical training to operate and maintain the rovers and the drilling equipment, in case of a system breakdown on extended EVA. The doctors are the pilots of the team, so they can traverse large distances quickly to react in emergencies.

Multiple qualifications will require many years of studies and preparation. Therefore astronauts will be in their mid-40's when taking off for the mission. Excess physical fitness is not a selection requirement as the astronauts can use exoskeletons.

While still being sufficiently physically fit in this age group, the likelihood of acquiring cancer in their lifetime is reduced. Also, an advanced age adds to mental resilience and experience.

Role	Primary Task	Secondary Task	Backup function
Engineer 1	Commander	Base Equipment maintenance	Vehicle maintenance
Engineer 2	Base equipment maintenance	Vehicle maintenance	Deputy Commander
Scientist 1	Scientific coordinator	Geologist	Biologist
Scientist 2	Geologist	Vehicle Maintenance	Base equipment maintenance
Scientist 3	Biologist	Medical	Pilot
Scientist 4	Doctor	Pilot	Biologist

Provided candidates of any gender are available for the required tasks the team should consist of mixed gender to increase the discipline of the group.

The team's qualifications are selected to provide multiple replacements for mission-critical roles or additional personnel in case the mission objectives have to be adjusted.

3.2 CREW ABILITIES AND TASKS

Engineer 1: Mission Coordinator
We assign the management of the mission to Engineer 1, as the functioning of the life support and resource production is essential for the survival of the group. His main task is to distribute the mission's resources between maintaining equipment & crew and scientific missions.

Engineer 2: Base operations and vehicle maintenance
The second engineer specialises in life support systems, resource production, maintenance and operations. The second task is to maintain the vehicles. In case the commander is out of base or not available, Engineer 2 replaces the commander.

Scientist 1: Scientific coordinator
As a geologist, Scientist 1 will coordinate the research objectives and schedule. As a scientific leader, he is not only an expert geologist but also an expert in biochemistry, which serves the aim of finding any traces of life.

Scientist 2: Geologist and technician
Specialisation in drilling and seismic experiments. Since the scientists will work outside the basecamp most of the time, they will need to be able to do simple repairs to the equipment without the engineers.

Scientist 3: Search for life and medic
Specialised on the search for life in cooperation with the geologists. Expertise in biochemistry also qualifies this scientist for being a replacement for the mission's doctor. For this function, training to operate the aircraft in emergencies is required.

Scientist 4: Flying doctor and biologist

The mission doctor is most of the time located in the basecamp, but has to be ready to fly to the rovers in case of emergencies to rescue injured astronauts. The knowledge of biology enables Scientist 4 to assist in the search for life, for which the medical analysing equipment of the base can be utilised.

3.3 WORKLOAD DISTRIBUTION

The engineers will mostly work in the base to keep the essential systems operational. They will join the EVA only occasionally.

The multitude of tasks for the team will be supported by 6 exoskeletons which will partly work autonomously for standard tasks like dedusting solar panels. If required the astronauts in the base can take control of exoskeletons with VR to support their colleagues anywhere, including on EVA. Therefore the useful time of can be maximised, i.e. astronauts can maintain the base instead of spending time driving to a drill site to provide expertise or physical help. Unlike operations from Earth, the exoskeletons will be controlled by VR in real-time.

3.4 COMMAND STRUCTURE AND EMERGENCIES

Ground control

A multitude of scientists and technicians will control and evaluate all mission data 24/7. Their task is to keep track of the energy and resource supply situation as well as to constantly evaluate progress in the different fields of scientific research. This way the ground team will free up much time for the astronauts allowing them to concentrate on practical work. As ground control has more time and human resources, much of the strategic planning of the mission will be done on Earth.

VR can help to simulate repairs on the hardware on Earth, providing the astronauts with updated and augmented reality programs for their missions and tasks. This way the astronauts will also be capable of performing complex tasks beyond their field of expertise if necessary. Given the nature of the mission, the ground control team can only give recommendations, as they have no way to enforce their decisions.

Mission commander

The commander is the team leader on Mars and represents the interest of the whole team towards ground control. The Mission Commander, therefore has the last say on any of ground control's suggestions. In case of technical emergencies, the commander assumes full responsibility instantly. As an engineer, the commander has the qualification to decide on priorities in life-threatening situations.

In the hostile environment of Mars, the survival of the team depends on the functioning of the technical infrastructure, therefore the commanding Engineer's decisions have priority over the interests of the science team. The commander or the deputy commanding engineer can call for the scientists if additional personnel for the operation of the base is required.

Science coordinator

Scientist 1 oversees the scientific projects in the field. The Science Coordinator can take quick decisions at any time if it is impossible to benefit from the expertise of ground control. Scientist 1 commands the team on EVA and assigns tasks in the lab. The Science coordinator can also call the doctor for additional lab resources.

Mission doctor

The doctor's priority is the health of the astronauts. The Mission doctor, therefore, has the indisputable power to send anybody to the sick bay if they consider that their life is in danger. This includes also the commander. In this case, the command powers are automatically transferred to Engineer 2.

Disputes
All astronauts are the product of a multi-year in-depth selection and training. We assume that psychologically stable and enormously motivated candidates will be available. However, we cannot ignore the possibility of major differences and animosities occurring. In this case, the mission commander has to adjust the EVA planning to compose teams in a way that avoids confrontations.

Nobody can exclude political tensions happening on Earth when the astronauts are in space. For multinational teams, this can be a problem, as they are sent as representatives of their nations. It is therefore important that all participants agree upfront that in such situations all team members continue to cooperate in a professional way. If necessary, the commander can reduce communications to earth and restrict any public appearance of the astronauts, except if they appear as a team.

A detailed set of conduct rules has to be agreed upon by all astronauts and their organisations on how to handle even the most unlikely situations without endangering the mission objectives. For example, if the commander is associated with a conflict party, the mission command will be transferred to a team member of a neutral country. In any case, team members are to avoid any nationalistic and political preferences while representing mankind on this important mission.

Religion and other beliefs
Religious beliefs are not a problem as long as their practice is not in conflict with any of the mission objectives. All team members will agree to respect each other's beliefs.

Severe illness or death of the team member
The tasks of the affected person are transferred to the other team members with relevant backup experience. The mission control and commander will have to adjust the workload and

reduce scientific programs if necessary. In case several team members become unavailable at some point, the survival of the remaining team becomes the highest priority.

Psychological issues
The mission doctor is also responsible for the mental health and stability of the team. If stress overburdens the team or individuals, the doctor can also prescribe extra rest time or in extreme cases isolation of team members and chemical treatment.

Rescues
All team members surely would help each other to the utmost of their possibilities. In the extreme environment of Mars with limited resources, however, team members need to agree that high-risk rescue attempts cannot be undertaken, when the survival of the team is likely to be compromised.

Extreme emergencies
When technical problems appear that create life-threatening resource constraints, so that not all astronauts may survive to the end of the mission, astronauts may volunteer to stay behind. If there are no volunteers, the ground control can give recommendations which remaining crew members would have the highest survival chance. Detailed rules of conduct have to be agreed upon by all team members upfront to avoid discussion in time-sensitive emergencies.

3.5 MISSION PLANNING

General mission planning
- A manned mission should not waste time on tasks that robotic missions or satellites could do.
- Situations in which rescue in case of an accident would not be possible have to be avoided. There should always be a backup plan, e.g. a second rover nearby.

- The radiation dose taken by the astronauts should be closely monitored and tasks should be assigned accordingly.
- At the end of the mission period, it would be acceptable to risk equipment, but never the life of the astronauts. An example of that would be sending the drones on one-way missions far out.

Mission phases

The mission will be divided into several phases, outlined below.

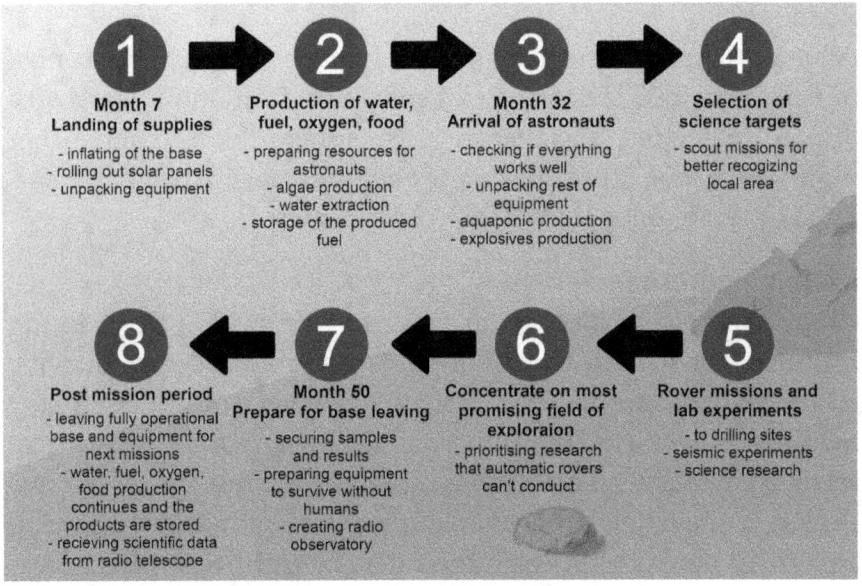

Phase 0—Launch of the supply ship—month 1

Phase 1—Landing of supplies and basecamp—month 7

A well-thought-out arrangement of payload allows most of the significant equipment to be automatically unpacked. The exoskeletons will be activated and distance controlled from Earth. The first task will be the rollout of the solar panels to secure power production and the setup of the ISRU plant.

Phase 2–Production of water, propellant, food and plastics
While waiting for the astronauts, rovers, fuel cells, photobioreactors and many more components work to prepare the base before the arrival of the manned mission. This solution offers us the possibility to check if all systems work well and avoid the risks of the ISRU systems failing during the main mission period and endangering the life of the astronauts. The extracted water is pumped into the base's inner layer to serve as a radiation shield. Propellant is stored in inflatable tanks. Algae are refined into nutrient powder and stored.

Phase 3–Arrival of the astronauts, finishing the habitat, start of explosives production and 3D printing, equipment tests–month 38
Although the base will be fully inflated, astronauts need to check that all systems are working within their parameters and then complete building up the habitat parts which require the highest precision, such as establishing the lab and unpacking the equipment. In that phase, the crew will begin testing the aquaponics system and start explosives production in order to prepare for upcoming science missions.

Phase 4–Selection of science targets and scout missions
Although research activities will be planned before humans arrive, scout missions will provide additional information to select targets for EVA. This will create an opportunity to better recognize the area and update previously acquired data.

Phase 5–Rover expeditions, lab and seismic experiments
The changing rover team will investigate the pre-selected sites and carry out drilling operations. Meanwhile, the lab team will be conducting experiments in the habitat and carrying out seismic research.

Phase 6—Concentrating on the most promising sites

Not all points of interest must prove valuable. In our mission, we assume a variable schedule depending on what will be found on-site. Finding traces of life can change the mission objectives considerably. Finding easily accessible resources can shift the emphasis to prospecting future landing sites for colonisation. The manned mission will prioritise research that automated rovers cannot conduct.

Phase 7—Securing samples and results, preparing for departure

When the mission will be coming to an end, the most interesting samples and other data-holding devices will be packaged for safe return to Earth. The base, vehicles and scientific equipment will be modified to survive without direct human interaction and switch to an automated mode When no more EVAs are planned, one rover and aircraft will be transformed into a radio observatory.

Phase 8—Post-mission period—from month 56

Our goal is to explore as much Mars as we can, but in addition to this, we want to leave a fully operational and equipped base and equipment waiting for the next mission. A significant majority of hardware can work longer than 4 years—the expected duration of the whole mission. Life support devices can continue to produce resources for future missions until machines are worn out or essential materials are depleted. The exoskeletons can perform repair work after humans leave. In order to leave the base in standby mode and suitable for future habitation, we propose the following solutions:

- Power production continues as long as solar panels are not degraded by radiation, or dedusting exoskeletons fail
- The radio telescope continues to work until power supply fails

- Water and propellant production continues and automatically fills up tanks
- Production of plastic granules continues until the chemical plant fails
- Photobioreactors continue working until they fail or fertilisers run out. The nutrient powder is automatically packed and stored
- Vehicles remain on standby mode for future missions

Relay/sensor towers scattered around the canyon will provide automated readings of temperature and atmospheric conditions over a long time span. Additional scientific research will be conducted using the radio telescope assembled from vehicle parts. The telescope will observe the sky in frequencies previously inaccessible to humans due to the Earth's ionosphere reflecting them. It will be possible to use the telescope in tandem with orbital or lunar radio telescopes, making the largest interferometer ever created, which could provide incredible results.

PART 4: COSTS

The Sputnik shock and Apollo programme generated great progress for the whole of mankind, outweighing the costs by far. We suggest viewing the cost of a Mars mission in the same way but making a more targeted approach to generate funds. We are not providing a detailed cost table because in our opinion, at this time, it is not feasible for us to reliably and accurately estimate the development costs of all the components of our mission. Besides that—these estimates would have not much meaning in the space industry anyhow, as going over budget happens on a regular basis (e.g. SLS). Here are some of our suggestions for reducing the cost of our mission:

INCOME STREAMS FROM DUAL-USE TECHNOLOGY DEVELOPMENT

Most technologies which we have described have a dual use on Earth. Flexible solar panels with robotic dedusting can be deployed on Earth's deserts, genetically improved algae and nutrient powders have multiple applications in the food industry and can greatly reduce stress on Earth's ecosystems. Exoskeletons are essential to keep an ageing workforce in industrialised countries productive as well as to provide expert support anywhere on the planet by VR without the necessity to travel. Lightweight fuel cells can generate electricity for aircraft, replacing jet engines. Polymers for 3D printing produced from CO_2 can replace conventional plastic and building materials while creating commercial demand for CO_2. Marketing of these innovations on Earth could end up creating a net profit before the mission even leaves our planet.

COST REDUCTIONS BY UTILISATION OF STANDARD TECHNOLOGIES

The mission will make use of upcoming commercial technologies, so no or little money will be required for adapting them for usage on Mars. Currently, billions are spent to improve battery designs and AI. Carbon-nano-tube-enhanced materials will gain popularity in the near future. We project that products with exotic properties today could be off-the-shelf by the launch date.

PROSPECTION OF FUTURE SITES FOR COMMERCIAL MINING

The prospect of commercial advantages for first-comers could greatly incentivise project sponsors. In case the mission can locate interesting mineral resources, it could then lay claim to them in order to capitalise space-mining corporations.

INCOME FROM THE UTILISATION OF EXTRA-TERRESTRIAL INFRASTRUCTURE

On Mars will remain several functional vehicles and storage tanks filled with fuel, oxygen, water and food. It will be an interesting question if we could sell these resources to other space agencies or private operators. Our automated basecamp would essentially become the first extra-terrestrial filling station in history, where you can top up your spacecraft while enjoying an algae sandwich. This could in fact create "astronomical" additional revenues.

COST REDUCTION BY REDUCING MISSION WEIGHT

The mission plan provides a number of potential weight reduction:

Reducing the number of inflatable gas tanks: Not all gases have to be produced upfront. Micromanaging the different chemical production streams could result in energy-intensive solids being prioritised during the unmanned period before the manned mission in order to reduce the number of required gas tanks capacities.

Reducing the number of drill heads: Depending on technical progress, drilling equipment could become more durable and lighter in weight.

Reducing or the use of lighter scientific equipment: Technical progress could lead to an enormous weight reduction of sensors, analytic devices or develop lab procedures which could require fewer consumables.

PART 5: WEIGHT ESTIMATES

Name of the component	Description / Notes	Weight [kg]	Power consumption [kW]	Total propellant consumed [kg]	Total water consumed [kg]
Crew	6 astronauts + private items	1 200	-	-	6 734
Base shell	Hull and compressors	1 000	1	-	200 000
Furniture	Partly packing material	250	-	-	-
Lab and medical equipment	Includes counters	3 000	10	-	5 000
Space suits, exoskeletons	Not including batteries	400	5	-	-
Food production facility	PBRs, fractionators	184	3	-	69 766
Lyophilised food		200	-	-	-
Life support systems	Only CO_2 removal and air conditioning	100	2	-	-
Solar panels	200 kW peak capacity	500	-	-	-
SOFC/ISRU	100 kW capacity	400	net 0	net 0	58 500
Batteries	100 kWh @ 0,3 kWh/kg	333	net 0	-	-

Name of the component	Description / Notes	Weight [kg]	Power consumption [kW]	Total propellant consumed [kg]	Total water consumed [kg]
Propellant tanks	Capacity for 150 tonnes	5 000	0	-	-
Water extraction equipment	2 rovers	460	100	-	-
Rovers	1 manned and 2 cargo	4 000	self-powered	30 000	-
Aeroplanes	2 planes	3 000	self-powered	100 000	-
Drilling equipment	6 drills	3 000	self-powered	10 000	-
Explosives production plant	Including expendable containers	1 000	35	not stored	not stored
Spare parts	Including duct tape	1 000	-	-	-
Vitamins, medicaments		500	-	-	-
SUM		25 527	156	140 000	340 000

APPENDIX: COMPETITION RESTRICTIONS

For our mission design, the main factors limiting the science output of the mission are the number of crewmembers and the number of vehicles. We have found that increasing the crew size results in a disproportionately small increase in the overall mission weight while increasing the science output linearly. Thus, we find the maximum of 6 astronauts imposed on us by the competition quite restraining. The 1,5-year stay duration limit is, in our opinion, reasonable.

Although our mission design has several tonnes of mass to spare, in our opinion the 30-tonne limit is inappropriate for the reality of an early 2030s launch date, as at this time higher capacity cargo transport to Mars will be made available by SpaceX's Starships. The first transport Starships would most likely remain on Mars as living quarters, changing the concept of including a basecamp in the mission.

The last restriction which we want to mention is the page limit of the original report. Amongst ourselves we have initially created much more content than could be included in the limits of the original report. We also would like to suggest that the set rules for the competition should be further refined and should be strictly obligatory for the teams as well as for the judges.

REFERENCES

1. Fueten, F., Flahaut, J., Stesky, R., Hauber, E., and Rossi, A. P. (2014), Stratigraphy and mineralogy of Candor Mensa, West Candor Chasma, Mars: Insights into the geologic history of Valles Marineris, J. Geophys. Res. Planets, 119, 331– 354, doi:10.1002/2013JE004557.
2. I. Mitrofanov, A. Malakhov, M. Djachkova, D. Golovin, M. Litvak, M. Mokrousov, A. Sanin, H. Svedhem, L. Zelenyi, (2022), The evidence for unusually high hydrogen abundances in the central part of Valles Marineris on Mars. Icarus, 374,1148053, https://doi.org/10.1016/j.icarus.2021.114805

3. Mcewen, Alfred & Dundas, Colin & Mattson, Sarah & Toigo, Anthony & Ojha, Lujendra & Wray, James & Chojnacki, Matthew & Byrne, Steph & Murchie, Scott & Thomas, Nicolas. (2013). Recurring slope linae in equatorial regions of Mars. Nature Geoscience. 7. 10.1038/ngeo2014.

4. A. Burden (2018): The evolution of East Candor Chasma, Valles Marineris, Mars: proposed structural collapse and sedimentation. Master thesis. https://dr.library.brocku.ca/bitstream/handle/10464/13896/Brock_Burden_Amanda_2018.pdf

5. J. W. Head, L. Wilson (2020): Sulphates on Mars: a pyroclastic airfall model for origin, emplacement, and initial alteration of Valles Marineris interior layered deposits (ILD), 51st Lunar and Planetary Science Conference, https://www.hou.usra.edu/meetings/lpsc2020/pdf/2048.pdf

6. R. Wordsworth, L. Kerber, C. Cockell (2019),Enabling martian habitability with silica aerogel via the solid-state greenhouse effect, Nature Astronomy, https://arxiv.org/abs/1907.09089

7. Heinicke, Christiane & Adeli, Solmaz & Baqué, Mickael & Correale, Giuseppe & Fateri, Miranda & Jaret, S. & Kopacz, Nina & Ormö, Jens & Poulet, Lucie & Verseux, Cyprien. (2021). Equipping an extraterrestrial laboratory: Overview of open research questions and recommended instrumentation for the Moon. Advances in Space Research. 68. 10.1016/j.asr.2021.04.047.

8. Photo: https://www.uahirise.org/hiwish/browse; map based on observations from HiRISE, CTX, MOC, CRISM and CaSSIS suggestions

9. Spaceflight Radiation Health Program at JSC, https://srag.jsc.nasa.gov/ Publications/TM104782/techmemo.htm
10. K. Reed, H. J. Willenberg (2004), Early Commercial Demonstration of Space Solar Power Using Ultra-Lightweight Arrays, Space Future, http://www.spacefuture.com/archive/early_commercial_demonstration_of_space_solar_power_using_ultra_lightweight_arrays.shtml
11. Rocket Lab (2022), IMM-α Space Solar Cell, https://www.rocketlabusa.com/assets/Uploads/RL-SolAero-Data-Sheet-IMM-Alpha.pdf
12. NASA (2020) High power density solid oxide fuel cell, https://ntts-prod.s3.amazonaws.com/t2p/prod/t2media/tops/pdf/LEW-TOPS-120.pdf
13. Dr. Alberto Ravagni, (2022) personal interview with expert
14. H. A.Tvete, D. Hill, T. Hildre (2021), Are solid state batteries the holy grail for 2030, DNV, Technology Outlook 2030, www.dnv.com/to2030/technology/are-solid-state-batteries-the-holy-grail-for-2030.html
15. J. Wiens, F. Bommarito, E. Blumenstein, E. Matt, T. Cisar, Water Extraction from Martian Soil, Lunar and Planetary Institute, https://www.lpi.usra.edu/publications/reports/CB-1106/csm01.pdf
16. A. B. Cunje, R. R. Ghent, A. Boivin, C-A. Tsai, D. Hickson (2018), Dielectric properties of martian regolith analogs and smectite clays, 49th Lunar and Planetary Science Conference, https://www.hou.usra.edu/meetings/lpsc2018/pdf/1805.pdf
17. E. Ethridge, W. Kaukler (2007), Microwave Extraction of Water from Lunar Regolith Simulant, https://www.

researchgate.net/publication/252915866_Microwave_Extraction_of_Water_from_Lunar_Regolith_Simulant
18. Cheng, D., Li, D., Yuan, Y. et al. Improving carbohydrate and starch accumulation in Chlorella sp. AE10 by a novel two-stage process with cell dilution. Biotechnol Biofuels 10, 75 (2017). https://doi.org/10.1186/s13068-017-0753-9
19. J. Falquet, The nutritional aspects of spirulina, https://www.antenna.ch/wp-content/uploads/2017/03/AspectNut_UK.pdf
20. Sun, XM., Ren, LJ., Zhao, QY. et al. Microalgae for the production of lipid and carotenoids: a review with focus on stress regulation and adaptation. Biotechnol Biofuels 11, 272 (2018). https://doi.org/10.1186/s13068-018-1275-9
21. Dr. Alberto Ravagni, (2022) personal interview with expert
22. E.S. Shatney, et al. (1948), Peroxide-glycerol-explosive, US Patent Office, https://patentimages.storage.googleapis.com/ef/8e/16/2ee970cd3c9061/US2452074.pdf
23. Rarata, G., & Smętek, J. (2016). Explosives based on hydrogen peroxide—a historical review and novel applications. Materiały Wysokoenergetyczne, T. 8, 56-62., https://bibliotekanauki.pl/articles/92653
24. Perry, Samuel C., Pangotra, Dhananjai, Vieira, Luciana, Csepei, Lénárd-Istvan, Sieber, Volker, Wang, Ling, Ponce De Leon Albarran, Carlos and Walsh, Frank C. (2019) Electrochemical synthesis of hydrogen peroxide from water and oxygen. Nature Reviews Chemistry, 3, 442-458. (doi:10.1038/s41570-019-0110-6).

25. Xu, H., Rebollar, D., He, H. et al. Highly selective electrocatalytic CO2 reduction to ethanol by metallic clusters dynamically formed from atomically dispersed copper. Nat Energy 5, 623–632 (2020). https://doi.org/10.1038/s41560-020-0666-x
26. Bahmanpour, Alimohammad (2017): Single-step conversion of synthesis gas into formaldehyde. Monash University. Thesis. https://doi.org/10.4225/03/58b784f4ca69c
27. Wikipedia (2022), https://en.wikipedia.org/wiki/Mechanical_counterpressure_ suit#MIT_Bio-Suit
28. Sarcos Robotics, https://www.sarcos.com/products/guardian-xo-powered-exoskeleton/
29. Dr. Jeff Hall, Big Wheels Inflatable Rover, https://www2.jpl.nasa.gov/ adv_tech/rovers/bigwheel.htm
30. http://www.aircraftdesign.com/Raymer_MannedMarsPlane_ASM2021_ paper.pdf
31. Ch. Hoftun, P. Lee, B. W. Johansen, et al. (2013), Deep Drilling on Mars: Two Concepts and Prospects, 44th Lunar and Planetary Science Conference, https://www.lpi.usra.edu/meetings/lpsc2013/pdf/2817.pdf

ARES-1
STUDENT DESIGNED MARS MISSION

SHRIYA SAWANT

CIAN MCNISH

UZAIR MOHAMMED

BRIAN BARTELO

OMARI HUDSON

SUMMARY

The first manned Mars mission would not only be a feat of science and engineering but mark a new chapter of human civilization: the establishment of a multi-planetary species. The landing location of this designed mission is Utopia Planitia, where a 4-person crew will stay for 355 Martian Sols or roughly an Earth year. The work accomplished in this mission will prove that off-Earth living is possible, and lay the foundations of subsequent missions and eventually permanent settlements. Much has already been learned about Mars from the data robots have collected, but one topic that these marscrafts weren't able to truly study would be the effects of the Martian environment on the human body, and the viability of long-term habitation on the red planet. The Curiosity and Perseverance rovers have made some contributions in this field through the RAD (Radiation Assessment Detector) and MOXIE (Mars Oxygen In-Situ Resource Utilization Experiment) instruments respectively. The Ares-1 crew themselves would serve as a significant scientific interest: studying these effects on the human body and how effective the used countermeasures are. This mission will demonstrate ISRU capabilities and perform demonstrations of experimental technology that could be developed or improved on for subsequent missions. The research found and technology used on Mars will be applicable for use on Earth as well and strengthen humanity's presence in space.

SCIENCE

The main objective of this mission is to study the long and short-term effects of Mars on humans, research can only be done by a human presence there and cannot be replicated by a rover, therefore the best use of the limited time the crew will have on the red planet. This research includes both physical and psychological changes that may occur while spending a large amount of time on Mars such as the effects of Martian gravity on humans, psychological effects of long term space exploration, the effectiveness of exercise on Mars for combating muscle atrophy, the effectiveness of Neuro-Muscular Electrical Stimulation on Mars, the occurrence of blood clots, the effectiveness of Martian-grown cops at sustaining humans long-term, the effects of the Martian calendar on circadian rhythm, and possible future use of commensal bacteria and other medical technology to overcome the effects of the Martian environment. These human studies were chosen as the main objective to provide data on how humans endure long periods in space far from Earth. The health of the crew is also a prioritized objective for the success of the mission and to prove that off-planet living is possible. This data will be collected in a variety of ways, such as having the astronauts journal their thoughts daily to express how they are feeling and how they believe their stay on Mars has impacted them psychologically. We will also have physical fitness and health screenings monthly to study how their stay on Mars has impacted them physically. None of the various measurements taken for human data require surgery in order to minimize the risk of a health issue arising.

Along with this main objective there are many other side objectives that our Astronauts would achieve during their time on the red planet, these include several objectives in the departments of Astrobiology, Meteorology, Geology, Agriculture/Life Support, and Planetary Science.

Since our mission relies heavily on the usage of Martian water-ice, we thought it would be beneficial to utilize some of this recourse to attempt to detect possible microbial life within the large ice deposits at Utopia Planitia. This is one of the reasons Utopia Planitia was chosen as the landing site. The region also possesses many locations of scientific interest such as its rich geological history from volcanic activity, as well as having relatively flat terrain that allows for a safe landing. Viking 2 and the Zhurong rover also landed in Utopia for similar reasons, and the spacecrafts' research makes the land more familiar to the Ares-1 mission. Utopia Planitia's large ice deposits are a very valuable resource for numerous reasons, one of which is the possibility that they may contain living or once living microorganisms. We plan to use an ALF (Agnostic Life Finder) device to determine whether or not Martian water contains evidence of life. The ALF can be installed to inspect collected water before it is processed. The Oxford Nanopore MinION, a portable DNA and RNA sequencing device, will also help in life detection. Our Martian ice experiments coupled with the possibility of a long-distance EVA mission to study hydrothermal vents make up our Astrobiology experiment section.

We also plan to study Martian weather such as dust storms and winds, as this would likely allow us to predict Martian weather patterns as we do on Earth. This would benefit not only our mission but also all future Mars missions as predicting Martian weather would allow astronauts to avoid events such as dust storms. We also plan on conducting geological experiments such as stratum data collection, observation of glaciers, analysis of ice layers, observation of mud volcanism, seismic activity data collection, and planetary internal temperature data collection. The samples collected on Mars will be brought back to Earth for further analysis as well.

Since our mission only plans to bring around four months' worth of food for our astronauts, we will also be growing our crops using an aeroponic greenhouse. We plan to grow a variety of crops such as Lettuce, Onions, Garlic, Chickpeas, etc. Along with our normal crop growth, we will also be conducting experiments such as crop growth in Martian soil, this would help us to better understand if Martian soil is a viable option for long-term farming. We will also experiment with different methods for Aeroponically growing crops. Plants are already resilient to unfavorable conditions, such as growing in the microgravity of the ISS, but minimizing the risk of a crop failure is key to the success of a Mars settlement. Experiments measuring how resilient plants are in off-Earth/space conditions, such as exposing the plants to cosmic radiation and seeing how they survive, will be conducted outside the greenhouse's protection. Samples of various GMOs (Genetically Modified Organism) with the advantage of producing higher yield or possessing resistance to factors like drought, pesticides (can become useful if pests have somehow infiltrated the seed payload), and certain diseases will also be tested to see if they produce the same results as they would on Earth. The collected data on how plants fare on this mission (regular crop cycle data or from experiments) can be used to develop new GMOs specifically tailored for use on Mars and outer space. These changes can include better resistance to this cosmic radiation, a useful advantage in the case the crops are accidentally exposed to it as the adaptation would reduce the likelihood of crop failure.

Our final set of experiments is Planetary Studies, these experiments will help us better understand the phenomenon on the red planet. We plan to study the movement of Martian moons and the effects they may have on the planet as well as investigate possible methane spikes that have been shown to appear on Mars.

Here is a breakdown of our mission plan, each section is about 35.5 Martian Sols (Note that all human effects information will be gathered monthly):

- Section 1: Set up Habitat and greenhouse, plant crops, set up drills for ice mining, gather ice/water, and conduct ALF experiments.
- Section 2: Gather ice/water, dust storm/weather analysis, and check crops (harvest if ready).

- Section 3: Stratum data collection, gathering ice/water, observation of mud volcanoes and volcanic history, checking crops (harvest if ready), and conducting ALF experiments.
- Section 4: Gather ice/water, measure the internal temperature of Mars, Long distance EVA to study lava tunnels, and check crops (harvest if ready).
- Section 5: Gather ice/water, study the core of Mars using the wobble of the north pole, observation of glacial formations, and check crops (harvest if ready).
- Section 6: Gather ice/water, conduct ALF experiments, grow crops in martian soil, and check crop growth (harvest if ready).
- Section 7: Gather ice/water, map out Martian moons and study their effects on Mars, conduct ALF experiments, and check crops (harvest if ready).
- Section 8: Gather ice/water, long-distance EVA to study hydrothermal vents, check crop growth (harvest if ready).
- Section 9: Gather ice/water, conduct ALF experiments, analysis of ice layers/cryosphere, and check crop growth (harvest if ready).
- Section 10: Gather ice/water, measure the seismic activity of Mars, and check crop growth (harvest if ready).

ENGINEERING

This section will encompass the engineering challenges of this mission as well as elaborate on experimental technology demonstrations that will be expanded on in future missions. Several methods of ISRU (In-Situ Resource Utilization) are used to decrease the amount of payload taken to Mars and increase the self-sufficiency of the Ares-1 base and mission. These methods of gathering resources found on Mars will increase the viability of an independent human settlement, as this would reduce dependency on Earth as a lifeline. Along with the human studies in Ares-1's scientific objectives, the success of this mission's technology establishes further evidence to support argument that future missions and a permanent settlement on Mars is viable.

HABITAT AND GREENHOUSE FLOOR PLAN

The 2-story inflatable Habitat serves as a home base for the astronauts. The fabric of the Ares-1 habitat consists of multiple layers of various materials such as kevlar and mylar to insulate heat, prevent leakage of air or water, and protect the crew from outside conditions. This fabric is reinforced with a collapsible aluminum-alloy framework built within the material. This framework utilizes lockable joints that subsequently unfold and snap into place when the Habitat is inflated, resulting in a rigid and strong structure that allows for a second floor and protects the crew from outside conditions. This configuration provides for easy deployment as it would require minimal manual labor. This concept was based on the design of a hybrid lunar inflatable structure by Rohith Dronadula of Rutgers University.

The Habitat is 30 by 30 feet and is 27 feet tall (Not including height of optical laser communication terminal or MEDA). The first floor holds the entrance to the building with an airlock, suit decontamination room, EVA prep room, medical bay, laboratory, and storage space. Note that most of the payload is stored in the lander, and using one of the two vehicles is transported to the Habitat when needed. A greenhouse (18 by 10 feet and 13 feet tall) is also connected to the Habitat on the first floor and is where the astronauts will grow their crops using aeroponic towers. It also uses the same design configuration as the Hab, a hybrid inflated structure reinforced by an aluminum framework. The laboratory is also the designated emergency shelter for the astronauts, as it is the most central part of the Habitat and puts the most mass between the crew and outside.

The second floor is the astronauts' living space and office and is accessed by the spiral staircase, as shown in the diagram. It holds the cabins, a recreational area, gym and laundry, food prep and dining area, bathroom, and an office and control center where the crew communicates with Earth or the two vehicles and can access the Habitat's Systems Operations.

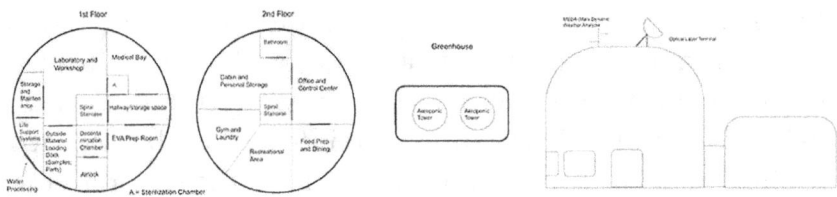

Figure 1: A rudimentary sketch of the floor plan of the Habitat and Greenhouse. Illustration by Shriya Sawant

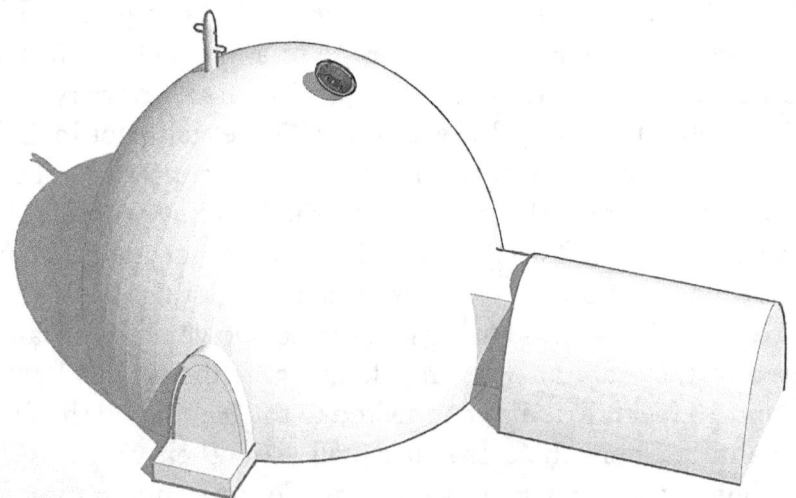

Figure 2: A 3D model of the Habitat and Greenhouse. Illustration by Shriya Sawant

MITIGATING MARTIAN REGOLITH

A problem the Apollo astronauts faced was lunar dust. Lunar dust is abrasive and electrostatically charged, which makes it very clingy to surfaces. The dust was impossible to brush off spacesuits and irritated astronauts' eyes and nasal passages. Since Apollo days, many technologies have been developed to combat this issue for future Moon missions but can be applied for Mars missions as well. Martian regolith is very fine and also electrostatically charged. Minimizing the amount of dust entering the Habitat is important, as over the course of time a buildup can damage electronics and affect the crew's health.

The outer layers of the EVA suits are designed to carry minimal dust using an Electrodynamic Dust Shield made from a network of carbon nanotubes. When a high-voltage charge is applied to this network, an electric field arises and levitates the electrostatic dust off the suit which then can be swept or blown away. Habitat and vehicle windows and suit visors are coated with a layer of Indium Tin Oxide, a material that can dissipate buildups of electrical charge, therefore reducing dust. This coating itself is not very heavy, as using a process called Atomic Layer Deposition, these layers can be applied to as thin as one atom thick. Electrostatic Precipitators will be used to filter air circulation by capturing floating dust particles as they travel along a gas stream, where two electrodes on either side of the stream pull out the charged dust.

VEHICLE AND FLOOR PLAN

The mission will utilize two vehicles, a 4-seater pressurized vehicle and a 2-seater buggy. Both utilize a radio wave communication system to communicate with the other vehicle, the Habitat, and to a satellite for Earth. The wheels of the vehicles are Nitinol Mesh Spring Tires. The tires use shape-memory to mold around obstacles and have excelled in simulations of lunar and Martian terrain, proficient in traversing both rock and sand. The terrain of Utopia Planitia is relatively flat allowing for easy travel and minimal obstructions of their view while driving. Topographic maps (discussed ahead in Navigation) will also inform the astronauts about dangerous terrain ahead.

The body of the 4-seat pressured vehicle is 23 feet by 8 feet and 12 feet tall. It has EVA capabilities, with a prep room, airlock, and miniature decontamination chamber, and also provides ample storage space for samples and collected water. A sample collection system seals samples in tubes to be later analyzed in the Habitat or stored on the Martian Ascent Vehicle. It has a small cabin area with 4 seats and 2 beds, as it is intended that the astronauts would take turns sleeping, so someone is always awake and alert in the case something were to occur. The vehicle's windshield has a retractable shutter in the case it is damaged. On the side of the vehicle is a hatch where samples can be directly transferred to the outside material loading dock of the Habitat's laboratory. At the back of the vehicle is a drill rig where a mechanical or hot-water drill can be attached. To aid in the search for ice deposits the vehicle is equipped with a ground-penetrating water radar. A modified version of the MEDA (Mars Environmental Dynamic Analyzer, from the Perseverance Rover) collects weather data and forecasts conditions. The vehicle will be used for long-distance travel such as for collecting water or samples at far but geologically unique sites. Its maximum speed is 30 miles per hour but it will normally travel at much lower speeds. It is powered by a rechargeable lithium-ion battery. Its life support system can sustain a full crew for up to six weeks.

The 2-seat buggy is 9 feet by 5 feet and is 6.25 feet tall and modeled after the lunar buggy and the Textron Wildcat X. It is an open-roof extreme-terrain vehicle meant for short-distance travel such as for transporting materials to and from the Habitat, lander, and the return vehicle. Just like the 4-seater, it also has a

Ares-1: Student Designed Mars Mission

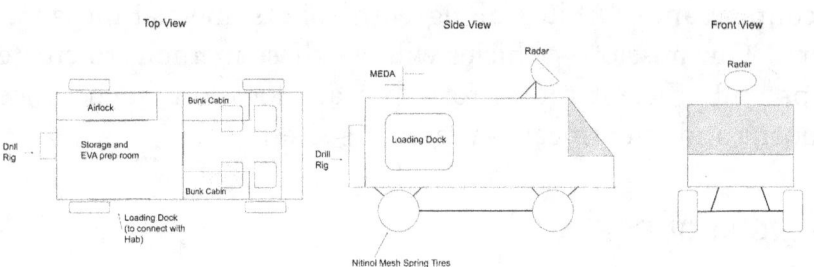

Fig. 3: A rudimentary sketch of the floor plan of the 4-seater vehicle. Illustration by Shriya Sawant.

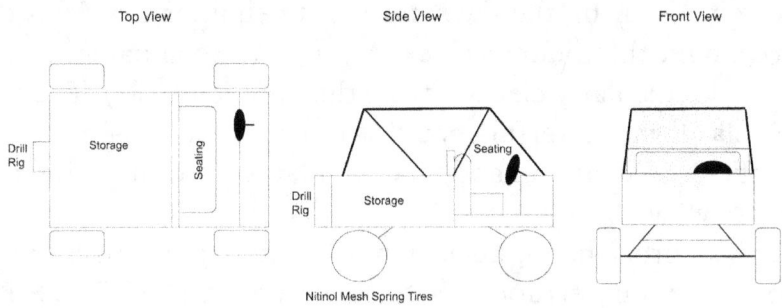

Fig. 4: A rudimentary sketch of the floor plan of the 4-seater vehicle. Illustration by Shriya Sawant.

suspension system, attachable drill rig, and ground-penetrating water radar. The buggy's maximum speed is 45 miles per hour (Again, it will normally travel at much lower speeds.) and like the pressurized vehicle is powered by lithium-ion battery.

NAVIGATION

Without a GPS in place for the red planet, the astronauts would navigate the Martian terrain using a combination of other systems. Methods of tracking mars rovers included topographic images, such as those taken by the HiRISE camera on the Mars

Reconnaissance Orbiter, along with robots' inertial measurements. Our mission's vehicles will use these methods to create maps and efficient routes to important locations such as ice deposits and scientifically-interesting sites.

ENERGY SOURCE

Nuclear energy is the most reliable source of power on a manned Mars mission. Solar power was not chosen for 3 main reasons: Limited sunlight, dust, and the amount of surface area needed to provide enough energy for the mission. Sunlight would only be received during the day, and Mars being farther from the Sun than Earth, would receive less sunlight. Solar panels would have to be regularly cleaned from dust accumulation. The size of a solar farm powerful enough to sustain the mission would be difficult to maintain and take up a large portion of the mission's payload.

On the other hand, nuclear power offers a compact, lightweight, and uninterruptible source of energy. The K.R.U.S.T.Y. (Kilopower Reactor Using Stirling Technology) was chosen for this mission for these reasons, as a 10 kWe reactor would stand at 11 feet tall and weigh only 4,400 lbs., and can be placed outside near the settlement. The kilopower reactor is more efficient than an RTG as it can convert 30% of fission heat to electricity. There is a very low likelihood that the reactor would pose a nuclear hazard, as the only way to reach that critical stage would be if the rod of the reactor had been accidentally removed. The reactor can also self-regulate its temperature in the case it becomes too low or high. This mission is powered by 2 K.R.U.S.T.Y. 10 kWe reactors. In the rare chance that the reactors fail, 2 lithium-ion batteries serve as a temporary backup power source until the primary source is repaired. The Habitat also has an energy-saving setting that reduces power usage to only necessary life support systems.

COMMUNICATIONS SYSTEM

This mission will utilize optical communication using the recently launched NASA LCRD (Laser Communications Relay Demonstration). Past missions have mainly used radio frequency communication which has a very limited data rate, preventing valuable information from being transmitted to Earth. Using optical communication larger amounts of data can be received quicker. A map of Mars that would usually take 9 weeks to be transmitted can be cut down to roughly 9 days by using lasers. This allows for the astronauts to have better coordination with researchers on Earth who can now analyze more data quickly, and actively advise them in their mission. For example, if a sample's spectrography has an interesting reading, researchers can request the astronauts to collect more samples from that location. Optical communication has the added benefit of having a bandwidth 10-100 times more than a radiowave system while also being smaller, lighter, and less power-consuming.

The Habitat will be equipped with a receiving and transmitting optical laser terminal that can communicate with spacecraft orbiting Mars to relay data to Earth. Data beamed to the earth-orbiting LCRD would then be relayed to either of currently two stations on Earth: Haleakalā, Hawaii, USA, and Table Mountain, California, USA, which were selected as they had minimal interference from clouds. With the Martian atmosphere 100 times thinner than Earth's, atmospheric interference would be rare. The Habitat also has a backup radiowave communication system. Crew spacesuits and vehicles will still use radio as surface physical obstructions will impede optical transmissions made to each other.

GROUND PENETRATING WATER RADAR

As mentioned in the Science section the landing location of Utopia Planitia, as detected by SHARAD (Mars SHAllow RADar sounder) on the Mars Reconnaissance orbiter, possesses dozens of large subsurface deposits at least ~10 meters beneath the ground and are 50-85% water ice by volume. To pinpoint the exact locations of these deposits a ground penetrating water radar based on the Perseverance rover's RIMFAX (Radar Imager for Mars' subsurFAce eXperiment) instrument, which as of today generally has a range of +10 meters. An updated (2030s) version of the radar is equipped on the 4-seater vehicle to help detect and locate ice/water deposits under the surface.

MECHANICAL AND HOT-WATER DRILL

The mission utilizes 2 types of drills. These are the mechanical drill and the hot-water drill. These drills can be attached to a drill rig on both of the mission vehicles. The mechanical drill can reach depths as low as +10 meters to collect samples or to reach ice/water deposits. Once a path is cleared to an ice/water deposit, the hot-water drill is deployed. This drill melts the ice in the deposit, creating a well that can be revisited by the crew to collect water.

RODRIGUEZ WELLS (RODWELLS)

After the hot-water drill has melted a sufficient amount of ice, a Rodriguez well is installed on the deposit. Used in the polar regions of Earth, the Rodriguez well is a pump submerged into a cavity of melted ice that cycles heated water to prevent the water from refreezing and to melt more ice in the deposit. The cavity's water is pumped up to the surface for reheating and can be transferred to a water storage tank, which the pressurized vehicle has. This water is brought back to the Habitat for processing.

WATER PROCESSING

Martian water potentially has perchlorates, a material hazardous to humans if consumed in large amounts. More than 99.9% of this perchlorate can be removed from water by adding a catalyst inspired by anaerobic microbes, which use molybdenum to lessen perchlorate. At room temperature, and without any combustion process required, the catalyst can swiftly break down the perchlorate by using hydrogen gas. The catalyst was developed by a team led by engineers from the University of California, Riverside.

Water can also be purified using activated carbon filters to remove sediments and heavy metals possibly present. It is assumed that the upcoming Perseverance Rover Sample Return will provide information on the composition of Martian soil and water, that this mission's water filtration system can be designed upon. This water then can be fed into an improved version of the International Space Station's Water Recovery System, part of the ECLSS (Environmental Control and Life Support System), which is discussed more in the Human Factors and Life Support section.

OXYGEN

Oxygen can be created by separating water into hydrogen and oxygen, using a Briny Water Electrolyzer developed by a team from Washington University. This electrolyzer, when operated in a simulated Martian environment and using the same input power, produced more than 25 times the amount of oxygen that was produced by the MOXIE (Mars Oxygen In-Situ Resource Utilization Experiment) instrument onboard the Perseverance Rover.

To recreate an Earth-like breathing mixture in the Habitat, imported tanks of Nitrogen would periodically release gas into the Hab to maintain balance. Trace gasses such as the byproducts of human metabolism are removed from the atmosphere using activated charcoal filters.

THE SABATIER PROCESS

Additional water can be created utilizing the Sabatier process. The Sabatier process takes hydrogen and CO2 to produce water and methane. The hydrogen needed for the reaction is available as the by-product of the briny water electrolyzer, and the CO2 is sourced from the exhalations of the crew, and if needed, intakes from the +95% CO2 Martian atmosphere. This additional water can be stored or used again in the briny water electrolyzer. This will increase the efficiency of our mission's water recycling system.

METHANE AS A POTENTIAL ROCKET FUEL

Methane, the other product of the Sabatier process, is a viable rocket fuel that Mars missions can use. Methane is more stable and can be stored at more practical temperatures (similar to liquid oxygen) than liquid hydrogen, the most common rocket fuel today, and has higher performance than most fuels. As methane is denser than liquid hydrogen and requires less insulation, storage tanks can be made smaller and therefore more economical. In this mission it is assumed that our return vehicle is already fueled before the crew landed.

RADIATION SHIELDING

Mars, unlike Earth, does not possess a magnetosphere which leaves the Ares-1 crew and future inhabitants vulnerable to radiation. The crew will encounter two types of radiation: GCRs (Galactic Cosmic Rays) and SPEs (Solar Proton Event. Galactic

Cosmic Rays are high-energy protons and nuclei stripped of their electron shells speeding through space at near the speed of light and are constantly bombarding Earth and Mars. Solar Proton Events occur when protons or other ions near the Sun are launched out to space during a solar flare. These are short-term events but would expose astronauts to elevated amounts of radiation. Activities outside the Habitat will be ceased until it is deemed safe to resume. In the case a crew member cannot return to the hab in time, they can find shelter by putting as much mass between them and open space as possible.

The best-known protectors against solar and cosmic radiation are hydrogenous materials, such as water and polyethylene, the latter used in the International Space Station to protect astronauts. Martian regolith has also been proposed as a method of blocking radiation but requires a structure to be buried in at least a meter of regolith to be effective. There is also the problem of secondary radiation, which is radiation resulting from the absorption of other radiation in matter. The atoms of a radiation shield itself could be broken down from the particles of original primary radiation, the collision producing particles of secondary radiation just as dangerous to human health. Heavy elements produce more secondary radiation than lighter ones, hence why hydrogen is the preferred radiation barrier as their atoms are harder to break down into the nuclear particles that make up secondary radiation.

There are multiple preventative measures in place to counter the radiation the crew will face, ranging from anti-radiation medicines to the materials the Habitat, 4-seater vehicle, and EVA suits are constructed from. The structure of inflatable Habitat is mainly made up of fabric with the exception of its aluminum framework. These layers of passive radiation shielding include current industry-standard materials as well as new inventions: HDPE (High-Density PolyEthylene), Kevlar, and 20%-hydrogen loaded BNNT (Boron Nitride Nanotube) woven into fabric. HDPE was chosen for its cheap but effective blocking of radiation. Kevlar, although expensive, is just as effective as polyethylene and is an extremely durable material that can protect the Habitat from outside conditions. BNNTs+20% hydrogen surpass polyethylene's ability and has excellent mechanical and thermal properties, possessing a higher elastic modulus, melting point, and thermal conductivity than the commonly-used alloy Aluminum 2195. Studies have also shown that Lithium Hydride (80% Li and 20% H) was able to widely outperform HDPE but due to its properties of being a powdery material, reactivity to water and oxygen, and harmful to human health in the case of direct exposure, it was not chosen for this mission.

The internal layers of the 4-seat vehicle are also made up of multiple layers of HDPE. The frame and exterior of the vehicle, just like most marscraft, is made from aluminum alloys. The EVA suits are also made up of HDPE, Kevlar, and BNNTS. This material, along with the liquid cooling garment, makes the suit capable of providing adequate protection against radiation. Later in this section, an experimental engineering demonstration will test the efficacy of a localized magnetic field created by a superconductor.

SPACESUIT DESIGN

The engineering section will focus on the basic design and a Human-Machine Interface for the spacesuit. Other aspects of the spacesuit are covered in the Science and Human Factors section of the report. The astronauts have two suits: The IVA (IntraVehiclaur Activities) suit is an adjustable mechanical counter-pressure suit based on the MIT BioSuit, while the EVA (ExtraVehicular Activities) is a partial gas-pressure suit that protects the human from extreme temperature, environmental conditions, and radiation while also having a life support system backpack, further discussed in the human factors section. This combination of both mechanical counter-pressure and gas-pressure is used to maintain suit pressure, and is a system likely to be developed and used by the 2030's. This system prevents decompression sickness as the astronauts will be under an earth-like pressure (14.7 PSI) at all times. Furthermore, a decompression procedure that includes pre-breathing pure oxygen is always done prior to EVAs.

Two technologies tested by the NASA Haughton-Mars are the Collins Aerospace IT IS (Information Technology Informatics System) and the Ntention Astronaut Smart Glove. The IT IS is an augmented reality display inside the helmet that lets the astronaut track their vitals, EVA elapsed time, the amount of oxygen they have left, maps, notes, task checklists, and other statistics. This allows the astronaut to be more self-sufficient as they are less dependent on external help for tracking their EVA. The Ntention Smart Glove uses gesture technology to control robots, eliminating the need for a hand-held controller.

DRONE

A drone is a vital tool on Mars as it can fly to places that no rover or vehicle could traverse safely. The drone can provide high-resolution video from above, acting as a second set of eyes for the astronauts. The drone can be controlled remotely either from a vehicle or the Habitat, or from the spacesuit's Ntention Astronaut Smart Glove.

SOLAR MONTGOLFIERE WEATHER BALLOONS

Current research of martian weather only happens from stations on rovers and spacecraft orbiting Mars. To collect more information about the atmosphere the crew will assemble, inflate (with Hydrogen), and release controlled Solar Montgolfiere

Balloons equipped with radiosondes, cameras, and dropsondes. The radiosonde will measure atmospheric variables (temperature, pressure, wind direction) while the camera will provide visual data of the balloon's journey. The balloon will attempt to deploy the dropsondes, which are lightweight dispensable devices used to study storms on Earth, over dust storms to study the inner workings of this planetary phenomenon. Every mission to Mars, manned or not, will expect some form of pollution left behind. This mission takes care to minimize this variable, as these dropsondes are the only planned debris to be left on Mars besides the EDL stage. These Montgolfiere balloons are also capable of soft-landing small payloads such as the aforementioned instruments or possibly small rovers. This ability wouldn't be of use in this mission, but in the future provide a way for astronauts to safely deliver packages in locations that themselves cannot reach or to other and future settlement locations.

3D PRINTER

Additive manufacturing expands the capabilities of ISRU and the industrialization of Mars as materials mined on the planet can be used to produce a near-infinite array of parts and tools, and in the future construct habitats and launch vehicles from scratch. In this mission a small (10x10 inch build plate) and compact 3D printer, preferably a simple design with minimal parts and easy assembly, and plastic filament powder are included on the payload. The crew's computers have CAD software to allow them to tinker with the technology.

Engineering Demonstrations- Active Radiation Shielding

There will be one major engineering demonstration done in this mission: testing a localized magnetic field created by a superconductor magnet. This technology would be useful in protecting astronauts, especially when they are traveling in deep space, from radiation. At their optimal temperature, superconductors are capable of producing stronger magnetic fields than conventional materials while being lightweight, making them an ideal method of active radiation shielding. High-temperature superconductors (above 321.1 F) can operate in similar temperature ranges to Mars's natural low temperatures, eliminating the need to import cooling agents to maintain their optimality. To determine the efficacy of a magnetic field generated by a superconductor, the crew will measure the dose of radiation inside the magnetic field, and compare the results to normal radiation levels and to the percentage of radiation that passive shielding would stop.

LIFE SUPPORT AND HUMAN FACTORS

The Life Support and Human Factors part of this mission deals with the astronauts themselves. We identified the jobs of these 4 astronauts and have taken into consideration their well-being. We have also identified the various life support systems and the physical and psychological needs of the astronauts.

CREW

- 1st Member (Commander): Pilot and Aerospace Engineer
- 2nd Member (Payload Specialist): Astrobiologist and Geologist
- 3rd Member (Mission Specialist): Nuclear Engineer and General Mechanic
- 4th Member (Mission Specialist and 2nd Commander): Botanist and System Operations

The crew's specialties will help them effectively carry out all objectives, as well as keep them safe and healthy during their stay on Mars. All crew members are fully trained for marswalks.

EVAs should always be carried out in at least pairs of 2. This buddy system ensures that one will be available to assist the other for their task or in an emergency.

The 1st crew member is the mission Commander, the leader of the mission and main coordinator with Mission Control. They serve as the pilot of the mission and along with the aid of autonomous systems are responsible for controlling spacecraft such as the lander and martian ascent vehicle. Being an aerospace engineer they are also responsible for any maintenance needed for spacecraft.

The 2nd crew member is an astrobiologist with a significant background in geology as well. As the payload specialist they will be the main conductor of completing the mission's scientific objectives, and have the most training in using the instruments and equipment brought to Mars. They will be the main communicator to researchers on Earth who study the data sent from Mars.

The 3rd crew member will be a nuclear engineer and general mechanic. They are responsible for ensuring energy is supplied to this mission by overseeing the operation of the K.R.U.S.T.Y. reactors. As a general mechanic they'll be the one to maintain and repair any broken equipment and assist the other crew members in doing so as well, such as helping the Commander to maintain spacecraft. They'll also be adept in using equipment such as the mechanical or hot-water drill.

The 4th crew member will be a Botanist and Systems Operations Expert. They will be responsible for directing crop harvests of the aeroponic towers and also manage the mission's life support and information technology systems. This includes ensuring the function of computer networks and communications, periodically checking the breathing atmosphere mixtures of the Hab are at safe levels, or monitoring various data loggers for strange activity (For indications that air is leaking out of the Hab somewhere, possible drinking water contamination, astronaut vitals, etc). This data is already monitored by a software program that will notify the crew of unusual activity and is also transmitted to Earth to be continuously supervised by experts who verify the safety and success of the mission.

All crew members will also be adept in first-aid, identifying health issues, and well prepared to handle serious medical emergencies with the guidance of professionals on Earth by telemedicine. As mentioned before, the astronauts' medical readings and tests are reviewed by these professionals on Earth to find any developments, both physical and mental, that threaten their health. This would help manage preventable conditions before they become a serious problem, such as identifying and treating thrombosis, or from psychological evaluations determining if an astronaut is at risk of depression. A medical bay is present in the Hab to treat injuries and to quarantine sick crew members.

The astronauts were selected irrespective of nationality or gender. The equipment and technology used in this mission can be built by international partners and private companies such as SpaceX or Blue Origin. Given the success these companies are having today, it is reasonable to project that they will have a large influence in Mars exploration, and one day have their own missions to the red planet.

The crew's schedules and tasks for the Sol are mainly predetermined by mission planners on Earth, but if the need arises for quick action the crew is trusted to make their own decisions. Shifts (sleep schedules and 1.5 day weekends) are allocated to always have at least one person awake and alert to monitor the Hab and mission status. Instruction manuals about the Ares-1 mission, emergency protocols, system operations, and health are all stored offline in the computer network and in hardcopy for consultation in the case Mission Control on Earth is unavailable.

RADIATION PROTECTION

The astronauts will be exposed to increased amounts of radiation, mainly throughout their journey in deep space, and to some degree on Mars. As mentioned before in the engineering section, several passive radiation shielding materials are used on this mission. Polyethylene is an effective blocker of radiation and cheap as well, with it commonly found in water bottles and grocery bags. BNNTs (Boron Nitride Nanotubes) are made up of Carbon, Boron, and Nitrogen, with Hydrogen interspersed throughout the empty spaces between these nanotubes. These nanotubes can be woven into a fabric for EVA spacesuits.

In addition to passive shielding, another method the astronauts can use to protect themselves from radiation can be in the form of medicine. A new treatment using an oral (via food) drug called PLX5622 can prevent brain damage after exposure to cosmic radiation, such as spending an extended period of time on an EVA. The drug has already completed successful trials on mice.

WATER

Treating the water taken from Mars for is a necessary step in keeping the crew healthy. 360 gallons of water are imported from Earth to sustain the crew for the first few months of the mission, giving them ample time to set up an ISRU water mining system explained in the Engineering section. It is assumed that by the 2030's a ~96% effective water recovery system will be developed. An improved ECLSS (Environmental Control and Life Support System) first used on the ISS will recover water from urine, brine, and other wastewater and revitalize the air inside our Habitat. This includes regulating the cabin's condensate and humidity levels. Components such as Argonide's NanoCeram filter can remove biological contaminants and small particles, and the recently implemented brine processor in the ISS ECLSS increases the portion of water recycled. This water recovery system will allow the mission to import less water from Earth, and we envision that subsequent missions to Mars will use a fully closed-loop system, recycling 100% of water.

FOOD

The amount of food imported from Earth would be 2000 pounds or ~4 months worth, more than enough to sustain the crew until the first aeroponic crop harvest. The first crop cycle will be complete at least a month into the mission, including the first few martian sols it will take for the crew to fully set up the Ares-1 base. Remaining imported food is reserved as emergency supply. Aeroponic systems were chosen to grow food for the mission for a multitude of reasons. Aeroponics uses the least amount of water and fertilizer compared to traditional farming methods and aeroponics. The two aeroponic towers used in this mission also operate independently of one another, which reduces the risk of both of them somehow failing. Aeroponically-grown crops also have significantly larger yields and shorter crop cycles than traditional growing methods, providing a quick and reliable source of food for the mission. Along with a healthy diet grown by this aeroponic system, astronauts will take supplements for any nutrients they cannot obtain enough of on Mars. Menu fatigue will be countered by growing certain crops at different times to bring variety and using different spices or seasonings, some of which can be grown aeroponically, to flavor the food. The farm is primarily tended to by the crew botanist, whose other expertise in systems operations helps them operate the growing system equipment. The weaker gravity of Mars would likely not pose a problem as aeroponic systems have successfully grown food on the microgravity environment of the ISS.

WASTE

The mission's trash and waste that cannot be further processed by the life support recycling systems will be stored in the return vehicle to be brought back to Earth so as to not excessively pollute Mars.

SPACESUIT–LIFE SUPPORT BACKPACK

The EVA suit's life support backpack includes a primary and emergency oxygen tank, a drinking water supply, a waste management system for urine, solid waste, and sweat, spacesuit monitoring system for detecting leaks or malfunctions, and a vitals monitoring system that measures parameters such as body temperature, heart rate, respiration rate, and blood pressure. The EVA prep room in the Habitat has all the materials and tools needed to properly don and duff the suit that is done with the help of another crewmate. A spare spacesuit is also accounted for in the mission.

HEALTH (OVERVIEW)

Keeping the crew healthy is another main priority of the mission. Being in space for an extended period of time in cramped quarters is not going to be a luxurious (but well worth it) journey for the astronauts. The 1 earth year spent on Mars along with transportation to and from the planet being ~7 months each results in a total combined time of ~2 years and two months spent off-Earth. This far exceeds the 437 days of the current record of the longest single stay in space. Furthermore, this record was achieved on the Mir space station which operated in low Earth orbit, much closer to help than this mission's journey on Mars and deep space.

The physical and psychological effects that this journey would have on the crew was a factor in why this mission chose to limit the stay on Mars to 1 earth year (355 martian sols) instead of the competition's maximum allowed duration of 1.5 years. But, the information gained on Ares-1 will lay the groundwork for future missions to extend their stay on Mars to 1.5 years and beyond, with the goal of an eventual permanent settlement.

PHYSICAL HEALTH

The crew will exercise 1-2 hours per day in order to prevent bone and muscle density loss. This number is based on the 2.5 hours ISS astronauts spend exercising to avoid these same complications. The 3 pieces of exercise equipment brought on this mission are also similar to what the ISS uses, a bicycle, treadmill, and weight training/ resistive exercise machine based on the ARED (Advanced Resistive Exercise Device). To imitate free weights in microgravity the ARED uses vacuum cylinders. This same concept will be applied to recreate weight-lifting on Mars. As more research has been done to downsize scientific instruments than exercise equipment, it is a hefty but important part of the mission payload. The data collected from exercise will be crucial to understanding how to make the human body better tolerate a long-term or permanent presence in space. For astronauts that are unable to exercise, NMES (Neuro-Muscular Electrical Stimulation) therapy is a temporary alternative. Commonly used to treat bedridden patients, NMES applies on the body a device that transmits electrical impulses to the nervous system, causing the muscle to contract. NMES can strengthen the muscle and therefore offset atrophy resulting from a period of disuse.

MENTAL HEALTH

The psychological health of the crew is just as important as physical health. Multiple factors such as isolation from the rest of humanity, the stress of work, and being in cramped quarters for so long can have a serious effect on the individual astronaut as well as the cohesion and camaraderie of the crew.

Monthly psychological evaluations can help document the astronauts' well being. As mentioned before, each crew member will also be provided their own private journal to write their thoughts down on. Each astronaut is allowed to bring 12.5 lbs worth of personal items and a selection of ebooks, video games, movies, and other media. Although Earth-Mars video calls and internet connection are unlikely to happen within the next decade, astronauts can communicate with their loved ones by email correspondence. The crew have a 1.5 day weekend (Can take place on any part of the week) to prevent burn-out. If possible, their workload will be reduced on birthdays and holidays.

COST

The cost estimate for this mission is around ~255 Billion USD. The cost estimate is based on current values of technologies used in this mission as well as how these prices may change ~10 years into the future, as this Mars mission takes place in the early 2030's. Certain technologies which already have commercial applications are more prone to have a reduced cost in the future, as they already have thorough research behind them and can be more easily produced. An example of this is the growing use of optical laser communication systems and the use of aeroponics. In turn, many of the technologies developed or improved for space exploration will find their uses here on Earth. Several cost and payload reduction methods are used in this mission such as ISRU-made water and oxygen.

Cost Breakdown
- Research and Development—$150 Billion
- Structures & Vehicles—$12.7 Billion
- Aeroponic Towers & Farming Equipment—$1.9 Billion
- Spacesuits—$8.3 Billion
- Life Support Systems—$27.14 Billion
- Scientific Equipment—$42 Billion
- Tools & Misc. Equipment—$13 Billion

Mission Weight Limit Spreadsheet (Total: 64680.598 lbs)

ITEM	TOTAL: 30 METRIC TON/ 66138 POUND LIMIT	
Inflated Habitat Structure	~27,000 lbs	12,246.994 kg
4-seat Pressurized Vehicle	~11,000 lbs	4,989.516 kg
2-seat Vehicle (2)	~1,700 lbs	771.107 kg
KRUSTY Nuclear Reactor (2)	~8,800 lbs	3991.613 kg
SUPPLIES AND TOOLS		
Drill	~Mechanical 265 lbs ~Hot Water Drill 2200 lbs	1118.105 kg total
Rodriguez Well Pump System	~350 lbs	158.757 kg
Solar Mongolfiere Weather Balloon (6)	58.07 total	26.340 kg
-Radiosonde (6)	~12 lbs Total	5.443 kg
-Dropsonde (Dust Storm Study) (6)	~5.16 lbs Total	2.3405 kg
-Hazard Avoidance and Imaging Cameras (6)	~4 lbs Total	1.814 kg
Drone	~10 lbs	
Instruments		
-High-Resolution Camera (2) Based off Mastcam-Z	~17.6 lbs	7.983 kg
X-Ray Fluorescence Spectrometer	~16.03 lbs	7.271 kg
Infrared Spectrometer	~3.84 lbs	1.742 kg
Gamma Ray Spectrometer	~67.2 lbs	30.481 kg
-Analysis Laser: Based off SuperCam	~23.1 lbs	10.478 kg
-Radiation Detector: Based off RAD	~3.3 lbs	1.497 kg
-MEDA (Mars Environmental Dynamics Analyzer) (2)	~24 lbs total	10.886 kg
Ground-penetrating radar (Based off RIMFAX) (2)	~13.2 lbs	5.987 kg
Lab Equipment (Microscopes, Incubators)	~100 lbs	45.359 kg
3D Printer	~60 lbs	27.216 kg
Plastic 3D Printing Material	~10 lbs	4.536 kg
Toolbox (Hammer, Screwdriver)	~30 lbs	13.609 kg
Ladder	~60 lbs	27.216 kg
Laser Comm. System (2) [Receiver and Transmitter]	~304.238 lbs	138 kg
Instruction Manuals (Book And Offline) on System Ops.	~5 lbs	2.268 kg
Briny Water Electrolyzer	~58 lbs	27.216 kg
ALF (2)	~6 lbs	2.722 kg
Mars Sample Containers (Empty)	~75 lbs	34.019 kg
Superconductor for Engineering Demo	~2 lbs	0.907 kg
LIFE SUPPORT		
Spacesuit (5)	~100 lbs IVA - 875 lbs EVA	442.253 kg total
Human Crew (4)	~836 lbs Total	379.203 kg
Greenhouse		
-Inflatable structure	~3,115 lbs	1412.94 kg
-Aeroponic System	~220 lbs	99.790 kg
-Seeds	~1 lb	0.454 kg
Packaged Food	~2,000 lbs	907.185 kg
Water	~3,000 lbs	1360.777 kg
Oxygen	~250 lbs	113.398 kg
Nitrogen (Won't need replenishing)	~462 lbs	209.56 kg
Water Recycling/Filtration System	~820 lbs	371.946 kg
Sabatier Reactor	~3.86 lbs	1.756 kg
Medicine		
-First Aid Kits (5)	~10 lbs	4.536 kg
-Medical Equipment (Stethoscopes, Defibrillator)	~50 lbs	22.680 kg
-Medicine (Antibiotics, Drugs, Supplements)	~10 lbs	4.536 kg
-Instructional Manuals (Book and Offline) on Health	~5 lbs	2.268 kg
Exercise Equipment		
-Bicycle	~140 lbs	63.503 kg
-Treadmill	~200 lbs	90.719 kg
-Weight Training/ Resistive Exercise machine	~250 lbs	113.398 kg
Miscellaneous		
Astronaut's Belongings (Books, Games, Personal Items)	~50 lbs total	22.680 kg

CONCLUSION

In this report, we described a mission centered on proving that human habitation on Mars is viable and worth investing into for its invaluable research, ISRU methods that can be used for eventual martian industrialization, and the survival benefit of becoming a multi-planetary species. From this mission comes a year's worth of documentation and data for the effects the Martian environment has on the human body and the successes and potential error or failures of the engineering and life support systems, paving the way for new and improved manned space exploration technologies and techniques built upon this mission. The research found on Mars and the technology developed to support this mission will find its way to improving lives back on Earth as well, and in the development of settlements on the Moon and elsewhere.

ACKNOWLEDGEMENTS

We thank the Mars Society, the volunteer mentor and judges, and our fellow student teams for making this project possible.

REFERENCES

SCIENCE

1. Greicius, T. (2016, November 22). Mars ice deposit holds as much water as Lake Superior. NASA. Retrieved July 29, 2022, from https://www.nasa.gov/feature/jpl/mars-ice-deposit-holds-as-much-water-as-lake-superior/
2. Frequently asked questions—vertical farming with Tower Farms. Tower Farms. (n.d.). Retrieved July 29, 2022, from https://www.towerfarms.com/us/en/faq

3. Horne, M. F. (2016, September 14). Drilling on Mars – mathematical model for rotary-ultrasonic core drilling of brittle materials. eScholarship, University of California. Retrieved July 28, 2022, from https://escholarship.org/uc/item/6zg2x2d8
4. Lupisella, M. L. (2016, June 24). Mars surface drilling study report.docx. Academia.edu. Retrieved August 5, 2022, from https://www.academia.edu/26469804/Mars_Surface_Drilling_Study_Report_docx
5. "mining" water ice on Mars–NASA. (n.d.). Retrieved August 5, 2022, from https://www.nasa.gov/sites/default/files/atoms/files/mars_ice_drilling_assessment_v6_for_public_release.pdf
6. ScienceDaily. (2021, June 4). A new water treatment technology could also help Mars explorers. ScienceDaily. Retrieved August 5, 2022, from https://www.sciencedaily.com/releases/2021/06/210604122505.htm
7. Cost analysis of life support systems summary report– ntrs.nasa.gov. (n.d.). Retrieved August 29, 2022, from https://ntrs.nasa.gov/api/citations/19730018345/downloads/19730018345.pdf
8. Carr, C.E., Bryan, N.C., Saboda, K.N. et al. Nanopore sequencing at Mars, Europa, and microgravity conditions. npj Microgravity 6, 24 (2020). https://doi.org/10.1038/s41526-020-00113-9
9. Oxford Nanopore Technologies . (2022, February 21). MinION. Oxford Nanopore Technologies. Retrieved August 29, 2022, from https://nanoporetech.com/products/minion

ENGINEERING

1. Dronadula, R. (2019). Hybrid Lunar Inflatable Structure. Rutgers University Community Repository. Retrieved August 29, 2022, from https://rucore.libraries.rutgers.edu/rutgers-lib/60141/
2. Bigelow Aerospace. (n.d.). B330. Bigelow Aerospace. Retrieved August 29, 2022, from https://bigelowaerospace.com/pages/b330/
3. Sierra Space. (2022, July 19). Life™ habitat: Inflatable space station design. Sierra Space. Retrieved August 29, 2022, from https://www.sierraspace.com/space-destinations/life-space-habitat/
4. Hoffman, S. J., Lever, J. H., Andrews, A. D., & Watts, K. D. (2020, October 1). Mars Rodwell Experiment final report—NASA technical reports server (NTRS). NASA Technical Reports Server. Retrieved August 5, 2022, from https://ntrs.nasa.gov/citations/20205011353
5. Hoffman, S., Andrews, A., & Watts, K. (2016, July). "Mining" Water Ice on Mars. Retrieved August 5, 2022, from https://www.nasa.gov/sites/default/files/atoms/files/mars_ice_drilling_assessment_v6_for_public_release.pdf
6. Stuurman, C. M., Osinski, G. R., Holt, J. W., Levy, J. S., Brothers, T. C., Kerrigan, M., & Campbell, B. A. (2016, September 15). SHARAD detection and characterization of subsurface water ice deposits in Utopia Planitia, Mars. American Geophysical Union Journals. Retrieved August 10, 2022, from https://agupubs.onlinelibrary.wiley.com/doi/full/10.1002/2016GL070138
7. SETI Institute, NASA Haughton-Mars Project, Ntention, Collins Aerospace, & Mars Institute. (2021, September 9). New Spacesuit Technologies for Moon and Mars

exploration tested in Oregon where Apollo astronauts once trained and tested spacesuits. SETI Institute. Retrieved August 5, 2022, from https://www.seti.org/press-release/new-spacesuit-technologies-moon-and-mars-exploration-tested-oregon-where-apollo-astronauts-once

8. Withrow-Maser, S., Johnson, W., Young, L., Cummings, H., Chan, A., Tzanetos, T., Balaram, J., & Bapst, J. (n.d.). An Advanced Mars Helicopter Design. Retrieved August 10, 2022, from https://rotorcraft.arc.nasa.gov/Publications/files/An_Advanced_Helicopter_Design_SW_ASCEND_final.pdf

9. Tibbits, S. (2022, March 30). Dava Newman presents 3D Knit BioSuit™ at 2022 Mars Conference. MIT Media Lab. Retrieved August 5, 2022, from https://www.media.mit.edu/posts/dava-newman-presents-3d-knit-biosuit-at-mars-conference/

10. Canadian Space Agency. (2006, August 18). What is decompression sickness? Canadian Space Agency. Retrieved August 27, 2022, from https://www.asc-csa.gc.ca/eng/astronauts/space-medicine/decomp.asp

11. Mohon, L. (2015, October 28). NASA tests methane engine components for next generation landers. NASA. Retrieved August 5, 2022, from https://www.nasa.gov/centers/marshall/news/releases/2015/nasa-tests-methane-powered-engine-components-for-next-generation-landers.html

12. Gayen, P., Sankarasubramanian, S., & Ramani, V. K. (2020, November 30). Fuel and oxygen harvesting from martian regolithic brine | PNAS. PNAS. Retrieved August 5, 2022, from https://www.pnas.org/doi/10.1073/pnas.2008613117

13. Ren, C., Yang, P., Sun, J., Bi, E. Y., Gao, J., Palmer, J., Zhu, M., Wu, Y., & Liu, J. (2021, May 18). A Bioinspired Molybdenum Catalyst for Aqueous Perchlorate Reduction. ACS Publications. Retrieved August 5, 2022, from https://pubs.acs.org/doi/10.1021/jacs.1c00595
14. Poston, D. I., Gibson, M. A., Godfroy, T., & McClure, P. R. (2020, June 4). Krusty Reactor Design. Taylor & Francis Online. Retrieved August 5, 2022, from https://www.tandfonline.com/doi/full/10.1080/00295450.2020.1725382
15. Gibson, M. A., Oleson, S. R., Poston, D. I., & McClure, P. (n.d.). NASA's Kilopower Reactor Development and the Path to Higher Power Missions. NASA Technical Reports Server (NTRS). Retrieved August 5, 2022, from https://ntrs.nasa.gov/api/citations/20170002010/downloads/20170002010.pdf
16. Wall, M. (2019, August 12). Nuclear reactor for Mars outpost could be ready to fly by 2022. Space.com. Retrieved August 5, 2022, from https://www.space.com/nuclear-reactor-for-mars-outpost-2022.html
17. Edwards, B. (2012, April). Overview of NASA's Laser Communications Relay Demonstration. Retrieved August 5, 2022, from https://cwe.ccsds.org/sls/docs/Work%20Completed%20(Closed%20WGs)/Optical%20Channel%20Coding%20and%20Modulations%20Birds%20of%20a%20Feather/Meeting%20Materials/2012_04_Darmstadt/Presentations/LCRD%20Overview%20for%20IOAG%20-%20Germany%20-%20April%202012.pdf
18. Baird, D. (2021, May 12). Laser Communications: Empowering more data than ever before. NASA. Retrieved August 5, 2022, from https://www.nasa.gov/feature/goddard/2021/

laser-communications-empowering-more-data-than-ever-before

19. Jones, J. A., & Wu, J. J. (n.d.). SOLAR MONTGOLFIERE BALLOONS FOR MARS. Retrieved August 5, 2022, from https://citeseerx.ist.psu.edu/viewdoc/download?doi=10.1.1.471.1250&rep=rep1&type=pdf

20. Jones, J. A., Cutts, J. A., Hall, J. L., Wu, J.-J., Fairbrother, D. A., & Lachenmeier, T. (n.d.). MONTGOLFIERE BALLOON MISSIONS FOR MARS AND TITAN. Pasadena; California Institute of Technology. https://www.cds.caltech.edu/~marsden/wiki/uploads/jplcdsmeetings/deploy/Jones_MontgolfiereBalloons_Inte.pdf

21. NASA. (2012, June 14). Mars Balloons Overview. NASA. Retrieved August 5, 2022, from https://www2.jpl.nasa.gov/adv_tech/balloons/mars_overview.htm

22. NASA. (n.d.). Reinventing the wheel. NASA. Retrieved August 5, 2022, from https://www.nasa.gov/specials/wheels/

23. NASA. (n.d.). Superelastic Tire. NASA. Retrieved August 5, 2022, from https://technology.nasa.gov/patent/LEW-TOPS-99

24. Narici, L., Casolino, M., Di Fino, L., Larosa, M., Picozza, P., Rizzo, A., & Zaconte, V. (2017, May 10). Performances of Kevlar and Polyethylene as radiation shielding on-board the International Space Station in high latitude radiation environment. Nature News. Retrieved August 5, 2022, from https://www.nature.com/articles/s41598-017-01707-2

25. Rojdev, K., & Atwell, W. (2016, July 10). Investigation of lithium metal hydride materials for mitigation of deep space radiation–NASA technical reports

server (NTRS). NASA Technical Reports Server. Retrieved August 5, 2022, from https://ntrs.nasa.gov/citations/20160003084

26. Cai, M., Yang, T., Li, H., Yang, H., & Han, J. (2022, January 27). Experimental and simulation study on shielding performance of developed hydrogenous composites. Space: Science & Technology. Retrieved August 5, 2022, from https://spj.sciencemag.org/journals/space/2022/9754387/

27. Singh, K. (2021, December). REVIEW OF BORON NITRIDE NANOTUBES FOR SPACE RADIATION SHIELDING . Retrieved August 5, 2022, from https://smartech.gatech.edu/bitstream/handle/1853/66179/SINGH-THESIS-2021.pdf?sequence=1

28. Thibeault, S. A., Fay, C. C., Lowther, S. E., Earle , K. D., Sauti, G., Kang, J. H., Park, C., & McMullen, A. M. (2012, September 30). Radiation Shielding Materials Containing Hydrogen, Boron, and Nitrogen: Systematic Computational and Experimental Study–Phase I. Retrieved August 5, 2022, from https://www.nasa.gov/sites/default/files/atoms/files/niac_2011_phasei_thibeault_radiationshieldingmaterials_tagged.pdf

29. Rask, J., Vercoutere, W., Krause, A., & Navarro, B. J. (n.d.). Space faring the radiation challenge–NASA. Retrieved August 5, 2022, from https://www.nasa.gov/pdf/284275main_Radiation_HS_Mod3.pdf

30. Groemer, G., Storrie-Lombardi, M., Sattler, B., & Hauser, O. (2011, February). Reducing biological contamination by a space suited astronaut ... ResearchGate. Retrieved August 5, 2022, from https://www.researchgate.net/publication/222722051_Reducing_biological_contamination_by_a_space_suited_astronaut_Laboratory_and_field_test_results_from_AoudaX

31. Manyapu, K. K., deLeon, P., Peltz, L., & Gaier, J. R. (2018, July). Spacesuit Integrated Carbon Nanotube Dust Removal System: A Scaled Prototype. Retrieved August 5, 2022, from https://ttu-ir.tdl.org/bitstream/handle/2346/74224/ICES_2018_278.pdf?sequence=1
32. Mackey, P. J., Johansen, M. R., Olsen, R. C., Raines, M. G., Phillips, J. R., Cox, R. E., Hogue, M. D., Calle, C. I., & Pollard, J. R. S. (2016, April). Electrodynamic Dust Shield for Space Applications. Retrieved August 5, 2022, from https://ntrs.nasa.gov/api/citations/20160005317/downloads/20160005317.pdf
33. Arias, F. J., & De Las Heras, S. (2018). Magnetic Mars Dust Removal Technology. Magnetic Mars Dust Removal Technology. Retrieved August 5, 2022, from https://www.hou.usra.edu/meetings/marssamplereturn2018/pdf/6003.pdf
34. Granath, B. (2017, June 22). Scientists developing technology to remove martian dust. NASA. Retrieved August 5, 2022, from https://www.nasa.gov/feature/kennedy-scientists-developing-technology-to-remove-martian-dust
35. Bos, B. J., & Scott, D. (2004). MARS HABITAT DUST CONTAMINATION FROM SIMULATED EXTRA-VEHICULAR SURFACE ACTIVITY. ResearchGate. Retrieved August 5, 2022, from https://www.researchgate.net/publication/267828651_MARS_HABITAT_DUST_CONTAMINATION_FROM_SIMULATED_EXTRA-VEHICULAR_SURFACE_ACTIVITY
36. Calle, C. I. (2017). Dust in Space. Dust in Space. Retrieved August 6, 2022, from https://www.nasa.gov/sites/default/files/atoms/files/sp-2017-01-009-ksc_ub_flyer_dust_mitigation_508.pdf

37. Junaedi, C., Hawley, K., Walsh, D., Roychoudhury, S., Abney, M. B., & Perry, J. L. (n.d.). Compact and Lightweight Sabatier Reactor for Carbon Dioxide Reduction. Retrieved August 5, 2022, from https://ntrs.nasa.gov/api/citations/20120016419/downloads/20120016419.pdf
38. Junaedi, C., Hawley, K., Walsh, D., Roychoudhury, S., Abney, M. B., & Perry, J. L. (2014, July). CO2 Reduction Assembly Prototype using Microlith-based Sabatier Reactor for Ground Demonstration. Retrieved August 5, 2022, from https://ttu-ir.tdl.org/bitstream/handle/2346/59643/ICES-2014-90.pdf?sequence=1
39. Dunbar, B. (2015, August 17). The Sabatier system: Producing water on the Space Station. NASA. Retrieved August 5, 2022, from https://www.nasa.gov/mission_pages/station/research/news/sabatier.html
40. Ambroglini, F., Battiston, R., & Burger, W. J. (1AD, January 1). Evaluation of Superconducting Magnet Shield Configurations for Long Duration Manned Space Missions. Frontiers. Retrieved August 5, 2022, from https://www.frontiersin.org/articles/10.3389/fonc.2016.00097/full
41. Archer-Boyd, A. (2014, July 21). Radiation shielding to protect a mission to Mars. Horizon Magazine. Retrieved August 5, 2022, from https://ec.europa.eu/research-and-innovation/en/horizon-magazine/radiation-shielding-protect-mission-mars#:~:text=Lightweight%20magnetic%20shields%20could%20be,travel%20to%20Mars%20or%20beyond.&text=Image%3A%20SR2S-,Lightweight%20magnetic%20shields%20could%20be%20the%20best%20way%20to%20protect,travel%20to%20Mars%20or%20beyond.

HUMAN FACTORS AND LIFE SUPPORT

1. Carmichael, S. C. (2015, December 28). The Research Is Clear: Long Hours Backfire for People and for Companies. Harvard Business Review. https://hbr.org/2015/08/the-research-is-clear-long-hours-backfire-for-people-and-for-companies
2. Frazier, S. F. (2015, September 30). How to Protect Astronauts from Space Radiation on Mars. NASA. https://www.nasa.gov/feature/goddard/real-martians-how-to-protect-astronauts-from-space-radiation-on-mars/
3. Dirks, M. L., Wall, B. T., Snijders, T., Ottenbros, C. L. P., Verdijk, L. B., & van Loon, L. J. C. (2013, December 12). Neuromuscular electrical stimulation prevents muscle disuse atrophy during leg immobilization in humans. Acta Physiologica (Oxford, England). Retrieved August 30, 2022, from https://pubmed.ncbi.nlm.nih.gov/24251881/
4. Mohon, L. (2017, September 11). ECLSS. NASA. Retrieved August 30, 2022, from https://www.nasa.gov/centers/marshall/history/eclss.html
5. Garcia, M. (2021, February 26). New Brine Processor Increases Water Recycling on the Station. NASA. https://www.nasa.gov/feature/new-brine-processor-increases-water-recycling-on-international-space-station/
6. Chowdhury, A. A. (2004). LSDA hardware–Advanced Resistive Exercise Device (ARED). Life Sciences Data Archive. Retrieved August 30, 2022, from https://lsda.jsc.nasa.gov/Hardware/hardw/1192
7. Krukowski, K., Feng, X., Paladini, M. S., Chou, A., Sacramento, K., Grue, K., Riparip, L.-K., Jones, T., Campbell-Beachler, M., Nelson, G., & Rosi, S. (2018,

May 18). Temporary Microglia-depletion after cosmic radiation modifies phagocytic activity and prevents cognitive deficits. Nature News. Retrieved August 9, 2022, from https://www.nature.com/articles/s41598-018-26039-7

8. Dunbar, Brian. "Progressive Plant Growing Is a Blooming Business." NASA, NASA, 23 Apr. 2007, www.nasa.gov/vision/earth/technologies/aeroponic_plants.html.

9. Suman Chandra, Shabana Khan, Bharathi Avula, Hemant Lata, Min Hye Yang, Mahmoud A. ElSohly, Ikhlas A. Khan, "Assessment of Total Phenolic and Flavonoid Content, Antioxidant Properties, and Yield of Aeroponically and Conventionally Grown Leafy Vegetables and Fruit Crops: A Comparative Study", Evidence-Based Complementary and Alternative Medicine, vol. 2014, Article ID 253875, 9 pages, 2014. https://doi.org/10.1155/2014/253875

N.E.W. E.R.A.
MARS MISSION DESIGN CLASS AND COMPETITION

AARYA OZARDE

BRIAN RIETKERK

CARL AUDRIC

GUIA MAYA

MICHAEL FRANK

VASHTI CHOWLA

VENKATA BHRUGUBANDA

VIBHAV CHATURVEDI

ABSTRACT

N.E.W. E.R.A. is a 1.5-year crewed mission on Mars. The acronym stands for the symbolic names assigned to the greenhouse ("Nourish"), the habitat ("Endure"), the spacesuits ("Wonder"), the rover ("Explore"), the balloon ("Reach"), and the truck ("Achieve"). Together, these components, alongside the crew of 5 Marsonauts, will pioneer a new era of exploration for humans as an interplanetary species. N.E.W. E.R.A. branches out to three scientific objectives: atmosphere and weather, life on Mars, and human sustainability. Utopia Planitia has emerged as the most appropriate landing site to achieve those. To study the Martian atmosphere, the balloon carries a hyperspectral imager and a microwave detector, and the rover holds a laser spectrometer. The search for life on Mars is supported through a metre-long drill on the remotely controlled rover to collect samples that instruments onboard can chemically analyse. This same system also supports the secondary objective of geologic exploration on the Mars subsurface. For human sustainability, the greenhouse is responsible for growing food, and the truck is responsible for three goals: drilling for ice, transporting the crew, and providing backup habitation. When the Marsonauts go outside the inflatable habitat shielded by Mars regolith bricks, they can rely on the hybrid gas-pressurised suits and mechanical counter-pressure suits for protection. The two sources of power are methane combustion for the base camp and solar power for the remote and methane production systems. Besides proving key technologies effective, the crew, at the end of the mission, will have set up a foundation that can be taken advantage of by the next generations of Marsonauts.

Keywords: atmosphere, food production, ice, methane, drilling, inflatables, extravehicular suit

OBJECTIVES

In humanity's quest to search for life beyond Earth, better understand other worlds, and evolve into an interplanetary species, this N.E.W. E.R.A. mission is landing on Utopia Planitia with 5 crew members on board. This proposed crewed mission aims to:

I. Study the Martian atmosphere and weather
   A. Gather atmospheric data for better predictions of weather and dust devils with the help of a balloon
   B. Map the distribution of compounds, particularly methane, in the atmosphere using hyperspectral imaging
   C. Detect rare lightning events on Mars with a microwave and kurtosis detector
   D. Use a gas in scattering media spectrometer to search for variations in methane level and methanogens
II. Search for life on Mars
   A. Drill into the ground and ice with a rover to search for organic chemicals trapped within the permafrost
   B. Detect extinct and extant life biomarkers with the Sign of Life Detector
   C. Search for 512 biological compounds to look for non-Earth-like life with the Microfluidic Life Analyzer
   D. Use a mass spectrometer to look for unnatural ions and repeating polymers on rock samples to find an Earth-like system of life
III. Ensure short-term and long-term human sustainability
   A. Harvest 95 to 100 thousand calories of crops (including mushrooms) per week via hydroponics
   B. Build a complementary power system that generates 75 to 90 kW/week using solar energy and methane combustion
   C. Install power generators relying on ice and compounds found on Mars

D. Determine locations unfrequented by dust devils for future base camps
　　E. Ensure minimum wastage and maximum usage of all available resources

SCIENCE

1. CASE STUDY ON METHANE

In 2003, a team at the NASA Goddard Space Flight Centre reported trace amounts of methane on Mars on a scale of several parts per billion (Methane on Mars, 2022). However, in a span of three years, there had been large differences between the measurements, suggesting that probably, the presence of methane is concentrated on one spot or it's seasonal. In 2014, the Curiosity rover repeated the experiment, and we found stranger results. From late 2013 to early 2014, there had been a tenfold increase in atmospheric methane, averaging around 7 parts per billion (Methane on Mars, 2022). The problem is that methane comes from an unknown source, considering there are no confirmed microorganisms like methanogens to produce that methane on Mars.

　　There are alternative attempts to explain this. There could be non-biological processes like water-rock reactions, radiolysis of water, and pyrite formation. It has also been shown that methane could be produced by a process involving water, carbon dioxide, and the mineral olivine, which is known to be common on the surface (Shekhtman, 2021). However, none has been confirmed thus far. An interesting hypothesis is that dust devils might be involved in distributing the methane on Mars, creating large discrepancies in measurement.

　　Scientists claim that dust devils generate hydrogen peroxide. Because the dust particles are rubbing against each other, small lightning discharges can trigger the production of hydrogen peroxide, which will oxidise or break down the methane in the atmosphere. This offers an answer to why some areas of Mars have lower levels of methane, and some have higher ones. If hydrogen peroxide is proven to be destroying Martian methane, then there will be more reason to believe that there once have been higher levels of methane than expected (Sanderson, 2006), pointing toward the possibility of methanogens once again (Atkinson, 2009).

There is no caveat in this mission. If dust devils are found to cause the uneven distribution of methane, then it's a piece of the puzzle of the strange methane distribution. Moreover, it can strengthen the argument that there is life on Mars. If these hypotheses were null, however, then the rovers have more reason to explore the chemical reactions that could be occurring on the rocks and underground. This will help unlock the mysteries of Martian methane and understand dust devils better, helping future missions predict and better prepare for dust devils once there is data on what chemical interactions to look for as warning signs.

The Mars Scout program has already pushed for a high-resolution atmospheric composition spectrometer that focuses on the detection of methane and its variations in accordance with dust activity (Farrell et al., 2006). A balloon will examine the atmosphere by observing the correlations among dust devils, electric fields, and methane. According to Farrell et al. (2006), the concentration of methane is hypothesised to decrease with increased dust devil activity, but using orbiting spectrometers would not be able to resolve smaller-scale interactions.

In order to study methane, Team N.E.W. E.R.A. proposes a two-part experiment: one with a balloon monitoring the dust devil from above and one with a rover examining the dust and rocks on the ground (see 4.2 and 4.3). Instruments such as the Hyper-Cam Methane and the Agile Digital Detector will do parallel measurements from an altitude of 10 km on the balloon for a closer look at the smaller-scale interactions in the Martian atmosphere. In addition, an upgraded version of the Tunable Laser Spectrometer derived from the Curiosity rover will be able to note the variations of methane levels on the ground during dust devil successions. As aerosols might destroy the methane on Mars, their use is not recommended. For that reason, the balloon and rover would get their power supply from the Sabatier reaction and solar energy.

One of the areas of interest for the balloon and rover is the northwestern part of Amazonis Planitia; with the higher likelihood of dust devils in flat desert plains, there can be more observations of dust devils, especially in the afternoons of spring and summer (Dust Devils, n.d.).

2. LANDING SITE

The location of the landing site was first narrowed down into the northern hemisphere of Mars because it has a less extreme seasonal climate as compared to the south (Martian Climate, 2018). For instance, winter would last for only four Martian months, allowing the Marsonauts to enjoy a more convenient spring and summer climate for thirteen months (Sharp & Gordon, 2022). Because ice would function both as a power source and a site for microbial research, the presence of ice was also a crucial consideration. Hence, the mid-latitudes from 30° N to 60° N were chosen for their ice-rich features. Higher latitudes promise more confidence that ice would be present, and while underground ice might be possible above 30° N, it is only above 40° N that ice and glaciers become certain (Secosky, 2021).

However, a compromise must be made to ensure that the landing site is still receiving an adequate amount of sunlight to support human operations. Because the 40° to 50° N latitude band already receives below 130 W/m2 of solar energy (UC Berkeley, 2022), going higher than 50° N will be impractical.

This amount of solar energy is sufficient as it will only be used as a secondary power source.

With these considerations, Utopia Planitia—the landing site of Viking 2—will be the location of both the landing site and the base of the crewed Mars mission. The place is suitable for landing as it has a low elevation as the largest impact basin in the solar system. With a diameter of around 3300 km, Utopia Planitia features intriguing textures and ice-related geologic deformations. The Brain Terrain, for instance, has ridges consisting of an ice core, which can be a water source. The Mars Reconnaissance Orbiter has also confirmed ice at the surface of the planitia or just below it, making its extraction much easier (NASA, 2016).

In terms of geologic research and in-situ resource utilisation (ISRU), Utopia Planitia's potential is immense. According to Secosky (2021), it features volcanoes, ancient lava pools, impact craters, tectonic faults, and river channels—areas that can potentially harbour life and can be traversed by an autonomous rover. Furthermore, Utopia Planitia is adjacent at around 40° N to Amazonis Planitia (Zigler & Ryan, 2005), which is a site of interest for its unusual presence of methane. At most, Utopia Planitia's crater at a longitude of 179° E would only be 45 km away from the nearest land in Amazonis Planitia.

In the dusty soils of Utopia Planitia, the oil-sample analyses of Viking 1 detected traces of iron, magnesium, calcium, sodium, and potassium (Utopia Planitia, 2019), minerals that can be utilised for growing plants on Mars—not to mention the traces of nitrogen (2.3%) and significant amounts of carbon dioxide (96.2%) found in the atmosphere (Oyama & Berdahl, 1977).

Living on Utopia Planitia would be a challenge. Its average surface temperature can go as low as 160 K during winter and as high as 240 K during summer (Cui et al., 2022). However, this is not a unique problem on the site because, on any part of Mars, the temperature can be extreme by Earth standards. With an efficient heating and power system in the habitat, the Marsonauts can maintain a stable environment that the human body can withstand.

ENGINEERING

3. MARTIAN BASE

3.1. Protection

The super-structures of the Endure habitat and the Nourish greenhouses will be 3D printed with the Martian regolith by robotic rovers that will be sent to the surface in a cargo capsule before the crew's arrival. The regolith structure will serve as a layer of protection from cosmic/solar radiation, and beneath this, there will be an internal, inflatable layer (carried from Earth) in which the crew will live and work. Inflatables are chosen because they are more flexible and compact, and they take up a relatively minimal volume when packed. The inflatables will be made of polyethylene, so they will have a higher strength-to-weight ratio, lower mass, and increased damage tolerance due to their flexibility

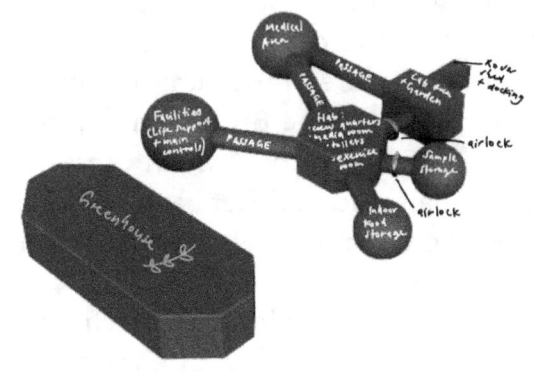

Figure 1: Model of the base

The trash disks (Gannon, 2013) made from disinfected faeces can be used as an intermediary/external layer of protection from radiation between the regolith and inflatables. However, this will mainly only be done if necessary or damage has occurred to the external structure.

3.1.1. Habitat

The outer layer of the Endure habitat will be a 3D-printed layer made from in-situ regolith material from the Martian surface. The second, internal layer will consist of high-density polyethylene (HDPE) fabric, whose total area will be around 976-980 m2. The thickness between the layers will be around 0.005 m, and this will also help the heat transportation system through the habitat. This material is chosen because it is lightweight, weather resistant, and more durable than low-density polyethylene (What is High Density, n.d.). With HDPE, the habitat will provide protection from extreme temperatures, high-energy radiation, solar storms, and dust devils. With the dimensions listed in Table 1, the habitat will allow enough space for repairing equipment such as robots.

Module/Area	Dimensions
Central Module	Diameter = 10m
Medical Module	Diameter = 6m
Sample Storage	Diameter = 4m
Facilities Area	Diameter = 8m
Lab Area	Base = 6m Height = 3.5m Width = 4m

Table 1: Dimensions of the base

The daily power requirement for the total area of the Hab will be between 75kW–90kW.

3.1.2. Spacesuits

Spacesuits are an integral part of any space mission as they protect Marsonauts from the dangers of space. On Mars, these are the lower temperatures and pressures as compared to those on Earth, as well as the "poor protection from ionising and non-ionising radiation" from the Martian atmosphere (Viúdez-Moreiras, 2021). As N.E.W. E.R.A. will be the first crewed mission to Mars, the Wonder spacesuits serve the additional purpose of preventing contamination. This is especially significant as one of the main objectives of our mission is to search for signs of current or past life on Mars. There have been many proposals for spacesuits by various companies and institutions in the past decades, but for our mission, it will be important to think about the weight of the suits on Mars as it has significantly stronger gravity than on the moon. This implies that the total weight on Earth, of the suits, must be lighter than that of previously used suits for Apollo missions. The suits must also allow the maximum possible mobility for the Marsonauts as part of the experiments involves drilling into the Martian surface.

In addition, a mechanism is needed for donning and doffing the suits so that Martian dust does not contaminate the habitat or rover. In this section of the paper, we will discuss the overall design of the intra-vehicular (IVA) suits and extra-vehicular (EVA) suits. As this is a mission with 5 Marsonauts, our team has elected to bring seven IVA and seven EVA suits so that the Marsonauts will have backups in case of an emergency.

In 2020, NASA sent 5 samples of outer layer material to Mars on Perseverance to be tested. They were tested in terms of how well they held up to the radiation throughout the mission. Currently, there is no available data on which materials were the best, but this gives a good idea in terms of the possible materials that could be used to construct a suit. Among the five samples was ortho-fabric, which is already in use for modern spacesuits. Ortho-fabric includes Nomex, Gore-Tex, and Kevlar—making it flame resistant, waterproof, and micrometeoroid-proof. This makes it ideal for the outermost layer of the suit. Furthermore, areas that are likely to undergo additional wear and tear such as the knees and elbows can be covered with Teflon which is very slick and hence harder to catch and tear.

It would be optimal for the gloves to be made of Vectran, as they have been in the past. Vectran is cut resistant but is ineffective "at keeping dust from penetrating layers beneath," hence it is probable that some solution will be needed to eject the dust from the suit, or possibly Tyvek could be used below the Vectran, trapping the dust between the two layers so that the dust could be ejected from time to time (Gaier et al., 2009). NASA also sent Teflon with a dust-resistant coating to be tested by Perseverance. However, due to its slick nature, it is not the best choice for gloves which need to have some traction to allow the Marsonauts to grip onto tools while conducting experiments on the surface.

For the helmet and visor, polycarbonate was included on Perseverance for its UV resistance to be tested, and this is an optimal material for the helmet as it bends when force is applied rather than breaking, retaining good optical properties. In addition, we will cover the helmet in a thin gold film to reflect UV and Infrared light while letting in visible light to protect the Marsonaut's eyes.

Finally, the suit will also be coated in blue Maya, which has a strong blue colour and is resistant to light, corrosion, fading, and moderate heat.

The above was an overview of the important parts of the suit, however as we are opting for an Extravehicular Mobility Unit (EMU) type suit. The suit will have 15 layers for maximum comfort and protection. For our design, these will be based on the outline in the paper "Approaches and Solutions for Martian Spacesuit Design" (Lousada et al., 2017). Here is the breakdown of the layers from the innermost to the outermost layers:

1. Soft fabric tricot lining for the Marsonaut's skin—white colour
2. Nylon with cotton and cooling garment—a layer of Spandex with plastic tubing which is slightly modified from

the traditional cooling garment to reduce the volume of water needed
3. Memory alloys which are "trained" to return to a fixed shape at a particular temperature, providing pressure to the suit and reducing its mass due to its lightweight nature
4. Dacron with cotton
5. Nylon coated with neoprene—good chemical stability and maintenance of flexibility over a range of temperatures
6. Nylon lined with urethane and Dacron
7. Mylar layer to protect against micrometeorites
8. Layer of liquid resin—which will harden on contact with oxygen gas to provide a seal should the suit experience a tear
9. Dense monolithic membrane
10. Orthofabric with blue Maya coating

In addition to all these materials, the Mechanical Counterpressure Layer which will be worn underneath the gas-pressurised suit will be made up of active material embedded into a non-active material. From the tests conducted by a team including Dava Newman from MIT (the proponents of the Bio-suit), they concluded that the most promising active materials to use in the suit would be a dielectric elastomer actuator (DEA) or a Shape Memory Polymer (SMP). A DEA consists of an elastomer film that is covered with a conductive layer on both sides, while SMPs are "polymers with shape memory characteristics that demonstrate deformation recovery capabilities" (Holschuh et al., 2012).

Both of these active materials are promising candidates as DEAs can produce significant strains which means they show promise for "artificial muscles" (Holschuh et al., 2012). SMAs demonstrate shape memory effects that are very useful for the fit of the suit.

Active Material Type	Nature of Active Material	Active Material Form	Possible Textile Architecture	Grade	Justification
Dielectric Elastomer	Controllable individual element strain	Ribbon or Band	Coarse weave (with active ribbons along the weft)	B	Directly utilizes active strain capabilities, but introduces interaction effects and electrical isolation issues
			Coarse braid (with active ribbons along each bias yarn)	C	Complex construction, inefficient compression mechanism, introduces interaction effects and electrical isolation issues
		Ribbon, Band, or Continuous Sheet	Non-woven sheath (comprised of continous active material)	A	Simplicity in pressure production mechanism, directly utilizes active strain capabilities
Shape Memory Alloy Shape Memory Polymer	Controllable individual element deformation	Small Diameter Fiber (spun into yarn)	Fine weave (with active yarn along the weft)	C	Unclear how to utilize deformation recovery to produce compression
			Fine knit (with active yarn along the warp or weft)	C	Unclear how to utilize deformation recovery to produce compression
			Fine braid (with active fiber along each bias yarn)	B	Material response scales with fiber thickness, biasing designs towards large fibers
			Fine looping / interlinking mesh (comprised of active yarns)	B	Material response scales with fiber thickness, biasing designs towards large fibers
		Large Diameter Fiber (wire or cable)	Coarse weave (with active wire along the weft)	C	Unclear how to utilize deformation recovery to produce compression
			Coarse knit (with active wire along the warp or weft)	C	Unclear how to utilize deformation recovery to produce compression
			Coarse braid (with active fiber along each bias yarn)	A	Textile architecture exploits material strengths (recoverable deformation)
			Coarse looping / interlinking mesh (comprised of active yarns)	A	Textile architecture exploits material strengths (recoverable deformation)

Because the materials have such different abilities and limitations, they must be dealt with in different ways. Although a concrete conclusion has not been reached yet as to how the active materials will be embedded, the team made a table with embossing techniques corresponding to the active materials. As of 2014, the BioSuit designed by Dava Newman at MIT was made from Shape Memory Alloy (SMA) coils integrated into a compression garment (Chu, 2014). However, it is clear that over the next decade more research and funding are going into the development of this suit and therefore we believe it will be possible to debut this design on our mission.

Another consideration of our spacesuits on Mars is that we are only bringing two extra suits. The mechanical counter-pressure inside the layers of the suits will be relatively light, and each Marsonaut will have a custom one to allow for proper compression. However, the gas pressurised sections of the suits are significantly heavier and hence will have to be adjustable

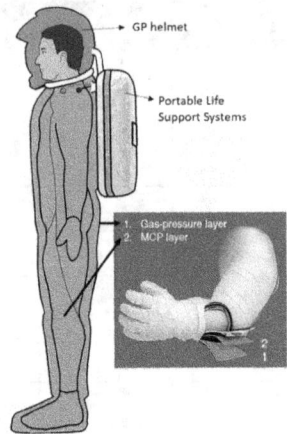

Figure 1.1. Hybrid MCP-GP Spacesuit Concept. *An inner MCP garment layer covered with a GP envelope is used to apply the adequate pressure to the astronaut. Image courtesy of Creare, LLC and Michał Kracik.* [14]

so that they can be used in case any of the crew members' suits experience an issue. NASA is currently developing an adjustable space suit with modular components on the chest and waist to allow for adjustability (Niiler, 2019).

Haptic footwear for space that helps Astronauts navigate around obstacles is currently being developed and it seems possible to be in use within the next ten years. "Researchers developed a device that spaced six haptic motors around each of a subject's feet—one motor each at the heel, big toe, and instep, and three motors along the outer edge of the foot" (Soon, 2016).

The Life Support System (LSS) of a spacesuit does exactly what its name suggests—it controls and provides the resources needed to support life in extraterrestrial environments during operations and missions. (Hamilton Standard, Division of United Aircraft, 2009). Since the first days of human space exploration, it has been one of the most important things to design and has constantly evolved and advanced to provide the most efficient and optimised service to astronauts. The biggest responsibilities of any life support system designed for space exploration consist of three things: oxygen and carbon dioxide regulation, controlling temperature inside the suit, and a pressurised atmosphere (MIT Department of Aeronautics and Astronautics, n.d.).

There are two major systems of maintaining pressure on the human body currently proposed: Gas-pressurised suits (GPs) and Mechanical Counterpressure suits (MCPs). Gas-pressurised suits are the ones that every space mission so far has used, in which gas such as oxygen is pumped into the suit to maintain pressure. Mechanical Counterpressure suits are another type of suit in which skin-tight garments are used to provide pressure against the skin, rather than gas (About: Mechanical Counterpressure Suit, n.d.). This paper proposes that the suits used on the mission would be made of an outer gas-pressurised layer and an inner Mechanical Counterpressure layer. This way, the suit is safer through redundancy, increases mobility for the Marsonauts, and reduces weight on the Marsonauts for easier EVAs (Huerta & Lluch, 2019). A neck dam would separate the GP helmet from the GP/MCP lower body.

The NASA Extravehicular Mobility Unit (EMU) and other designs pump 100% O2 into the suit and remove CO2 with "scrubbers" (National Aeronautics and Space Administration, n.d.). This requires a lot of oxygen to be stored in the PLSS (Primary Life Support System) and thus, creates a lot of weight. A more efficient idea on Mars, suggested previously by Dr. Larry Kuznetz, would be to keep pumping pure O2 into the helmet, but pump the Martian atmosphere (95% carbon dioxide, 3% nitrogen, 1.6% argon, and trace amounts of other gases) into the upper and lower torsos (Arizona State University, 2020). The pressure in the helmet would be kept higher than that in the lower body to not allow CO2 to escape into the helmet. The pre-breathe requirement for the Marsonauts would be about 30 minutes. A dense monolithic membrane would be placed against the suit to stop any Martian life from contaminating the suit, and from any Earth life from going out to keep the Martian environment pure while conducting studies looking for life.

The weight of the MCP suit itself is expected to be around 25% that of existing GP suits, around 19 lbs. The PLSS is expected to be around 75% the weight of the A7L PLSS, coming out to about 93.75 lbs (Gorguinpour et al., n.d.). The outer GP lower body suit would weigh around 90 lbs, as it would be less than the wet weight of the EMU at 110 lbs (Harris & Chandler, 2008). Sweat would be dealt away by a thermal micrometeoroid garment, protecting the astronaut and also allowing heat to dissipate away into the environment, circumventing the need for a Liquid Cooling and Ventilation Garment (Stroming & Newman, 2020). Adding the Helmet Assembly, Visors, and other required items would amount to at most another 15 lbs (Lunar and Planetary Institute, 2017). In total, the combined suit weight would come out to about 217.75 lbs, or around 99 kgs. As the Martian gravity is about 0.375 that of Earth, on Mars, the suit would weigh about 82 lbs, or 37 kgs (NASA, 2019).

The waste management and maintenance systems on our space suit will be relatively simple, both male and female Marsonauts will be wearing Maximum Absorbency Garments to collect urine and faeces for the duration of their EVA.

3.2. Essentials

3.2.1. Power

There are two main sources of power in the habitation and general systems of the mission. During the start of the mission, solar panels will be used as the primary power source until the process of creating/burning methane is fully operational. When the camp is running at full capacity, it will use methane produced from the Sabatier reaction, using 15,120 MJ of energy per week at about 16950 moles of methane per week. All of the parts of the methane production (being Ice drill, mini

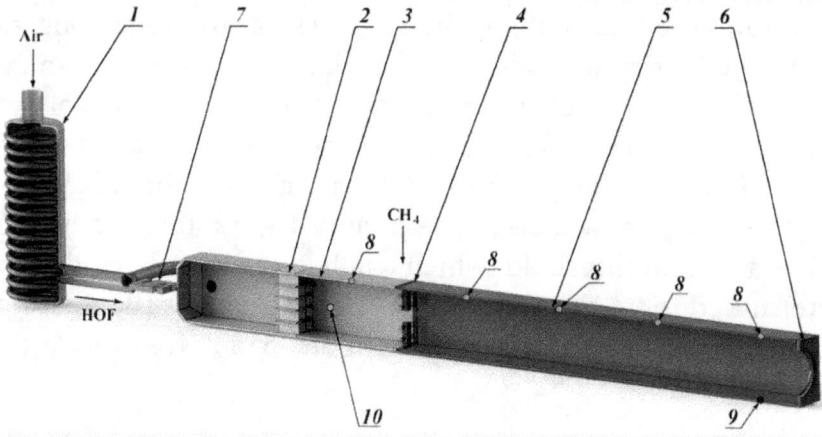

Figure 1. Experimental facility scheme. 1—heat exchanger; 2—rectifying element; 3—crossover joint; 4—methane supply pylons; 5—channel of constant cross-section; 6—throttler; 7—longitudinal force sensor; 8—static pressure sampling points; 9—pressure pulsations sampling point; 10—HOF temperature measurement point.

Figure 3: Combustion chamber to use heat exchanger for steam (Grishin et al., 2022)

rover, filter, electrolysis chamber, and the Sabatier generator) are going to run on solar panels to avoid overreliance on methane production at base camp. Due to the methane generator only working at up to 72% efficiency on Mars (Catapano et al., 2016) with some of the product being lost as heated steam, we seemingly need to produce more methane to power our base. Fortunately, by using the steam to support the heating on the hab (using pipes to guide the steam and with controlled input), little energy is wasted from the intensive methane production. Since the greenhouse also needs methane to function but it is such a central system to the survival of the mission, a backup solar panel array will be attached to make sure food production is always in stable condition from a power perspective.

Outside of the base, solar power and batteries function as the primary energy input of the rover, truck, balloon, and spacesuit (charged on the truck). This allows us to be completely remote from the home base for a short time to conduct research, repair the camp, and take the crew on field missions to visit sites for biological and geologic research. This independence allows for unprecedented mobility in our mission, where as long as the needed amount of food is packed, two Marsonauts can go about 100 miles of camp in any direction and still be able to make it back home safely. All solar panels will be cleaned using pressurised air canisters that will be attached to the solar panels. The canisters will clean the panels if they start producing below a certain threshold (which will have to be independently determined for each specific panel). This prevents the wasting of energy/resources through cleaning the panels for every little speck of dust.

3.2.2. Water

The average water intake for a Marsonaut would be 4.55 litres or 1 gallon per day—taking into account drinking, cleaning, and preparing the food (Schuhknecht, 2022).

One of the overarching aims of our mission is to create as much of a complete loop as possible, with regard to sustainability and the usage of resources. Wastewater collected from processed urine, hab humidity condensate, and any unused, remaining water from the greenhouses will all be passed through a water processor and purity sensor—and will accordingly be stored or delivered into the water. Some of this water may also be used for the hydroponics system that will be set up to study plant life. On any necessary taps (on the water dispenser/in the toilet), the tap flexibility will be limited, so that water wastage is kept at a minimum. The water used for the basin (e.g. washing hands or brushing teeth) will be the same water used to flush the waste.

Water from the Sabatier Reactor will be recycled back through the electrolysis centrifuge to be split into hydrogen

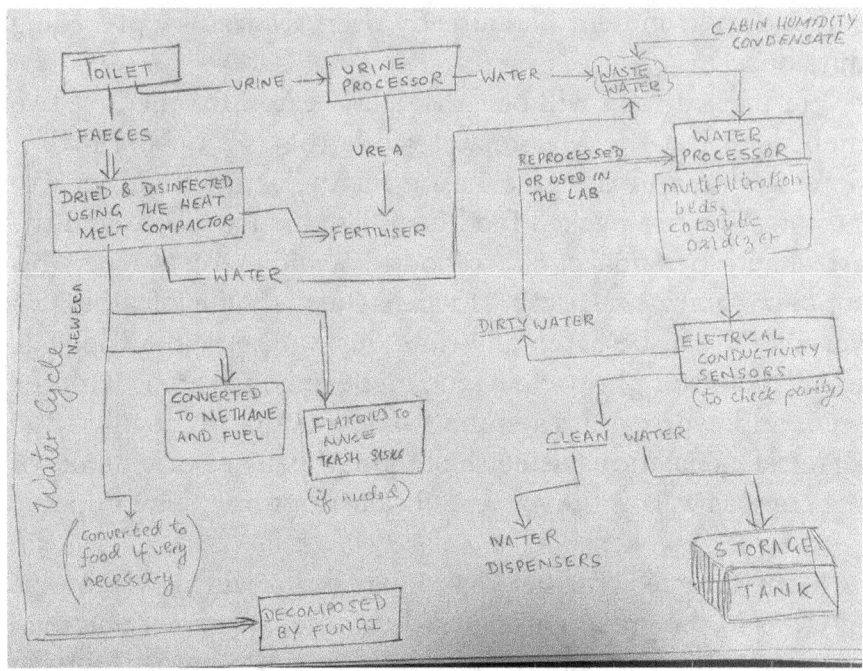

and oxygen, and the hydrogen will be put back into the Sabatier Reactor to continue producing methane.

These separate cycles allow us to stay efficient in the production and use of water while still having a backup plan of sourcing every bit of water needed from the drill. This is crucial because, in case of emergencies or unprecedented vehicle missions, an extra 10 gallons worth of ice can be stored daily.

3.2.3. Food

The system for growing food is hydroponics. The reason aeroponics was not chosen is that plants in aeroponics are more likely to decay faster before a malfunction in the system can be fixed. Although both are almost equally efficient, hydroponics is more reliable, considering the fact that this is the first crewed mission to Mars. Aeroponics would make more sense in future missions which could afford more risks by the time a stable environment had already been secured by preceding missions.

Pre-packed food will be carried and eaten for the first two months to last the Marsonauts while they set up the hydroponics system in the greenhouse for the actual plant growth to start. The pre-packed food includes "luxury foods" and the astronauts' personal comfort foods to avoid menu fatigue. This supplementary pre-packed food has a shelf life of around 4 years so it can be eaten any time during the whole trip. The total amount of pre-packed food on the payload along with the seeds and hydroponics systems would amount to roughly 1200 kg (after calculations using the required daily caloric intake of the crew, as well as the harvested calories from the hydroponic crops).

Menu fatigue is further kept at bay by growing a wide range of crops in the greenhouse including potatoes, sweet potatoes, carrots, lentils (each taking 8 weeks to grow), tomatoes, spinach (6 weeks), soybeans, rocket leaves (4 weeks) and mushrooms (1 week). These crops would be rotated depending on the time they take to grow. This makes sure that crops are not stored for longer periods of time as harvesting everything at once would take time to consume entirely, thereby ensuring that the crops are kept as fresh as possible. There will be one greenhouse having 8 batches, including all of the aforementioned crops except mushrooms since mushrooms require a cooler, darker environment. The mushroom growth will start after the first harvest. The left-over plant material (i.e. plant parts that we do not consume) is stored in the boxes that are used to bring the seeds to Mars. Mushroom mycelium is grown in a lab on a sterilised petri dish before it's added to the compost, which also contains human faeces, to grow. These mushrooms will be high in protein and potassium.

Each crew member requires around 2800 calories per day—roughly 15,000 in total per day for five crew members; hence, one harvest would be 95,000–100,000 calories a week. This number has been made slightly higher so as to make sure that we never run out of food, as well as to help the Marsonauts, who would be adjusting to the harsh conditions on Mars—which is when they'll be requiring more food to survive, especially considering the gravity and the recovery needed after a 5-7 month long journey in zero gravity.

The greenhouse is designed the same way as the hab. It will share air and heat regulation systems with the living modules, but will not be directly connected to the hab (it will have its own entrance, to avoid risks of contamination in the living quarters). It is protected with 3D-printed regolith bricks, as well as an inflatable inside. In addition, the plants will be supplied with artificial light using LEDs powered by the Sabatier reactor.

The plants will be fertilised in two main ways. One way is with urine. When applied to soil, urea reacts with water to form ammonia, which makes the nitrogen within the fertiliser available to plants. Urea fertilisers deliver one of the highest amounts of nitrogen at 46%, with little phosphorus or potassium. On the other hand, human faeces is rich in phosphorus and potassium, which are important plant nutrients. The urine produced in the 7-month trip to Mars is collected in water cycle pipes (connected to the commodes) and then used directly in the hydroponic circulation. The urine, along with the faeces, complement each other as one provides a certain significant nutrient that the other does not. In this manner, it's ensured that the most is made out of waste products.

The utensils used with regards to food—like largely foldable cutlery and crockery—can be reused, as well as a set of steel mugs and straws assigned to each Marsonaut with spares available. Two water dispensers and warming ovens will be used in the central hab by the crew, to heat and rehydrate their pre-packed meals.

3.2.3.1 Biochemistry Research

Majority of the biochemistry research (other than the geochemical research) done on Mars would include studying the plant growth and nutrient content, environmental conditions, temperature, and pH balance. This also includes the mushrooms, as well as the mycelium that is used to start the mushroom growth. This is to ensure that the plants are healthy and suitable for human consumption; finding any abnormalities may help us detect possibilities of low gravity or other factors affecting the plants in some way. Human waste will be examined regularly to check for any abnormalities or changes in its composition providing more data points for the crew's health.

Name:	Nutrients:	Calories:	Time To Grow
Potatoes	**Carbohydrates,** Vitamin C, Vitamin B6, Potassium, Fibre, Protein, Magnesium, Calcium	200-300	8 weeks
Sweet Potatoes	**Carbohydrates,** Fibre, Vitamin B6, Vitamin A, Vitamin C, Iron, Folate, Sodium, Sugar, Protein, Magnesium, Calcium	110-150	8 weeks
Carrots	**Vitamin C,** Fibre, Vitamin B6, Magnesium, Potassium, Calcium, Sodium	30	8 weeks
Lentils	**Protein,** Fibre, Fat, Iron, Potassium, Vitamin B6, Magnesium, Carbohydrate	200-230	8 weeks
Tomatoes	**Vitamin C, Potassium,** Vitamin B6, Fibre, Magnesium	30	6 weeks
Spinach	Vitamin A, Vitamin C, Vitamin K, Iron, Folate, Potassium	30	6 weeks
Soybeans	**Protein,** Fat, **Omega-3 fatty acids, Vitamin D,** Fibre, Antioxidants	224-300 (100g)	4 weeks
Rocket Leaves	**Vitamin C, Vitamin E,** Vitamin B, Vitamin K, Amino Acids, Fibre, Magnesium, Potassium, Calcium, Copper	20	4 weeks
White Mushrooms	Protein, Potassium, Vitamin B6, Vitamin C, Iron, Vitamin D, Magnesium	22 (100g)	1 week

Table 3: Nutrients Table

Food intake and waste would be studied closely, taking into account the time spent exercising by the Marsonauts. This is to ensure that they are getting enough nutrients and are hydrated—both to exercise and stay healthy in the Martian environment.

3.2.4. Oxygen

Oxygen—along with hydrogen, carbon dioxide, methane, and diatomic nitrogen—will all be stored in cryogenic tanks in liquid form under 50 atm. For the safety of the crew, all the gases, especially oxygen, will be stored outside the hab, where if a catastrophic malfunction were to occur, the crew would be unharmed. The oxygen will be obtained from electrolysis as will the hydrogen gas. Carbon dioxide gas will be filtered and pumped into another cryotank, and methane will be obtained from a reactor, whose sole purpose is to react carbon dioxide from the atmosphere with the hydrogen obtained from electrolysis. Figure 6 has a picture of what the electrolysis chamber will look like. It can act as a centrifuge to apply forces on the water undergoing the process (Lomax, 2022). This is present to prevent the buildup of gaseous bubbles on the cathode and anode rods of the chamber, as they form more regularly in microgravity environments.

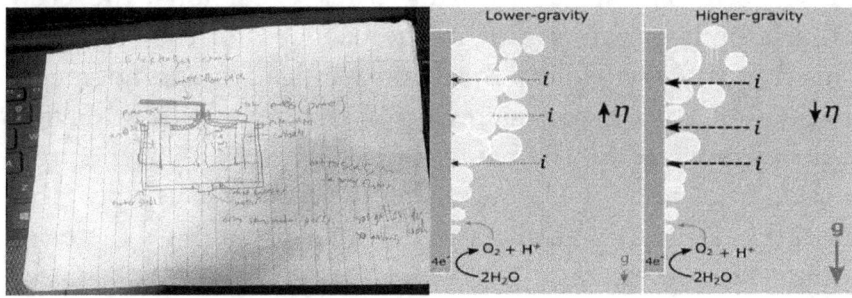

Figure 6 displays the bubbling process

By getting the chamber to spin fast enough, the rate of production will increase greatly while the size of the camber can decrease, saving weight

Additionally, small amounts of carbondioxide exhaled by the Marsonauts from the hab or the atmosphere will be pumped into the greenhouse. and atmosphere (for any extra needed) to ensure the crops grow healthily and to prevent the crew from asphyxiating from CO2 poisoning.

3.2.5. Heating

As Mars' surface is much colder than Earth, the Marsonauts will need a thermal regulating system rather than a heating/cooling system. The hab and greenhouses will share the atmosphere and temperature regulation systems—though the controls and inputs might vary.

A system much like the Active Thermal Control System (ATCS) on the ISS will be used in the Hab and will consist of 3 components; the heat collection subsystem, to collect heat from both the methane-powered generator and the excess heat produced from the Sabatier reactor, the heat transportation subsystem—that will have a pathway between the layers of the hab—and the heat rejection subsystem. The heat rejection subsystem will use radiators that will be placed in the greenhouses since any excess heat can be utilised there.

3.2.6. Communication

On the Martian surface, during truck excursions, the crew will use built-in ham radios in the headgear of the spacesuit. This frequency will allow vocal communication and telemetry that will be stored in a microchip in the same built-in device. Beacons required for the ham radios will be placed in the pressurised truck and the Hab, allowing the crew to have a portable beacon as well as a stationary one, with each having a radius of about 150-200 metres.

Considering that the N.E.W. E.R.A. mission is set around 10 years in the future, the crew will be able to carry foldable cell phones that will be placed in a specific, accessible place in the spacesuit, though they will only be used in an emergency so that they are kept as shielded from unnecessary radiation. The cell phones can be used as an additional emergency tracker apart from the one already on the suit. The two computers in the media room, as well as a spare cell phone in the medical room, will also have the tracking (and TBIRD) systems.

A High Gain Antenna (HGA) will be used as a communication set-up to contact Earth. HGA uses the Mars Endeavour satellite and sends data to Earth through radio waves that are converted to, and from, binary form. This set-up consists of an amplifier, a radio transmitter, and a radio receiver—which will be stored in the passage connecting the medical and central modules, to be protected from radiation while not in use.

Moreover, laser communication can be used to send visual and recorded data to Earth if its range and power usage are deemed reliable before mission launch. This will help maximise the available data storage space on devices on Mars, as the TBIRD laser communication system (Nasa, 2017) will utilise Martian satellites like the Odyssey Orbiter to relay the information to Earth.

VEHICLES AND INSTRUMENTS
TRUCK
4.1. Pressurized crewed Truck "Achieve" and Portable Modules

4.1.1 Truck "Achieve".
The pressurized vehicle was created with the need to have a flexible vehicle that could tackle most large problems the crew could face while on their mission (estimated to weigh 6.6 tonnes). Its ability to transport the methane energy production system and be able to support the crew with the habitation module makes the truck a great backup system in case something goes wrong with the main habitation. For compatibility's sake with each module—namely the cryotank gas storage, methane production system, and electrolysis centrifuge—the crewed rover will be battery-powered with a solar panel to increase the battery life and range of the vehicle. The mobile lab will also have solar panels for the same reason and an enlarged dish for

communication with orbital infrastructure. This will enable long-range communications with the main habitat at the main mission site and connection with the command back at Earth for any last-minute scientific research. The truck is built for a two-person drive with access to external space suits built into the sides where traditional doorways exist on earth trucks.

4.1.2 Portable Module

The first main module is made for drilling the water ice on mars as it is a mission-critical component. The large drilling equipment for mining ice is extremely heavy and bulky (mining module expected to weigh 4 tonnes). The system includes a rotary drill made of tungsten carbide (which chips instead of breaking, allowing drilling to occur even if the drill is damaged) that takes ice out of the ground in cylindrical core sample shapes up to a depth of 5 metres. This drill will produce 420 gallons of water per week for various uses around the base. 80 gallons are used for methane production for the hab, 30 gallons are for drinking, 300 gallons are for food production, and 10 gallons are kept in storage for backup. The drill system will also crush the cylinder and use evaporation to filter the water, which is a slow but reliable form of filtering. Then the now liquid water will go through the Electrolysis Chamber and Sabatier Process Generator, and then it's combusted to create power. Having the drilling equipment transportable by the truck was necessary and the idea to have the drilling module independent of the rover made the modularity component of the truck significantly simpler. Moreover, it adds the benefit of the drilling equipment being able to operate without a need for the Achieve truck and being able to move the drill in case insufficient ice is present at the drill site. Using the data from the SWIM missions on mars, the crew will always be able to move the drill to a new area and use the Explore rover to check for the presence of ice before digging, saving resources and time.

N.E.W. E.R.A.

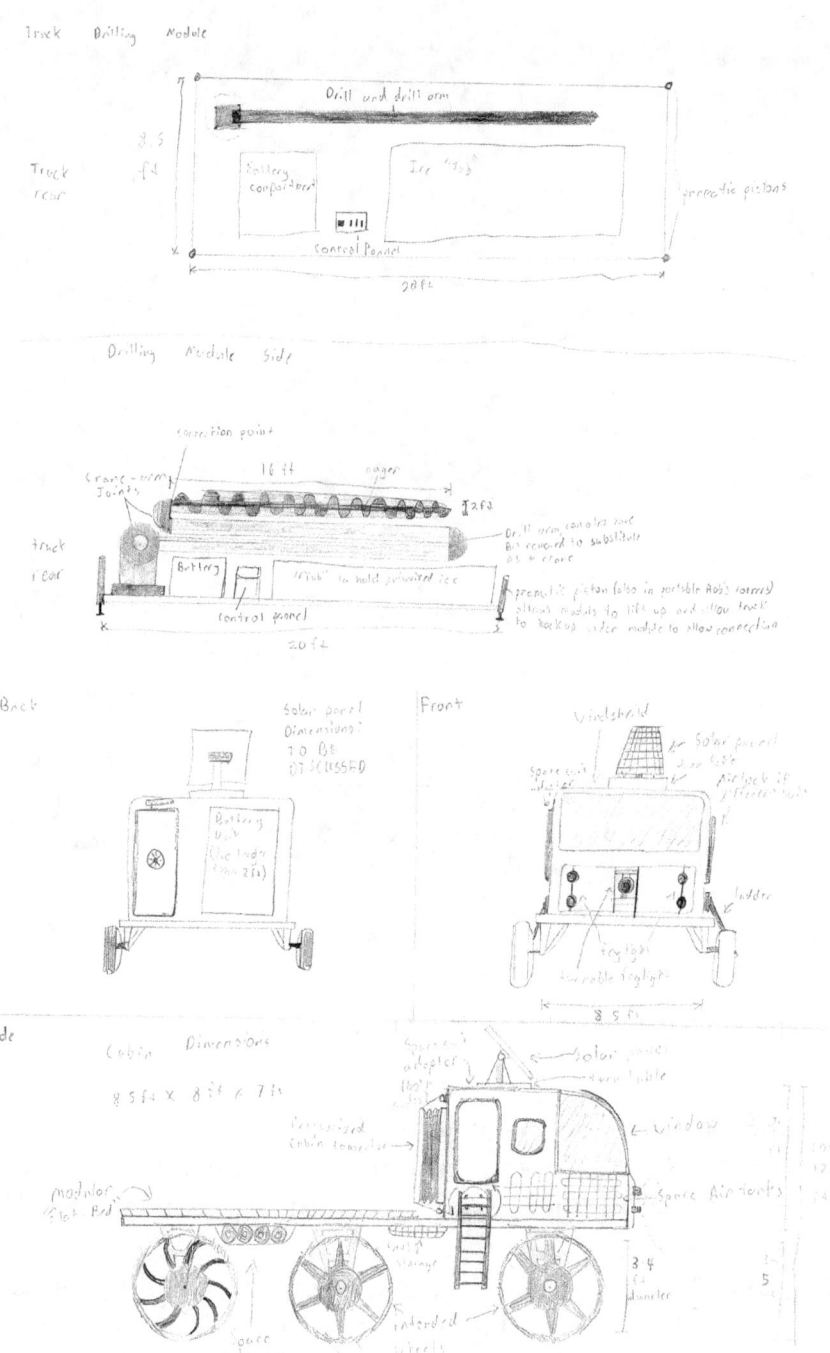

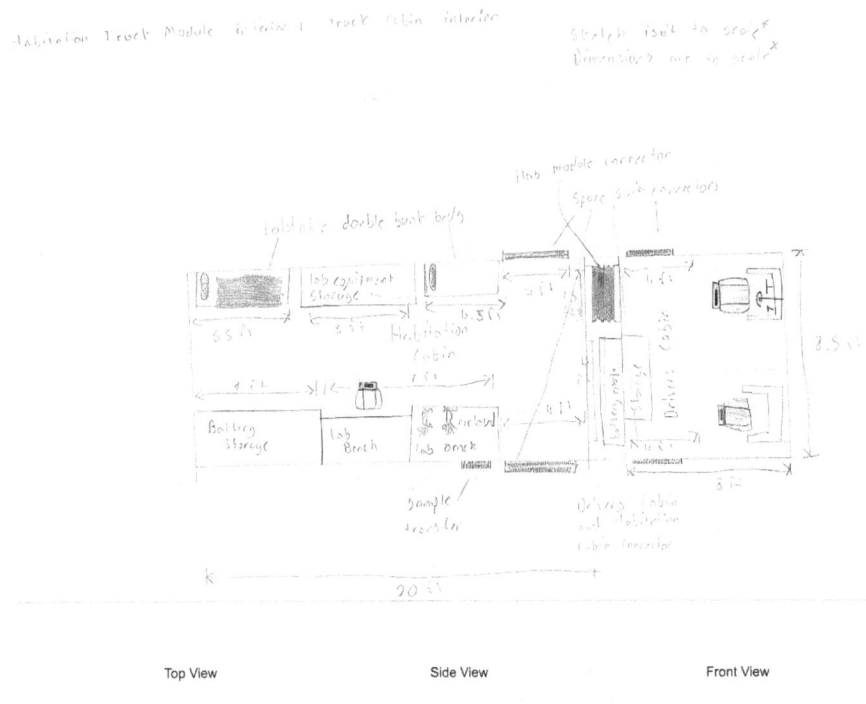

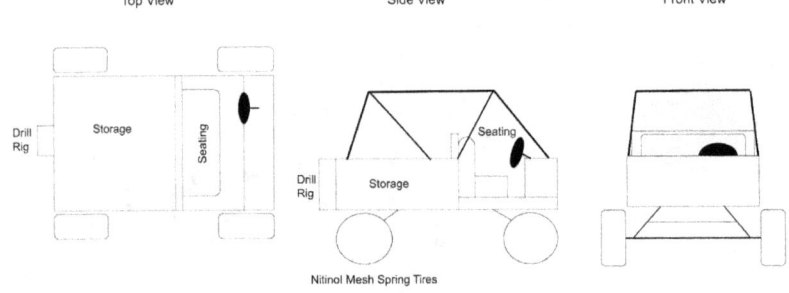

Figure 7-10: Sketches of the Achieve pressurized crewed truck

Additionally, another concept for a module is to have an enlarged cabin to allow the crew to embark on longer extended journeys for scientific research, in which an unpressurized ATV style of vehicle wouldn't have the range to allow long-term journeys. This approach was taken when approaching the issue of a portable Habitat, which can perform its duties as a mobile laboratory without the need for a truck. (The mobile hab is expected to weigh 2.3 tonnes).

4.2. Crewed Mars Exploration and Reconnaissance Rover "Explore"

4.2.1. Design
The Explore rover's role is to find any sign of life on Mars entombed within Martian permafrost where the mission will be digging to supply the mission's need for water. The rover will be equipped with instruments to detect samples of geological interest and any organically produced chemicals trapped within the ice. To obtain samples, the rover will use a rotary-percussive, very similar to that found on the Insight lander proposal by JPL. It escapes the problems the Insight mission's drill ran into by being mobile and having a temperature sensor at the bottom of it. This allows the onboard computer system to detect a change in the drill material, which also allows the rover to relocate to prevent getting stuck at an angle like the insight lander. By scouting ahead of time, the Explore rover prevents the larger drill system on the Achieve truck from getting stuck as well.

This rover will be controlled by the mission personnel on-site, but after the mission's conclusion can continue to operate as it has solar panels similar to that of the Spirit rover but will be equipped with an air compressor to clean off the solar panels. Although this air compressor will be significantly weaker as compared to its counterparts on Earth, the air spray should be more than powerful enough to spray debris off the solar panels lining the back of the rover. While the crew is on Mars, the rover will be remotely controlled and once they leave, it will join Curiosity and Perseverance in their format of exploration.

Although this rover is separately designed from NASA's rovers it still uses the same principles and technology as many of its ancestors. All the communication systems are taken from the Curiosity and Perseverance missions. The methane detection systems and life detection systems are derived from previous NASA projects and although all of them are not tested on Mars, many of them are designed for future Mars missions. Even the newest aspects of the rover (the drill and connected geologic tools) are designed for a Mars mission and are built to avoid the previous downfalls of the Insight Lander mission through built-in mobility and obstacle detection logic programmed into the drilling computer. The drive system of the rover is based on Curiosity and Perseverance and is adjusted for the more durable spring tires used in the rover. With the direct monitoring capabilities of the crew, this rover is designed to assist both the survival of the mission and conduct efficient scientific research at a rate still unseen in landed Mars rovers.

4.2.2. Instruments for Methane

For the purposes of methane detection in northwestern Utopia Planitia, the ground rover will hold a Tunable Laser Spectrometer (TLS) with a new feature for Gas in Scattering Media Absorption Spectroscopy (GASMAS). The TLS measures light absorption at different wavelengths to measure the concentrations of compounds such as methane in the atmosphere of Mars. It has a chamber or Herriott cell and mirrors where a laser beam passes through the gas sample 81 times, making the measurement and analysis extremely efficient for a 20-cm sized instrument (Greicius, 2014)

The mechanism of Curiosity's TLS will be upgraded to accommodate GASMAS, a method that can detect gas "hidden" inside dust particles (Sjöholm et al., 2001). The limitation of using TLS alone is that any interference would reduce its detection capabilities. With GASMAS, the situation can be improved by increasing the interaction length of light with the gas, enhancing the performance of the technique especially in

Name	Weight	Purpose	Location	Additional Info
MILA	8 kgs	Look for Life	On back rotating platform	
SOLID	7 kgs	Look for life signs	On back rotating platform	2.2 Watts used on average
Mini mass spectrometer	10-18 kgs	Analyse the chemicals inside of a sample	On back rotating platform	Uses nano tach to analyse. Still in development but almost ready
Sample collection	50 kg	Bring back interesting cores to earth	On back rotating platform	
Body	1,800 kg	Connecting everything on the rover	Middle of the rover	
High gain Antenna	1kg	Transmitting data directly to and from base	Back right corner	
Ultra-High Frequency Antenna	1kg	Transmitting Data to base through Mars Orbiters	Between the front and back rotary platforms on the right	
Low-Gain Antenna	1kg	Receiving Data	Back left corner	
Spring Tires	198 kg	Prevent tires from breaking and provide mobility	Tires spots	Aluminium springs
Drill (Auger)	22.5 kg	To reach the ice provided on the planet	Front middle of the rover	For more cohesive or sticky samples, the drill can engage percussion, which would help to dislodge small rocks
Computer	10 kg	To process the data from the sensors and sample collectors	Middle left of the rover	Uses VxWorks (multitasking)
Pneumatic Tube/System	2 kg	To transport all of the samples to the testing areas.	Connecting the sampling system to the testing chambers. The pressure chambers are in the front and right side.	Place the tube in the air over a fixed spot and use the spinning plate to get the right machine. The sample then gravity falls directly into a cup.
Bit Temp Sensor	N/A	To measure the changes in temp on the ground while digging, to make sure nothing gets stuck and everything is efficient.	At the end of the Auger/ drill and on the inside top of the bit.	The temp reading can be used to learn the subsurface geology of Mars, which is important to understanding its geothermal situation.
Bit Electrode	N/A	To measure the electrical conductivity	At the end of the Auger/drill and above	Can be used to determine the presence of salts in the water

Table 4: Rover and Tools Specs, Location, and Purpose.

detecting trace species (Tunable Diode Laser, n.d.) The laser is directed to a sample containing gas cavities, and a narrow-bandwidth laser scans the gas to generate its absorption lines, thereby recording its transmission profile (Panaviene et al., 2022).

The combined weight of the TLS and GASMAS instruments is generously estimated at 10 kg (SAM, 2022). The TLS will have two lasers with wavelengths of 2.78 μm and 3.30 μm each and a vacuum pump that pumps Martian air in and out of the device to perform readings at different pressure levels (Dunbar, 2012). This avoids complications when the detector is saturated at a certain pressure (Lakdawalla, 2012). Moreover, the GASMAS instrument uses a laser light falling under the Class I category. This does not only imply that the instrument does not pose any human hazard during a long-term mission, but it also means that the instrument uses a very low output power of a few microwatts (Maltais, 2020).

4.2.3. Instruments for the Search for Life

For the purposes of searching for life, there are three main instruments on the rover. The Sign of Life Detector (SOLID) has two main components to it. The Sandwich microarray immunoassay (SMI), and a Competitive microarray immunoassay (CMI). CMI to detect extinct life molecular biomarkers and other small molecules, and SMI to detect extant life molecular complexes (proteins, EPS, nucleic acids, whole cells, etc.) (Garcia, Castilla, Rodriguez-Manfredi, Rivas, 2015). By having such a board detection system for Earth-like life, we will be able to determine the nature and some chemical processes of life if it is to be found. The detailed analysis will make it easier to study this new system of life without harming the astronauts or their life. The total weight of the instrument (SPU plus SAU) is 7 kg, and the instrument can be transported in a suitcase bearing 12 V rechargeable batteries. The peak of energy consumption is next to 90 W just for 1 min periods during ultrasonication and 45 W for image acquisition (Garcia, Castilla, Rodriguez-Manfredi, Rivas, 2015).

The second instrument is the Microfluidic Life Analyzer (MILA). Designed to look for evidence of life, these tools include the Wet Chemistry Laboratory, an instrument developed by NASA's Jet Propulsion Laboratory that flew on the 2007 Phoenix mission to Mars. While diabetics, for instance, may monitor their blood sugar with a device that detects the presence of a single molecule (glucose), the rover instrument will search for 512 different biological compounds (Landau, 2015). This will allow Explorer to look for life dissimilar to that on earth, like amino acids that are left-handed, in very small amounts. This search for amino acids is one step removed similarly to life on Earth and if only this system goes off, then information will already be collected about Martian life.

The final instrument for the search for life is a small, mass spectrometer being developed by MIT. This will allow the rover to look for life with NASA's broad definition of a chemical system that can undergo Darwinian evolution. By looking for unnatural ions and repeating polymers in the samples from the rover, it can account for the possibility of a foreign system of life that developed on Mars that still resembles our definition.

If found, possible microorganisms present in ice would need to be isolated and the equipment sterilised.

4.2.3. Instruments for Ice and Geology

For the purposes of digging into the ground, a large 1 metre-long drill with a specialised drill bit will be used to dig into the ground and a pneumatic tube will transfer and save up to 30 lbs worth of samples in storage for the crew to analyse later.

The bit is special due to the temperature sensor and electrode on it. See Figure 11 for more info on the use and design. The data from this bit will allow the large drill to work more efficiently, as the conductivity and temperature parameters can be used to make sure that the big drill doesn't get stuck on ice, as the solubility of the salts in the ice can change the melting point. Being close to the melting point can make it faster to drill, so this rover will test drill rates to make sure nothing gets stuck.

In the process of biting the drill is periodically retracted from the hole, the cuttings are transferred to an instrument, and the drill is lowered back into the hole to acquire the next bite as shown in Figure 12. This process allows for the rover to take accurate temperature readings of the subsurface of mars, which has yet to be done at the time of writing and will give geologists a new understanding of the subsurface world of mars. It will also prevent the rover from getting stuck in the ground if it drills too deep.

The pneumatic is slightly pressurised to push samples along the tube and drop them over the back of the rover, where a rotating platform will have the tube hung slightly above the inputs for the life detection tools and sample storage container. The gap is present to make sure that the rover is not in violation of NASA's Planetary Protection Office (Conley, 2011), as the drill has to meet required cleanliness standards. The rover carries life-detection instruments, so the drill and sample delivery system must meet stringent contamination requirements to prevent false positives. The rover can carry up to 50 kgs of samples in the collection system.

4.2.4. Instruments for Communication and Rover Body

For communication, three major instruments (all of which are on Curiosity) are used. The Ultra-High Frequency Antenna (UHA), the Low-Gain Antenna (LGA), and the High-Gain Antenna (HGA) are all used for different communication on the rover. Using UHA allows the rover to communicate directly with earth and send data as a back system to the hab if needed.

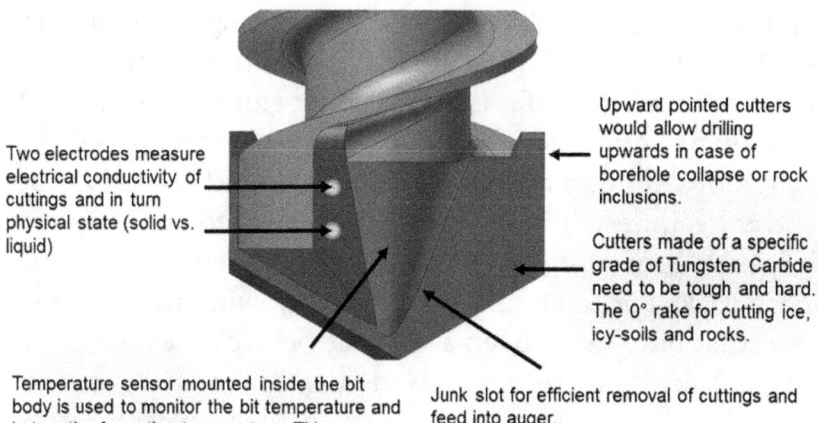

Figure 11: Drilling bit

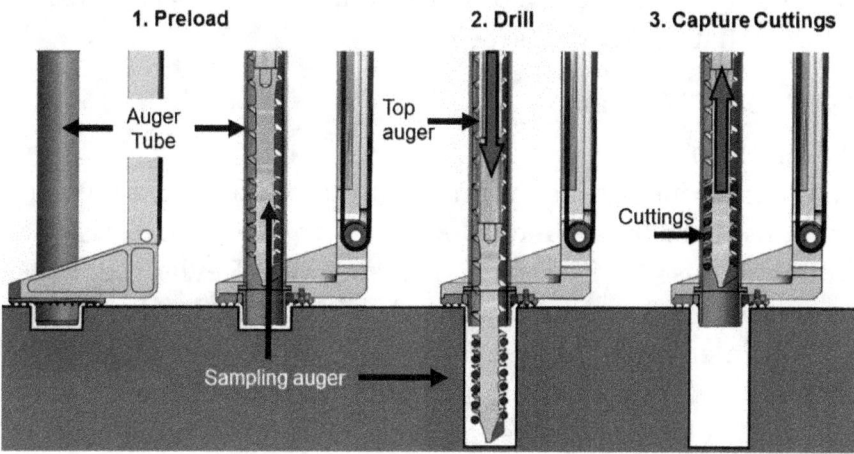

Figure 12: Biting process

The LGA allows for direct communication with the rover, and it is a one-way connection from the hab to the rover to send commands. It is redundant with the HFA as that allows communication to the hab back and forth through the satellites in the Martian orbit. This will allow for future communication with the rover, even if it is on the other side of the planet.

A small computer weighing about 10 pounds will be in charge of communicating the data back and forth to the hab (and earth if need be). Spring tires will be used on the system as they have been tested in fields to be less likely to break due to sharp rocks and such on the surface, allowing them to go into areas that have never been accessible before and still go at high speeds. Since the rover is crewed, it will be reaching speeds of up to 50 kilometres per hour, as the primary reason rovers on mars are currently slow is to avoid taking damage from unseen hazards. By putting a camera on the rover as well, the crew will be able to pilot the rover manually to wherever it needs to go, allowing the crew to save energy as they do not have to explore exclusively on the crewed Truck, but can only visit sites of interest that the rover discovers.

4.3. "Reach" Balloon

4.3.1. Design

To observe dust devils that reach up to 8 km from above, the balloons must fly around 10 km high to keep a safe distance from any dust devil that might form (Dust Devils, n.d.). Taking reference from the Mars Aerial Platform (MAP) mission of Zubrin et al. (1993), the Reach balloon will circumnavigate Mars 20 to 50 times, with the number dependent on the varying wind velocities that range from 30 to 60 kph. In a span of 1.5 Martian years, the data to be collected will provide a vast wealth of information about the planet's atmospheric composition. It will be left flying until something goes wrong with its systems or it crashes totally.

In either case, a substitute balloon stored in the hab will be deployed by a Marsonaut specialising in being a mechanic. The balloon must be inflated slowly (20 g/s) for the first 20 seconds to prevent damage to the balloon fabric and faster (170 g/s) for the rest of the time until the desired diameter of 4.103 m is reached. (Given a pressure difference of 0.3168 (Zubrin, 1993) to fly the balloon at a constant altitude, the Buoyancy force equation indicates that the mass of the balloon film has to be 5.388 kg with a radius of 4.103 m.) The fabric will be made of a 12-micron thick biaxial nylon 6 film, which is already being done by Winzen Balloons of San Antonio Texas. The estimated mean life before any significant damage would be beyond the 1.5 years of the crewed Mars mission. Conveniently, the lifetime is the longest (~3000 sols) when the balloon is in the northern hemisphere.

For basic atmospheric measurements, the balloon will feature miscellaneous atmospheric monitors such as temperature and pressure monitors, a sun sensor, and an accelerometer. The location of the balloon will be given by a tracking device, which will also provide information on the speed and direction of the winds at any point in time. Moreover, there will be a monitor for the water vapour concentration and the mean size of dust particles in an area to investigate the dynamics of dust and water on Mars. These instruments will have a total mass of 62.8 kg, all powered by a solar array on the balloon generating 43 W-hr/sol of power (assuming a 100 W/m2 solar incidence). This power will be stored on a battery with a capacity of 18 W-hr so the balloon can continue operating at night.

The data from the balloon will be transmitted using an aerostat transmitter system, with a radio receiver listening to a beacon from a current communications satellite. This beacon prompts the balloon to send up signals to an orbiter, using up to 18 W of power to generate a 401 MHz signal and send 64 kb/s data. The remaining power in the balloon's battery can be used for contingencies such as a drop in solar levels.

To sum, the team chose a balloon for the mission due to the immense data that it can provide by circumnavigating Mars. Having balloons on site will allow the crew to gain more scientific knowledge about the Martian atmosphere: this is with a closer view and lesser power requirements than an orbiter while reaching higher altitudes than a drone. In other words, the balloon offers a better range of view of the Martian atmosphere while achieving the mission's scientific objectives efficiently.

Component	Mass (kg)
Main Parachute System	15.9
Balloon	5.4
Balloon container and gas cans	5.9
Solar Array (40 W-hr, 0.22 m^2)	0.5
Radio Transmitter	1.1
Miscellaneous Atmospheric Monitors	0.1
Main Scientific Instruments	62.8
TOTAL (per 1 balloon)	91.7

Table 5: The breakdown of the mass of one balloon

4.3.2. Instruments

A Hyper-Cam Methane will be mounted to look for traces of methane around the areas where a dust devil is occurring or has recently occurred. There will be no shortage of data as the Perseverance rover has in fact recorded approximately 300 dust devils in just a year (Tomaswick, 2021). The current Organic and Toxic Analyzers have a wide range in detecting methane (CCAC, n.d.), but a new instrument in the form of the Hyper-Cam Methane combines the two analyzers while maintaining their wide range and detecting atmospheric compounds more precisely in low concentrations. The Hyper-Cam methane is a hyperspectral spectrometer (i.e., non-invasive remote sensing) specifically for monitoring methane gas even at low flow rates (Methane Gas Detection, 2015). From a balloon, it can visualise methane in real time and localise the source and direction of the methane gas. This will provide new data on the mysterious methane distributions on Mars. Conveniently, the instrument can withstand changing weather conditions of the planet's harsh outdoors, making the Hyper-Cam handy for dust devil studies.

The Hyper-Cam Methane is a Michelson-type interferometer, so it needs power to produce a laser (Methane Gas Detection, 2015). It features a Stirling Cycle Cooled Detector that can make operations possible at a temperature of 75 K (Stirling Cooled, n.d.). Because it does not need liquid nitrogen like traditional technology, the Hyper-Cam is an ideal instrument for outdoor, remote, and autonomous vehicles like the balloon. It weighs 40-50 kg in total and requires 30 W of power (Wuhan Joho, n.d.).

There's also an interesting study that found very rare lightning events on Mars, unexpected events due to the sheer dryness of the planet. Why these are a key point of interest is thoroughly discussed in Section 1. Essentially, rubbing dust particles are hypothesised to be producing small-scale electrical discharges, which might be breaking down and redistributing methane in the Martian atmosphere. Scientists speculate that thermal radiation is involved in triggering the electrical discharges, so aside from the Hyper-Cam Methane, the balloon will also carry a microwave detector that is capable of finding signs of electrical discharges to confirm their occurrence within active dust devils. Due to the increased friction of dust particles within dust devils, they are the perfect site to detect rare lightning events on Mars and understand their role in methane production.

The University of Michigan has already procured such a microwave detector called the Agile Digital Detector (ADD), which can distinguish natural thermal emission signals from radio frequency interference (Misra et al., 2010). The ADD uses microwaves as they can penetrate easily through dust devils with negligible attenuation (Dong et al., 2013). However, unlike the Hyper-Cam Methane, the ADD is not designed for the harsh weather conditions of Mars. For protection from dust and moisture in the upper atmosphere, the ADD will be covered with a non-metal protective oxide film, which would not interfere with the readings of the instrument (How to prevent corrosion, 2021). To accommodate turbulence or shock, a rubber cushion will be added on the surface where the ADD is fixed to absorb shock caused by sudden gusts of wind.

For a more precise data collection, the ADD will also be paired with a Kurtosis Detector, which is already in use on Earth-based observatories. Bringing one of them to Mars will give atmospheric scientists a front-seat view of smaller-scale lightning events that might be invisible to Earth-based instruments. According to Ruf et al. (2010), the Kurtosis Detector processes signals by differentiating between thermal and non-thermal radiation, allowing it to pinpoint the said lightning events. The ADD and Kurtosis Detector weighs around 17 kg and requires 120 W of power (Morris, 2019).

HUMAN OPERATIONS

5. CREW SELECTION

Apart from flexible criteria like an age range (preferably adults around 26-35 to maximise natural physical capabilities even after years of mission training) and a height range (around, but not limited to, 5'6"–6'3"). If someone fits the mission well but does not come within these ranges, the adjustable spacesuits can still be tailored to their needs as choosing the N.E.W. E.R.A. crew will extensively consider a person's abilities over anything else. The regular process of applications, followed by NASA and the ESA, will be conducted, with interviews and intense physical and medical assessments of all candidates. After narrowing the field, the remaining candidates will undergo conceptual application and theoretical tests. The 30 top candidates will then perform the next round of tests, which include exposure to radiation, decision-making and problem-solving in high-pressure situations, and communication skills. This will be short-listed to 10 people who will all train for the mission. However, the primary N.E.W E.R.A crew—consisting of the top 5 members—will be chosen by performing in-depth psychological tests to understand a person's natural tendencies, see the extent to which a person tends to think positively, assess how they work as a team and, last but not least, get an idea of their personalities. A person's experience will influence their application, but ultimately the final assessments will be the deciding factor.

The selected crew needs to state their consent to the tolerance of any possible outcome of the mission, and something that will also be considered is their non-professional interests. For instance, team morale benefits from a Marsonaut who enjoys cooking, playing the guitar, crocheting, or likes languages. They should be trained to handle higher-than-average amounts of radiation and should be able to adapt to situations while staying as composed as possible. The reason for this is that during the mission, the Marsonauts will have to manage a heavy, extreme workload as well as long hours of restlessness, boredom, and isolation. An astronaut's nationality or sexual identity does not affect whether they are chosen to be part of the crew, and N.E.W E.R.A's final candidates will be chosen in the most representative and diverse manner possible.

Finally, the qualifications of the N.E.W. E.R.A. crew should be aligned with the three main objectives of the mission: life on Mars, atmosphere and weather, and human sustainability.

A crew size of 5 was chosen as it allows an optimal balance between the diversity of necessary skills and the adequate distribution of resources (food, backup spacesuits, etc.) The ideal qualifications of each crew member are as follows:

1. Climatologist/Lead Engineer (Captain, in consultation with TWM)—in charge of setting up the balloon, leading methane-related activity, and performing rover functions
2. Geochemist/Secondary Engineer (will replace the captain if needed)—will go on the truck with Marsonaut 4 and work on the ice; in charge of setting up and using the rover
3. Botanist/Psychologist (Team Welfare Manager [TWM])—in charge of maintaining the greenhouse and the crew's nutritional income; will monitor crew mental health and advise the captain regarding team welfare
4. Ecologist/Lead Medic—will work with Marsonaut 2 on the ice extraction and research; will act as first contact for the crew in case of extreme medical emergencies
5. Biochemist/Secondary Medic—will carry out the biochemistry and food-related research in the greenhouse; in charge of air regulation and life support systems

For most team decisions, a democratic system will be used, but considering the mission is for a 1.5-year period, each crew member shall be in charge of a specific area of command. Marsonaut 1 (M-1), the captain, will make the final calls in critical situations. Marsonaut 2 will make important decisions regarding truck excursions and will step up as captain if M-1 is rendered incapable. Marsonaut 3 will have the deciding statement on the mental health of a crew member and has the authority to denounce the captain if they are not fit. Lastly, Marsonauts 4 and 5 will perform any medical procedures should emergencies arise. The geochemist and the biochemist in the team will also oversee ensuring the documentation of all scientific findings.

Three of the crew members will be fully trained in piloting the landing spacecraft, while the secondary engineer and lead medic will train on driving the pressurized truck. However, the rest of the crew must be aware of how it is done as well. Two crew members should preferably enjoy cooking/culinary practices, as that will help prepare food for the crew once crops can be harvested on Mars. The selected crew will be trained in data handling and coding (e.g., in case modifications to the rover or any system need to be made manually) as well as in-depth medical assistance and urine/blood sample testing. All crew members should be able to communicate efficiently; this ability is significantly considered during the crew selection. To adapt to any technical issues, the crew will need to undergo courses on engineering/scientific concepts and mechanical/electrical skills.

6. SCHEDULE

Because the Marsonauts are expected to leave Earth during its conjunction with Mars, the crew must stay on the red planet for 550 days or 1.5 years. After that period, Earth and Mars will be in conjunction again, thereby minimising the amount of fuel needed to go back to Earth (Zubrin, 1996). The N.E.W. E.R.A. mission must take full advantage of the 1.5 years afforded to the crew for Mars exploration.

Hence, a sol on Mars, for the crew, would be busy as demonstrated by Table 6. To make the crew feel more accustomed to their routine, a clock—designed as a typical Earth clock, but with a slightly bigger scale to fit in the 39 extra minutes available on Mars—could be used.

A minimum sleep time of 8 hours is required for the crew to function healthily, as well as sticking to regular mealtimes, to sustain the workload they need to perform. This schedule makes the best use of physical space and resources available to the crew.

6:30am - 7:00am	Wake-up and do the essentials	- take waking heart rate and perform the required breathing exercises
7:00 am - 8:20 am	Physical exercise (they can rotate between treadmills/bike/skipping)	- cardio and mentally prep for the day
8:30am - 8:50am	**BREAKFAST**	
9:00am - 11:45am	Morning experiments/work	
11:45am - 12:30pm	Interviews/Report-writing/etc.	
12:30pm - 12:50pm	Short nap	:)
1:00pm - 1:30pm	**LUNCH**	
2:00pm - 5:45pm	More work	Crew members can choose to workout for an hour anytime between 4-7pm so that the exercise room is not crowded at once.
5:45pm - 7:00pm	Workout	- strengthening
7:00pm - 7:45pm	Relax/call family, friends/check email/ or do more work	
7:45pm - 8:15pm	**DINNER**	(everyone eats together)
8:20 ish pm - 9:15pm	Catch-up on the day's work and plan for the next day/ do more work	
9:20 ish pm	Alone time/ meditation	For half an hour/40minutes
10:00pm	**Sleep**	

Table 6: A sol on Mars

Apart from weekly, fortnightly, and monthly checks and tests, the crew will have monthly goals of the experiments and objectives to be reached within the respective month. The crew should also make time to play word games, watch movies, listen to music, and eat together to maintain the levels of trust and comfort in each other's company.

5-8 days of each month must be dedicated to cleaning equipment (on a rotatory basis). However, the Marsonauts must give themselves at least one day off each month for recuperating and rejuvenating.

As this is a multi-year mission, it would be necessary for the crew to clock 10-12 hours of revisional training every month, just so that they keep in contact with mission objectives and performance. Towards the final quarter of their mission, the crew will start performing certain training exercises (that are possible on Mars, like virtual simulations) to prepare for space-travel again.

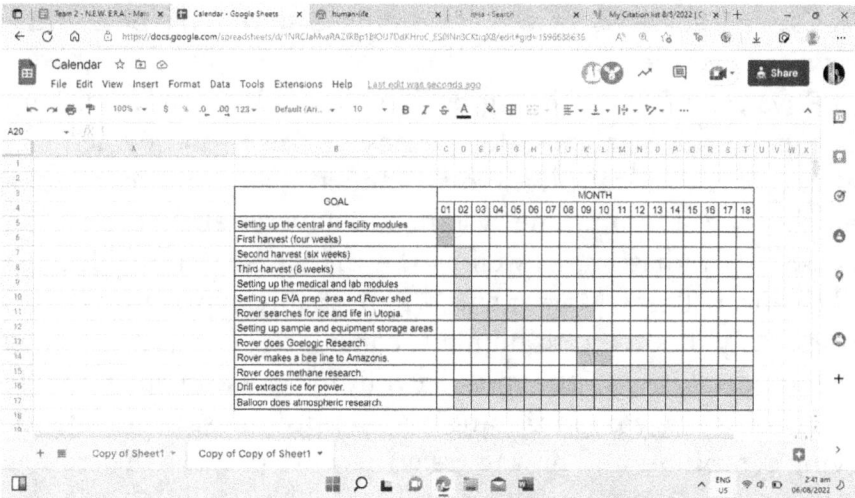

Table 7: 18-month schedule of the crewed Mars mission.

The initial months of the N.E.W E.R.A mission will be focused on setting up the central module and the facility module including the greenhouses. The latter part of this first phase will overlap with the assembling of the rover and truck, which will allow ice and atmospheric research to be conducted. Secondary modules like the lab and storage area, as well as the rover shed and EVA prep room, will be set up during this time. Atmospheric and ice research will be conducted over the course of the mission. Once the truck can manage without the rover for ice research, the rover will move on to geologic research during the middle of the mission and methane research towards the second half.

7. MARSONAUT HEALTH

7.1 Physical and Mental Health

A Marsonaut's day should include an intake of around 2,800 calories, 2.5 litres of water and 2-2.5 hours of physical exercise (as well as a minimum period of sleep time, as mentioned before)—this should continue once they land on Mars. Available exercise equipment on Mars will include the ARED (Advanced Resistive Exercise Device), treadmills, a stationary bike and a rowing machine.

Physical effects of living on Mars include a likely build-up of nutrient deficiencies, due to lack of fresh food (which will affect psychological/physiological functions), alterations in the efficiency of the immune system and adverse effects on vision caused by radiation, as well as the increased risk of illnesses like cancer. These Marsonauts will probably experience things previously unknown to humans, considering the journey they are undertaking, so the mission training must include a wide range of dietary conditioning and supply the skills of identifying symptoms and how to treat them—to prepare the crew as much as possible.

Considering this mission is one that will be physically and mentally challenging to boundaries unknown by humans before, it is required that the Marsonauts also spend time understanding themselves and learning how to train their minds. (for example, visualising the possible challenges they might face on their mission and how they can respond to it, breathing exercises, etc.) This process, however, has to start cohesively with the mission/physical training for the Marsonauts to feel it will make a difference and to understand how it works. Small things like taking their waking heart rate (HR), maintaining a journal and making sure they spend some alone time daily, are habits that the Marsonauts need to adapt. To add to this, the crew could create a motivation jar, or have a pinboard in the central module where they pin/stick up anything that they like: it could vary from memes and photographs to observations and research.

The lighting and colour/interior of the hab will play a big role in the crew's mental health. It would be ideal for the crew to have continuous access to solar light on Mars for optimum preservation of health, but with protection from radiation being a priority; interior lighting within the hab will have to make up for natural light and be set up so that it provides the crew with a sense of comfort and helps maintain their Circadian rhythms. Hopefully, over time, a protected space can be developed where the crew can spend some time observing the Martian sky.

7.2 Testing and Protocol

A certain medical protocol will be kept in place and followed by the Marsonauts in training. For example, if someone is sick, they must remain isolated in their bubble for a minimum of 3 days, or till symptoms subside, while nutritional supplies will be passed to them through the flap doors. If the parameters for the below-mentioned tests are not in the normal range, the required measures will be taken to help the person recover.

Urine and blood sample collections, as well as Fluid Shift tests, will be done at fortnightly intervals. Each crew member will be trained in how to take these tests, for themselves as well as for another individual, making the process viable. The tests can take place in the medical module and the samples will be tested in a corner of the laboratory module.

While lactate testing is part of the first aid kit, it can also be done at intervals to check the efficiency of oxygen delivery in a Marsonaut's body. To monitor the cleanliness of the equipment, hab swabbing and rover checks will take place at weekly intervals.

During the mission, Mission Control on Earth might schedule spontaneous cognitive, spatial or physical sensory tests that will appear on certain devices, and gauge the immediate attention and stress levels of a Marsonaut. There will also be a website/document available on all of the Marsonauts' devices so that medical advice and procedures will always be accessible to the crew. In addition, the protocol will include maintaining a personal journal to prevent the build-up of emotions, as well as recording and listening to their own voices to keep in contact with themselves.

7.3 Medical Module and Monitors

The medical module on the Mars base is directly connected to the central, living module. It will contain 2 inflatable beds (only used if necessary), and a monitoring screen that will project the vital parameter readings of the crew at all times. (Data storage and transfer activities will happen in the medical module, except when the beds are in use).

For this to be possible, each Marsonaut will have monitoring devices on them—such as a watch and a secondary, monitoring strip—that will make sure the respective crew member's data is kept track of at all times. A first aid kit (including bandages, thermometers, a lactate testing kit, etc.) will be kept in each crew member's bubble (beneath their bed) which they will need to carry on the truck in the case of excursions. The kit will also contain smaller, lighter ultrasound devices (Editor, Space Ref, 2021) that will allow the crew to access the test images from their cell-phone.

The majority of the medicine supply taken for the Marsonauts will be stored in the medical module, however, the spare oxygen tanks will be stored in the colder, regolith shelter near the preserved food.

8. DISPOSAL PLANNING

8.1 Human Waste

The toilets for the Marsonauts, built on Mars will be self-cleaning toilets. These commodes will be made of metallic (i.e. Titanium) enclosures and will be slightly adjustable in terms of vacuum-ability due to the reduced gravity of Mars. Its structure will somewhat resemble NASA's Universal Waste Management System (UWMS) (Elburn, 2019), and the vacuum-ability will also ensure minimal use of water and help the segregation of urine and faeces.

A reactor called the Heat Melt Compactor (Jones, Pace, & Fisher, 2013) will process this waste to produce water, oxygen, and other gases. The remaining waste will be biologically inactive and can be disinfected using ammonia. Faeces will be used in the greenhouse to supplement the growth of mycelium, while the remaining faeces can be used to shape trash disks which will be stored until needed as radiation protection or fuel. In the urine processor, the urea will be collected and directed to the greenhouses where it can be used as fertiliser.

The Maximum Absorbency Garments (which resemble adult diapers) used by the Marsonauts during EVAs will be disposed of and kept in a storage area. However, with the emergence of more sustainable solutions to historically disposable ones, biodegradable diapers like those made by the company 'Unique Wellness' can be burned with no adverse effects and used as fuel without posing any risk to the soil (Unique Wellness, n.d.). In future missions, the equipment could be taken to disinfect the used garments and turn the waste into usable compost.

8.2 Packaging

Packing for such a long mission, will take up at least a tonne of the weight on the payload. In cases of machinery, plastic packaging cannot be avoided, but for certain food and other matter, lightweight materials like bamboo, corn starch, or mycelium could be used. Biodegradable materials like these are yet to be tested in space for their longevity, but using packaging that is edible, plantable or compostable in the Martian soil (to study the activity of microorganisms) would save accumulation of waste—as well as reduce the payload for the return journey, and ensure no littering on Mars. Even recycled materials on Earth could be used to attain packaging for equipment and food. Beverages, however, will have to be stored as usual in airtight containers as powders to avoid inconveniences caused by spillage.

8.3 Clothing

Considering the crew will stay on the Martian surface for around 18 months, they will use each piece of clothing for the maximum amount of time that is possible. However, there should also be a system that allows these clothes to be cleaned. What makes this possible is dry cleaning, using liquid CO2, (Rodriguez, 2022) which is non-toxic and non-flammable. This process does not require any water, thereby not using up essential resources required by the Marsonauts.

Cleaning Process/Solvent	Electricity Use (KWh/kg Textiles)
GreenEarth® (decamethylcyclo-pentasiloxane D5)	1.195
Hydrocarbon	0.783
LCO_2	0.681
PERC	0.586
Wet cleaning	0.205

8.4 Spare and broken parts

There is a high probability of damage occurring to the devices and machinery on Mars. There are backup systems but, for example, if a rover or shield stops functioning, their metallic structure can be used, along with polyethene, to store fresh crops and samples.

For example, the landing spacecraft may initially be used as storage space or shelter, and the components inside it will be reused based on their functionality.

CONCLUSIONS

The first cost that we accounted for, was for the unmanned rover as we can easily provide an estimate by looking at the budget for the Curiosity rover. We subtracted $1 billion (accounting for the spacecraft) from Curiosity's $2.5 billion budget because the N.E.W. E.R.A. mission does not consider the launch (Planetary Science Mission Directorate, n.d.). Since the truck and the habitat mostly feature new components, the cost for them was more challenging to estimate. However, the truck's technological complexity, relative to the unmanned rover, makes $5 billion reasonable. By the same logic, the most important living

Component	Mass	Cost	Power Required
Habitat and Appliances (exercise equipment, computers, etc.)	4,000 kg	$10,000,000,000	75-90 kW/hr
Greenhouse	2,700 kg		3.5 kW/hr
Pre-packaged Food	1,200 kg		N/A
Electrolysis	750 kg		15 kW
Combustion Chamber	100 kg		N/A
Filtration	100 kg		35 kW
Manned Truck	6,600 kg	$5,000,000,000	1.65 kW/mi
Habitation Module	2,300 kg		75-90 kW/hr
Drill	4,000 kg		4 kW/hr
Gas Tanks (4 pc.)	1,200 kg		1.5 kW
Spacesuit (7 pc.)	560 kg	$700,000,000	3.3 kW/hr
3D Printers	500 kg	$300,000	0.115 kW/hr
Sabatier Reactor	600 kg	$4,000,000	7 kW/hr
Solar Panels (90 m^2)	1,000 kg	$250,000	N/A
Balloons (2 pc.)	200 kg	$100,000	self-maintained
Unmanned Rover	2200 kg	$1,500,000,000	self-maintained
TOTAL	28,010 kg	$17,204,650,000	

Table 9: Summary of Weight, Cost, and Power

quarters must at least be double the truck's cost, so we set $10 billion for the habitat.

The prices of the remaining components were based on their current commercial prices. For instance, each spacesuit costs around $100 million, so bringing seven of them will be $700 million (Mendoza, 2021). Likewise, 90 m2 of solar panels (calculated using data corresponding to energy consumption and production methods) corresponds to around $250,000. The same estimation applies for the 3D printers, the Sabatier Reactor, and the hot air balloons.

9. RECOMMENDATIONS/POTENTIAL FOR FUTURE RESEARCH

Using Aquaponics in future missions is a project we propose. Relying on it on the first mission seems neither plausible nor logical despite the advantages and convenience it brings. It would only be highly beneficial once Mars's population starts growing when we'd need more things to rely on and maintenance would be significantly easier.

The Reach balloon and Explore rover used on this mission will gather data while performing their experiments and will most likely help humans immensely with our understanding of dust devils. This will prove important in the future as the following missions will be able to take dust devil activity into consideration when choosing landing sites, base, and experimental locations. Furthermore, we could conduct more research into creating colonies on Mars by bringing small mammals such as mice or rats on board with us and testing the effects of Martian gravity on their overall but especially reproductive health. Going to Mars will also prove insightful for human life on Earth as to how we can maximise, protect and appreciate our resources.

The most important outcome of exploring Mars will be the development of a new branch of a self-sufficient human civilisation, individual from that on our home planet. Shaped by the physical, psychological and technological challenges on the new frontier, and liberated from Earth's established history, these explorers could freely navigate the future by benefiting from centuries of knowledge and progress. This mixture of challenge and freedom should also allow people to discover entirely new definitions of citizens' rights and obligations, as well as new ways of organising society.

We are in the front seat for a new era of both science and society.

REFERENCES

1. About: Mechanical counterpressure suit. (n.d.). Dbpedia.org. https://dbpedia.org/page/Mechanical_counterpressure_suit
2. Abramov, I. P., & Å Ingemar Skoog. (2003). Russian spacesuits. Springer ; Chichester, Uk.
3. 28 Advantages and Disadvantages of Aeroponics and Hydroponics https://www.1001artificialplants.com/2019/09/29/the-advantages-and-disadvantages-of-aeroponics-and-hydroponics/
4. Arizona State University. (2020). Mars Education | Developing the Next Generation of Explorers. Asu.edu. https://marsed.asu.edu/mep/atmosphere#:~:text=Mars
5. Atkinson, N. (2009). Lightning detected on Mars. Universe Today. https://www.universetoday.com/32858/lighning-detected-on-mars/

6. Brown, M. (2022). New study solves a major problem with living on the Moon and Mars. Inverse. https://www.inverse.com/innovation/mars-city-moon-electrolysis

7. Catapano, F., Di Iorio, S., Sementa, P., & Vaglieco, B. M. (2016). Analysis of energy efficiency of methane and hydrogen-methane blends in a PFI/DI SI research engine. Energy, 117, 378–387. doi:10.1016/j.energy.2016.06.043

8. CCAC Oil and Gas Methane Partnership" Methane Emissions Detection and Measurement Techniques, Equipment and Costs. (n.d.). U.S. Environmental Protection Agency. https://www.epa.gov/sites/default/files/2016-04/documents/mon7ccacemissurvey.pdf

9. Chu, J. (2014, September). Shrink-wrapping spacesuits. MIT News | Massachusetts Institute of Technology. https://news.mit.edu/2014/second-skin-spacesuits-0918

10. Conley, C. (2011). Planetary Protection at NASA: Status and Issues. NASA Planetary Protection. https://science.nasa.gov/science-pink/s3fs-public/atoms/files/ConleyPPstatusMay11v1_-_TAGGED_-_UPDATED.pdf

11. Cui, Z., Jia, L., Li, L., Liu, X., Xu, W., Shu, R., & Xu, X. (2022). A Laser-Induced Breakdown Spectroscopy Experiment Platform for High-Degree Simulation of MarSCoDe In Situ Detection on Mars. Remote Sensing. 14. 1954. 10.3390/rs14091954.

12. Dong, Q., Li, Y., Xu, J., Zhang, H., & Wang, M. (2013). Effect of Sand and Dust Storms on Microwave Propagation. IEEE Transactions on Antennas and Propagation. 61. 910-916. 10.1109/TAP.2012.2223446.

13. Dunbar, B. (2012). Pieces of the tunable laser spectrometer. NASA. https://www.nasa.gov/mission_pages/msl/multimedia/webster1.html

14. Dust devils. Dust Devils on Mars | Exploring the Planets | National Air and Space Museum. (n.d.). https://airandspace.si.edu/exhibitions/exploring-the-planets/online/solar-system/mars/wind/dust-devils.cf
15. Editor, S. R. (2021) *Space Health Institute demonstrates self-reliant performance of the Butterfly IQ portable handheld ultrasound system in Space.* SpaceRef. https://spaceref.com/press-release/space-health-institute-demonstrates-self-reliant-performance-of-the-butterfly-iq-portable-handheld-ultrasound-system-in-space/
16. Elburn, D. (2019). *Boldly go! NASA's new Space Toilet.* NASA. https://www.nasa.gov/feature/boldly-go-nasa-s-new-space-toilet-offers-more-comfort-improved-efficiency-for-deep-space/
17. Enhanced water bottles filter water on the go. (n.d.). NASA. https://spinoff.nasa.gov/Spinoff2013/cg_1.html
18. Gannon, M. (2013). *NASA turns astronaut trash into Space Radiation Shield.* Space.com. https://www.space.com/19111-astronaut-trash-space-radiation-shield.html
19. Greicius, T. (2014). Tunable Laser Spectrometer on NASA's Curiosity Mars Rover. NASA. https://www.nasa.gov/jpl/msl/pia19086/
20. Grishin I., Zakharov V., & Aref'ev K. (2022). Experimental Study of Methane Combustion Efficiency in a High-Enthalpy Oxygen-Containing Flow. Applied Sciences.12(2):899. https://doi.org/10.3390/app12020899
21. Gorguinpour, C., Leclair, R., Carval, D., Estes, M., Hsieh, A., Howe, K., Rodriguez, C., Saffuden, M., Saylor, S., & Yen, Y.-R. (n.d.). Advanced Two-System Space Suit. https://www.lpi.usra.edu/publications/reports/CB-1106/ucb01.pdf

22. Hamilton Standard, Division of United Aircraft. (2009). PORTABLE LIFE SUPPORT SYSTEM (p. 1). https://www.hq.nasa.gov/alsj/LM15_Portable_Life_Support_System_ppP1-5.pdf
23. Harbaugh, J. (2017). *Deep Space Optical Communications (DSOC)*. NASA. https://www.nasa.gov/mission_pages/tdm/dsoc/index.html
24. Harris, W., & Chandler, N. (2008, March 24). How Astronauts Work. HowStuffWorks. https://science.howstuffworks.com/astronaut7.htm
25. Holschuh, B., Obropta, E. W., Buechley, L., & Newman, D. (2012, September 11). Materials and Textile Architecture Analyses for Mechanical Counter-Pressure Space Suits using Active Materials. ResearchGate; unknown. https://www.researchgate.net/publication/268570032_Materials_and_Textile_Architecture_Analyses_for_Mechanical_Counter-Pressure_Space_Suits_using_Active_Materials
26. How many calories should I eat in a day? (2018)
27. https://www.nhs.uk/common-health-questions/food-and-diet/what-should-my-daily-intake-of-calories-be/
28. How to prevent corrosion, shock and dust on field instruments? (2021). Vacorda. https://www.vacorda.com/news/how-to-prevent-corrosion-shock-and-dust-on-field-instruments/
29. Huerta, R., & Lluch, I. (2019). Feasibility and Analysis of a Hybrid Spacesuit Archietcture for Planetary Surface Exploration. https://scholar.colorado.edu/downloads/6108vb59f

30. Jones, H & Pace, G & Fisher,. (2013). Managing Spacecraft Waste Using the Heat Melt Compactor (HMC). 10.2514/6.2013-3362.
31. Knowlton C., Veerapaneni R., D'Elia T., & Rogers S. Microbial analyses of ancient ice core sections from greenland and antarctica. Biology (Basel). 2013 Jan 25;2(1):206-32. doi: 10.3390/biology2010206. PMID: 24832659; PMCID: PMC4009855.
32. Lakdawalla, E. (2012). More than you probably wanted to know about curiosity's Sam Instrument. The Planetary Society. https://www.planetary.org/articles/curiosity-instrument-sam
33. Lind, R. (2012). Next Generation Vehicle for Space Exploration Driving New Tech Here On Earth. NASA. https://www.nasa.gov/exploration/technology/space_exploration_vehicle/index.html
34. List Of Common Agricultural Fertilisers (2017) https://www.gardenguides.com/12405093-list-of-common-agricultural-fertilizers.html
35. Lomax, B. A., Just, G. H., McHugh, P. J., Broadley, P. K., Hutchings, G. C., Burke, P. A., Roy, M. J., Smith, K. L., & Symes, M. D. (2022, February 8). *Predicting the efficiency of oxygen-evolving electrolysis on the Moon and Mars.* Nature News. Retrieved August 6, 2022, from https://www.nature.com/articles/s41467-022-28147-5
36. Lunar and Planetary Institute. (2017). NASA EXTRAVEHICULAR MOBILITY UNIT (EMU) LSS/SSA DATA BOOK Publicly released per JSC-E-DAA-TN55224. In https://www.lpi.usra.edu/lunar/constellation/NASA-EMU-Data-Book-JSC-E-DAA-TN55224.pdf

37. Maltais, J. (2020). Laser Classes & Laser Safety—What You Need To Know. Laserax. https://www.laserax.com/blog/laser-safety-laser-classes-explained
38. Martian climate. Planetary Sciences, Inc. (2018). https://planetary-science.org/mars-research/martian-climate/
39. Mathias, G. (2020). Hydrogen production through electrolysis. Process Ecology. https://processecology.com/articles/hydrogen-production-through-electrolysis
40. Methane gas detection using hyperspectral imaging: Sphereoptics en. Methane Gas Detection using hyperspectral Imaging | SphereOptics EN. (2015). https://sphereoptics.de/en/methane-gas-detection-using-hyperspectral-imaging/
41. Methane on Mars. (2022). Wikipedia. https://en.wikipedia.org/wiki/Methane_on_Mars
42. Misra, S., De Roo, R., & Ruf, C. (2010). Evaluation of the kurtosis algorithm in detecting radio frequency interference from multiple sources. 2019–2022. 10.1109/IGARSS.2010.5652321.
43. MIT Department of Aeronautics and Astronautics. (n.d.). Life Support. Web.mit.edu. http://web.mit.edu/16.00/www/aec/lif_sup.html#:~:text=and%20reliability%20requirements.-
44. Mendoza, J. (2021). How much does a NASA spacesuit really cost? Grunge. https://www.grunge.com/624909/how-much-does-a-nasa-spacesuit-really-cost/
45. Monaghan, H. (2018, June 19). *O2O: 2023*. NASA. https://www.nasa.gov/directorates/heo/scan/opticalcommunications/o2o/
46. Morris, V. (2019). Microwave Radiometer Handbook. U.S. Department of Energy. https://www.arm.gov/

publications/tech_reports/handbooks/mwr_handbook.pdf

47. Nanoceram filters. Argonide Advanced Water Filtration Systems. (n.d.). https://argonide.com/products/nanoceram-electropositive-water-filters

48. NASA. (2016). Location of large subsurface water-ice deposit in Utopia Planitia, Mars – NASA mars exploration. NASA. https://mars.nasa.gov/resources/8183/location-of-large-subsurface-water-ice-deposit-in-utopia-planitia-mars/

49. NASA. (2017). https://www.nasa.gov/sites/default/files/atoms/files/tbird_fact_sheet_v2.pdf

50. NASA. (2019). Planet Mars. NASA's Mars Exploration Program; NASA. https://mars.nasa.gov/all-about-mars/facts/

51. National Aeronautics and Space Administration. (n.d.). Suited for Spacewalking An Activity Guide for Technology. https://www.nasa.gov/pdf/188963main_Extravehicular_Mobility_Unit.pdf

52. Niiler, E. (2019, October 16). NASA's New Space Suits Will Fit Men and Women Alike (for Once). Wired; WIRED. https://www.wired.com/story/no-more-spacewalk-snafus-nasas-new-space-suit-fits-everyone/

53. Oyama, V. & Berdahl, B. (1977), The Viking Gas Exchange Experiment results from Chryse and Utopia surface samples, J. Geophys. Res., 82(28), 4669– 4676, doi:10.1029/JS082i028p04669.

54. Panaviene, J., Pacheco, A., Schwarz, C. E., Grygoryev, K., Andersson-Engels, S., & Dempsey, E. M. (2022). Gas in scattering media absorption spectroscopy as a potential tool in neonatal respiratory care. Nature News. https://www.nature.com/articles/s41390-022-02110-y

55. Parro Garcia, V., de Diego Castilla, G., Rodriguez-Manfredi, J., Rivas, L., et al. (2011). SOLID3: A Multiplex Antibody Microarray-Based Optical Sensor Instrument for In Situ Life Detection in Planetary Exploration. Astrobiology. 11. 15-28. 10.1089/ast.2010.0501.
56. Perez, M. (2015). 'Chemical Laptop' Could Search for Signs of Life Outside Earth. NASA. https://www.nasa.gov/feature/jpl/chemical-laptop-could-search-for-signs-of-life-outside-earth
57. Planetary Science Mission Directorate (n.d.). NASA. https://www.nasa.gov/pdf/345951main_4_Planetary_Science_FY%202010_UPDATED_final.pdf
58. Rodriguez, J. (2022). *How to get the best results from your dry cleaner, according to experts.* Good Housekeeping.
59. https://www.goodhousekeeping.com/home/cleaning/a38885055/what-is-dry-cleaning/
60. SAM. (2022). NASA. https://mars.nasa.gov/msl/spacecraft/instruments/sam/
61. Sanderson, K. (2006). Whirling dust devils bust martian methane. Chemistry World. https://www.chemistryworld.com/news/whirling-dust-devils-bust-martian-methane/3004306.article
62. Schuhknecht, K. (2022). How much water can an astronaut on the ISS consume each day? ILLUMINATION. https://medium.com/illumination/space-day-saturday-ae1cda0625b5
63. Secosky, J. (2021). Periodic climate changes on Mars. Marspedia. https://marspedia.org/Periodic_climate_changes_on_Mars
64. Sharp, T. & Gordon, J. (2022). What is the temperature on Mars? Space.com. https://www.space.com/16907-what-is-the-temperature-of-mars.html

65. Shekhtman, L. (2021). First you see it, then you don't: Scientists closer to explaining Mars methane mystery – NASA mars exploration. NASA. https://mars.nasa.gov/news/8976/first-you-see-it-then-you-dont-scientists-closer-to-explaining-mars-methane-mystery/
66. Signs of Life Detector (n.d.). SOLID. http://auditore.cab.inta-csic.es/solid/en/instrument/
67. Sjöholm, M., Somesfalean, G., Alnis, J., Andersson-Engels, S., & Svanberg, S. (2001). Analysis of gas dispersed in scattering media. In Optics Letters 26(1). p.16-18. https://lup.lub.lu.se/record/2259401
68. Soon, space boots to prevent astronauts from tripping over. (2016, July 28). Deccan Herald. https://www.deccanherald.com/content/560690/soon-space-boots-prevent-astronauts.html
69. Southern, T., & Moiseev, N. (2019). Commercial EVA Space Suit System Development. https://ttu-ir.tdl.org/bitstream/handle/2346/84710/ICES-2019-26.pdf?sequence=1
70. Stirling Cooled Detectors. Infrared Associates, Inc. Infrared Detectors & Accessories—Stirling Coolers. (n.d.). http://www.irassociates.com/index.php?page=stirling-coolers
71. Stroming, J., & Newman, D. (2020). Thermal Modeling of Mechanical Counterpressure Spacesuit EVA. https://ttu-ir.tdl.org/bitstream/handle/2346/86447/ICES-2020-234.pdf?sequence=1&isAllowed=y
72. Tabor, A. (2017). Mars Rover Tests Driving, Drilling and Detecting Life in Chile's High Desert. NASA. https://www.nasa.gov/feature/ames/mars-rover-tests-driving-drilling-and-detecting-life-in-chile-s-high-desert

73. The Sabatier System: Producing Water on the Space Station. (2011). NASA. https://www.nasa.gov/mission_pages/station/research/news/sabatier.html
74. Tomaswick, A. (2021). Perseverance has already detected over 300 dust devils and vortices on Mars. Universe Today. https://www.universetoday.com/152599/perseverance-has-already-detected-over-300-dust-devils-and-vortices-on-mars/
75. Tunable Diode Laser Absorption Spectroscopy—Limitations and Means of Improvements (n.d.). https://www.liquisearch.com/tunable_diode_laser_absorption_spectroscopy/limitations_and_means_of_improvements
76. UC Berkeley. (2022). For human settlements on Mars, solar power may beat nuclear energy. SciTechDaily. https://scitechdaily.com/for-human-settlements-on-mars-solar-power-may-beat-nuclear-energy/
77. Environmental Friendly—Adult Diapers. (2022.)
78. Wellnessbriefs.com. wellnessbriefs.com/why-unique-wellness/environmental.
79. Utopia Planitia (2019). Encyclopædia Britannica. https://www.britannica.com/place/Utopia-Planitia
80. What a high density polyethylene sheet?—HDPE FACTS: A&C plastics. What is High Density Polyethylene Sheet?—HDPE Facts (n.d.). A&C Plastics. from https://www.acplasticsinc.com/informationcenter/r/what-is-hdpe-sheet
81. Wuhan Joho Technology Co., LTD. (n.d.). Stirling Cycle Cooling Dual-FOV Cooled HgCdTe FPA Thermal Imaging Camera For Video Monitoring System. https://www.eo-irsystems.com/

sale-14369700-stirling-cycle-cooling-cooled-hgcdte-fpa-thermal-imaging-camera.html
82. Zacny, K., Paulsen, G., McKay, C., Glass, B., Dave, A. Davila, A., Marinova, M., Mellerowicz, B., Heldmann, J, Stoker, C., Cabrol, N., Hedlund, M., & Craft, Jack. (2013). Reaching 1m Deep on Mars: The Icebreaker Drill. Astrobiology. 13. 10.1089/ast.2013.1038.
83. Zigler, J. & Ryan, D. (2005). USGS Scientific Investigations Map 2888. U.S. Geological Survey. https://pubs.usgs.gov/sim/2005/2888/sim2888.pdf
84. Zubrin, R. (1996). The Case for Mars: The Plan to Settle the Red Planet and Why We Must. Touchstone: New York, NY.
85. Zubrin, R., Price, S., Gamber, T.. Clark, B., & Cantrell, J. (1993). The Mars Aerial Platform mission—A global reconnaissance of the Red Planet using super-pressure balloons. https://www.researchgate.net/publication/234368375_The_Mars_Aerial_Platform_mission_-_A_global_reconnaissance_of_the_Red_Planet_using_super-pressure_balloons/citation/download

POLEMOS

PEYTON HEMANN

SEBASTIAN SHOUP

ANIESSH MEDHYAL

MAXIMUS TREST

LUCAS A. BARUN

NICOLE DE BEAUCHAMP

JOSHUA DE BEAUCHAMP

INTRODUCTION

The Polemos program is focused on laying the groundwork for future Martian colonies. For Polemos I, the ice-laden scarps of Milankovič Crater will be the setting for a deep dive into surface geology and biology; the feasibility of using the Martian atmosphere, regolith, and water ice to support human and plant life; and a proving ground for robotic technologies that could someday be the backbone of a colony's fuel production. The astronauts chosen will be able to conduct experiments across disciplines, prove new technologies, and perhaps even find hard evidence of past life on the Red Planet. Polemos I will require landing only 28.5 metric tons of cargo on the Martian surface, so it is well within the launch capacity of heavy lift rockets currently in development, such as SpaceX's Starship.

ENGINEERING

LOGISTICS AND TIMELINE

Polemos I astronauts will stay on the surface for the full 550 days (roughly 18 months) their transfer window allows; it is assumed that this is a conjunction-class mission. The team has assumed that the MITHRIL program will be proceeding along concurrently with the Polemos program, according to the timeline the MITHRIL team has illustrated in their paper (Auster et al., 2022); this would put Polemos I, with its precursor shakedown program for one of MITHRIL's components, in a window from 2030 to 2034. Launch windows, therefore, open in 2031 and 2033. The first 30 days will be allotted to setting up the Hab and its components, as well as mapping routes for rovers and starting to mine for water.

LANDING SITE

Polemos I will land near the western rim of 815A30 (aka. Milankovič), a large crater located in Arcadia Planitia. Milankovič's 118-kilometer diameter offers plenty of space to land in, but the landing site at 54.3°N, 148°W was chosen to give the crew easy access to the most interesting features of the crater. Reducing the transit time to and from areas of interest should help maximize their scientific output during their 50-day stay on the surface.

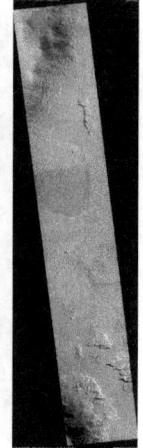

Infrared image of Milankovič Crater (L), alongside a HiRISE image of the crater (R) with the ideal landing site marked by an "X".

Scientific Requirements

Milankovič Crater was chosen in part because of the diverse set of geological features all located within its rim. Polemos I will be able to explore lava flows, eolian deposits, and a massive central peak, all within driving range of the landing site [1]. However, the most exciting feature is located at the landing site itself.

SUBSURFACE ICE

All of Arcadia Planitia is known as a promising area to look for subsurface ice, but Milankovič Crater is among 8 sites identified by a study as locations where large amounts of ice could exist especially close to the surface, in scarps located at Polemos I's landing site [2][3]. While discovering and utilizing ice on Mars would allow future missions to generate fuel for their return trip to Earth, this discovery would also have important scientific ramifications. An objective of Polemos I is to search for evidence of past life on Mars, and if microbial life still exists on Mars, it is likely to be found in ice deposits or briny deposits [3].

Practical Requirements

Polemos I will need to land in an area flat enough for astronauts and rovers to traverse it easily. According to orbital surveys, the floor of Milankovič is composed of smooth, flat plains [1]. This is perfect for rover operations since the visibility and stability this offers will allow crewed rovers to travel safely at high speed. The relatively flat crater floor will also make it easier to maintain line-of-sight radio communication between all of the elements of Polemos I.

Entry, Descent, and Landing Considerations

Polemos I will land within 20 kilometers of the rim of Milankovič Crater, which will require a high level of precision during the landing so as to avoid impacting the crater rim or landing too far away from the subsurface ice mentioned above. Fortunately for this mission, the recent landing of the Perseverance rover has demonstrated that it is possible to land a payload on Mars with far more precision than the 200 km by 70 km landing ellipse of the Pathfinder lander back in 1997 [4]. A version of the Terrain Relative Navigation software tested on Perseverance will also be able to assist in landing Polemos I on target while avoiding crashing into the crater rim or the icy scarps the mission is meant to land close to.

Impact on Future Mars Missions

Since there is a high likelihood that Polemos I will confirm large deposits of subsurface ice in Milankovič Crater, future manned and unmanned missions to Mars will likely also land in the area. Polemos I will be able to extensively survey the crater on the ground and during landing, which will allow later missions to more accurately navigate during their landing approach and while on the surface.

MARS HABITAT REQUIREMENTS

An ideal Mars habitat design must protect the health and safety of the crew while sustaining productivity. Mars is a challenging planet for human exploration and so too is the design for a Martian habitat. Factors that must be considered when designing a human habitat on Mars include life support systems, radiation protection, ease of both intravehicular activity (IVA) and extravehicular activity (EVA), habitat space, cost, and more [29]

FIRST STAGE

A first stage habitat will be temporary, mainly a place to stay during the building of the more permanent second stage habitat [32].

TransHab

TransHab was a NASA inflatable habitat concept developed in the 1990s, with the rights to this concept now owned by Bigelow Aerospace. TransHab has four levels featuring an airlock, exercise area, first aid station, personal hygiene area, crew quarters, mechanical room, and kitchen [30]. TransHab is not specifically designed for the surface of Mars but the design could be and has been modified and repurposed to allow for this [29]. TransHab may not be viable for a mission launching in the early 2030s as NASA is no longer developing the concept and Bigelow Aerospace is unlikely to finish the development of TransHab by the 2030s. In addition, TransHab does not offer substantial benefits over using a lander as a temporary habitat.

Lander
Using a lander as a temporary habitat is an approach many companies are considering taking for a mission to Mars as it is simple, efficient, and the most cost-effective [32]. The lander would be used as a habitat for a short time while the main habitat would be constructed.

SECOND STAGE

The second stage habitat is a more permanent habitat meant for longer term stays [32].

Dome
While a staple of Mars imagery, domes are extremely impractical for a permanent habitat on Mars. They are difficult to build, are not space efficient, nor do they offer any radiation protection.

Underground
An underground habitat was proposed by engineers in the 1990s but was found to be impractical [33]. Building an underground habitat on Mars would require more equipment and time when compared to any other proposed habitat design. One advantage that an underground habitat does have is a virtually unlimited amount of room and excellent protection from radiation.

Custom Habitat

For Polemos I, our team proposes a custom habitat design to fit the criteria of the mission. Taking design cues from the NASA Habitat Demonstration Unit and other Mars habitat designs, to keep costs low, our team proposes a custom habitat design which features a water tank at the top of the hab to protect against radiation. In addition, the habitat would be connected to a greenhouse through a pressurized tunnel for ease of access. Amenities include a hygiene module, a geo-lab, a medical station, a maintenance workstation, a robotics workstation, an airlock, and a separate inflatable crew area [34]. The habitat will come pre-assembled for the crew with little setup required, and will weigh a total of approximately 16 tons [35]. NASA has not provided an estimated cost of a habitat on Mars; however, the cost should not be excessively high, since similar designs and prototypes have already been researched and developed.

Artist's vision of the Polemos I custom habitat design, showcasing the placement of the water tank and Kilopower reactors.

Life Support

For the crew habitat, the habitat will be pressurized to 101.3 kPa (14.69psi). The habitat atmosphere will be 80% nitrogen and 20% oxygen. Nitrogen can be extracted from the Martian atmosphere through a condensation process [36].

PACKING FOR THE RED PLANET

SPACESUITS

For spacesuits, Astronauts on the Polemos I mission will use a modified version of the Z series spacesuit. The suit's components are meant to work with the systems in both the habitat and the pressurized rover, which will allow the crew to explore larger areas of the Martian surface more easily.

Design Requirements

The calculated weight of the spacesuit design will be approximately 13.5 kilograms (30 pounds). In addition, the life support system and oxygen needed for an EVA weighs 22.5 kilograms (50 pounds). This comes to a total weight of around 36 kilograms (80 pounds), making maneuvering easy. The suits will have an integrated hatch (aka. a "suitport") on their backpacks, allowing the astronauts to seal their suits to a docking port and enter the habitat and the pressurized rover. This system prevents outside contamination and minimizes the amount of Martian dust crewmembers are exposed to since the exterior of the suit never enters a pressurized area [5]. A thin layer of gold on the visors of the helmets will assist with blocking ultraviolet radiation and protect the occupant.

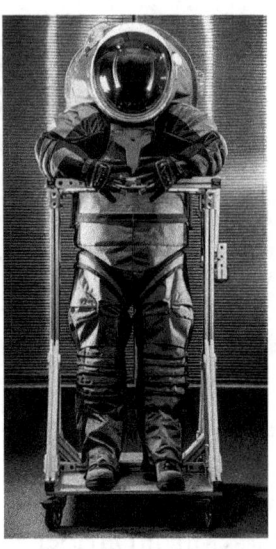

A picture of the NASA Z-2 spacesuit prototype

Materials

The suit will be made out of a nylon tricot base, Kevlar, and Nomex blend, while the gloves will incorporate Spandex for extra flexibility.

MARTIAN PRESSURIZED ROVING VEHICLE

The Polemos I astronauts will be able to easily explore the areas within several kilometers of their base camp on foot, but they will need a vehicle to transport them and their equipment to areas of interest further from the habitat. The Martian Pressurized Roving Vehicle (MPRV), which is loosely based on the rovers from NASA's Austere Missions to Mars plan, will satisfy this requirement [6].

Specifications
With a top speed of 20 kilometers per hour (roughly 12 miles per hour) and its ability to support a crew of two for up to three weeks, the MPRV will significantly increase the area the mission will be able to study and therefore augment the amount of data returned as well. However, since no EVA suit can sustain its occupant for such a long period of time, the MPRV will have to allow its occupants to take their suits off inside the rover.

PRESSURIZATION AND LIFE SUPPORT

The most important feature of the MPRV will be its pressurized cabin, which will be able to house two astronauts and their life support systems for up to three weeks. The consumables required for a journey this long will weigh 819 kilograms (1806 pounds), but since they will be produced on the surface, they do not need to be factored into the weight of the vehicle during landing. Astronauts will enter and exit the rover by attaching the aforementioned "suitports" of their EVA suits to hatches at the back of the rover [6]. The MPRV will have five of these hatches, so the entire crew can use the rover in an emergency. However, the life support system would only be able to support five astronauts for one week, so this feature will only be used if the habitat is seriously damaged. The atmospheric composition inside the rover will be the same as that of the EVA suits and the habitat: 20% oxygen and 80% nitrogen. This will reduce the time it takes to prepare for EVAs by removing the need to pre-breathe oxygen before exiting the rover. Excess carbon dioxide will be removed by reusable zeolite crystal filters, which will be heated regularly to release the trapped CO_2 into the Martian atmosphere [7].

SCIENTIFIC CAPABILITIES

The MPRV itself will be equipped with weather sensors and visible and infrared cameras, as well as ground penetrating radar similar to the RIMFAX experiment on NASA's Perseverance rover. The radar will be used to search for features hidden up to 10 meters (33 feet) under the surface, including underground ice deposits like the ice in the scarps by the landing site [8]. The rover will also have ample space on the exterior to store equipment for astronauts to use during EVAs. This inventory will include core sampling drills, shovels, and cameras. Additionally, the crew will be able to store any samples they collect on EVAs in containers on the exterior of the rover, reducing the risk of contamination.

POWER

The MPRV will be powered by a 5 kilowatt Stirling RTG, similar to the Advanced Stirling Radioisotope Generator and NASA's Kilopower reactors [9]. Unlike solar panels and batteries, the RTG produces electricity constantly, so the rover will be able to operate at all times of day, and will never need to be recharged. The generator will power individual electric motors driving each of the six wheels of the vehicle. The excess heat from the RTG will be dissipated by radiators on the roof of the rover. Since the RTG converts the heat from the radioactive decay of plutonium-238 into electricity, it will never need to be refueled during Polemos I's stay on the surface. Additionally, as the plutonium decays, the RTG's power output will only diminish by 0.787% every year [9]. As a result, a future mission to Milankovič Crater may be able to re-use the MPRV, if the remainder of its systems are still functional.

SIZE

To accommodate all of these features, the MPRV will be 8 meters long and 6 meters wide, with a ground clearance of 0.6 meters (2 feet). Combined with a fully independent suspension, this will enable the MPRV to drive over most small rocks. To accommodate the cooling systems for the RTG, the rover will be 4 meters (13 feet) tall in total.

Logistics and Cost

To fit within the 30 metric ton (66,138 pounds) weight budget of Polemos I, the MPRV will weigh about 5 tons (11,023 pounds). This light weight will be enabled by the use of advanced composite materials in the pressure hull and ISRU production of consumables. As a result of its 8-meter length and 6-meter width, the rover will not be carried on the same descent stage as the habitat and will instead land separately nearby. Based on the estimated cost of a similar rover in NASA's Austere Missions to Mars, the first MPRV is likely to cost about $1 billion, including research and development costs [6]. However, the reliability, safety and possibility of re-use make this a worthwhile investment.

DRILLING FOR WATER ICE

RedWater is a system designed for harvesting water from subsurface Martian ice, and the Polemos I landing site is an ideal

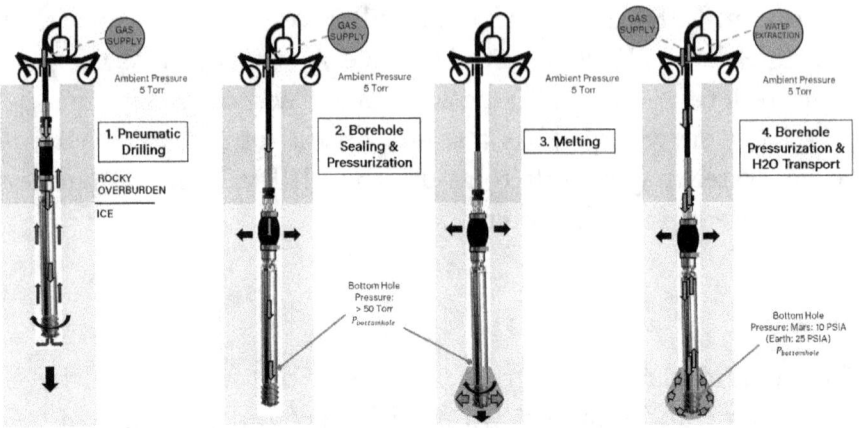

A diagram of the drill system's stages of operation.

site for the first application of RedWater. Milankovič Crater falls squarely in one of the regions highlighted by Honeybee Robotics' RedWater team as a region of interest for drilling for water ice, and in many areas, the 10-20 meter ceiling of the drill's reach will not be required [26]. However, we will still overcompensate for overburden (regolith over the ice) depth, and pack a full 20 meters of tubing.

Operation

The system initially uses pneumatic CT drilling to advance below the surface into about a meter of ice, then seals off the hole. Using runoff heat from a hose run to a nearby Kilopower reactor (the reactor placement will account for this), the Rod-Well system begins cycling hot water through the drill head into the bottom of the hole to melt a well. Once the ice is sufficiently melted, some is cycled back, while the rest of the water fills the tank on top of the Hab.

Materials

Most of the RedWater system will simply be something like milled aluminum, and custom electrical and drilling equipment contained in the BHA. For the water pipelines to the Hab (RW-Hab) and the reactor (RW-KP), thermoplastic composite pipes or TCP were originally considered. These pipes, manufactured by Strohm for use in oil drilling applications, can resist high temperatures up to 80°C and high pressures up to 689 bar (10,000 psi), and as no other statistic was listed on the website, we assumed they were stable in cold temperatures and went forward with getting weight and cost estimates from the company. An email sent out to Strohm has sadly confirmed that TCP is only good down to -20°C, and an alternative is required.

This application may require a custom tubing design, using some blend of woven steel, a special cryo-silicone developed for the medical industry [37], and plasticized PVC to produce a design that does well with high pressure differentials and varying temperatures. To remove the high ceiling of the temperature extremes, we plan to hook both ends of the RW-KP line into the bottom of the Kilopower reactor and have an internal, rigid metal loop carry the water from there; to provide some insulation, we will bury both lines under several centimeters of regolith. Additionally, we can embed heaters in the outer layer of the RW-Hab line, to keep the water warm and flowing on its journey through the ALF and into the Hab tank.

Logistics

The system will weigh 10 kilograms, not including the pipelines. This is in line with the scale models tested by Honeybee, which are about five times smaller than the TRL-5 design requirements they set for the system and can drill down ~1 meter into the ice, disregarding overburden.

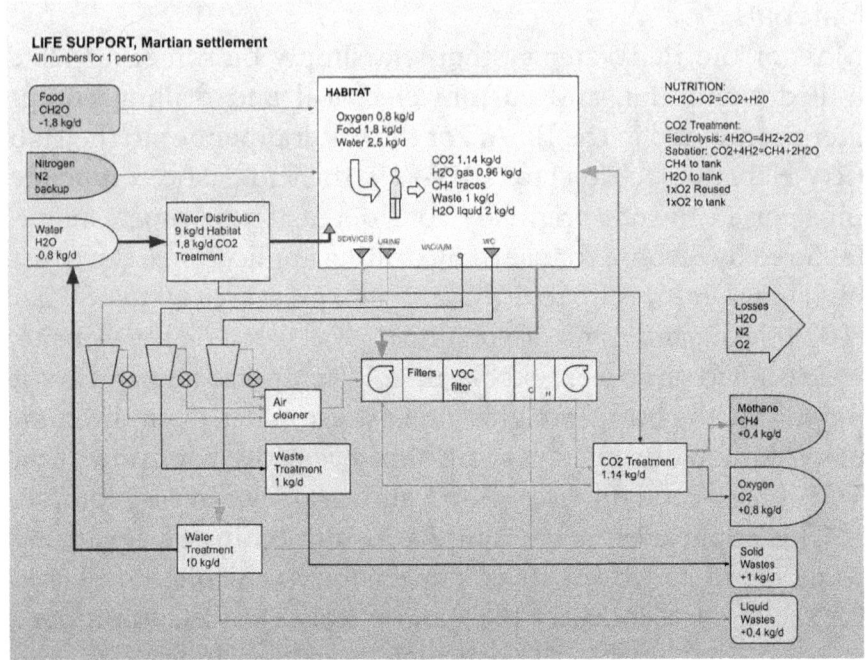

LIFE SUPPORT

The life support system in the habitat will convert 1 ton of CO2 per day into oxygen from human respiration, which is then supplied back to the crew. The air recycler system must remove the CO2 and supply 1700lbs of new oxygen per day, or a total of 617.3 tons of oxygen per year. The humidity will be kept between 20% and 40%, and the temperature kept at around 21 C. Daily, humans use 100W of power, so the life support system of a settlement which includes food production will require approximately 100W/1% = 10,000W to 20,000W of average power per inhabitant.

One person will intake 0.8 kg of oxygen, 1.8kg of food, 2.5kg of water and will give out 1.14kg of CO2, 0.96kg of H2O gas, 1kg of waste and 2kg of H2O liquid.

MARS POWER REQUIREMENTS

As humans come closer to setting foot on Mars, we have to answer a key question: how are we going to power an extraterrestrial habitat and make fuel for the trip home? There are many considerations regarding requirements for the power source including weight, cost, output, and design simplicity. NASA estimates that 20 kWh of power will be needed to power a Martian base. Proposed power options for a Martian base include solar panels, Kilopower nuclear reactors, and radioisotope thermoelectric generators.

Solar Power

Solar panels are seen as a quick and dirty solution to power an extraterrestrial base but they have many downfalls. They only produce power during the day, a limited amount of power is produced due to dust storms, the distance of Mars to the sun is great, and diurnal oscillation in solar flux reduces efficiency even further. In total, the efficiency of the solar panels would be approximately 20%, a low number that would mean an enormous amount of solar panels would be required in order to power a base on Mars [12].

Kilopower Reactors

Kilopower reactors are a type of nuclear reactor designed by NASA for space travel. An initiative first started in 2015, Kilopower reactors can generate anywhere from 1-10 kWh depending on their size [10]. Kilopower reactors have been tested and are seen as the answer to powering a base on Mars. Depending on power requirements, NASA estimates two Kilopower reactors would be required to power a Martian base [10]. The only other downfall of Kilopower reactors is heat dissipation, which can be solved by adding a large radiator to the top of the reactor [10]. The generated heat will also be used to melt ice for mining.

A Kilopower reactor sits on the surface next to a concept Mars base (not Polemos I's).

RTG Reactors
Radioisotope thermoelectric generators, or RTGs, are a type of nuclear battery used in most unmanned space missions [13]. They aren't viable for use on a manned Mars mission's habitat due to their limited power output.

Energy Source for Polemos I
For the mission Polemos I, Kilopower reactors will be used to power the base. Kilopower reactors are small, efficient, and cost-effective. The mission will bring 2 Kilopower reactors, weighing a total of 6.61 tons [10]. NASA says it's still too early to give a price tag for the reactors, but the demonstration reactor KRUSTY cost 20 million dollars, including R&D.

SCIENCE

PLANNING FOR THE FUTURE

The Polemos program, from the start, emphasizes the importance of building a foundation for future missions and eventual colonies. As such, the goal of Polemos I is not purely science return, but data return. Astronauts on the surface will have access to capable scientific instruments and ground transport, enabling a study of Martian geology, climatology and possible biology at higher resolutions, sample sizes, and certainty than a robotic mission could ever hope to achieve. Additionally, the mission calls for an extra engineering study revolving around the spider-like rover Alala, as well as an effort to test the feasibility of large-scale water ice ISRU. The knowledge the Polemos I astronauts will reap from the Red Planet will serve to further Mars exploration on multiple fronts.

SURFACE STUDIES

Polemos I has four scientific goals: to study Martian geology, investigate the history of the Martian climate, search for evidence of ancient life on Mars, and to determine whether any life-forms have persisted to the present. These cover the fields of geology, climatology and paleontology, and astrobiology. Thanks to their advanced equipment and diverse skill set, the crew of Polemos I will be able to accumulate more data than any robotic mission could in the same period of time, and analyze it more effectively.

Exploration

Assuming the crew cannot find a way out of Milankovič Crater, they will have approximately 11,000 square kilometers of Martian land to explore in only 550 days. To allow for a more in-depth study of the most scientifically interesting areas, the

Month	Tasks
Month 1 (Sols 1-29)	Base setup; equipment testing; surveying the area near the habitat
Months 2-4 (Sols 30-117)	Drilling for ice in the scarps by the habitat; AOS testing near the habitat
Months 5-6 (Sols 118-177)	Exploring the southwestern crater rim; AOS tests in the same region
Months 7-9 (Sols 178-265)	Exploring a smaller crater in the plains to the east of the landing site; testing Alala's ability to climb crater walls
Months 10-12 (Sols 266-354)	Studying the lava flows around the central peak
Months 13-15 (Sols 355-443)	Investigating the central peak with the rover and Alala
Months 16-17 (Sols 444-502)	Exploring the northeastern crater rim
Month 18 (Sols 503-535)	Cataloging samples for future missions and selecting some to bring back to Earth

Areas of interest are marked in red on a photo of Milankovič Crater (top), above a possible schedule for the scientific aspects of Polemos I (bottom).

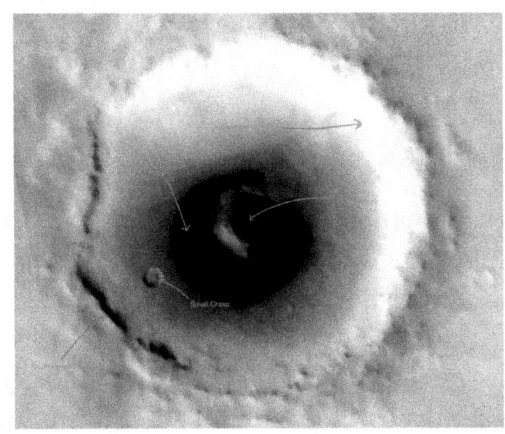

astronauts will spend 2 to 3 months investigating each of 6 areas of the crater instead of trying to explore every square centimeter of the crater floor.

EVA EXPLORATION

The scarps at 54.3°N, 148°W are only a short walk from the habitat, so the crew of Polemos I can collect rock samples and ice cores from the area during EVAs. Ideally, two crewmembers will be on one EVA at a time, so that astronauts on the surface will have help in case of an emergency. However, astronauts in EVA suits will not be able to travel far from wherever they started out, so a better way of exploring larger areas will be necessary.

ROVER EXPEDITIONS

The pressurized rover mentioned earlier will be used to reach other areas of Milankovič. During each two-week expedition, the rover will be crewed by two astronauts, one with the necessary training and knowledge to repair the rover, and one with a scientific background. The rover's sensors will be used to survey large areas of the surface in detail and to map underground features, but more detailed exploration of specific locations will require the rover crew to go on EVAs. Since each rover trip will last up to two weeks and astronauts will have 2 to 3 months to survey an area, multiple rover expeditions will travel to the same general area.

ANALYSIS AT THE HABITAT

Astronauts on EVAs will not be able to carry many tools, and the rover will not have enough space for every piece of equipment required to study an area, so EVAs and rover trips will collect small rocks, rock and soil samples, and ice cores to return to the habitat for further analysis. At the habitat, an alpha particle x-ray spectrometer and a laser-induced breakdown spectroscopy system will be used to study the composition of rock samples [15][16]. A Signs of LIfe Detector (SOLID) and Compact Color Biofinder will be used to search rocks for biological material, while an Agnostic Life Finder will be used to search ice samples for polyelectrolytes similar to DNA [17][18]. The water from the RedWater drilling rig will also be filtered through a different ALF before use [18]. Additionally, astronauts in the habitat will have the equipment to measure the chemical composition and electrical conductivity of ice cores, as well as test for any gasses trapped in the ice. This will allow the crew to determine the age of the ice cores, as well as gather data on the history of the Martian climate [19]. The habitat will also be equipped with small weather sensors like the rovers, as well as a seismometer to record any marsquakes.

Returning Samples to Earth

It is assumed that the Mars Ascent Vehicle (MAV) provided for Polemos I will be able to take some cargo back to Earth in addition to the crew. However, the astronauts are likely to collect far more rock and ice samples than the MAV can carry, so the crew will have to select the most interesting samples to bring back to Earth with them during the last weeks of their mission. The rest of the samples will be cataloged and left in containers inside or outside the Hab, to make it easier for any future missions to retrieve them.

Human Health Studies

Living on Mars for a year and a half will likely affect the health of the astronauts in some way, and these effects need to be understood before larger numbers of humans are sent to the red planet as part of a permanent colony. Some can be anticipated based on the experiences of astronauts on the International Space Station, but there's really no substitute for landing people on Mars and observing their health.

HEALTH MONITORING

Every astronaut will always wear two bracelets: a personal active dosimeter, and a physical fitness monitor similar in size to a smartwatch. These devices will be used to monitor their health and recommend any necessary treatments or more involved tests.

PERSONAL ACTIVE DOSIMETER

This instrument is a second-generation version of the European Crew Personal Active Dosimeter, an experiment installed on the ISS in 2016 [38]. The dosimeter will measure the amount of radiation the astronauts are exposed to throughout the mission, and provide the astronauts with real-time data about their exposure [39]. While the first generation EuCPAD was a large device installed in the Columbus module of the ISS, the second-gen version on Polemos I will be a wearable device that each astronaut will have on at all times.

PHYSICAL FITNESS MONITOR

This device will track the heart rate, blood pressure and quality of sleep of every astronaut. This data will be analyzed by both the medical specialist on Polemos I and doctors on Earth to determine the overall health of each astronaut.

MEASURING MUSCLE MASS

The reduced Martian gravity will likely impact the muscle mass of the astronauts on Polemos I [40]. Without the extra resistance from Earth gravity, their muscles will atrophy, even though the astronauts will devote time every day to exercise. This effect will be most noticeable on "antigravity muscles," such as the quadriceps and back muscles [41]. A bioelectrical impedance analysis system will be used to measure the muscle loss of the astronauts by sending a weak electrical current through their body [42]. Since this is a simple and quick process, BIA testing will be performed about once every three weeks [43]. Testing at this frequency means that all the astronauts can be tested at the same time, after two crewmembers return to the habitat from a rover expedition.

ATHLETE OPERATIONAL SHAKEDOWN

Through NASA's RASC-AL contest, the Illinois Space Society in collaboration with Honeybee Robotics has created the mission plan for MITHRIL (Mars Ice Thermal Harvesting Rig and ISRU Laboratory). One component of the mission, which aims to mine subsurface water ice and refine it via a Sabatier reactor, is the ATHLETE rover. This spider-like robot, which has already been partially developed by NASA JPL, will be used to carry and place cargo, deploy other MITHRIL components, and determine the placement of the STING (Subsurface Targeted Ice miniNG) system [8]. The ATHLETE system is critical to MITHRIL's success, and throughout this mission, a scale model named Alala will be tested during the AOS (ATHLETE Operational Shakedown) program to ensure that Earth-based operators can interpret and understand the rover's autonomous decision-making and "handling" in situations that require human input.

The massive full-scale ATHLETE, depicted next to a fully deployed MITHRIL plant in a render by the ISS team.

Evaluating Capabilities

The main objective of the AOS is to troubleshoot and evaluate the performance of ATHLETE's two main navigation suites, as well as the rover itself. ATHLETE must be able to traverse rough terrain on its mission to set up MITHRIL, and the icy scarps of Milankovič Crater will serve as both a geological curiosity and a navigation testbed. No equipment will be used for the AOS besides Alala, the operator's controller (software run on their personal laptop), and the pressurized rover.

AUTONOMOUS DRIVING

ATHLETE's autonomous driving capabilities are powered by an advanced version of ENav, the suite used on the Perseverance rover to determine the best path to a point using data obtained from stereo cameras. Short routes on the outskirts of the Milankovič scarps will be pre-planned from camera data during EDL, and Alala's ENav decisions will be measured against them. This part of the program is designed not to test ENav itself, but to develop a manual of sorts for future MITHRIL operators. During normal operations, they will need to understand the types of pathing decisions ATHLETE makes; during troubleshooting or an emergency, understanding what led ATHLETE to choose a faulty path can help influence the rescue effort as well as tweaks to the software.

DRIVER OPERATION

A second, JPL-developed suite called the FootFall Planning System allows an operator on Earth (or during this mission, on Mars) to directly control the placement of each of ATHLETE's legs. If the rover gets stuck or cannot find a way over rough terrain by itself, this program can help it continue on its path.

Principal investigator Brian Wilcox stands in front of a 1:4 scale ATHLETE model.

During this part of the AOS, the Milankovič scarps will be used as an obstacle course for Alala, and the operator will learn and document the challenges FootFall faces in the Martian gravity, terrain, and atmosphere.

Logistics and Planning

Fortunately for the AOS, a 1:4 scale ATHLETE has already been constructed by a team at JPL [22]. Based on the dimensions of the full-scale ATHLETE described in the MITHRIL paper, Alala will only weigh 442.5 kilograms (975.5 pounds), with a volume of 1.35 cubic meters (47.7 cubic feet) when stowed. Alala will ride on a sort of "bike rack" on the side or back of the pressurized rover when stowed, so astronauts will not need to drag it off the roof when deploying it.

Impact on Future MITHRIL and Mars Missions

MITHRIL was designed as a fuel-mining hub, capable of producing and storing 50 tons of propellant a year for future Mars missions. Eventually, whole colonies might depend on MITHRIL facilities, and by extension, the autonomous maintenance capabilities of ATHLETE. When entire crews depend on MITHRIL's ISPP capabilities for their rides home, control teams must comprehend the robot's autonomous processes and human-influenced elements, and the ways in which errors in these components can be resolved.

ISRU-POWERED FOOD PRODUCTION

Hydroponics is an efficient and relatively undemanding agricultural system that is capable of producing an extensive variety of traditional produce for future Martian astronauts. The system utilizes aerated nutrient-dense water, sourced from Martian ice, to supply plants with adequate nourishment. It consists of tubing that distributes water to growth trays containing plant roots which can be stacked atop each other, conserving valuable space. The plants would then be exposed to purple grow lights to facilitate plant growth and quality. Unlike other alternatives, the structure has a simple assembly and is not labor intensive, making it an especially appealing option for the mission. Additionally, the system has been shown to harvest plants 50% faster and conserve 10 times the amount of water compared to traditional farming practices.

Image depicting an active indoor hydroponics system.

Botanical Grow Lights
The hydroponic grow lights will produce a magenta light frequency as it combines the benefits of both red and blue light. [23] Red light has been shown to be beneficial in producing taller and leafier plants due to the increase in the production of the hormone meta-topolin, which prevents the breakdown of chlorophyll, generating more nutrients. Additionally, blue light promotes leaf expansion, sprouting, and root development which are all important factors in the quality and efficiency of plant growth [27].

Hydroponic Nutrient Solution
Due to hydroponics not requiring soil, the plants need to get their vital nutrients through the water circulating throughout the system. The nutrient solution generally contains a mixture of macronutrients, such as nitrogen, phosphorus, potassium, calcium, sulfur, and magnesium. The three most important for a plant's development are nitrogen for vegetative growth as well as for the production of chlorophyll and amino acids, phosphorus for tissue formation and cell division, and potassium which promotes photosynthesis and other essential developmental processes.

Maintenance
A hydroponics system requires very little maintenance, especially when compared to other options, such as aeroponics and traditional farming. Maintenance includes draining and refilling the hydroponic nutrient solution about twice a month as well as simple cleaning measures to ensure the system stays in its proper condition.

HUMAN OPERATIONS
CREW SIZE AND COMPOSITION

The Polemos I mission will consist of five astronauts, each from a separate space program: NASA, ESA, JAXA, CSA and KARI. There will be a designated commander; two specialists trained for specific EVA duties; two specialists trained to service all life support systems; two specialists trained in geology, microbiology, and paleontology; two specialists with knowledge of how to fly the MAV or lander in an emergency; and two specialists capable of servicing the mission's electrical components. In addition to this, every astronaut will have a non-essential specialty or focus to aid in their assigned duties. There will be considerable overlap in the fields these astronauts are trained in; however, since it is impossible to tell the exact skillset of the crew until individuals are selected, the jobs each specific astronaut will have are not yet set in stone. Every astronaut will be trained in first aid and made aware of the exploration goals and inner workings of the mission.

In addition to pure skill, astronauts will be screened on their natural ability to work well with others, as well as their ability to try to work with the rest of the team and learn new fields during the training process. No astronaut will be perfect, but they must be willing to get as close to it as possible by launch day, while seeing their fellow crewmates as colleagues, friends, and maybe friendly competition.

CONSENSUS, CONFLICTS, AND COMMAND

While it is encouraged that the commander listens to every crew member when making decisions, in the end, it is their executive decision to make, and all crewmembers must follow. While voting on an issue is certainly more democratic, in a stressful or emergency situation these meetings can take precious time away from potentially life-saving procedures. The commander will also be responsible for breaking up physical or verbal conflicts; since one cannot simply send someone home from the surface, confinement to quarters would be the highest possible punishment.

Certain main computer commands, like shutting down all life support, can only be accessed by the commander; in case the commander is dead or incapacitated, a secret second-in-command can take over. Any non-incapacitated crew must unanimously agree that the commander is gone, and notify the computer. Until it is verified that the commander cannot function, the second-in-command position is not revealed, to prevent any fights about the command hierarchy.

LIVING ON THE SURFACE

The ISS allows 1.5 kilograms (3.3 pounds) of personal items, but for the sake of the astronauts' sanity, this will be upped to 4 kilograms (8.8 pounds). Additionally, each astronaut will have a personal laptop with 16GB of RAM and 1TB of storage, which will be pre-loaded not only with the technical programs each requires for the mission or prefers to use but with any kind of digital entertainment they want.

In addition to personal computers, a large monitor will serve as an access point for the main computer, which handles weather data, systems data, and piped-in data from external components like the rover, reactors, drill, and Alala. This "family PC" setup is in a meeting room with seats for all five astronauts; they can even have a movie night using the monitor as a TV, as they do on the International Space Station.

This room is where a Polemos astronaut starts and ends their day: breakfast in the morning with the crew to go over the day's schedule, and dinner in the evening before everyone heads back to their quarters. This friendly routine will serve to give the crew a sense of normalcy in the least normal place humanity has ever set foot.

REFERENCES

1. Geologic map of the Diacria Quadrangle of Mars | U.S. Geological Survey. (n.d.). Www.usgs.gov. Retrieved August 5, 2022, from https://www.usgs.gov/maps/geologic-map-diacria-quadrangle-mars
2. Than Putzig–Intl Mission to Mars Design Course & Competition (2022)–The Mars Society. (n.d.). Www.youtube.com. Retrieved August 5, 2022, from https://www.youtube.com/watch?v=lCKTKR0t_nA
3. Dundas, C., Bramson, A., Ojha, L., Wray, J., Mellon, M., Byrne, S., McEwen, A., Putzig, N., Viola, D., Sutton, S., Clark, E., & Holt, J. (2018). Exposed subsurface ice sheets in the Martian mid-latitudes [Review of Exposed subsurface ice sheets in the Martian mid-latitudes]. In Slideshare. American Association for the Advancement of Science. https://www.slideshare.net/sacani/exposed-subsurface-ice-sheets-in-the-martian-midlatitudes
4. https://www.jpl.nasa.gov. (n.d.). Mars Probe Landing Ellipses. NASA Jet Propulsion Laboratory (JPL). Retrieved August 5, 2022, from https://www.jpl.nasa.gov/images/pia24377-mars-probe-landing-ellipses
5. Wikimedia Foundation. (2022, February 5). Suitport. Wikipedia. Retrieved August 4, 2022, from https://en.wikipedia.org/wiki/Suitport
6. Wayback Machine. (n.d.). Web.archive.org. Retrieved August 5, 2022, from https://web.archive.org/web/20100206135703/http://trs-new.jpl.nasa.gov/dspace/bitstream/2014/41431/1/09-3642.pdf

7. Freudenrich, C. (2011, February 22). How is carbon dioxide eliminated aboard a spacecraft? HowStuffWorks. https://science.howstuffworks.com/carbon-dioxide-eliminated-aboard-spacecraft.htm
8. mars.nasa.gov. (n.d.). Radar Imager for Mars' Subsurface Exploration (RIMFAX). Mars.nasa.gov. https://mars.nasa.gov/mars2020/spacecraft/instruments/rimfax/
9. Wikipedia Contributors. (2019, November 13). Radioisotope thermoelectric generator. Wikipedia; Wikimedia Foundation. https://en.wikipedia.org/wiki/Radioisotope_thermoelectric_generator#Life_span
10. Gibson, M. A., Oleson, S. R., Poston, D. I., & McClure, P. (n.d.). NASA's Kilopower Reactor Development and the Path to Higher Power Missions. NASA Glenn Research Center & Los Alamos National Lab.
11. Poston, D. I., Gibson, M. A., Godfroy, T., & McClue, P. R. (2019, December 18). KRUSTY Reactor Design. NASA Glenn Research Center & Los Alamos National Lab.
12. Behrens, C. B. (2019, November 21). Solar power is never going to work on Mars, and everybody knows it. Medium. Retrieved August 1, 2022, from https://medium.com/swlh/solar-power-is-never-going-to-work-on-mars-and-everybody-knows-it-b2fb221722b1
13. NASA. (2018, September 25). Radioisotope thermoelectric generators (rtgs). NASA. Retrieved August 1, 2022, from https://solarsystem.nasa.gov/missions/cassini/radioisotope-thermoelectric-generator/
14. mars.nasa.gov. (2019). APXS | Instruments – NASA's Mars Exploration Program. NASA's Mars Exploration Program. https://mars.nasa.gov/msl/spacecraft/instruments/apxs/

15. Wikipedia Contributors. (2022, June 26). Laser-induced breakdown spectroscopy. Wikipedia. https://en.wikipedia.org/wiki/Laser-induced_breakdown_spectroscopy
16. Spanish Astrobiology Center. INSTRUMENT | SOLID. Retrieved August 5, 2022, from http://auditore.cab.inta-csic.es/solid/en/instrument/
17. Misra, A. K., Rowley, S. J., Zhou, J., Acosta-Maeda, T. E., Dasilveira, L., Ravizza, G., Ohtaki, K., Weatherby, T. M., Trimble, A. Z., Boll, P., Porter, J. N., & McKay, C. P. (2022). Biofinder detects biological remains in Green River fish fossils from Eocene epoch at video speed. Scientific Reports, 12(1), 10164. https://doi.org/10.1038/s41598-022-14410-8
18. Spacek, J. (n.d.). How the Agnostic Life Finder (ALF) Searches for Life on Mars – The Primordial Scoop. Retrieved August 5, 2022, from https://primordialscoop.org/2021/02/11/how-the-agnostic-life-finder-alf-searches-for-life-on-mars/
19. Stoller-Conrad, J. (2017, August 16). Core questions: An introduction to ice cores – Climate Change: Vital Signs of the Planet. Climate Change: Vital Signs of the Planet; NASA. https://climate.nasa.gov/news/2616/core-questions-an-introduction-to-ice-cores/
20. Auster, A., Arostegui, A., Bansal, I., Bojinov, A., Davis, G., Dayal, G., Frankenthor, M., Kesarwani, S., Kosciarz, J., Kulcsar, A., Lauer, B., Lim, E., McCarthy, S., Miheve, Z., Moy, K., Odeen, M., Patel, K., Porwal, A., Raju, A., … Wang, A. (2022, May 29). Mars Ice Thermal Harvesting Rig and ISRU Laboratory. Urbana-Champaign; University of Illinois.

21. The Hindu. (2020, December 17). All about Hydroponics. YouTube. Retrieved August 1, 2022, from https://www.youtube.com/watch?v=wBcnUUkdavE
22. Wilcox, B. H. (2015, June 30). ATHLETE: A Cargo and Habitat Transporter for the Moon. Pasadena; California Institute of Technology.
23. Discover how LED lighting color spectrum affects plant growth. SpecGrade LED. (2022, April 29). Retrieved August 1, 2022, from https://www.specgradeled.com/news/how-the-lighting-color-spectrum-affects-plant-growth/#:~:text=Violet%20or%20purple%20light%20has,of%20a%20plant%27s%20leafy%20vegetation
24. Marspedia. (2021, July 6). Life support. Retrieved August 2, 2022, from https://marspedia.org/Life_support#:~:text=On%20Mars%20an%20artificial%20life,the%20same%20time%20is%20required.
25. Anderson, M. S., Ewert, M. K., & Keener, J. F. (2018, January). Life Support Baseline Values and Assumptions Document. NASA.
26. Mellerowicz, B., Zacny, K., Palmowski, J., Bradley, B., Stolov, L., Vogel, B., Ware, L., Yen, B., Sabahi, D., Ridilla, A., Nguyen, H., Faris, D., van Susante, P., Johnson, G., Putzig, N. E., & Hecht, M. (2022). Redwater: Water Mining System for Mars. New Space, 10(2), 166–186. https://doi.org/10.1089/space.2021.0057
27. Littlewood, N. (2021, April 20). Why are some grow lights purple? 3 key reasons why we think you should. Urban Leaf. Retrieved August 3, 2022, from https://www.geturbanleaf.com/blogs/lighting/why-are-some-grow-lights-purple
28. Staff, T. (2022, February 10). Hydroponic nutrient solution–the essential guide. Trees.com. Retrieved

August 3, 2022, from https://www.trees.com/gardening-and-landscaping/hydroponic-nutrient-guide

29. Cohen, M. M. (2015). First Mars Habitat Architecture. Pasadena, California; AIAA.

30. Wikimedia Foundation. (2022, July 4). Transhab. Wikipedia. Retrieved August 4, 2022, from https://en.wikipedia.org/wiki/TransHab

31. Petty, J. I. (2006, June 27). TransHab Concept. ISS History. Retrieved August 4, 2022, from https://web.archive.org/web/20060627190940/http://spaceflight.nasa.gov/history/station/transhab/

32. Habitat. Marspedia. (2021, July 5). Retrieved August 4, 2022, from https://marspedia.org/Habitat

33. Artificial cave. Marspedia. (2019, August 2). Retrieved August 4, 2022, from https://marspedia.org/Artificial_cave

34. Dunbar, B. (2010, August 24). Habitat Demonstration Unit (HDU) facts. NASA. Retrieved August 4, 2022, from https://www.nasa.gov/exploration/analogs/hdu1_pemfacts.html

35. NASA. (n.d.). Habitat Demonstration Unit – Deep Space Habitat.

36. Atmospheric processing. (n.d.). Marspedia. Retrieved August 6, 2022, from https://marspedia.org/Atmospheric_processing

37. APLT: Ultra low temperature silicone tubing. AdvantaSil Ultra Low Temperature Silicone Tubing. (2001). Retrieved August 27, 2022, from http://www.advantapure.com/aplt-ultra-low-temperature-silicone-tubing.html

38. DLR–Institute of Aerospace Medicine–EuCPAD: Hardware for radiation tracking now on the ISS.

(n.d.). Www.dlr.de. Retrieved August 28, 2022, from https://www.dlr.de/me/en/desktopdefault.aspx/tabid-1752/2384_read-47145/

39. A new approach to measuring radiation in space – iriss mission blog. (n.d.). Retrieved August 28, 2022, from https://blogs.esa.int/iriss/2015/09/02/a-new-approach-to-measuring-radiation-in-space

40. Johnson, M. (2020, January 7). Bone and Muscle Loss in Microgravity. NASA. https://www.nasa.gov/mission_pages/station/research/station-science-101/bone-muscle-loss-in-microgravity/

41. B, L. (2004). NASA INFORMATION National Aeronautics and Space Administration. https://www.nasa.gov/pdf/64249main_ffs_factsheets_hbp_atrophy.pdf

42. Buckinx, F., Landi, F., Cesari, M., Fielding, R. A., Visser, M., Engelke, K., Maggi, S., Dennison, E., Al-Daghri, N. M., Allepaerts, S., Bauer, J., Bautmans, I., Brandi, M. L., Bruyère, O., Cederholm, T., Cerreta, F., Cherubini, A., Cooper, C., Cruz-Jentoft, A., & McCloskey, E. (2018). Pitfalls in the measurement of muscle mass: a need for a reference standard. Journal of Cachexia, Sarcopenia and Muscle, 9(2), 269–278. https://doi.org/10.1002/jcsm.12268

43. Walter-Kroker, A., Kroker, A., Mattiucci-Guehlke, M., & Glaab, T. (2011). A practical guide to bioelectrical impedance analysis using the example of chronic obstructive pulmonary disease. Nutrition Journal, 10(1). https://doi.org/10.1186/1475-2891-10-35

THE NIGER VALLIS MISSION

AARON SMITH

AIDAN EMMONS

ANKITH TIRUMALA

JAYDEN RIGGIN

NATHAN HARBUT

1.0 HUMAN OPERATIONS

1.1 LOCATION

On Mars, every metre of the planet is different. While deciding a landing site, every factor must be considered.

Using a program developed by NASA with information about the planet and different areas, we decided on a spot located at -35.49 Latitude 92.34 Longitude. The Site is along the *Niger Vallis*, an area to the east of *Hellas Planitia*. This site was found using NASA's Mars Trek in which we used its tools to find a site with Ice, Gullies, and Potential for microcellular palaeontology. Additionally, the large flat area surrounding the valley will make an ideal landing zone. The crew will be allowed a 20 kilometre work radius so that they can find any needed information within their short stay. Plenty of ice can be found around the area, so ice coring will be quite efficient. Although the area is not very level throughout the whole area, there is enough flat area to land and set up the base. From there, multiple hills are present but they are small enough that a basic rover can traverse them.

1.2 THE CREW

For a Human Mars Mission to happen, a crew must be put together with members whose skills can work together to accomplish everything required. Every piece of equipment must have someone who knows how to operate said technology.

For this mission, the crew will consist of five members, each of which being at least 37 years of age, and 48 years at the most. The first member will be a glaciologist from the National Snow & Ice Data Center (NSIDC), in Antarctica. Therefore they will know what to look for in the ice cores, and as asort of bonus, they will know enough to operate the drills if something happens to the member that is supposed to control them. On that note, said member would be our engineer. He would be tasked with controlling the drills, keeping all of the technology in order, and would accompany our geologist on their journeys. Our engineer is also the captain of the Mars Mission Crew. Our geologist will be manning the seismometer, as well as venturing out in the rover for research. The fourth member is the biologist, who is tasked with keeping track of how the algae is doing, and figuring out how to deal with any problems that may occur. They will also be helping to keep the HAB as clean as possible. Finally, we have the doctor. With a decent amount of knowledge in various medical fields, she would obviously be making sure every crew member is in good health throughout the mission. She would also be there if anyone got in an accident of some sort. As a personal interest of hers, she would also be helping with the climatology aspect of the mission.

While our crew is on the planet, events may happen that the crew members disagree on. Each and every one of the crew members has their ideas, so to solve disputes, the team will use a democratic system, involving voting on what will be done about whatever topic is being discussed. Anything that even one of the crew members disagrees with should be discussed, and eventually settled. While the engineer will be the captain, the only time he can make a truly superior decision is in an emergency situation that does not have any time to be discussed.

1.3 NUTRITION

The Food consumed by the astronauts on this mission would be a combination of MRE's, Potatoes, and Multivitamins. The daily nutrition for the astronauts would consist of 1 MRE, 4.5 Baked Russet Potatoes, and enough multivitamins for the day. This will provide our astronauts with a caloric intake of 2000 calories per day. Due to the fact that cosmic radiation would break down the multivitamin they would increase the amount of multivitamins they are consuming. Another measure would be to create an extremely potent mixture of multivitamins that once degraded due to radiation would provide the correct amount. Additionally, various species of algae and seaweed will be raised and kept in the base. These are high in both fibre and protein, along with numerous micronutrients vital to the sustained health of the astronauts. The algae would also allow for a more varied and diverse diet, improving both morale and general satisfaction among the astronauts. In terms of mass, not much would really be needed. The average mass of the potatoes is about 220 grams each. Each MRE would be about 623 grams, and a bottle of multivitamins would weigh about 200 grams at the most. For the total mission, we would only need about one and a half tons, including added weight for storage. For the algae and seaweed, about a half ton would be needed, which includes a small amount of water for the vats. Overall, all of the food weighs about 1.04 tons.

1.4 MAINTAINING MORALE

The Mars mission crew will need to stay positive since a crew with low morale can not do their job as well. The food selection is not great for the team, as they will be eating quite a few potatoes over the course of the mission. Having the algae and seaweed is an enormous help since it's a completely different type of food. Although the suits that the crew will be wearing are meant to make it so space won't have it's normal effects on the human condition, the crew may still want to exercise, so basic equipment for that purpose will be provided. With two treadmills and multiple different weight related items, this adds about 250 kilograms to our mission.

2.0 SCIENTIFIC STUDY
2.1 OBJECTIVES

The entire point of a Mars mission is to learn more about the planet itself. There are multiple scientific areas that can be researched, but only a few can be chosen. For this mission, the crew will be looking for life, either past or present, in the ice cores that we bring up from the drills. Along with that, they will be observing how the Algae does in the Martian atmosphere. While we're sure that it will survive, whether or not it truly thrives or not is not yet known. Our crew will also have weather equipment for climatology, but it will be a lesser study, as weather studies are already on numerous crafts on Mars, such as the Perseverance Rover and the InSight Lander.

2.2 GEOLOGICAL SURVEYING

One of the primary objectives of the Mars base will be to study the terrain of the *Niger Vallis*. The area appears to have several landforms which could only have been carved via sustained water erosion. The high ice content of the surrounding soil also seems to support this theory. Through the use of a coring drill, brought along from Earth, personnel would be able to look for the layered sedimentation which is typical of lake beds. If this is found, it would be substantial evidence toward the area formerly being a lake or river of some kind.

2.3 PRODUCING OXYGEN

Oxygen production on the Martian surface will be an interesting challenge. While artificial methods of air scrubbing exist, an exceptionally effective method can already be found in nature. The numerous species of micro and macroalgae produce up to 60% of the free oxygen in Earth's atmosphere and oceans, and we believe they can be used for this purpose on Mars as well. Through a controlled experiment utilising vats of algae and seaweed, their use as a solution for oxygen production on Mars could be tested. Studies from the BIOS-3 experiment, conducted at the Institute of Biophysics in Russia, showed that only $8m^2$ of various algae in the genus *Chlorella* were needed to filter the air for a single human. By scaling this process up, we could provide not only sufficient oxygen for the crew, but a source of nutrition as well, as the algae contain almost 50% protein, along with numerous fats and proteins. This however, would need to be properly prepared and eaten, as the tough cell walls of *Chlorella* would need to be broken down to allow for digestion. The findings from this experiment could be used not only on later Mars expeditions, but voyages to other places in the solar system and beyond. If successful, future Mars habitats could gain a significant portion of their nutrition and oxygen from algae.

2.4 ARCHAEOLOGY

The *Niger Vallis* is believed to be a dried up outflow channel, meaning it presents an interesting archaeological opportunity. On Earth, outflow channels typically become a gathering place for sediments, many of which contain the remains of marine life, be they micro or macroorganisms. There is no reason to assume a similar process could not have happened on ancient Mars, meaning that if life did evolve, some form of remains would be left here. The crew will routinely take core samples from this area, and be on the lookout for any areas of rock which seem different from the surrounding. Astronauts will be looking for tracks or other trace fossils, and will be equipped with archaeological equipment such as trowels, picks, and brushes, along with microscopes for any potential microorganism fossils. The crew's core drill will be quite light, weighing in at a mass of 18.1 kilograms.

2.5 SEISMOLOGICAL MONITORING

The question of whether Mars still has some form of interior activity will be a subject of study during this mission. The astronauts will be equipped with various seismographs and other vibration sensing equipment. This will not only be able to detect potential marsquakes, but could be used to measure the effect of impacts on Mars. If a small meteoroid were to hit the planet, its effects would be measurable through this network. With a seismograph with a mass of about 70 kilograms, our crew can add this to their objectives for an easy bonus.

2.6 IN-SITU WATER PRODUCTION

One of the most valuable traits the *Niger Vallis* region of Mars has is the apparent presence of large amounts of water ice in its soil. This ice can be collected and purified into water, both for drinking and other needs, through various methods. The method which we have chosen for this mission is first obtaining an amount of ice, which will then be placed inside of a distiller. Using heat from the onsite KiloPower nuclear reactor, this material will be boiled and then the water vapour will be separated out through a filter. In order to get rid of the perchlorates in martian water, this water will then be processed with reverse osmosis. Following this, the water can be used for any multitude of tasks, such as growing algae. Additionally, recyclers similar to the ones on the I.S.S. will be used to recycle wastewater and improve filtration.

3.0 ENGINEERING

3.1 THE HAB

The habitation module, or "Hab" will be a cylindrical inflatable structure capable of housing the 5 person crew and their supplies for the duration of the mission. It will be 8 metres tall and 12 metres wide, with a 2 floor layout. Though the mission will only last 150 martian sols, for safety reasons the habitat will be rated for a minimum of 200. The inflatable structure would be made of 3 layers of 0.5 inches of kevlar fibres, fitted to a triangular tiling that would act as the floor, incorporating hinges with a limit of 180°. This entire structure would be sent to Mars folded and deflated, before being deployed on the surface and inflated to its full size. The structure would be supported by a combination of air pressure and aluminium beams in certain critical points. This design allows for the structure to withstand the harsh martian climate, while still being light enough to be shipped with little hassle. When fully inflated, the Hab will be 2 floors, with a total of just over 226 m^2 of usable floor space. Additionally, the Hab would be surrounded by both water storage and several layers of bismuth infused acrylic panels, providing more than adequate radiation protection. Due to Kevlar being a reasonably light fabric, the Hab itself would be about 3.1 metric tons. Inside the Hab, five cots are set up on the tops of storage containers that are about 0.75 cubic metres in size. These would be on the upper level near the walls. Also on the upper level are multiple computers for processing the research that has been acquired. On the lower level, the algae tanks are held and the oxygen is transferred to the oxygen tanks right next to them. All of this will weigh another ton and a half or so.

3.2 THE ROVER

The aspect of a rover on mars is a desired prospect for any mission for many reasons. Whether it's transport, cargo, or maybe even experiments on the go, a rover will be very useful. For our mission, we designed a small unpressurized rover with capacity for a cargo of experiments, samples, scientific equipment, and other items. It would be powered by an electric motor being fueled by both solar and recharged battery banks, able to be recharged either through the panels or back at the base. The rover comes with a detachable trailer to haul along additional cargo to new areas, potentially setting up at sites of interest far from base. The rover's mobility allows us to cover a much wider area of the martian surface, meaning sites which would normally not be accessible are now well within reach. Even with the small design, the rover is still easily the heaviest single item on the mission. It would weigh in at 3.4 metric tons, and the trailer adding another half a ton.

3.3 THE SUITS

The suits that the mission crew will be wearing will be quite similar to Dava Newman's "BioSuit". It is made out of a Shape Memory Alloy (SMA), which can be returned to its original position after being changed. Designs on the suit are made to apply mechanical counterpressure, resulting in the gas pressure being avoided almost entirely. Since the human condition can be seriously affected by radiation, this design will be a huge help for our crew. The difference between our design and Dr. Newman's design is that we have a slightly bulkier helmet, and a medium sized oxygen tank on the back, both of which would be attached. The oxygen is then spread out into the helmet and the rest of the suit. Having a slim suit like this is also incredibly helpful because it removes many possible injuries caused by wearing a large suit like those on the Apollo missions to the moon. While those were great designs, they were quite heavy and required the crew to expend a large amount of energy that could be used for other research purposes. Since the SMA is incredibly light, we only need about a half ton at most for the all of the suits.

3.4 ENERGY PRODUCTION

Energy production on Mars will be a challenge, as the solar panels typically used for spacecraft will function at only 40% capacity in the best case scenario, will not work at all during the martian night, and will need to be routinely cleaned of the fine martian dust. Radioisotope Thermoelectric Generators (R.T.Gs) like those on the Curiosity and Perseverance rovers, provide too little power for a large base, and would be difficult to replace or remove in case of emergency. In order to alleviate these issues, our base design will utilise a currently-experimental technology from NASA, the Kilopower Miniature Nuclear reactor. Though current models are only capable of producing 1 Kilowatt, NASA anticipates future models will be able to produce up to 50 kW for a period of 12-15 years. Only one of these 50 kW reactors will be required for our base, which will be situated 1.5 km from the habitation module in a downwind direction, in case of leakage. This entire reactor is expected to weigh only 1.5 tons, 226 Kg of which will just be the core.

4.0 CONCLUSION

Even though this mission is only six months in length, the crew has a lot of work to do. All the different equipment will be set up and maintained, as well as used of course. A shorter mission makes the need for a strict timeline, but lots of research can still be done. Quite a bit of thought must be put into every aspect of the mission, and we have done exactly that. The experimental parts are ideas that could very possibly be put into play in only a few years, and will improve the efficiency of the mission quite a bit.

Overall, the equipment, Hab, and rover are all quite light. Although individually the items seem quite light, the total weight of the mission is about 12.9 metric tons, or 12,900 kilograms. Extra mass can be used for the personal belongings of the crew, as well as any sudden changes in how the item is made resulting in more weight.Cost is a little harder to calculate since much of this is experimental. For the Hab, just getting the material would be an easy 3 to 4 million dollars US Dollars. The rover would be tens of millions of dollars. In total, our final cost would most likely be somewhere between 1 and 1.5 billion dollars.

REFERENCES

1. Location: https://trek.nasa.gov/mars Dava Newman Suit: https://news.mit.edu/2014/second-skin-spacesuits-0918
2. Kilopower: https://www.nasa.gov/directorates/spacetech/kilopower/ Ice Drills and Information: https://icedrill.org/equipment

GROUP A MARS MISSION

ALDEN SANTOSO

JAMES MITCHELL

JAY MITCHELL

JACOB MITCHELL

TIM ROMANENKO

KYLER MCCORMICK

SCIENCE

A. SCIENTIFIC EXPLORATION

There are many places where life can be found. The location for the landing site contains a lot more frozen water underground than any place in the middle area of Mars. Ice under the surface of Mars can be obtained via a cylindrical drill that can extract cylindrical blocks of ice for further research and soil tests for mineral contents and possible signs of life in Martian regolith. The crew can use an electrothermal drill to remove a piece of cylindrical ice. The ice cylinder would be taken by the crew members to be further researched under a microscope. Another part of the exploration will be testing whether plants can survive with mars soil and transparent roofs that let in

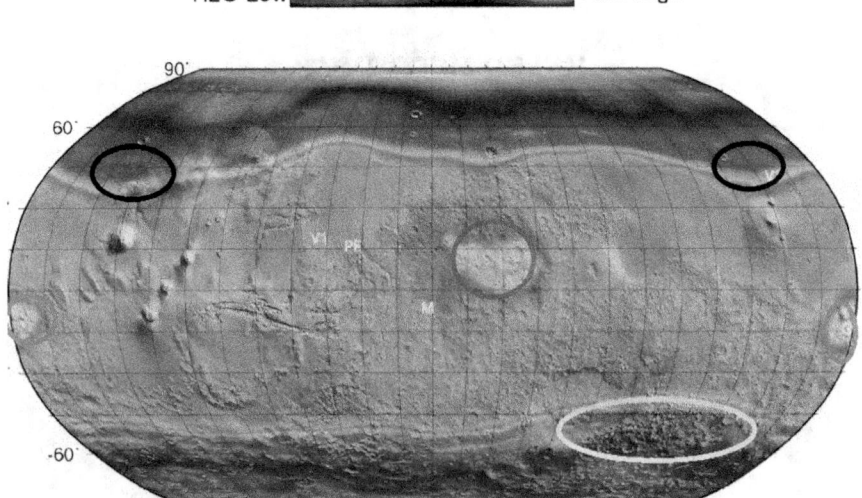

A map of good landing sites, determined by water location.

martian sunlight but not the excess radiation, therefore relying on mars's conditions more for agriculture.

B. LANDING SITE

Winds are the fastest along Martian crater rims and the volcanic highlands. Additionally, basalt formations are found throughout the surface of Mars. Flat land would be more desirable. Considering all these factors, the top right black circle is the best place. The general coordinates of this location are latitude 180 and longitude 57.

C. WASTE MANAGEMENT

Waste management is some of the most important aspects of life in space. The luxuries of life on Earth are not afforded in space, and because resources are so limited, almost everything on the space station and on human missions to mars are going to be reused or recycled in some way. Water is one of the most scarce resources in the solar system, and Mars only has difficulty accessing water in the form of ice under the surface. To save on energy costs as well as time, and overall maximizing efficiency, the waste and water recycling systems put in place on long term space satellites like the international space station can be used on Mars.

The first step to recycling water, and having a closed loop system, is to capture all of the water which is released as waste from the human body. This includes sweat, moisture from a person's breath and even recycling water from urine. After the liquid has been collected, any particulate must be filtered out. Once it can be confirmed that no particulate is left, impurities from the water also must be removed. This includes chemicals which are not healthy, bacteria, and other complex outputs that come from human processes. Despite the fact that there

The Urine Process Assembly and Water Process Assembly

are chemicals which make urine completely unhealthy to ingest, it actually contains roughly 95% water. This large water content allows systems to recycle as much as 87% of the water from this particular waste product.

On the ISS there are two main components that go into recycling water. Titled the Urine Process assembly(UPA), this machine is responsible for extracting the water from the urine. Once the water is extracted, it gets run through the water process assembly, which serves as the method of purification for the water. Once water gets run through the water process assembly, it is safe to drink again. The water process assembly is not only useful for water from the urine process assembly, but also serves as the purification method for all of the other water sources that can be found in a space mission.

Physically, there are a few processes which the water goes through to reach a pure state. These processes are quite similar when compared to the water treatment that water goes through on Earth before it reaches the final destination. The water assembly process and the urine assembly process have nearly identical orders when compared to each other. The UPA first sends the collected urine into a distillation tank which evaporates the urine and condenses it into a more compressed form. An important process which is found in the UPA is a pump which pulls out air from the process. This is important because air from the process can build up the pressure and can impede the efficiency of some of the tools, including the distillation tank. This comes with the added bonus of condensing water

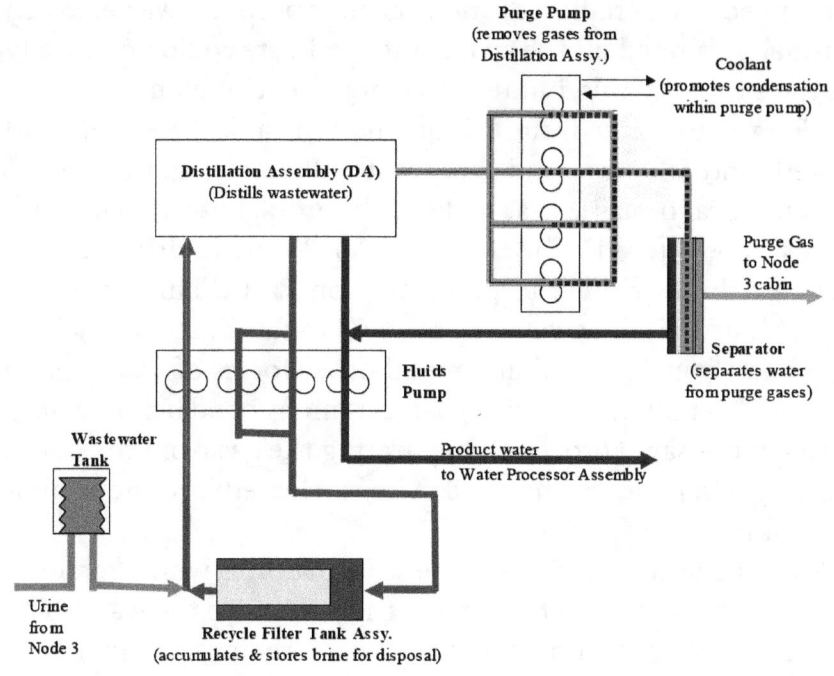

The Urine Process Assembly (UPA)

vapor from the released air, but there is still a combination of gas and water. The gas, depending on conditions could be released into the habitat, or it could be sent to a separator which separates the gas and water. The air gets the odor removed through a special device, and the water can be sent through the water process assembly later.

Through all of this, it is important to keep in mind that the urine from the distiller assembly gets more and more concentrated. At a certain concentration, the urine gets pulled out and stored. Once enough is stored, it is compressed into a brine filter which, as the name states, filters out the brine. It is important for the UPA to be as efficient as possible, so the result of the brine filter is sent back into the distiller assembly to get evaporated and repeat the process again. Every once in a while, the brine filter needs to be replaced, and this filter becomes waste, which is usually shipped off the space station. There could potentially be ways to reuse this, but it needs more development.

The waste water from the distillation tank is sent off and stored, and is considered dirty water. Water which is free of the chemical of urine that makes it harmful, but the water still needs to be filtered to be clean and 100% safe to drink. This is the part that is similar to processing on Earth. This tank contains all of the dirty water from the habitat. That will include humidity from the habitat, and all other forms of water listed above. This tank will contain gas, so as mentioned before it goes through the same process of separating the gas from the liquid with a gas separator. The gas can be rereleased into the habitat as a source of oxygen.

Now, as in life the water is sent into a filter which removes any particles that may have made their way into the water. The water is then sent into a filter which can remove any contaminants which are too difficult to see, and may have dissolved into the water. To be safe, the water is sent into a filter like this twice. These filters do need to be replaced. This is one of only two waste products from the water purification process. The dirty water is now almost entirely clean, except for volatile organic compounds. Man-made chemicals which are used in the production of everyday objects. To remove these, they need to be passed through the volatile removal assembly (VRA) which is part of the water process assembly. This process requires heat, but this can be rather energy intensive. To complete this process, pre-existing heat from the ISS is used, which aids in heating the water. Once this process is complete, the water goes through a regenerative heat exchanger that brings the temperature of the water even higher. This source of this heat is actually the heat of the water from the previous process. The water is heated up to 263 Celsius, which it then flows through a reactor. Oxygen is introduced in this reactor which cancels out the volatile organic compounds. After this, the hot water is pushed through the regenerative heat exchanger so that the energy can be recycled. Then the oxygen is separated and returned to the bases cabin. The water is repeatedly fed through the heat exchanger so that the maximum amount of heat energy can be recycled on other water. Once the water is cool enough, it gets stored in a clean water storage tank.

For general trash, there are a couple of options that have been or can be used. This includes compressing the trash into cubes and disposing of them. Another idea which has been developing is breaking down small pieces of trash. Putting them into a reactor, and breaking them down into more usable products which may include water or oxygen. Either way, the best developed way of dealing with trash requires a way of reducing it in size and dealing with it via varying methods. Anything that can be reused in any way should be.

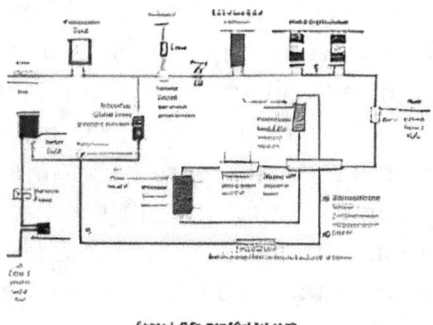

The Water Process Assembly (WPA)

D. IN SITU RESOURCE UTILIZATION

When designing a long term interplanetary mission, scientists must think about how the crew will sustain themselves. Being able to function without the help from scientists on Earth is key to ensuring a more permanent stay, and eventual colonization on Mars. One way to ensure sustainability on Mars is using available sunlight as a source of energy. A prime example of this is the International Space Station, known for its massive solar panels to harness energy and keep every instrument on board up and running. Mars's solar irradiation is 43.1% that of Earth, which means that solar panels on mars must be 2.32 times as large as those on Earth in order to supply the same amount of energy.

A more sustainable resource on mars is its regolith, which could prove helpful in the mission. Martian regolith differs greatly than that of Earth's, which could open the door to new ISRU opportunities. JSC Mars-1, a compound used to simulate Martian regolith, is 25% magnetic, and it is estimated that Martian soil actually contains up to 7% magnetic compounds. With this information, researchers on Mars can harness these resources with various rovers, accurately determining their chemical properties in the process. As astronauts learn more about Mars, our crew members can better adjust to the environmental conditions on the Red Planet throughout the course of the mission.

E. INTERPLANETARY COMMUNICATION

Crew members on a Mars mission need to be able to communicate to Earth in some form or another. Typically communication to Earth takes approximately 5-20 minutes since Mars is far away from Earth. Unfortunately there are no current technologies that allow humans to communicate between planets in a faster time. Group A is going to have a vehicle such as a rover or lander type machine that has two DSN antennas. A high-gain and low-gain antenna, that essentially allows radio waves to be sent and received. The antennas are approximately 37 yards and 76 yards tall. If a message was sent from Mars, the message would be sent via a radio signal. It would first reach one of the satellites orbiting Mars. The satellite would send the message to another satellite orbiting Earth and finally, the radio message would be sent to a receiver that would then decipher the message. Typically scientists create a scheduling system to ensure that the mission's priorities are met.

ENGINEERING

A. HABITAT

The astronauts going to Mars will need a habitat that can withstand the high winds, intense solar radiation, extreme temperature changes, and lack of oxygen. Additionally, every 6–8 years, Mars experiences huge dust storms that cover the entire planet. The materials used to construct the habitat will feel the effects of these forces and start to deteriorate. This factor leaves an importance in the material that is used to construct the habitat.

There are two ways that the habitat can be built: underground or above ground. Underground has quite a few benefits including protection against solar radiation, high winds, and dust storms. Lava tubes are also quite spacious so this leaves the astronauts as much space as they would ever need. It even leaves room for expansion. One of the biggest benefits to a cave is water. There is a high likelihood that ice is in caves relieving a lot of pressure of a reliable water source for not only drinking water but food and the various other uses. Though there are a lot of natural benefits, there are some huge disadvantages, the biggest of which being the fact that it's an enclosed space. It will be hard to get materials into the cave and collapse at the entrance is not uncommon. The plants needed for food and research would also need sunlight to thrive and a cave or lava tube doesnt have much light, making it hard to grow anything.

Another way of habitation is above ground. Now there is a lot more opportunity with this method, however, the drawback stems from the fact that there isn't any natural protection that a cave can provide. The designers of habitats have all made their habitats in a round-like shape, similar to a dome or cylinder. This is because this style of housing is able to withstand the tensile forces a lot better. Additionally, material used in the habitat can shield the inhabitants from a great deal of forces.

As previously stated, the material will need to be very resilient, however, another factor is the size of the habitat. People are going to be living in this environment every single day so the habitat has to be quite large. This means that the material will have to come from Mars itself. The habitat in this mission will utilize a few different materials, first being basalt. Basalt in itself is quite a good material because, if mixed with martian regolith. The resulting concrete will have a low permeability rate as well as natural strength. Another material added to the habitat material will be polyethylene. This material will be useful as it is able to seal walls and ensure impermeability. The right mixture of polyethylene can provide benefits to the structure like radiation blocking, a non-porous boundary layer to keep the interior airtight, shielding from potential toxic materials in the Mars regolith and overall insulation. This material can also be used as a byproduct of already existing uses. As an extra precaution the habitat will have an outer and inner shell, providing extra shielding from fluctuating temperatures, leaks, and corrosion.

The method of creating the habitat will be 3D printing. A rover will be mounted with excavation tools, a 3D printing arm as well as a concrete mixer to create the concrete for the habitat. The reason the habitat will be 3D printed is because it is efficient with a lot of potential for quick habitation. It can also be done without human interference and it saves a considerable amount of weight. The final measurements for the volume of the habitat is 754 feet cubed. The structure is also 15 feet tall and 8 feet in width.

This is the habitat pictured on Mars.

B. POWER SUPPLY

1. Power supply options

Our power supply is perhaps the most crucial thing to get right for this mission. There are many variables to take into account when deciding how our power system will function such as, heating, lighting, energy storage, excess energy usage, weight, cost, safety, lab use, and recreational energy use. Solar power is a great method for some aspects of our mission; however with less than 37% of the available sunlight reaching the panels and frequent dust storms, our habitat cannot rely on solar power. Solid state fuel is too heavy and costly to bring a years long supply to mars, so that is unfeasible. This narrows our options down to wind power, and nuclear power. While wind is prevalent on Mars, the lack of strong data on its frequency does not make me confident in its ability any more than solar. Along with the extra weight and upkeep of the turbine equipment. I am not confident in its ability to power the habitat. The only option left to power our habitat is nuclear power.

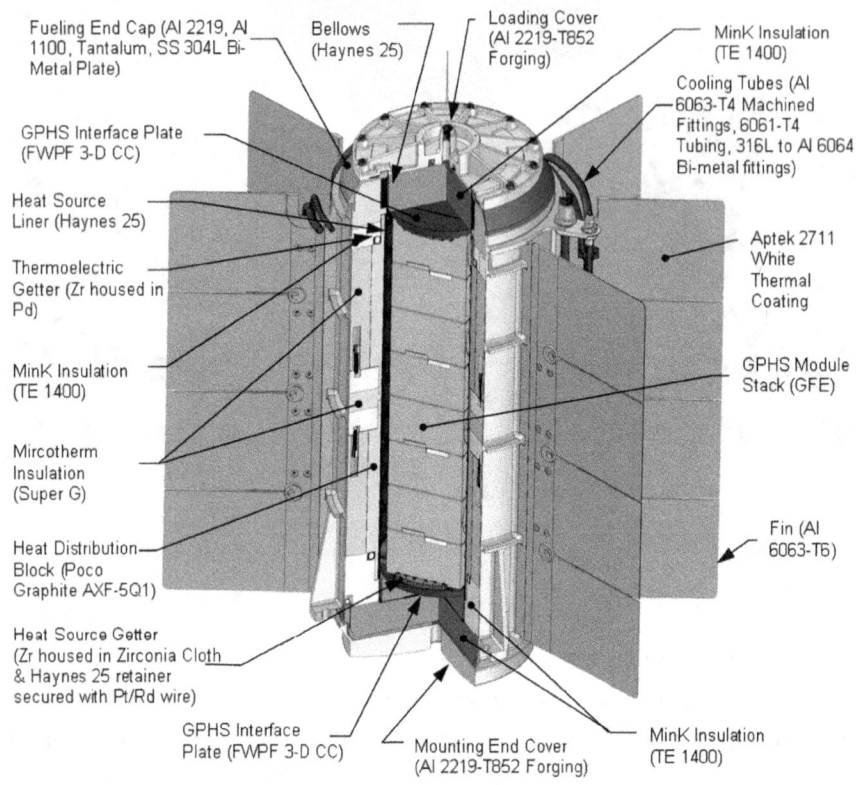

2. Nuclear power

Nuclear power has been reliably used in missions in space and on other terrestrial bodies, most prolifically by the martian rovers of recent. The basic principles for a small radioisotope thermoelectric generator to function are as follows. A radioisotope will slowly decay into a lighter, more stable element and as the isotope decays it releases powerful charged particles that release heat into the system. The generator will then absorb the heat using a thermoelectric device and use the Seebeck effect/ Thermoelectric effect to generate an electric current from the heat. RTGs are notoriously inefficient, they provide an average 6.2% of the thermal power.

3. Power Diversity

Relying on one source of power throughout the entire mission is simply put, putting all your eggs in one basket. When using equipment, especially power sources that require constant upkeep, problems can occur that can have devastating consequences. Other power sources that we can use are solar and wind, why these? As discussed before in "Power Sources", solar is limited by low sunlight, and wind is limited by frequency. Despite these problems, solar and wind are still substantial sources of power. We plan to use nuclear power as our primary generator in the habitat; however our vehicles, which will be outside the habitat, would be a large burden if we had to manually charge them from the habitat. To solve this problem, our vehicles will be powered by lithium ion batteries charged by solar panels that will be mounted to the vehicles directly. This removes the burden of charging them from the habitat, and removes the possibility of becoming stranded without power a long distance from the habitat in search of rare earth minerals. Wind power will primarily be used as an extra source of power in the habitat and the greenhouse, the turbines mounted outside the habitat will slowly charge lithium ion batteries in the habitat and when we need, we can divert our energy consumption from the radioisotope generator, to the turbines. This is an example of a small, lightweight turbine we can mount outside the habitat. This model stands a little more than ten feet tall or three meters.

4. Experimental Power Generation, CH4

In a reaction called the Sabatier reaction, carbon dioxide and hydrogen are transformed into water and methane. The International Space Station has a machine called the Sabatier CO_2 methanation reactor where this process can be done. Essentially, with the presence of a catalyst, high pressure, and high temperatures, hydrogen and carbon dioxide that were put into the reactor turn into water vapor and methane gas. The water vapor is then funneled into a condenser where it is condensed into water that can be reused for uses such as drinking, growing plants, creating oxygen, and more. The methane gas can be condensed into methane liquid which can be used for rocket fuel or alternatively, the methane gas can be used in another reaction to create polyethylene, a material that is highly radiation absorbing. The hydrogen is obtained from the oxygen generators which split water into hydrogen and oxygen while the carbon dioxide can be easily extracted from the atmosphere of Mars since Mars' atmosphere is 95% carbon dioxide.

C. OXYGEN SUPPLY

Oxygen is an essential resource that is needed to support human life on Mars. It is not a viable solution to transport enough oxygen to Mars for a year and a half mission. Ultimately, that would take up a lot of space and weight that is needed for other essential materials. One way to solve this problem would be to use an oxygen In-Situ Resource Utilization (ISRU) system. An ISRU system would use resources that can be found on Mars, like H_2O and CO_2 and separate the chemical from the oxygen molecules.

CO_2 is a gas that is highly abundant in the atmosphere of Mars. Oxygen can be made from the CO_2 using an ISRU system that extracts the carbon dioxide from the atmosphere of Mars and performs Solid OXide Electrolysis (SOXE) to separate the carbon monoxide molecule from the two oxygen molecules. As a result you are left with two gasses, carbon monoxide and oxygen. NASA has built an oxygen ISRU system called the Mars Oxygen ISRU Experiment (MOXIE). Unfortunately MOXIE does not create enough oxygen for it to be a viable option in this Mars mission.

Group A Mars Mission

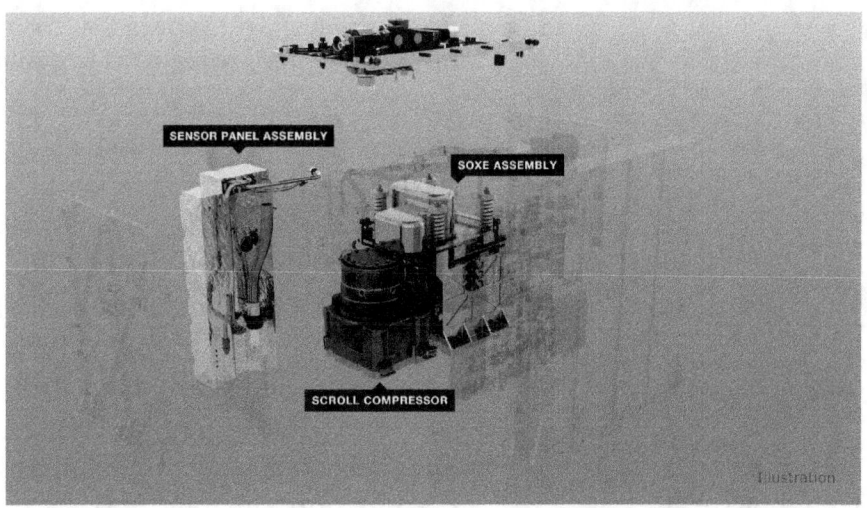

This picture is a blueprint of MOXIE. It is around the size of a car battery and weighs around 14.14 pounds on Mars (37.7 pounds on Earth). MOXIE was implemented on the Perseverance in the year of 2020 and has proven to work on Mars. Currently MOXIE can only make around 10 grams of oxygen per hour but scientists say that by the time a Mars Mission will occur, it will be improved to produce around 200 times the current amount or 2000 grams of oxygen per hour.

A second option is to use an ISRU system that can separate the oxygen molecule from the hydrogen molecules in H_2O. Water or H_2O is a resource that can be found and harvested on Mars. The water can be used for consumption but also for oxygen. In a method called electrolysis, the two hydrogen molecules and one oxygen molecule in H_2O are split. Afterwards both gasses are split into separate chambers. The oxygen is pumped into a storage oxygen tank while the hydrogen gas is pumped into the atmosphere. A machine called the Elektron utilizes this form of conversion on the International Space Station. The Elektron intakes water that has a little salt (for conductivity), the electrolysis then splits the water into hydrogen gas and oxygen gas.

Both gasses are separated into different chambers and the oxygen goes through a pipe into an oxygen tank while the hydrogen is pumped into outer space.

The Elektron is around 4 feet tall and 1.5 feet wide. One Elektron alone can generate 79 liters of oxygen an hour which is able to sustain 3 humans on a year and a half mission with 16 liters of oxygen an hour left to spare. Approximately 860 watts is needed to power the Elektron. Under normal circumstances, the hydrogen would be discarded into outer space like on the ISS but on Mars, the hydrogen gas and carbon dioxide from humans and the Mars atmosphere can be used in a reaction called the Sabatier reaction to create more usable water and methane gas which could be condensed into liquid and used for rocket fuel. The water could also be combined with carbon dioxide to create ethylene gas which could be used to support growth in the greenhouse or used to create polyethylene plastic that is very efficient at absorbing radiation. One Elektron uses 8 liters of water a day.

A third option could be using a form of chemical reaction that creates a byproduct of oxygen. To perform this reaction, powder iron is ignited and heated up to specific temperatures. Use the fire to burn powdered sodium chlorate to create sodium chloride (salt) and the byproduct of oxygen. A fourth option would be to mine rocks off the surface of Mars and put the rocks into a machine that will run 450 amps through the rocks which breaks the rocks down. When the rocks are broken down, usable oxygen is released from the rocks. The final option is to bring all the oxygen 4 humans need to sustain themselves for a year and half.

For the Mars Mission Group A, we decided that the best option would be to use two water oxygen generators. The water oxygen generators would be similar to the Elektron. With the combined effort, both machines are able to sustain all 4 of the humans on Group A's mission with 1.6 liters of oxygen an hour left over. If both water oxygen generators worked all hours of the day, it would produce too much oxygen to store and would be considered a waste of energy, space, weight, and water therefore both generators would need to run 13 hours a day and be turned off the other 11 hours. The generators would use a total of 8.68 liters of water a day to produce the oxygen needed to sustain the 4 crew members. All of the water recycled from human urine, the water recycled from the leftover hydrogen, and extra water obtained from the mechanical drill will flow into the oxygen generators. The water undergoes electrolysis and the two gasses are separated into two chambers. The oxygen is pumped into an oxygen tank which is used for oxygen supply in the habitat/pressurization system. The hydrogen gas is pumped into a different tank with carbon dioxide and used in a reaction called the Sabatier reaction to create water and methane gas. The methane gas that was a result from the Sabatier reaction can be used to fuel the rocket back to Earth or used to make polyethylene while the water is recycled to the oxygen generators. To supply carbon dioxide for the Sabatier reaction, a simple machine would suck in carbon dioxide from the atmosphere of Mars and pump it into the tank. Furthermore, to maintain fresher oxygen in the habitat, a simple air circulation system that uses air ducts and fans to circulate the air in the habitat with the air in the greenhouse and other stories of the habitat. By doing this, the plants would have carbon dioxide to perform photosynthesis while the humans would have oxygen and need less oxygen input and energy to maintain acceptable oxygen levels. In the event that the water oxygen generators fail, the best solution would be to bring a backup SFOG oxygen generator that uses powder iron and powder sodium chloride to create oxygen, the leftover salt can be used to increase conductivity of the water for the water oxygen generators. Group A is going to bring enough of the powders to supply the crew for half a year. In total, this system could efficiently ensure that the 4 crew members have an efficient oxygen supply for the year and a half mission on Mars with a backup in case the water oxygen generators fail.

D. WATER SOURCE

A renewable source of water is one of the most important things to consider when developing a mission to Mars. It is simply not feasible to continually transport water to Mars, and so methods of sourcing water from the planet itself should be analyzed.

That presents a few challenges though. The first one being that Mars does not have reservoirs of water—flowing or not. The water cycle is very different from Earth, and the planetary conditions are such that only ice exists on Mars. Either in the ice capes of the planet, or on an axis very far north or south of the equator. Alternatively, subsurface ice exists across the planet, and should allow for a wider range of possibilities when it comes to finding a source of water which is in a suitable location for the other factors necessary for a mission to Mars.

Given that the mission will include at least 4 astronauts as well as other systems like plant growth, the water source needs to be consistent enough to maintain that level of usage.

This is the water map of Mars, along with a map of past landing sites on Mars. The further north and south, the more ice there is. To find optimal locations, a map of past landing sites and this map of subsurface ice could be cross referenced to look for successful past landing sites which also have a high amount of ice.

When looking at the landing sites, it is easily noticeable that there have been landings on quite a wide range of landings. Some very far north, and quite a few around the center of the planet. This shows

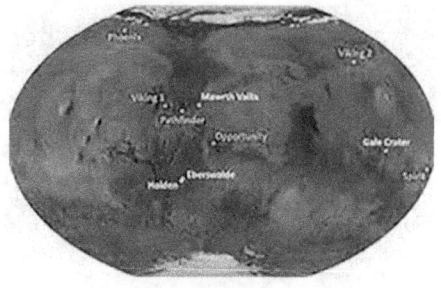

Maps of Past Rover Landings and Underground Ice Locations

that trying for a landing site further north where the density of water is higher is a possibility. The small spots of light blue which are located on the left and right of the water map also have had rovers land close to, like the spirit rover. This area is a possibility. Lastly, the larger dot of light blue area in the center of the water map could definitely be landed in or very close to, as there have been many rovers in that area before.

In this diagram, there are four different colors marked out. The circles colored black are 1 option for landing. This area was chosen because they have a lot of water, and are the furthest south out of anywhere in the northern section. The circle in the center colored in red contains an area of medium H_2O content but is located nearly in the center of the planet which will be very good as the temperatures will be less extreme. The third

Water Map
2001 Mars Odyssey Gamma Ray Spectrometer

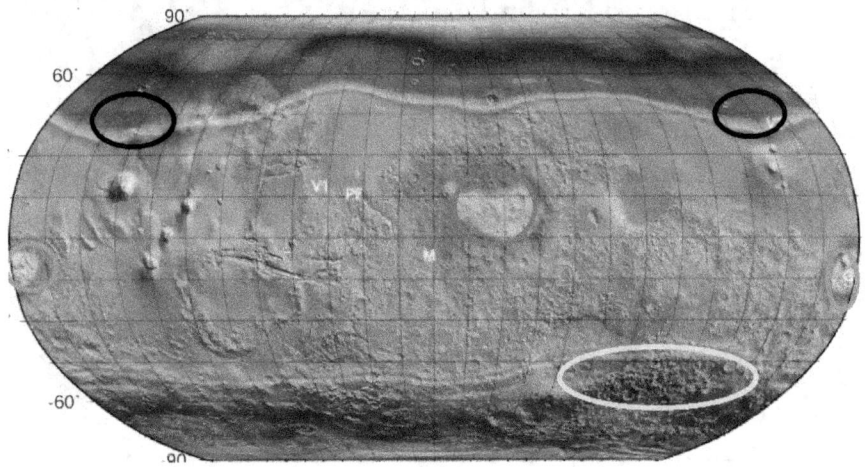

Map which shows Potential Locations that have Water

option marked out in purple also contains medium levels of H_2O content, the only difference is that they are slightly further south than the red circle. The last area marked in a light pink color is located in the southern part of the planet, and was chosen for how far north it is compared to the rest of the southern part in dark blue. The drawback to the two potential locations for water in the north and south is that they will be experiencing more extreme temperatures and conditions given that they are closer to the poles. All of this will be looked at in further detail in the landing sites section of the report.

It should also be considered the depth which ice is available at. The maps above show the quantities of water available in certain areas, but do not mention how deep the ice i

Group A Mars Mission

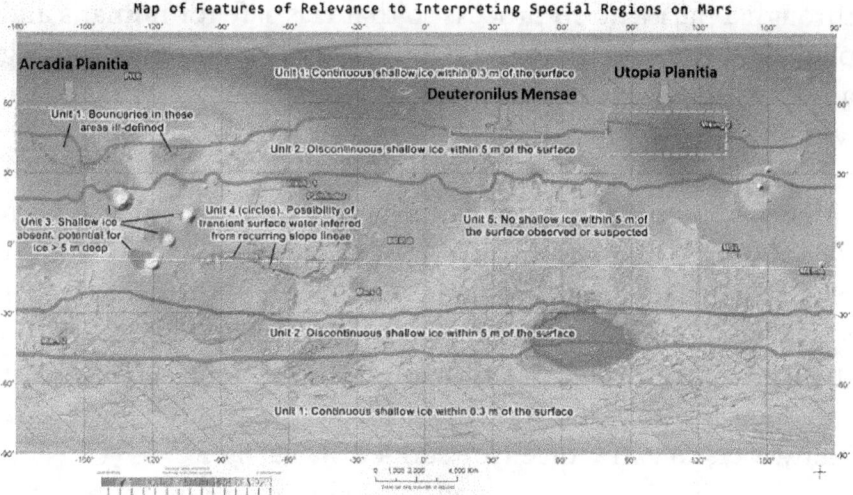

A Map which shows Estimated Ice Depth

The image above is an analysis of an ice map of mars, and also has divided the map into sections describing how deep the ice is. From the diagram of potential locations, it can be assumed that the northern and southern locations circled have ice between .3 and 5 meters deep. The other locations may *potentially* have ice below 5 meters deep, but is much more likely that the ice will be greater than 5 meters deep. Using this information, it can be assumed that our ice mining device must reach at least 5 meters underground, but it is most preferable if the device can mine ice that is much deeper than even that.

Now that the location options have been analyzed, the final part which still needs to be sorted out is how the water will be acquired. The largest reservoirs of water are located underground, and so a device which has the capability to mine out the water, which is in solid form, and transport it back to the surface needs to be developed. The water may also need to run through a purification process so that it is safe for humans and plants alike. Again, one of the most useful resources is looking at what already exists either on Earth or what has been used on Mars in the past missions.

There have not been many studies done on the process of gathering deep ice, but concepts have been developed. A popular concept is the use of a drill to get through the initial layer of rock which does not contain water ice. Once the drill reaches ice it is extracted, and another device is sent down and melts the ice. The now liquid is transported to the surface, where it can then be stored and purified into usable water. There are many ways to extract ice from under the surface.

Similar to oil mining rigs, pumps can be used to quickly extract melted ice, and move it to a portable, or permanent storage area (as seen in the diagram below). Another concept is to have a container, which after the ice is melted in a large underground reservoir, is lowered down and brought back to the surface containing the melted water. There has also even been an idea where the ice is melted to where it evaporates, and a hopper like item is at the top of the drilled hole to catch the gas, and condense it back into a liquid form.

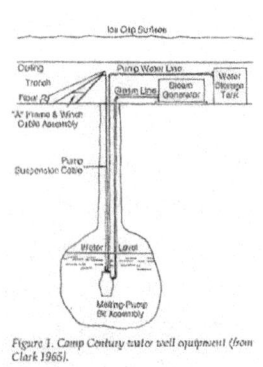

Figure 1. Camp Century water well equipment (from Clark 1965).

A Diagram of Water Extraction

There are also different types of drills to use. The standard mechanical drill, which works as expected and can drill through ice itself. There are hot water drills which can ONLY work on ice but is easily adjustable, allowing for wider or deeper holes. Hot water drills work by shooting a jet of hot water out of a nozzle, which melts the ice and can allow it to be collected. This can be very energy intensive though. There are also electrothermal drills which only work on ice as well. Electrothermal drills melt a ring around the ice it will collect. After the hole is dug, and the ice is melted and collected, the purification process is needed.

The purification of the extracted water is actually quite a simple process. The first thing to do is to get rid of all the material from the drilling and the surrounding martian soil. Simply run the water through a multi-layer mesh system to filter out the particulate. Then the resulting liquid gets run through a reverse osmosis filtration system. It sounds complicated but essentially what a reverse osmosis system is running the water which needs purification through a membrane which only allows the water to filter through, leaving behind any very small particulate. Thus, purifying the water into a drinkable and usable form. It gets its name as it is similar to, if not the reverse of, osmosis in a cell. There are a few modifications that would need to be made to the revers osmosis system used in purifying salt water, but all things considered it would not be as difficult because a lot of the system is already designed on Earth.

There are actually two designs of ice and water extracting that we will use. Both of the designs will use a mechanical drill to get through the rock on the surface and reach the solid ice under the crust. Once the hole is drilled out, and the drill as been reversed from the hole, a probe is sent down to melt the water. This is where the designs differ. One design will use a pump to pump out the melted ice and transport it directly into the habitats water storage. The flaw in this singular design is that it is difficult to transport, and so the drilling would happen only very close to the habitat. The pump, depending on the location will only need solar power to run, using 450 watts on the high end, per hole dug, assuming that the drill can drill the hole in about an hour.

The second design that we have decided to choose, is one which is much more portable. It also uses a mechanical drill to drill a hole to the ice pocket. After that, solar energy is magnified down the hole until it can evaporate the water. After which, a hopper which is covering the hole's opening, condenses the water vapor into water and it is then sent to a portable storage, which can then be transferred to the main habitat storage. This design comes with the added benefit that it does not require any energy to melt the ice, and it is quit transportable, as all it requires is a mechanical drill. The rest of the process is done at the surface. Notably, the energy costs of this design are much less, as it does not require any more than the 15-50 watts per hour that the mechanical drill requires. The drawback to this is that it can be quite slow, as it takes quite a bit of time to heat water to a temperature at which it starts to evaporate. Some water also may be lost in the process of evaporation, but it shouldn't be so significant as to greatly impact the ratio of drinkable water to energy usage when compared to the other design.

These two designs should be able to provide enough water for 4 people considering each person uses 3-5 gallons of water each day. That totals to 12-20 gallons of water per day. There is also the bonus that much of that water can be reused through processes shown and described in the waste management section, which also covers some water reusability.

E. PRESSURIZATION

Pressurization is generally classified as the pressure put on an object by the surrounding air. Humans cannot live without pressurization for a multitude of reasons. Therefore the habitats and space suits of Mars and the Moon need to be pressurized. Furthermore in order to leave the habitat on Mars, the pressurization inside a room needs to match the outside/inside pressure otherwise there would be a strong vacuum effect.

First off, the habitat needs to be pressurized. There is a simple solution to this problem. Oxygen can be funneled into the habitat that not only allows the crew members to breath without an oxygen tank but also generates enough pressure that the crew can live on. Group A can do this by attaching multiple pipes to the oxygen tanks that came from the oxygen generators and pump the oxygen into the habitat in multiple areas such as the bottom floor and the top floor. This method of distributing air will take around 480 watts of power. There will be a ventilation system that connects the greenhouse to the habitat that allows the greenhouse to also have efficient pressure and oxygen.

Second is airlock systems. Group A has decided that connecting the habitat to the greenhouse would be the best option therefore only the habitat requires an airlock system. The best airlock system for the habitat would be the Nanorack Bishop Airlock Module (NBAM). The benefits of having this system would be the size and the weight. Currently this airlock module is one of the smallest airlocks designed at 6 feet and 7.3 inches in diameter and 5 feet and 11 inches in height. Although this means that the crew can only enter and exit the airlock at around two at a time, it also means that less air is needed to pressurize the module. Not only that but the system weighs significantly less compared to its counterparts, weighing at only 2,335 pounds. This airlock module utilizes 350 watts to power it.

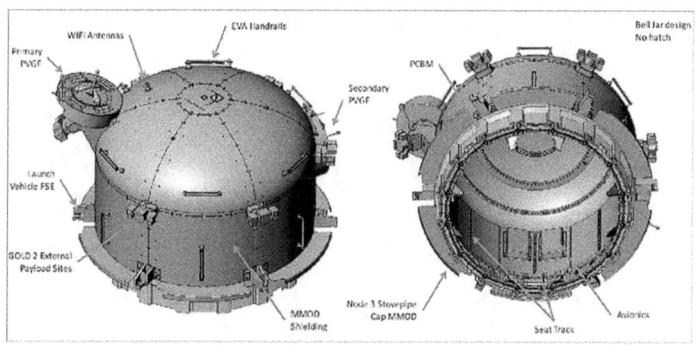

F. VEHICLES

1. Personnel vehicle

On Mars, our scientists will have a difficult time traversing the harsh terrain on foot to reach sites of interest whilst wearing cumbersome suits. It is pivotal that we provide a fast, reliable, and easy to manage vehicle for everyday needs. I introduce this design for our martian personnel vehicle. It is powered by a medium sized Radioisotope Thermoelectric Generator in the front, this power is stored in a lithium ion battery at the base of the chassis. The battery powers a motor that turns the drive shaft which will convert its power into the airless tires. The airless tires are inspired by many modern designs and even have aluminum cleats to grip the surface rock. These tires are all connected to the vehicle via an independent suspension system, this system will ensure the best performance on rough terrain. The vehicle is non pressurized, meaning our scientists must wear suits at all times whilst inside the vehicle. This was done to ensure the lightest weight possible, and to not overcomplicate what's simple in principle. Inspired by many military contracted vehicles of the past, this has a medium sized trunk bed with a tool box and of course many useful tools to help with any unforeseen damage or terrain difficulties.

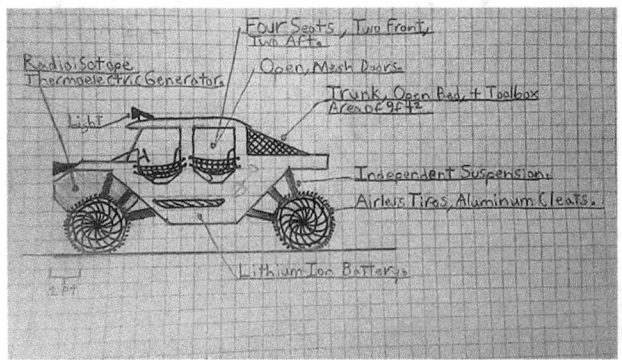

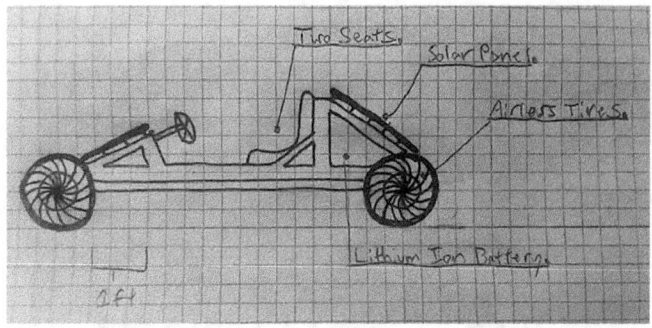

2. Double Passenger Roving Vehicle

Our scientists will need to travel across the martian terrain frequently, and the larger vehicle may be inoperable or used elsewhere. This vehicle is by all means, a spare. It is very lightweight, has the capacity to seat two people. The vehicle is powered by two solar panels and the power is stored in a lithium ion battery. The tires are airless. The vehicle is around 8 x 2.5 x 3.5 feet, a scale is provided

3. Reusable Weather balloons

Our mission is to conduct as much experimental research as possible with our requirements. In doing so we have decided to explore the weather of mars like never before. On our mission we will have five reusable weather balloons. We aim to explore the layers of the atmosphere, the patterns of air currents, the chemical makeup of the atmosphere and explore the effect of air density on the balloons. This weather balloon is a very hefty instrument, including: a radiosonde, infrared spectrometer, electrochemical sensor, ground and horizontal facing cameras, and a catalytic diffusion sensor. To ensure the equipment runs at full capacity, we have installed an automatic radioisotope heater unit. This is all powered by two solar panels, one on the top, and another on the left side; the power is stored in a lithium ion battery inside. The balloon is an experimental design of a reusable system. The neoprene balloon will inflate and expand

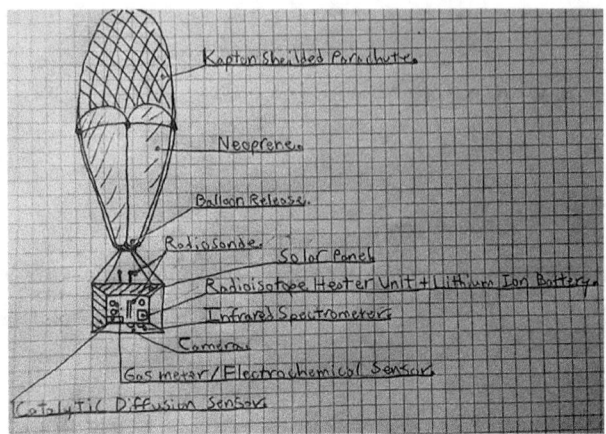

and burst as all weather balloons do; however this has a large "not drawn to scale" parachute installed atop the balloon. Once the balloon bursts we expect the parachute to capture the air and make its descent to the surface where it may be retrievable. We will use this to track air flow and to experiment on parachutes in an atmosphere that is less dense than that of earth.

4. Triangulated Surface Imaging Drones

An aspect we hope to explore on Mars is drone coordination, and imaging. I have introduced a drone to perform coordinated thermal and optical imaging sweeps at high and low altitude of the martian surface. This drone will travel in a group of three, they will be given an objective to reach and they alone, along with data from satellites and "later to be introduced" Mars Link Rovers, will travel long distances and take imaging data, and return to base. These drones are powered by small solar panels covering the top side of their frame, and the power is stored in small lithium ion batteries. This will power the instruments on board and three toroidal propellers. Toroidal propellers have been demonstrated to be more efficient and quieter than normal propeller blades. These drones will charge during the evening hours and rest for the night, then resume the objective in the morning. As the drones will have to make regular trips to the surface without human help, they may encounter rough and unstable ground. These drones will have a gyrostabilizer that will "feel" the level of the drone as it lands, the dynamic tripod legs on the rover will move to support the drone and help place the drone at near perfect level.

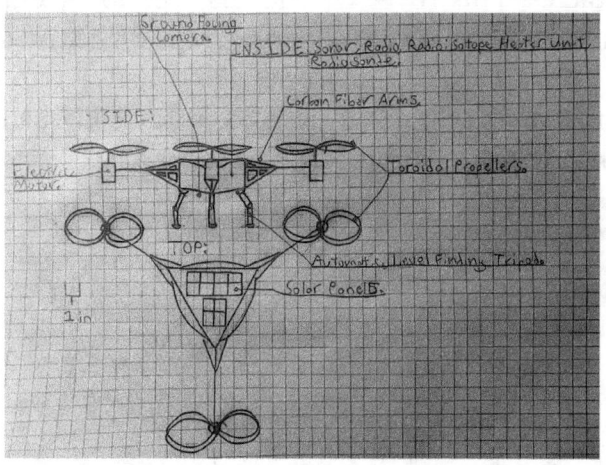

5. Rare Earth Element Detecting Rover

As our primary objective is to find deposits of rare earth elements on mars, we need a rover to help in the search. This rover will orbit our camp and continue searching for rare earth elements as long, or perhaps even after our scientists leave Mars. This rover will use varying frequencies and Ground Penetrating Radar to sense elements deeper underground. The rover is also equipped with a four foot long sample gathering arm. This arm, inspired by the perseverance rover, has a magnet, an abrasion tool for gathering small particles off of rocks, and a claw for picking up rocks it finds interesting. Inside the rover is a sample collection and analysis bay, where it will use an infrared vapor spectrometer to analyze the chemical makeup of its samples.

This data will be sent back to base with its large antenna. This rover is powered by a radioisotope thermoelectric generator in the rear and the power is stored in a large lithium ion battery inside. The rover will navigate using a 360 degree optical camera and several lidar sensors. The tires are airless and mounted in a way to prevent the vehicle from getting stuck on medium sized obstacles. This rover will have a secondary objective, to sample the soil for life sustaining properties. The rover will take a detour to one of the several ancient riverbeds and test the soil for potential signs of ancient life and fertile soil qualities. This rover is around 10 × 4 × 5 feet, it is not drawn to scale.

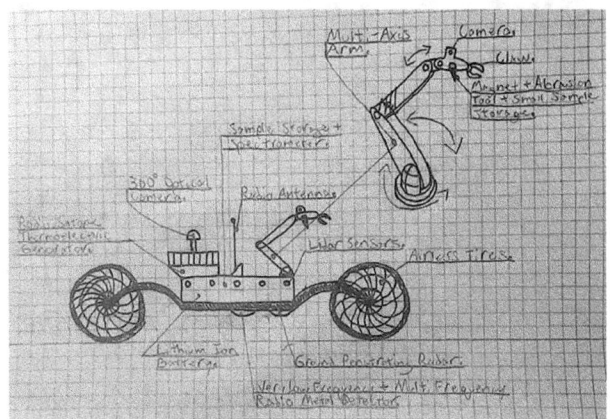

6. Load Bearing Rover

During the construction of the habitat, our scientists will need to move massive amounts of equipment across long distances. I have introduced what is in principle, a programmable construction vehicle. This load bearing rover will take heavy objects placed inside of it, along a programmed route, and deliver the items to the new location automatically. This rover is powered by a radioisotope thermoelectric generator. The power is stored in a large lithium ion battery at the bottom of the chassis. The vehicle has six airless tires, each with a motor and suspension that can elevate, or lower the entire body to make loading easier for a person. The vehicle has a large hatch that acts as a loading ramp. The vehicle is around 12 × 5.3 × 8.6 feet, a scale provided.

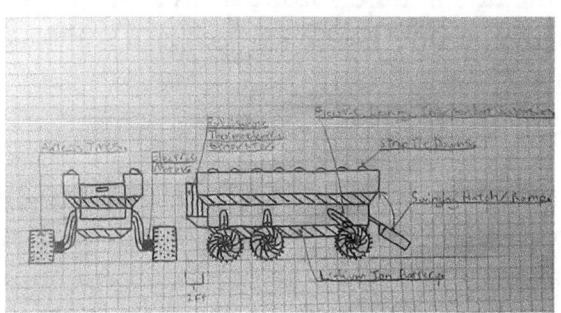

7. Mars Link Rovers

Mars is very devoid of fast communication, and there are very few satellites to redirect signals to distant targets. Our scientists are going to have many rovers and drones across long distances and it will be difficult to contact them remotely. I have introduced what is simply a mobile radio signal relay rover. These small, lightweight rovers will span the distance between sights of interest that would normally be very hard to communicate signals too. Like the world wide web of earth, they will find the fastest route to relay communication from transmitter to receiver. These rovers are powered by solar panels that store their energy inside a lithium ion battery. In case of high winds,

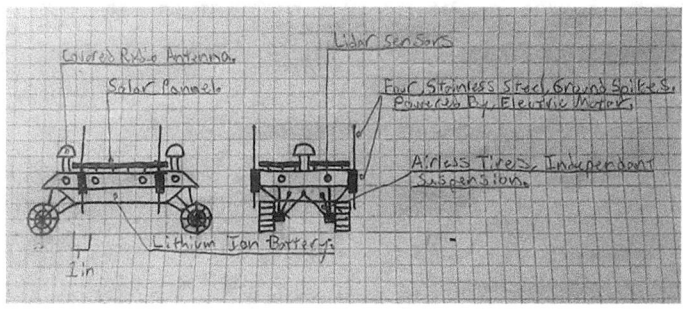

these rovers have four, long, stainless steel rods that can be driven into the ground to lock the rover in place. The rovers will navigate the Martian surface using Lidar sensors. These rovers also include a radioisotope heater unit for the electronics. The rover is around 12 × 7 × 8 inches, a scale is provided.

G. GREENHOUSE

The greenhouse will include a few parts to actually function, first of all being the greenhouse itself. It will be partly foldable and non-transparent while being made of Aluminum, carbon fiber reinforced polymers and polyethylene for the outer walls, making the radioactive-proof and very durable, the entire greenhouse will have a semi-cylinder structure that will fold into itself using unfoldable polymer fabrics for the stretching part with three main hard parts that will go into each other, the earlier mentioned non-transparency will be counted measured with uv lamp fixtures above the plants.

   The walls will be lined with pots with a water circulation system coming between the bottom of each pot row and next uv light fixture, this will provide water to the plants by piping it directly into the soil and venting the unnecessary water out the bottom, sending it back to the minor filter system that uses nanofiber fabric to take away radiation and other unnecessary minerals.

   A large plant seed pack will also be necessary for backup seeds for both starting and replacing plants in the greenhouse gardens. It will be made of an airtight packing used by nasa made of Nylon, polyethylene, and Ethylene vinyl alcohol. Along with dehumidifiers to avoid damaging the seeds

   The final part of the greenhouse will be a smaller off branch of it with a transparent roof made of ETFE (Ethylene Tetrafluoroethylene) as it is highly durable, lightweight, and capable of strong radiation resistance. The frame of this building will consist of Aluminium alloy for it's resistance to radiation and strength. This sector will use the martian sunlight and soil to grow plants being a testing section for how plants can cope on mars, the building itself will be detachable and attachable to the main greenhouse building via extendable airlock.

The total weight of this sector is 11 metric tons and 25 kg

III. HUMAN OPERATIONS

A. LIFE SUPPORT

Despite being closer to the sun than Earth, the temperature on Mars is typically around negative 70 degrees fahrenheit. Human life cannot survive in this cold of temperatures therefore the habitat requires a heating system. Heating in the habitat is usually obtained through heaters and radiators but sometimes the habitat may get too hot. In this case, an efficient heating system has been implemented on the International Space Station that could be used on Mars. This system is called the Active Thermal Control System (ATCS) and it uses excess heat from equipment, electronics, and more and essentially removes the heat. The ATCS gathers the heat from equipment through ammonia coolant and water pipes which is then disposed of into space via a radiator. On Mars, instead of disposing of the heat, it can be looped to a radiator in the habitat to keep the place warm but if the temperatures rise too high, the system can switch to a method of disposing the heat into the atmosphere of Mars.

Another basic life support need is health care. Onboard this mission, there are the basic life support needs in case of an injury like a med kit. One major health issue on Mars is osteoporosis. To combat this issue, the habitat can hold medicine that can help fight osteoporosis if a crew member were to get a severe case of it.

B. CREW SCREENING

Efforts to train crew have already been implemented with CHAPEA, a 1700 square foot 3d printed simulation of a Mars habitat. Crew train in these simulated environments for over a year, 378 days to be exact, and NASA monitors their physical, behavioral, and emotional traits throughout the mission. Because crew members will spend extended amounts of time in an area isolated form Earth, Crew members must be healthy, and have no known chronic medical issues. Scientists will screen the family members of the crew to determine any risk of genetic disease, especially as the stay on Mars will take several years. Medical procedures such as ECGs, Xrays, blood tests, and ultrasounds will be performed to ensure that the crew member is in peak physical health. In terms of mental health, crew members will see neurologists, psychologists, and therapists to ensure that the crew member is in peak mental health. Due to NASA's history, crew members must be fluent in English. This ensures that they can communicate as effectively as possible with NASA mission control.

C. CREW LIFE

In any Mars mission, it is integral that crew strictly follow a fixed routine in order to maximize the efficiency of the mission. Because Mars is an entirely different habitat than that of Earth, astronauts must adjust heavily to the unfamiliar conditions on the Red Planet. Most importantly, 1 day on Mars lasts 24 hours and 37 minutes. Though this may seem like a minor change from the typical Earth day, this can have adverse effects on the performance of the crew and the mission as a whole. Because our biological clocks are fitted to the 24 hour cycle, an adjustment of 37 minutes every day is enough to cause jet lag throughout the mission, as our body clocks constantly lag behind by almost one hour every day. As a result, scientists have developed a way to keep time on Mars. A Sol is used to describe one solar day on Mars, or the time it takes for the Sun to appear in the same point in the sky on Mars. The issue of sleeping on Mars can be solved by integrating environments from Earth with the Red Planet. Scientists can position the habitat in such a way that the sleeping areas are close to windows to provide a source of natural light in the morning. However, the natural light from the sun may be too dim considering Mars's distance from the Sun. As a result, timed artificial sun lamps overhead can supply the necessary light for astronauts to maintain a healthy sleep schedule on Mars, maximizing crew efficiency and morale in the process.

Additionally, exercise is integral to the physical health of the crew members. For hundreds of thousands of years, human life has evolved and thrived under Earth's gravity, or 9.81 meters per second squared. However, Mars's gravity is around one third that of Earth's. Let's put this in perspective. Imagine a 10 kilogram object (22 pounds). That same object would feel like 3.7 kilograms (8.15 pounds) on Mars. This can have adverse effects on the health of crew members. When working in an environment with a gravitational force less than that of Earth's, muscles in the legs and back will weaken because they no longer support the weight of the astronaut on Earth. In other words, our muscles do less work when the force of gravity is weaker. To prepare for these missions, astronauts train in deep pools or zero g planes to simulate microgravity environments. Space can also affect sleeping patterns and the biological clock of the astronauts, causing nausea.

Luckily, there is a way to combat these adverse health effects, and that is exercise. Astronauts must exercise several hours each day in order to counter the negative effects of zero gravity in order to maintain physical health and proper muscle growth. This has already been implemented successfully on extended space missions such as the ISS missions, with the TVIS(Treadmill Vibration Isolation System). Astronauts typically spend 2.5 to 3 hours per day on the modified treadmill, which covers the daily exercise requirement necessary to maintain muscle and bone strength. Scientists can implement this unique solution on a mission to Mars, as TVIS weights one metric ton.

D. ENTERTAINMENT AND INTERNET

When performing any high stakes mission, astronauts must remember the importance of relaxation time. This can increase morale as well as mission effectiveness, as crew will be able to destress and unwind after performing in a high pressure environment. In previous missions to space, astronauts have read books, watched movies, and played games, similar activities and one would do on Earth.

Additionally, astronauts on Mars can use a form of interplanetary internet to communicate with people on Earth, connecting them to the planet they call home, or as a form of entertainment. This idea has already been put forth with the idea of the IPN (Interplanetary Network). With this resource, crew members can communicate, though slowly, with peers, colleagues, and family on Earth. Due to the speed of light and the changing distance between Earth and Mars over each orbit, communication between Mars and Earth can lag from anywhere between 8-40 minutes both ways. New technologies such as DTNRG are innovating new ways to communicate in deep space, Take the example of a remote outpost, imagine an isolated Arctic settlement with electricity, one or more computers, but no communication connectivity. With the addition of a simple wireless hotspot in the village, plus DTN-enabled devices on, say, dog sleds or fishing boats, a resident would be able to check their e-mail or click on a Wikipedia article, and have their requests forwarded to the nearest networked location on the sled's or boat's next visit, and get the replies on its return. However, the best solution for communication between Earth and Mars is through caching data from servers on Earth to servers based on Mars. In doing so, scientists on Earth can send in 'mission critical' data to the crew on Mars, which can greatly benefit the mission. A connection of networks between each habitat is also important. Crew members must communicate effectively with one another to ensure maximum productivity as well as safety. Various options for establishing Marsnet include communication through satellites, or internet cables laid out on the surface. By using the same technologies implemented on Earth, astronauts can establish websites, forming the first Martian communication network. The Internet on Mars is valuable in the sense that it gives crew the opportunity to entertain themselves and communicate effectively with their counterparts on Earth.

E. PSYCHOLOGICAL FACTORS

The crew will be isolated for a long time, especially considering the mission is more than a year. This could result in a large variety of negative emotions. There will be tension between the crew, depressive symptoms and disturbed sleep cycles could all happen. Scott Kelly has stated that he dealt with loneliness by doing a few things. First, it is important to give time for rest. He stated that a scheduled time to stop working has helped him a lot. New hobbies would also be a good method for combating loneliness. Lastly, making plans with other crew members or friends and family would help the crew with loneliness. This would help them to keep it touch and feel more connected. There is also a way to deal with the anxiety that astronauts face. This is exercise. Physical activity of up to two hours every day can both improve the state of the body mentally and physically. Students have shown that activity and eating well have positive effects mentally. Bad sleep can also affect the crew. In the past, the ISS has faced this by having fixed lighting, noise cancelation with earbuds, sleep masks, relaxation time in schedules, and cozy sleep pods will help with bad sleep. Lack of light can also cause fear. This can simply be fixed by enough lighting and possible roof lighting in the habitat. It can also be important to mentally prepare for the mission beforehand as well as do field expeditions with the team and individual training sessions. Experiencing different cultures, socializing, watching movies, playing board games, and celebrating occasions can all be important to the crew mentally.

Many things affect the mental health of an astronaut including disturbed sleep patterns, team dynamics, exposure to radiation and psychosocial stressors. Solid communication with family and friends can help as well as time for meal preparation, entertainment, gardening, artificial sunlight. These Mars missions will be very stressful and critical at times, so entertainment will be very integral to the crew. Entertainment can release and distract from the stress from everyday life up on Mars. It can also help with relationships. The crew themselves need to be on good terms with each other which can be done by sharing entertainment. Good sleep can improve attention and concentration which will be needed throughout the entire day. It will also leave undesirable sleep behaviors behind. It will also form a routine and especially good techniques which promote good sleep.

F. CLOTHING

Space suits have come a long way since the first time they were ever used. The suits from the mission to the moon are much more bulky and have many designs which are outdated. One of the most recent space suits that have been announced to the public is called AxEMU or Axiom Extravehicular Mobility Unit and has been designed for the next mission to the moon. There are some differences between this suit and what would be optimal for a suit on a mission to Mars, but it has features which will be helpful in all places.

The most important aspect of any space suit is the oxygen carrying capabilities. Normally by having tanks that hold the air. The space suit should have a pack on the back, which contains a fan which assists with air circulation inside the suit. The space suit should also have some type of life support system on it which is accessible. On the back, the space suit should also contain a water storage for use on long missions outside of the habitat. The last thing that would go on the back of the space suit, and one which is semi-unique to Mars, is a contamination control device which would prevent the fine Mars dust from contaminating the inside of the suit.

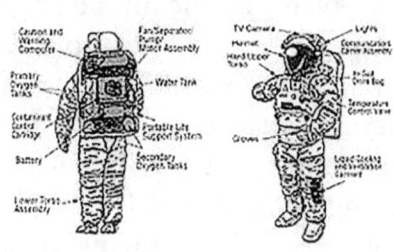

A Diagram of Useful Space Suit Components

There are also other accessories necessary on space suits. Lights, communication devices, and ventilation for cooling liquid running through the suit. There are also some quality of life accessories as well as necessities needed on space suits designed for Mars. Of course, no part of the astronaut can be at all exposed to the outside as it can have damaging, sometimes long lasting effects. Gloves and boots are a necessity, and they would preferably be attached entirely or very securely to the rest of the suit. It would also be nice for the suit to be very lightweight and slim fitting so that operating equipment and moving is easier and faster for the astronaut.

As far as what space suits are physically made of, there is quite a wide range of materials, including nylon, synthetic polymers and other fabric-like materials as well as many types of metals and electrical equipment needed to build the life support systems and other systems needed for a space suit to work properly.

Given that the mission to Mars will be a long period of time, it may be a good idea to have other clothes that are made out of fabrics that are more radiation resistant, as a way of preserving the health of the astronauts, especially as they will be returning to Earth. Experiments have been conducted around using a mixture of lead, resins and fillers to create a very flexible piece of vinyl which has the capability of being radiation resistant. This has huge potential as an extra layer of protection against radiation so that, if need be, a mission in the future could be even longer and the risk of radiation could be even less than normal.

G. FOOD

A key factor for plant growth is air. Plants need air while at the same time absorbing water and nutrients. Hydroponics is a system that uses water to grow plants, without the use of soil. Aeroponics is very similar, however, the roots are in the air and receive nutrients by a mist. Both of these methods are good for space as there is no soil to transmit disease, expanding the lifespan of the plant. Aeroponics has a few more benefits than hydroponics in terms of space exploration. One factor is the water itself. Versions of aeroponics use drastically less water as well as space. In fact, water usage can be reduced by 98 percent. Plants have also been known to grow quicker with aeroponics. This paired with the fact that plants grow faster in space would increase yields heavily. From these factors it can be determined that aeroponics is a good choice for space and plant growth on Mars.

The Aeroponics system is able to grow most plants with some of the best being scallions, microgreens, tomatoes, peppers, and sprouts. If these plants were combined with other plants, the result could be food that is healthy, nutritional and full of energy for the astronauts. With a greenhouse, the astronauts could have a wide variety of foods every day.

Furthermore, a culture of spirulina can be kept somewhere in the habitat. The culture of spirulina can be turned into a supplement that is able to be consumed.. Spirulina is an algae that is highly beneficial for humans to consume. It proves many great health benefits and other nutritional values that can keep the crew members healthy.

With the combination of foods being grown and already brought to Mars, the four crew members are able to survive off of 2,500-3,000 calories a day per crew member. This includes about 3 meals a day for all crew members.

Cost
300,008,205- 355,008,205
Weight
22.563-23.613 metric tons

SOURCES AND CITATIONS

A. WATER

1. Dunbar, B. (n.d.). *Human needs: Sustaining life during exploration.* NASA. https://www.nasa.gov/vision/earth/everydaylife/jamestown-needs-fs.html#:~:text=Because%20electrical%20power%20for%20the,(11%20liters)%20per%20day.
2. *Extracting drinkable water from the Mars Surface.* Northeastern University College of Engineering. (n.d.). https://coe.northeastern.edu/news/extracting-drinkable-water-from-the-mars-surface/#:~:text=The%20

water%20is%20pumped%20into,in%20the%20water%2C%20Hibbard%20says.

3. LLC, A. L. (n.d.). *Puretec industrial water: Deionized water services and reverse osmosis systems.* Reverse Osmosis | Puretec Industrial Water. https://puretecwater.com/reverse-osmosis/what-is-reverse-osmosis

4. Map of Mars showing global concentrations of near-surface water ice 13 ... (n.d.-a). https://www.researchgate.net/figure/Map-of-Mars-showing-global-concentrations-of-near-surface-water-ice-13-Locations-marked_fig3_228628199

5. "mining" water ice on Mars–NASA. (n.d.-b). https://www.nasa.gov/sites/default/files/atoms/files/mars_ice_drilling_assessment_v6_for_public_release.pdf

6. Special REPORT95-10–university of wisconsin–madison. (n.d.-c). https://user-web.icecube.wisc.edu/~araproject/radio/drilling/thermal_rodwell_crrel.pdf

7. *Thermal drill.* Ice Drilling Program. (n.d.). https://icedrill.org/icebits/topic/thermal-drill#:~:text=The%20Electrothermal%20drill%2C%20aka%20the,to%20the%20pressure%20melting%20point.

8. *Water Pump Energy Calculator: Watts and kwh.* Water Pump Energy Calculator: Watts and kWh. (n.d.). https://www.energybot.com/energy-usage/water-pump.html#:~:text=How%20many%20watts%20does%20a,%2C%20size%2C%20or%20other%20factors.

B. CLOTHING

1. Dunbar, B. (n.d.). *Spacesuits.* NASA. https://www.nasa.gov/audience/forstudents/nasaandyou/home/

spacesuits_bkgd_en.html#:~:text=A%20fan%20moves%20the%20oxygen,Extravehicular%20Activity%20Rescue%2C%20or%20SAFER.
2. Lloyd, V. (2023, March 15). *Spacesuit for NASA's Artemis III Moon Surface Mission debuts*. NASA. https://www.nasa.gov/feature/spacesuit-for-nasa-s-artemis-iii-moon-surface-mission-debuts/
3. *What are Space Suits made of?–VTI*. Vinyl Technology. (2023, May 17). https://www.vinyltechnology.com/what-are-space-suits/#:~:text=They%20are%20typically%20constructed%20from,to%20form%20the%20innermost%20layer.

C. WASTE AND HUMAN WASTE

1. Guardian News and Media. (2022, January 29). *NASA asks public to help solve waste recycling for Mars Trip*. The Guardian. https://www.theguardian.com/science/2022/jan/29/nasa-asks-public-to-solve-waste-recycling-mars-trip#:~:text=The%20four%20waste%20products%20Nasa,least%20two%2C%20maybe%20three%20years.
2. Schlieder, S. (2022, March 3). *NASA seeks ideas for handling waste on future human missions to Mars*. NASA. https://www.nasa.gov/ideas-for-handling-waste-future-mars-missions
3. YouTube. (2021, June 12). *The ISS Water Recycling System*. YouTube. https://www.youtube.com/watch?v=AzZxg-hCyZs

In Situ resource utilization
1. "Overview: In-Situ Resource Utilization." *NASA*, 2023, www.nasa.gov/isru/overview. Accessed 22 July 2023.
2. Allen, Carlton, et al. *MARTIAN REGOLITH SIMULANT JSC MARS-1*.

D. CREW SCREENING

1. "Step Closer to Crew Selection for Simulated Mars Mission." *Esa.int*, 2023, www.esa.int/Science_Exploration/Human_and_Robotic_Exploration/Mars500/Step_closer_to_crew_selection_for_simulated_Mars_mission. Accessed 21 July 2023.

E. CREW DAILY ROUTINE

1. Fraeman, Abigail. "Sols 3889-3891: It's Still Rock and Roll to Us!" *NASA Mars Exploration*, 2023, mars.nasa.gov/msl/mission-updates/9439/sols-3889-3891-its-still-rock-and-roll-to-us/. Accessed 19 July 2023.
2. admin. "Solving Space–Running in Space–Space Center Houston." *Space Center Houston*, 4 Aug. 2021, spacecenter.org/solving-space-running-in-space/. Accessed 24 July 2023.

F. ENTERTAINMENT

1. "Free Time in Space." *NASA*, 2015, www.nasa.gov/audience/foreducators/stem-on-station/ditl_free_time/. Accessed 24 July 2023.
2. "Internet." *Marspedia*, 2020, marspedia.org/Internet. Accessed 24 July 2023.
3. "Interplanetary Internet." *Marspedia*, 2020, marspedia.org/Interplanetary_Internet. Accessed 24 July 2023.

G. PRESSURIZATION

1. ISS Payload Hosting Opportunities on Bishop Airlock (nanoracks.com)
2. Nanoracks Bishop Airlock–Wikipedia

3. Nanorack Bishop Airlock Module—Bing images
4. How Much Electricity Does A Sump Pump Use? Find Out—Build Better House

H. OXYGEN SUPPLY

1. Modeling Oxygen Production on Mars | NASA
2. MOXIE Sets Consecutive Personal Bests and Mars Records for Oxygen Production—NASA Mars
3. Components of MOXIE (Illustration) – NASA Mars Exploration
4. Mars Oxygen In-Situ Resource Utilization Experiment (MOXIE)—NASA Mars
5. James Oberg's Pioneering Space
6. How is oxygen made aboard a spacecraft? | HowStuffWorks
7. This Reaction Could Let Us Live on Mars—YouTube
8. How to Make Water and Oxygen on Mars | Science News | Naked Scientists (thenakedscientists.com)
9. Math and Science at Work—Student Edition (nasa.gov)
10. Whole House Ventilation Strategies for Existing Homes | Building America Solution Center (pnnl.gov)

I. INTERPLANETARY COMMUNICATION

1. Phoning Home: Communicating from Mars—Bing video
2. Communications with Earth—NASA Mars
3. Communications with Earth | Mission – NASA Mars Exploration
4. How the Mars Exploration Rovers Work | HowStuffWorks

J. VEHICLES

Links:
1. https://mars.nasa.gov/mars2020/spacecraft/rover/electrical-power/#:~:text=Without%20power%2C%20the%20rover%20cannot,decay%20as%20its%20

Perseverance Rover Power supply
1. http://large.stanford.edu/courses/2017/ph240/black1/#:~:text=To%20date%2C%20the%20two%20energy,been%20sunlight%20and%20radioactive%20decay.

Stanford paper, powering mars mission
1. https://www.newark.com/pdfs/techarticles/tektronix/LIBMG.pdf

Lithium Ion Battery Maintenance
1. https://citylabs.net/technology-overview/nuclear-battery-technology/

Nuclear battery
1. https://www.bas.ac.uk/project/detecting-rare-earth-elements-with-remote-sensing/

REM remote sensing
1. https://blanchard.engr.wisc.edu/res/batteries.htm

Atomic battery
1. https://marsed.asu.edu/mep/wind#:~:text=Scientists%20have%20made%20only%20a,per%20hour%20(62%20mph).

Wind power
1. https://en.wikipedia.org/wiki/Multi-mission_radioisotope_thermoelectric_generator

Radioisotope generator

K. POWER SUPPLY

1. Sabatier Reaction–YouTube
2. Microsoft Word–ICES 2011_Sabatier Revised Manuscript_ID 1021595.doc (nasa.gov)

L. SCIENTIFIC EXPLORATION

1. Electrothermal Drill | Ice Drilling Program
2. Geothermal Drilling Costs | The Driller

THE FIRST MANNED MISSION TO MARS
M.A.R.T.I.A.N. MISSION—MARS ASTRONAUTS RESEARCH TRAVERSE ISRU AND KNOWLEDGE MISSION

ANIKA JHA

TISYA SRIVASTAVA

HANCHEN LIU

GUANGXU ZENG

Jha, Srivastava, Liu, Zeng

ABSTRACT

M.A.R.T.I.A.N. Mission (Mars Astronauts Research Traverse ISRU And kNowledge Mission) represents a groundbreaking endeavor by The Martian Warriors to execute the first manned mission to Mars. This comprehensive scientific report presents a detailed plan for the mission, which encompasses three principal sections: Science, Engineering, and Human Operations(i). The mission's objective is twofold: to conduct extensive scientific exploration and ensure the safe return of the Marsonauts (human crew). Mars, being Earth's closest potentially habitable neighbor, offers promising opportunities to study its dynamic geophysical processes, search for signs of past and present life, and gather critical data about its geological, climatological, and meteorological aspects. The M.A.R.T.I.A.N. Mission is driven by the innate human desire for exploration, knowledge, and the advancement of our civilization into an interplanetary species.

INTRODUCTION

The human spirit of exploration has always been driven by an insatiable thirst for knowledge, constantly seeking to expand our understanding of the cosmos and our place within it. As technology rapidly advances, the dream of sending manned missions to other planets has transformed into an imminent reality. In this context, The Martian Warriors have meticulously crafted M.A.R.T.I.A.N. Mission (Mars Astronauts Research Traverse ISRU And kNowledge Mission), heralding humanity's first venture to Mars.

This report provides an in-depth and structured account of the M.A.R.T.I.A.N. Mission, encompassing three vital domains: Science, Engineering, and Human Operations.(ii) The mission is set to commence in 2029 with two distinct phases: Precursor + cargo launch in 2029, followed by the crew + equipment launch in 2031. The primary objectives of the mission are to undertake extensive scientific exploration and, most importantly, ensure the safe transit and return of the Marsonauts, the intrepid human crew.

M.A.R.T.I.A.N. Mission presents an opportunity to answer one of the most profound questions in human history: Are we alone in the universe, or is life a common occurrence beyond Earth? By seeking evidence of past and present life on Mars, this mission may shed light on humanity's place in the cosmic fabric.

As we set our sights on Mars, we are poised to enter a new phase of human evolution—one that entails becoming an interplanetary species. The success of the M.A.R.T.I.A.N. Mission will be a testament to our capability, resilience, and scientific prowess, inspiring a cascade of future space missions that will strengthen our understanding of the universe and, perhaps, lead to the eventual colonization of Mars and other celestial bodies.

While various space agencies have embraced the idea of a manned mission to Mars(iii), the M.A.R.T.I.A.N. Mission is unique in its comprehensive plan focused solely on reaching the Red Planet. This report delves into the intricate details of the mission, elucidating the roles of the Science, Engineering, and Human Operations departments. The successful execution of the M.A.R.T.I.A.N. Mission will be one small step in our space exploration journey, but one giant leap in our civilization.

SCIENCE

MISSION OBJECTIVES

The scientific/mission objectives for M.A.R.T.I.A.N. Mission are:

1. Search for Life and Indication of Habitability
   a. Paleontology: The search for past life
      i. To find evidence of past life on Mars
      ii. To explore geomorphic features
      iii. To find and study features that suggest that Mars once had a habitable environment
      iv. To find and study features that reveal more about when Mars became/was habitable/inhabitable
      v. To find and study features that show evidence of liquid water on the surface of Mars (recurring slope lineae)
      vi. To perform archeology – looking for imprints, fossils, organic evidence, etc.
   b. Astrobiology: The search for present life
      i. To find evidence of present life on Mars
      ii. To examine and understand recurring slope lineae (RSL)
      iii. To explore Martian habitats that possibly have microbial life:
         1. Caves
         2. Salts and brines
         3. Ground ice
   c. Indicators of First Genesis life, past and present (similar to life on Earth):
      i. To find presence of liquid water/water ice
      ii. To find organic compounds
      iii. To find other signs of First Genesis life
   d. d. Indicators of Second Genesis life:
      i. To detect and observe abnormal behavior in environmental components (regolith, atmosphere, etc.)
2. Geology & Geography
   a. Samples

i. To conduct tests and experiments on samples and observe their behavior
ii. To understand their composition (presence of certain elements, organic compounds, minerals, etc.) and infer other information from this data
iii. To find out more about the precious metals and other elements present on Mars, and in particular areas (making geologic maps)
iv. To begin mapping the distribution of elements on Mars (this mission will be particularly focused on Erebus Montes and other surrounding areas in Arcadia Planitia, but future missions can continue mapping them)
v. To bring samples of Mars back to Earth

b. Water & Ice
   i. To verify areas of SWIM ice consistency maps, predictions for where water ice exists on Mars, and other beliefs/predictions/expectations of subsurface water ice
   ii. To make more specific and detailed maps of water ice on Mars (future missions can continue what we start in Erebus Montes and map ice all over Mars in detail)
   iii. To check for signs of past/present life in/around water ice
   iv. To check the purity of water ice, and the impurities present (from which we can infer more about Mars)
   v. To take some quantities (in solid and liquid form) back to Earth for further comparison and investigation
   vi. To check whether there are any abnormalities or differences with water ice from different areas of

Mars, different depths underground, etc. and find patterns
    vii. To analyze and observe RSL
1. See whether they are flows of liquid water, brines, or other material
2. See if different RSL are made of different material and find patterns
3. See how long and frequently RSL occur
4. Record RSL behavior and videotape/photograph them

c. c. Martian History
    i. To explore, experiment on, analyze, and understand Hesperian Noachian terrain and rocks
    ii. To determine the age of different areas, samples, rocks, etc. in and around Erebus Montes using geochronology methods like potassium argon dating (which can, with future missions, be done all across Mars to better understand Mars's history)
    iii. To track the age of subsurface ice (and any other water found) on Mars To understand since when RSL have been occurring

d. Geological Features
    i. To explore, understand, analyze, and learn more about the geological features of Erebus Montes and other intriguing features nearby:
1. Glaciation & ground ice
2. Broad, piedmont-like lobes
3. Filled/buried craters
4. Lobate debris aprons (LDAs)
5. Impact craters (some even expose ice)
6. Lava tube caves (and caves in general)
7. Amazonian lava flows
8. Lineated valley fills (LVFs)

9. Dust devils and their tracks
10. Polygonal patterned ground
11. Ancient river valleys
12. Linear ridge networks
  e. Maps of Erebus Montes (that can extend to make maps of Mars via future missions)
    i. To initiate the development of different types of maps of Mars that are much more detailed than our current maps (all these maps will be available online and offline, and online maps will have interactive features like search options):
      1. Water ice presence/density map (already in progress with the SWIM mission, we will begin making the map more detailed and filling in data gaps in the Erebus Montes region, soon spreading to others)
      2. Life probability map (a map that highlights areas on Mars where it is/was more probable to support life)
      3. Geological map
        a. Distribution of rocks, soil, and sediment
        b. Distribution of rock types
        c. Distribution of elements and compounds
        d. Rock history
3. Climatology & Meteorology
  a. To take detailed observations of Martian climate, weather, and atmosphere (atmospheric conditions)
  b. To observe, analyze, and learn more about strange/infrequent/seasonal weather occurrences on Mars (like rare lightning, dust storms, aurorae, precipitation, etc.)
4. Humans on Mars

a. To explore the feasibility of human settlement on Mars
b. To demonstrate and verify equipment and techniques to sustain human life on Mars, including but not limited to:
  i. In situ resource utilization (ISRU)
  ii. Agricultural experiments (aquaponics, hydroponics, and algae growth)
  iii. Life support technology
  iv. Recycling strategies

LANDING SITE SELECTION

The M.A.R.T.I.A.N. Mission's landing site will be Erebus Montes (central coordinates: 35.66°N, 185.02°W), a group of mountains located in Arcadia Planitia (Figure 1). The unique SROIs and RROIs it possesses make it a convenient location to land and study. These include exposures of Hesperian-Noachian transition terrain; Ice-rich LDAs; Amazonian-aged subsurface ice abundance in the region; Home to multiple recent ice-exposing impact craters; Contact between multiple episodes of Amazonian volcanism; Strong possibility of lava tube caves; Mountains present an interesting point for geographical research; It is near the dichotomy boundary of Mars, which is extremely important for us to learn more about; Methanogens may be present in the region. All of these unique characteristics listed are also easily accessible from our landing location in Erebus Montes.

Compared to other alternatives, Erebus Montes is what has all the necessary (and additional) features, thus making it the best location for the first manned mission to Mars as it is explored, but not thoroughly, and has all the necessary resources for M.A.R.T.I.A.N. Mission. Other candidates that were debated upon includes: a relatively unexplored place in

Arcadia Planitia (which is what we chose: Erebus Montes), Arsia Mons (abundant subsurface water ice is not confirmed), Meridiani Planum (did not have as many SROIs as Erebus Montes), and an area in Hellas Planitia (terrain is complicated to land on, launching off of it will prove to be difficult as it is a crater, in case of failure the humans will be trapped).

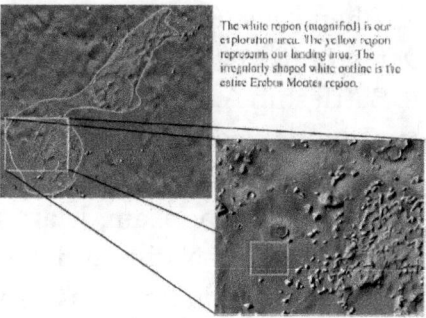

Figure 1: Erebus Montes, mission landing site

SCIENTIFIC INSTRUMENTATION TO TAKE

There is a vast amount of scientific instrumentation that we must take to fulfil our scientific objectives, conduct the necessary experiments & analysis, gather essential data, and maintain communication. Below are the scientific instruments we will be bringing to Mars (All of these technologies will certainly advance in the future, so our mission will use the latest technology as long as it doesn't weigh more. All the vehicles will have communication apparatus that include high-gain and low-gain antenna, receiving and transmitting antenna, transponders, repeaters, etc.):

Collector (one of our two unmanned rovers): Gamma-Ray Spectrometer Suite (GRS), Radar Imager for Mars Subsurface Experiment (RIMFAX), Mars Odyssey Neutron Spectrometer (MONS), Chemistry and Camera (ChemCam).

Finder-Catcher (one of our two unmanned rovers): Planetary Instrument for X-ray Lithochemistry (PIXL), Scanning Habitable Environments with Raman & Luminescence for Organics

& Chemicals (SHERLOC), SuperCam, Complex Molecules Detector (CMOLD), Sample Analysis on Mars (SAM).

Battleship A, B, C, & D (our four unmanned drones, different combinations of the following instrumentation will be docked on the drones based on where they will be primarily flying): Mastcam-Z, SuperCam, Mars Environmental Dynamics Analyzer (MEDA), Nadir and Occultation for MArs Discovery (NOMAD), Radiation Assessment Detector (RAD), Shallow Radar (SHARAD), Mars Color Imager (MARCI).

Scientific equipment that the Marsonauts will use, in the Laboratory Module, during EVOM exploration, and other places: Scanning Electron Microscope (SEM), Raman Spectrometer, Qubit 4 Fluorometer [for DNA, RNA, and Protein quantification], Petrographic Microscope, typical geology laboratory equipment (rock splitter, wafering saws, grinding and polishing wheels, a vacuum impregnation system, an ultrasonic bath, hot plates and an oven), Water Photometer, geochronology instrumentation, necessary experiment apparatus supplies (flasks, test tube holders, Bunsen burners, etc.)

OBSERVATIONS/ANALYSIS/DATA-GATHERING TO ACCOMPLISH

The aim of M.A.R.T.I.A.N. Mission is to accomplish as much scientific exploration as possible. Below is the data and observations/analysis we will be gathering/conducting:

Microbial Studies: Collection of samples from potential Martian habitats like caves, salts, brines, and ground ice, followed by on-site analysis and experiments to detect and study potential microbial life.

Recurring Slope Lineae (RSL) Studies: Detailed observations and analysis of RSL to determine their composition, behavior, and frequency of occurrence, which could provide insights into the presence of liquid water on Mars.

Water Ice Analysis: Comprehensive analysis of water ice samples, including checking for signs of past/present life, assessing purity, identifying impurities, and comparing ice from different regions and depths to identify patterns.

Precious Metal Exploration: Investigation and analysis of the distribution of precious metals and other valuable elements on Mars to understand the planet's resource potential.

Climate/Atmospheric Data and Anomalies: Monitoring and analyzing Martian atmosphere and climate, including weather occurrences such as rare lightning, dust storms, aurorae, and precipitation to better comprehend Martian climatology.

Human Mission Data: Gathering data on the feasibility of human settlement on Mars, including testing in situ resource utilization (ISRU) techniques, agricultural experiments, and life support technology. This data will help assess the challenges and requirements for sustaining human life on the planet.

Geological Feature Studies: In-depth exploration and analysis of various geological features, such as glaciation, ground ice, lobate debris aprons, impact craters, lava tube caves, and ancient river valleys, to understand the planet's geological history.

Martian History and Age Determination: Using geochronology methods like potassium-argon dating to determine the ages of different Martian areas, samples, rocks, and subsurface ice, shedding light on Mars's geological timeline.

Development of Detailed Maps: Initiate the development of detailed maps of Mars, including water ice density maps, life probability maps, and geological distribution maps. These maps will provide valuable information for future missions and scientific research. Human Health and Psychological Studies: Continuous monitoring and analysis of the physiological and psychological health effects on the crew during the mission to understand the impact of long-term space travel on humans.

Technology Assessment: Evaluation of the performance and reliability of the mission's technological instruments, spacecraft, and equipment, which will aid in future mission planning and improvement.

Communication and Data Transmission: Ensuring reliable communication and data transmission between Mars and Earth throughout the mission to ensure the successful retrieval of valuable scientific data.

Assessment of In-situ Resource Utilization: Detailed evaluation of the effectiveness and efficiency of ISRU techniques to determine their viability for future missions and potential human settlement on Mars.

Remote Sensing Data: Collection and analysis of remote sensing data to study Martian surface conditions, including soil properties, temperature variations, and potential hazards. Robotic Exploration and Imaging Data: Analyzing and using imaging, catalog, and other data from the unmanned vehicles to augment the understanding of Mars' surface, atmosphere, and geological features.

ENGINEERING

CHALLENGES

There is an abundance of engineering challenges for the first manned mission to Mars. This report will thrive to tackle these challenges including but not limited to: Fuel and trajectory; Habitat construction & design; Vehicles (manned and unmanned); Spacesuit for Marsonauts; Food, water, and air provisions; Sanitation for the Marsonauts and their habitat; Recycling systems; Planetary protection; Overall weight and cost constraints; Optimization and redundancy.

Mission Timeline, Trajectory, & Launch Windows

Before delving deep into these topics, we must clarify our trajectory and time on Mars. The mission timeline is as follows:

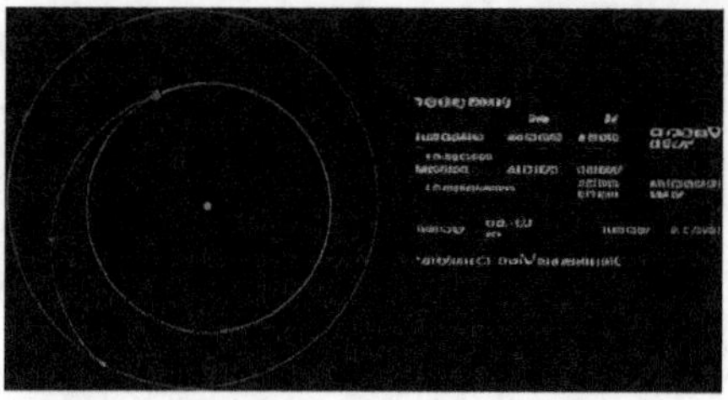

Precursor + cargo launch (Figure 2.1):

Launch date/Earth departure → January 16th, 2029 (Buffer time: 2 weeks) Arrival on Mars → July 11th, 2029

Transfer period: 176 days

Time on Mars: indefinite

Figure 2.1: Precursor + cargo launch

Crew + equipment launch (Figure 2.2):

Launch date/Earth departure → March 11th, 2031 (Buffer time: 2 weeks) Arrival on Mars → October 5th, 2031

Departure from Mars → January 11th, 2033 (Buffer time: 4 weeks)

Reentry on Earth → July 22nd, 2033

Transfer period1,EM (Earth departure): 208 days

Transfer period2,ME (Mars departure): 192 days

Time on Mars: 1.27 years (ample to conduct extensive scientific research and minimal enough for the first humans on Mars to experience reasonable intensities of the unavoidable physiological and psychological effects of space, explained in the Human Operations section)

We will use LOX/LH2 (liquid oxygen and hydrogen) propellant for both launches from Earth, but the ascent vehicle on Mars (for the crew and their returning equipment e.g., samples) will use LOX/LCH4 (liquid oxygen and methane) propellant to use in-situ resource utilization and reduce weight, as SPEM (Sabatier Process and Electrolysis Machine) will make methane and oxygen using the abundant carbon dioxide on Mars.

Precursor + Cargo Launch

Now, we must discuss the first launch. The precursor + cargo payload, launching on January 16th, 2029 and reaching Mars on July 11th, 2029, will land in Erebus Montes in Arcadia

Planitia (32.800, -178.830). It will carry the technology that creates the habitat (the MIML) and the unmanned vehicles (Collector, Finder-Catcher, Battleships A-D).

HABITAT

Our mission's habitat, a crucial facet of any manned mission to Mars, is called MIM, which stands for "Made in Mars". This is because our habitat will be created almost solely with the materials already available on Mars. Here is the detailed plan for habitat creation:

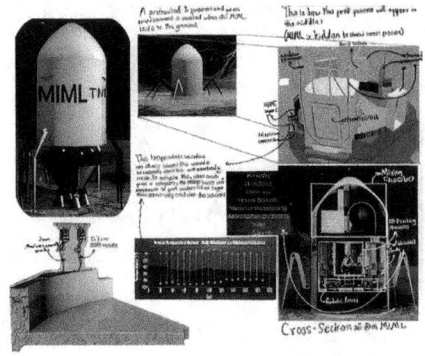

Figure 3.1: MIML design, description, print process, and details

In the precursor + cargo launch, the MIML (Made in Mars Lander) will be sent to Mars along with our autonomous and remote-controlled rovers and drones. The design of the MIML is shown in Figure 3.1.

The MIML is a rounded cone (8 m by 8 m) containing advanced 3D printing nozzles with premade architectural pieces. It has spider-like metal limbs that provide mobility. Equipped with an ASRG, solar panels all over, and pre-charged battery, it is able to generate the necessary power it needs (3 kWh + 70 kWh/kg to melt HDPE). One of our 2 unmanned rovers, Collector, has sensors (labeled in Figure 5.1) that allow it to find necessary resources to create Martian concrete. Martian concrete is a material made from ice, calcium oxide, and

Martian aggregate, which are all found easily on the Red Planet, hence demonstrating ISRU. These materials will be collected by Collector, which we will launch along with the MIML, and fed into the mixing chamber within it. The details of the mixing chamber are shown in Figure 3.2.

After developing Martian concrete, the MIML's high resolution cameras will help the mission control center walk it to a flat and wide terrain to start building the habitat. It will land in Erebus Montes, but it needs ample space to construct our habitat modules, which it will scout in its surroundings. Once we drive it to the desired location (most likely right beside the landing point), it will seal to the ground and create a pressurized and protected print environment that will hold against Martian dust devils and storms, rapid temperature changes, and other harsh climate factors.

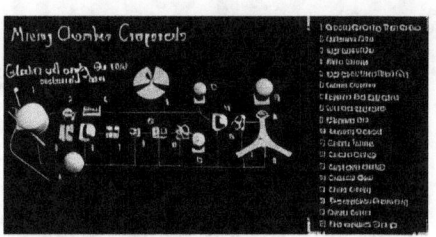

Figure 3.2: MIML Mixing Chamber

Finally, it will start printing the first module (the designs will be programmed into its system) base up, using two printing nozzles that are placed 3 cm apart: one printing HDPE (a highly recyclable thermoplastic that provides temperature insulation and radiation protection) and one printing the Martian concrete (which enables further radiation protection, stable structure, and the capability of creating sloped overhangs). During the print process, robotic arms within the MIML will place lightweight prefabricated parts (airlocks, window structures, glass, pipes, toilets, sinks, shelves) wherever necessary.

This process will repeat to create three modules interconnected via airlocks that serve various purposes to our Marsonaut crew, and a fourth that is separated from the system.

Speaking of which, MIM's design is depicted in Figure 4. It is a modular habitat with 4 main hexagonally structured areas. All modules have basic communication apparatus and a storage compartment. It is expected to have a power consumption of

9 kWh on average (max usage 12 kWh). It will have a foldable solar panel supply extending 180 sq. m which can provide 2 kWh, and a 10 kWh Kilopower unit.

The central unit, which is the largest (7.3 m in diameter and 6 m tall), is called the Communal Module. As the name suggests, this is the place that all four Marsonauts will use for everyday activities. It consists of: a main lounge for discussion, self-entertainment, recreational activities, relaxation, and/or recuperation; four separate bedrooms for the Marsonauts; two bathrooms with bathing, hygiene, and toilet facilities; laundry and clothing storage; a kitchen; and a yoga and exercise station. There is a mezzanine level accessible by a ladder that stores spare parts, a small 3D printer, and extra supplies (oxygen, food, water, hydrogen, nitrogen, seeds, fish eggs, and spacesuits) for backup that can last the Marsonauts over one month in case all fails. There is an airlock-bound room before exiting the module which stores the four spacesuits to protect the internal habitat and living space from Martian dust and possible pathogens. Adjacent to the suits is a sanitation facility using liquid nitrogen spraying that ensures the suits remain usable and relatively clean. The suits will be cleaned once every week, and more/less frequently if required.

The Communal Module is directly connected to food and water resources (Life Module) on its left, and the lab (Laboratory Module) on its right.

The Life Module (5 m in diameter and height) is where the hydroponics garden and aquaponics experimentation will be set up. It boasts the largest window in the entire habitat, providing direct sunlight to the plants. This window will be openable so that the Martian atmosphere's carbon dioxide can be used by plants initially, if human-generated carbon dioxide is not enough to sustain them (there will be a filter installed in the open part to ensure that CO_2 is the only thing that enters). An additional artificial light will be installed for when dust storms block the window (which will be manually cleaned whenever required). The Marsonauts will not be exposed to extreme radiation when in the Life Module as the window is made of UV-resistant glass and coated with a thin layer of gold to reflect and absorb most of the excess radiation.

It also has some biology, botany, and scientific equipment to conduct tests and experiments on the aquaponics system, and parts of the hydroponics system as well. It has some shelves (storage facility) to store scientific equipment borrowed from the Laboratory Module, and packed food.

The air between the Life Module and the Communal Module is shared to maintain a symbiotic relationship with the Marsonauts and their food: the oxygen generated by the plants will be used by the humans, and the carbon dioxide exhaled will be essential to the plants. The module's exit airlock has two pump areas on the door to collect water harvested from SPEM (Sabatier Process and Electrolysis Machine) and SIXUR (Subsurface Ice eXtraction Using RedWater) in the water-storage canisters to streamline the water collection process (so that the Marsonauts need not exit and enter frequently only to retrieve water).

The Laboratory Module (6 m in diameter and 5 m in height) has all the scientific, technological, and advanced communication equipment. It is the main link point in the habitat for communication with Earth, although all modules are capable of this. It has 4 advanced computing stations (for all four Marsonauts) with a laptop, desktop, tablet, phone, clock, mouse, keyboard, and digital notebook at each one. The center has all sorts of analysis screens and scientific equipment (as mentioned in the Science section), with graphs and data regularly updated by the crew that are constantly transmitted back with Earth. The Laboratory Module shares air with the Communal Module, but to conserve air and power, the airlock is only opened when the module is being used.

Finally, the Storage and Emergency Module (5 m in diameter and 4 in height), disconnected from all other modules, is a backup separate habitat module that can be activated in case of emergency to provide the Marsonauts a pressurized, warm, and breathable environment until MIM can be fixed, using a separate ASRG for power. It will be used to safely store the Martian samples we are returning with Earth after scientific analysis and experimentation is done on them in the Laboratory Module. (Equipment stored in the mezzanine level of the Communal Module is also stored here, and more can be retrieved as the mezzanine level is accessible from both inside by ladder and outside via an opening hatch at the top.)

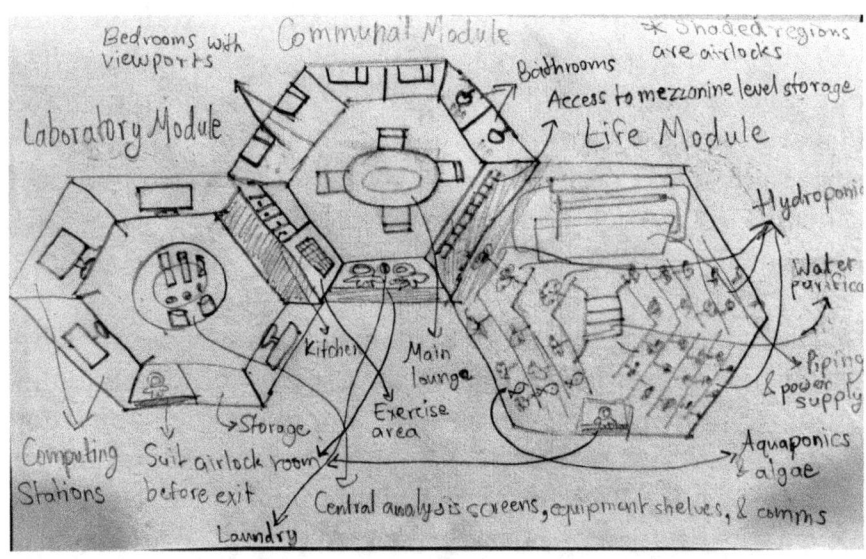

Figure 4: MIM Habitat design (corners are sharp for drawing purposes, real habitat will be rounded and having dome overhangs)

Vehicles (in the precursor mission + cargo launch)

Let us reinstate the point that along with the MIML, 2 self-driven rovers (Figure 5.1, 5.2) and four autonomous drones

(Figure 6) will also be launched. Collector is the first rover, which has the sole purpose of collecting resources for the MIML and perhaps the Marsonauts. Finder-Catcher is the second rover, which will scout the terrain in and around Erebus Montes before the Marsonauts arrive. All our machinery is shielded with aluminum/lead layers to protect them from radiation.

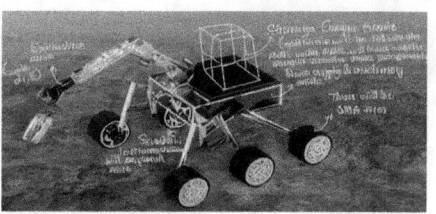

Figure 5.1: Collector rover design

Collector (Figure 5.1) will be designed to be as lightweight, fast, durable, compact, and efficient as possible. It will carry empty and light chambers to store materials and resources to bring them back to the MIML and/or the Marsonauts. Its instrumentation will allow it to locate ice, calcium oxide, and aggregate for Martian concrete, along with robotic arms and drills that extract them. It will also keep a data catalog that tracks where all these resources were available (using the Mars relay network to determine their location), how deep they were in the ground (the drill measures distance), and how much was found (mass). It will have a usage of about 3 kWh/100 km + 2 kWh for scientific equipment, which its ASRG and overhead solar panels will provide.

Finder-Catcher will be designed similarly to Perseverance, but will have SMA wheels, lack some of Perseverance's scientific equipment, have a larger sample storage chamber, and will be smaller and lighter. Finder-Catcher has certain instrumentation (as mentioned in the Science section) to search for biosignatures, other evidence of past and/or present life, gather data about elements in Martian geology, find clues about Mars's history via geomorphic features, take note of locations where Marsonauts should visit and explore, and record weather. It has roughly the same power consumption as Collector and will

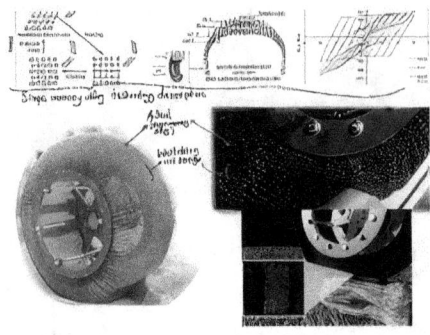

Figure 5.2: SMA Tires

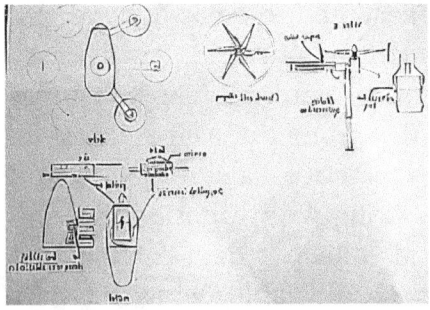

Figure 6: Battleships (drones) design

have the same power supply components.

Both rovers (and the manned vehicle, EVOM) will use a new type of wheel design currently being developed by NASA termed Shape Memory Alloy (SMA) tires (Figure 5.2). These tires are composed of a nickel and titanium alloy (nitinol) that is ductile like other metals but has a special atomic structure that resumes its original shape upon bending, stressing, or deformation. This specific arrangement of atoms requires the least amount of energy compared to alternative arrangements, which causes the atoms to naturally fall back into this arrangement when deformed (as once the energy is no longer being applied, the atoms go back to their low-energy state). This wheel technology allows our vehicles to easily traverse over jagged rocks and tough Martian terrain, while also providing significant traction.

Meanwhile, the drones (Figure 6) will primarily be used for mapping and imaging Martian landscape, locating subsurface water ice, examining the Martian atmosphere, and communication (they have receiving and transmitting antenna equipped with repeaters and transponders).

The drones (named Battleship A, B, C, and D) are useful to the mission as they collect valuable and insightful data about the

Martian environment and provide a reliable and quick method for this mission's communication. The orbiters that currently surround Mars are primarily used for communication with Earth. So, instead of using them for mission communications between the Marsonauts on the surface (as that will most likely prove to be inconvenient, complicated to set up, and unnecessary), these 4 drones can help the Marsonauts communicate with one another within the mission. This is also advantageous as built-in radio communication within the spacesuits is too close-range (although these will remain available for their simplicity, and also in case of emergencies).

Regarding the design of Mars drones, there is not much difference from drones on Earth, except for higher lift requirements. Each drone will have six rotors, each with six slender blades, and an external culvert with a large opening on the top and a slightly restrained middle and lower part. Such a structure improves lift. The center of the propeller has a downward-extending shell that spans the connection of the transmission shaft, reducing dust accumulation. (The heat dissipation port can be closed.) The motor casing has a downward sloping opening to provide heat dissipation for the motor. Of course, dust cannot be completely avoided, so the casing can be disassembled and cleaned at the base if required. There is a hidden retractable landing gear inside the rotor arm. In order to take off and land on any terrain, the laser rangefinder will measure when landing, adjust the height of each landing gear, and prevent the drone from falling down on the slope. The laser rangefinder is below each motor. In case of a dust storm, the laser rangefinder cannot be used. So, during landing, each landing gear will feel pressure. When a landing gear is subjected to significant force and the gyroscope senses the inclination of the drone, the height of that landing gear can be lowered, until all landing gears are under pressure, and the same applies to other landing gears. Two modes cannot be activated simultaneously. If encountering a dust storm, it is best to land before it engulfs the drone, close the heat sink, and prepare for dust prevention.

Each drone uses 6 kWh for flight and instrumentation. There are 4 small solar panels on the side of the drone (adds up to 8, two opposite sides add up to 16). Each drone operates for 2 hours, and then lands to recharge. Recharging takes 2.5 hours. When the Marsonauts arrive, the drones can come back to MIM to charge, as recharging at the base only takes 1.5 hours. There is a backup battery on each drone that can be used to fly them back to the habitat for safety in case solar power is not available. There is a universal connection port under the drone which will carry various scientific research equipment as needed (50-70 kg capacity). The antenna above each drone is directly connected to MIM, the Marsonauts' phones, the EVOM (our manned vehicle), and SIXUR for mission communication.

The reason we are sending these unmanned vehicles to Mars, just before the MARTIAN Mission, is to conserve the Marsonauts' time and effort: Locating unique/ interesting/ promising locations around the landing site beforehand, developing an active mission enclosed communication system, taking samples of interesting rocks and storing them for further research, and preparing and keeping track of the activities in Erebus Montes allows the Marsonauts to immediately maximize their potential and accomplish much more work knowing the first particular places to explore and what samples to experiment on arrival, using their time in a much more efficient and effective way. We don't want the crew to waste time doing things that autonomous robots can. The Marsonauts can use their time much better with this autonomous and working machine-human integration as compared to reaching Erebus Montes without a solid plan for investigation and little-to-no idea of what to look for/what might be found.

CREW + EQUIPMENT LAUNCH

Let us shift to the primary part of M.A.R.T.I.A.N. Mission: the crew + equipment launch. The hydroponics and aquaponics set-up, scientific payload, packed food, backup & spare materials, spacesuits, recycling & sanitation systems, and the Marsonaut crew will be sent in a launch on March 11th, 2031 and reach Mars on October 5th, 2031. They will spend 1.27 years on the Martian surface, before leaving on January 11th, 2033 and reentering Earth on July 22nd, 2033. The Marsonauts will spend the first seven Sols of the mission setting up their habitat, and they will be equipped with sufficient food and water supply for this time period. The landing coordinates will be determined based on the data collected by the precursor + cargo launch to ensure that the site is a safe distance away from the landing site of the previous launch, provides easy accessibility to water, is a flat terrain, and is near the habitat.

SPACESUITS

When planning a manned mission to Mars, human safety is of utmost priority. When our Marsonauts will stand on the surface of Mars, they will inevitably be faced with multiple threats to their physiological health: the unparalleled solar and cosmic radiation, extreme temperatures, low pressure, microgravity, lack of breathable air, food and water scarcity, and toxic compounds hidden in regolith. Mars's hostile environment will be an arduous challenge to overcome, but not impossible. It is our responsibility to develop a perfect spacesuit that can withstand all these harsh conditions and provide comfort, dexterity, and essentials for extended time periods during EVAs. Here is how we accomplish this:

Figure 7: MIT BioSuit Technology, Design, and Details

The BioSuit, which is a spacesuit currently being designed by students and professionals at the Massachusetts Institute of Technology (MIT), is promising for missions to Mars. It is forecasted to be formally developed, tested, and fit for our mission by 2031, so we plan to use its technology (Figure 7).

Instead of traditionally using gas to pressurize an astronaut's body (which limits the range of mobility and comfort), our spacesuits will use a form-fitting combination of powerful elastic fabric and structure to provide at least 4.3 psi/29.648 kPa of pressure (one-third of sea-level atmospheric pressure on Earth, approximately the pressure felt on Mount Everest). Not only will this approach allow for incredible dexterity and comfort, but it will also be safer and more redundant. If an abrasion or micrometeoroid puncture were to occur, sudden decompression would not happen. Instead, the tear could be covered with a specially engineered bandage.

The inner layer is the skin-tight pressurizing bodysuit, and the outer layer is a combination of various fabrics and materials that provide radiation protection, thermal insulation, structure, and micrometeoroid, water, and flame resistance. The spacesuit will be coated with a thin layer of fluorescent cyan pigment to make spotting Marsonauts easy with a bright color contrast against Mars's background.

The complete suit utilizes an advanced technique of multilayered 3D knitting to deliver compression. It leverages versatile polyethylene fibers that possess both flexibility and high tenacity. These fibers enable the suit to offer pressure, regulate temperature, and provide partial protection against radiation. They also contain an inertial measurement unit, an accelerometer, a gyroscope, and onboard machine-learning algorithms to provide real-time sensor information. To enhance the ease of donning/doffing the suit, a two-layer design was employed for the 3D knit sleeve. It consists of an inner base layer with a zipper and an outer high-compression layer that can be securely closed using a magnetic ratchet mechanism. To prevent decompression sickness, the Marsonauts who will be exiting MIM/EVOM will pre-breathe oxygen during the night, and we expect this spacesuit technology to develop enough to reduce the duration required for pre-breathing. We will bring 6 spacesuits to ensure redundancy.

VEHICLES AND EQUIPMENT (IN THE CREW + EQUIPMENT LAUNCH)

For the majority of the mission, the Marsonauts will be traveling to various places around the landing site to conduct scientific experiments, analysis, and explore. Therefore, they

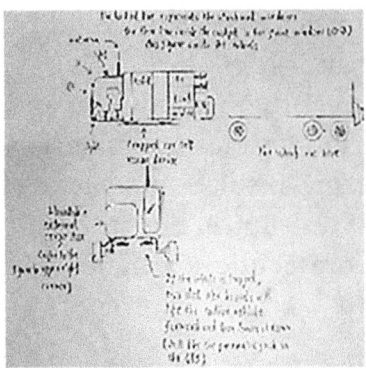

Figure 8.1: EVOM Design (typo in the design: RTG will be replaced by an ASRG)

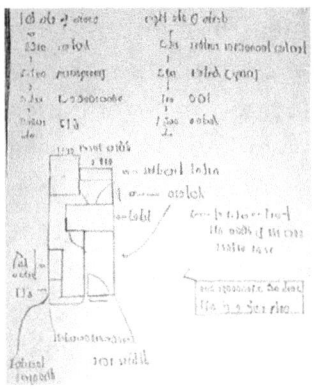

Figure 8.2: EVOM Layout (typo in the design: RTG will be replaced by an ASRG)

require a safe, pressurized, thermally regulated, breathable, fast, and durable vehicle for transportation. The EVOM, Exploration Vehicle on Mars, is exactly this (Figure 8.1, 8.2). It can allow the Marsonauts to go on journeys that last for up to one month, as it has an advanced Stirling radioisotope generator as its primary power supply (65 kWh/100km + 3.5kWh) during low sunlight periods and a solar array covering the entire roof to provide power when the sun is available (to conserve the ASRG's power usage for when it is required).

Inside, the rearmost compartment has a bathroom facility along with supplies, spacesuit, food, water, and oxygen storage (airtight containers) with a capacity (120 kg food[iv], 280 L water[v], 48 kg oxygen[vi]) that can last four Marsonauts up to two weeks with no additional provisions (and if only two Marsonauts planned to go, they could travel for about a month). The front compartment has four spacious seats for the driver, co-driver, and passengers. Underneath the control panel (which has communication, music, GPS, analysis, driving, and other control functionality) and between the seats is space to store scientific instrumentation. It will usually be driven at a speed of 40 km/hr, but has a maximum speed of 60 km/hr. To protect the Marsonauts from radiation, the

EVOM's body is made of HDPE with a thin lead and aluminum coating to reflect and absorb most radiation. The windshield is made of Lexan with a UV-blocking polycarbonate coating (high impact strength, UV-resistant, flame resistant, chemical resistant, transparent). This also makes the vehicle relatively lightweight. The EVOM is slightly larger than a cargo van, measuring about 5.1 meters long, 2.6 meters wide, and 2 meters tall. Two airlocks (on the left and right of the front portion, and one at the back) are present for entry and exit, and the storage compartment has an airtight cabinet to store the spacesuits and ensure that regolith does not enter and circulate within the EVOM. A separate cabinet contains a medical kit, spare tools, and has space for a mini 3D printer to be taken if required. The EVOM will have six individually steerable wheels that have 2 modes: turning in place and regular driving. They will use the same wheel design as Collector and Finder-Catcher: durable nitinol SMA tires.

The Marsonauts will be taking the hydroponics and aquaponics equipment with them in this launch (along with sanitation supplies, a packed food supply, and other equipment). However, during the travel period, they will already set up the hydroponics system and grow plants. This will be incredibly useful, as it will allow them to carry less packed food since they will thrive off of the produce. Our plan is to provide the crew with four months of packed food while they are setting up and cultivating the plants, and when the plants are ready for consumption, the remaining packed food is kept for backup. When they need to shift the hydroponics system into the Life Module after landing, they will harvest the present plants and store them, and pump the current water in the hydroponics system into multiple compact tanks. They will then detach the main large components so that it can be carried out and fit through the Life Module's airlock door, and reassemble it once inside. This process will not be too tedious, as the system's pipes are conveniently detachable, so very little disassembly and reassembly will be required. Meanwhile, the aquaponics system and algae growth extension will be established upon landing itself.

FOOD AND WATER

Our mission will primarily use hydroponics technology to provide food to the Marsonauts. Our hydroponics system revolves around the concept of soil-less cultivation and water recirculation. Plants will be grown in hollow horizontal pipes supplied with nutrient-rich water, eliminating the need for soil, herbicides, or pesticides. This method conserves water as it is filtered and periodically replenished with nutrients, preventing unnecessary absorption by soil. Hydroponics promotes faster and healthier plant growth, subject to analysis by scientists and agriculturists on Earth. The crew will diligently monitor factors like temperature and pH balance to ensure optimal conditions. Hydroponics offers the advantage of rapid adaptation to extreme conditions, a crucial aspect for our mission on Mars.

The hydroponics circulation system and machinery will undergo some changes. Two stations will be introduced: i) for filtering circulating water to eliminate harmful microorganisms like bacteria and mold, and ii) for periodically adding required nutrients to the water for the plants. It will share the Life Module's solar & radioactive power supply upon landing, and use an RTG during space travel periods.

As the hydroponics system will be initially set up during the Earth-to-Mars transition period, the pipes will be detachable to make them easy to carry to MIM's Life Module upon landing.

Our scientific objectives include studying aquaponics and algae growth as well. So, we will be taking a small, portable aquaponics setup connected to an algae growth station to fulfill this target. It can also serve as a redundant element for food supply. Aquaponics is similar to hydroponics in the fact that it maintains plants in water-filled pipes. However, unlike hydroponics, the water in aquaponics contains minimal added nutrients, as the primary source of nutrients comes from the waste of marine life, typically fish. This creates a small ecosystem within the setup. The potential of aquaponics as a self-sustaining system makes it a significant subject for study on Mars. By employing this aquaponics + algae setup, astronauts can explore and analyze marine and microbial life on Mars in greater depth.

The water for these two agricultural systems will be provided either from the water generated through the recycling and waste management systems or from the water we extract from Martian ground. This is a segue into a vital aspect of our mission: providing water.

Water is extremely crucial for us on this mission as it will also be the source of oxygen and food for us. We plan to use a vehicle we have developed (Figure 9) called SIXUR (Subsurface Ice eXtraction Using RedWater) to extract water from Mars. It has a 5 kWh power usage, and is equipped with a rechargeable battery and solar panels to supply this.

Collector, Finder-Catcher, and Battleships A-D will scan the area in and around Erebus Montes to detect water ice reserves on Mars. SIXUR will be brought in the crew + equipment launch, so the best areas to drill will be determined by then. SIXUR will be operated by one Marsonaut, and a driving compartment. The driver's den will feature two gates on both sides and will be subdivided into two

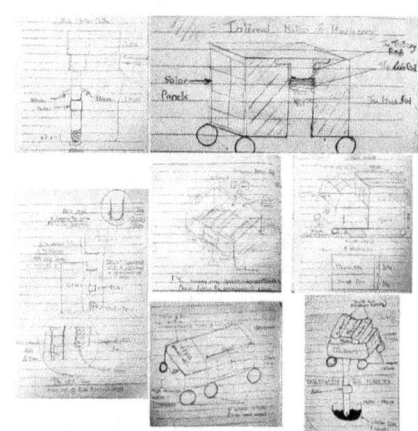

Figure 9: SIXUR Design

sections: i) the driving compartment and ii) the storage area. The driving compartment will occupy 75% of the space, while the storage area will occupy the remaining 25%. Additionally, the driver's den will be equipped with retractable steps, a roof, and windows. These windows and the roof will provide protection to the driver and the den in the event of a dust storm, aligning with the primary objectives of this scientific investigation. The machine itself is waterproofed and has 3 main layers:

1. The two containers to store water, along with space for the pumps, communication machinery, and two retractable antennas for communications will be found in the first layer. To optimize performance in the harsh Martian environment, all components will be coated with a silver surface to efficiently reflect and manage heat, radiation, and light, thus ensuring the equipment's longevity and functionality in extreme conditions.
2. The second layer has the main machinery for the drill (compressed within it), a high quality surveillance camera (connected to MIM), and durable SMA wheels to withstand wear and tear.
3. The rod itself will have a complex system to drill and heat the ice, as well as a pair of blades along the rod that cut through the ground so that we can wedge it out if it is jammed.

The working is explained below:

The SIXUR machine, which will be handled by a Marsonaut, first reaches its destination, after which the drill is sent down from the machine with the help of metal compressors lying within the sub-rod that can be controlled to compress and decompress the rod. Using the drill tip of the rod, it pneumatically drills into the Martian regolith and rocks to reach the subsurface water ice reserves. Once it reaches the ice, an inflatable packer seals the water ice from the atmosphere to avoid sublimation. The heater at the end of the drill's nozzle is then turned on, which gradually melts the ice. After the required amount of ice has melted, the liquid water is sucked into the rod by adjusting the pressure and is directed to the containers, one of which will store water for human use, and the other for oxygen generation. SIXUR will have a penetration rate of 1 m/min. It has a capacity of yielding 2 liters/minute of water extraction from the borehole and will be able to extract 120 liters in an hour. Each container's capacity is this value. After the water is collected in the tanks, the driver will bring the mobile machine back to MIM. This water will be used for our agricultural systems, consumption, hygiene, and oxygen generation.

PLANETARY PROTECTION, RECYCLING, FILTERING, PRESSURIZATION, THERMAL REGULATION, WASTE MANAGEMENT, AND SANITATION SYSTEMS

The NASA-led International Space Station (ISS) serves as a model for human survival in space, maintaining reliable instruments and conditions. The atmospheric pressure on the ISS is maintained at 14.7 psi, equivalent to sea level pressure on Earth, ensuring a steady environment. The 'Environmental Control and Life Support System' (ECLSS) is responsible for maintaining this pressurization. It includes filters to purify the air, scrubbers to remove CO2, and equipment for temperature and humidity regulation. The system also provides and recycles water, as it extracts and purifies water from astronauts' sweat and urine. For our

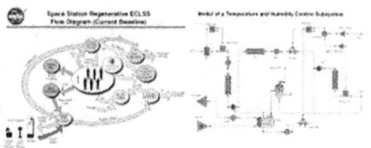

Figure 10: ECLSS Water Recycling and Thermal Regulation System

mission, we will adapt three components (Figure 10) of the ECLSS system for usage in M.A.R.T.I.A.N. Mission: water recycling (UPA, WPA), temperature control (ATCS), and oxygen generation (OGS & OGA, this is part of SPEM). We will also be deriving a lightweight and simpler solution for an FDS in our mission, and scrubbing. Our scrubbing system will direct the CO2 and volatile organic trace gases in MIM to the Life Module. The pressure in our habitat and vehicles will not require much maintenance as they are sealed shut, and air lost during entry and exit can be easily replenished with our oxygen generation and nitrogen supply.

M.A.R.T.I.A.N. Mission strives to avoid pollution on Mars and harmful components from Mars reaching our crew and Earth ("nothing gets in, nothing goes out"). In order to meet these expectations, there will be a rigorous sanitation system for the habitat and machinery, along with top-tier sterilization and decontamination procedures that will occur on a monthly

basis and before returning to Earth. The spacesuits and habitat will be inspected and cleaned weekly, the former with liquid nitrogen spraying and the latter by the crew.

The astronauts' clothes will be cleaned using 80 Wash's nearly waterless and detergent-free laundry technology to increase their lifespan. This laundry machine is based on patented ISP steam technology that kills bacteria (sterilizes) using low-frequency (non-ionizing and non polarizing) radio-frequency based microwaves, and further removes stains, dirt, and odor with the help of dry steam generated at room temperature. It can wash 5 clothes using half a cup of water and no detergent in 80 seconds, and the cycle can be repeated multiple times if needed. The technology is already available for B2B commercial usage and is extremely low cost.

The spacesuit sanitation room features a liquid nitrogen spray that removes about 95% of Martian regolith on the suit using the Leidenfrost Effect. To clean MIM, the Marsonauts will follow procedures similar to the ISS, such as using disinfectant wipes to clean materials touched by hand and dusting off ventilation grids. The Marsonauts will have frequent full body medical check-ups and mental health updates. All samples and spacesuits will be sealed in ampules/airtight containers once unusable/before Earth reentry to ensure no contamination. To maintain the chain of protection, the Marsonauts' module will be transported (while closed) to the enclosed astronaut facility before it is opened and the crew is released on Earth.

FUEL, OXYGEN, AND WATER–SPEM (SABATIER PROCESS AND ELECTROLYSIS MACHINE)

When returning to Mars, we will be using LOX/LCH4 propellant (as mentioned earlier), which demonstrates in-situ resource utilization and greatly reduces the weight and cost of the mission.

The atmosphere of Mars is rich in CO_2 (~95%) and humans generate lots of it as waste. By performing a controlled reaction with this CO_2 and hydrogen[vii] with the Sabatier Process, we can generate methane (sent to tanks for methane storage) and water (a quarter of the water will be pumped into a storage vessel for human use and backup, while 75% will be directed by a different pump into the electrolysis chamber) which will both be stored in a condenser. The water generated can be further split into hydrogen (which will go back into the reaction, creating a closed loop cycle) and oxygen (75% of the oxygen will be used for breathing, and the last quarter will be saved for the propellant) in the electrolysis chamber.

This will all be done using SPEM, the Sabatier Process and Electrolysis Machine (Figure 11). Each of SPEM's 4 reaction units has a water production rate of around 7 l/hr and a methane production rate of around 6.6 kg/hr. As SPEM will be automated and constantly supplied with power (solar and radioactive), human supervision will not be required at frequent intervals. In case of failure, the machine is programmed to halt all processes and send a signal to MIM and EVOM (it is highly improbable that the entire crew will leave the habitat for a long expedition, the EVOM signaling is just a backup) before shutting down, which ensures rapid recovery of the system as human assistance will arrive almost immediately and none of the internal components will remain active during failure.

The Sabatier Process and Electrolysis Machine (SPEM) is a cylindrical device that utilizes the Sabatier reaction to produce methane. Liquid carbon dioxide and liquid hydrogen are introduced from the upper interface. The carbon dioxide will be filtered, and then the carbon dioxide and liquid hydrogen will pass through the diversion pipeline to each reaction unit, go down through the heater, and pass through a diversion pipeline again to enter each reaction kettle. The reactor is high-temperature and high-pressure, and nickel or ruthenium can be pre added as a catalyst. The generated methane and water leave the reactor and gather below the reaction unit. The pipelines of each reaction unit converge again and pass into the condenser to obtain water and methane. The heat generated by the reaction can be used to heat liquid carbon dioxide and liquid hydrogen, and can also drive a Stirling engine. The number of reaction units and size of the reaction kettle can be changed based on the size of the entire machine in future endeavors, but SPEM has 6 reactors per unit and 4 reaction units. It shares the habitat's power supply (and has its own Stirling engine) for its 1.5 kWh usage. The electrolysis component of the machine is derived from the ISS's ECLSS's oxygen generation system (OGS) and assembly (OGA). The separation of water and methane naturally occurs via downward displacement of water, and a more detailed description is written in Figure 11. Additionally, the water in the electrolysis chamber will also be fed in by SIXUR. The "oxygen to cabin" step will be replaced by another pump that directs oxygen inside MIM, as SPEM is outside the habitat to access Mars's CO2.

HUMAN OPERATIONS

CREW CRITERIA

In preparation for this vital mission, the selection of the most qualified personnel is crucial. To achieve this, we have established specific criteria for choosing the four crew members. The crew will have these primary designations in some combination: Astrobiologist/Chemist/Scientist, Geologist/Meteorologist, and Technician/Engineer. Additionally, they should all be experienced in either medical or mathematical and physics fields. A Public Relations/Communications expert will also be part of the crew. To be eligible, all crew members must excel in a comprehensive test that checks their cognitive ability. Educational qualifications require a master's degree in a STEM field from an accredited institution, along with at least two years of relevant professional experience or 1,000 hours of pilot-in-command time on jet aircraft after degree completion. Language proficiency is essential: the crew members must be fluent in at least two languages, English being mandatory. Physical fitness and medical certification are of utmost importance, and astronauts must meet specific medical benchmarks. These benchmarks include 20/20 vision (naturally or with corrective lenses), blood pressure not exceeding 140/90 in a sitting position, a height between 157 and 190 cm (62 and 75 in), and a weight between 50 and 95 kilograms (110 and 209 lb). Additionally, astronauts must have no past addictive history, be psychologically stable, and able to maintain long-distance relationships. Lastly, the crew members should be comfortable consuming meat and seafood while being highly adaptable to a vegan or vegetarian diet.

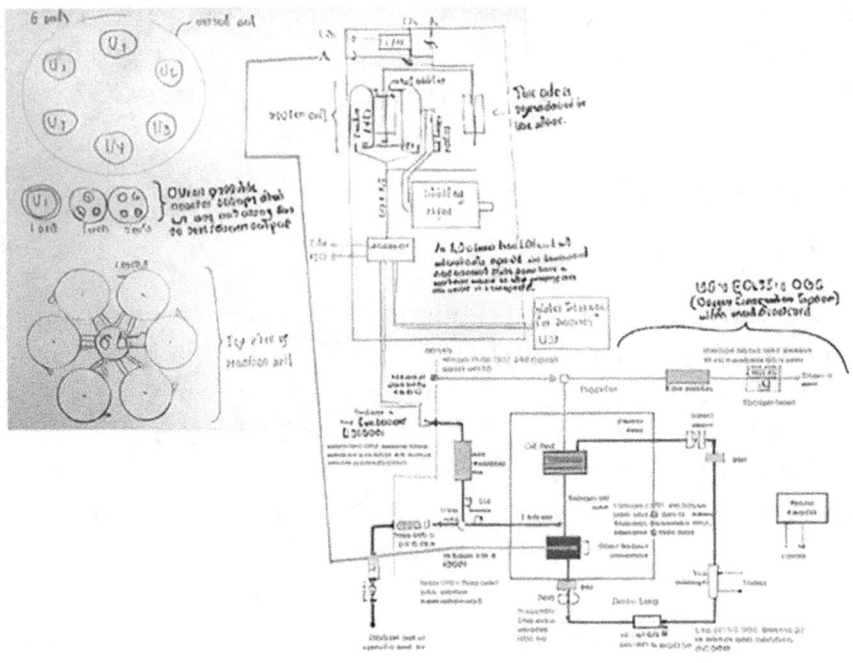

Figure 11: Sabatier Process and Electrolysis Machine (SPEM) Design

OXYGEN

As mentioned in the Engineering section of the report, we will be using SPEM (Sabatier Process and Electrolysis Machine) to generate oxygen from water. Breathing 100% oxygen at normal pressure causes acute oxygen poisoning, leading to symptoms like fluid in the lungs, hyperventilation, chest pains, and uncontrollable coughing with possible blood. To prevent this, the Marsonauts will have to breathe air that contains a mixture of oxygen and nitrogen. To accomplish this, nitrogen will be compressed into specialized containers, ensuring its stability during the journey through space. Cryogenic storage will be leveraged to maintain nitrogen in its liquid state and prevent any loss during transit (when containers are opened, nitrogen will automatically evaporate and mix with the air). Additionally, the Marsonauts that will be going on EVAs will have their airlock-bound bedrooms' air gradually drained of nitrogen throughout the night. Essentially, they will be pre-breathing while resting to save time and avoid decompression sickness during EVAs.

FOOD

In our mission to Mars, we will implement two significant food cultivation methods: hydroponics and aquaponics + algae. Hydroponics will serve as our primary source of food, while aquaponics will be used for experimental purposes and to study the survival of marine life on Mars. For the journey to Mars, we will limit dairy products onboard, with only feasible options like cheese, to reduce weight and optimize resources. To ensure each astronaut receives sufficient nutrients, a medically certified doctor will prescribe individualized sets of medications, including nutrient supplements, multivitamins, painkillers,
or sleeping pills if needed. These medications will be periodically updated by doctors on Earth.

Hydroponics requires constant monitoring, and astronauts will adhere to a scheduled check up routine for this purpose. The Marsonauts will grow a variety of plants (Figure 12) with high nutritional values to ensure that they do not suffer from menu fatigue and get their necessary caloric & nutrient intake (white mushroom, strawberries, spinach, potatoes, turmeric, basmati rice, peas, Brussel sprouts, beetroot, chickpeas). Additionally, there will be 4 months' worth of packaged food for the whole crew to consume while hydroponics food is growing/in emergencies.

PSYCHOLOGICAL EFFECTS AND MITIGATION

The main challenge for a manned mission to Mars is maintaining astronauts' mental well being. The mission to Mars will force four astronauts away from home for 2 and a half years in which they are confined in a small area.

In space, human communication is challenging. Humans are able to conceal their thoughts from others, leading to misconceptions and potentially fatal mistakes. While in such a risky environment, astronauts also have to combat issues such as isolation, depression, homesickness, and disputes with mission control. Selecting resilient and well-prepared astronauts through rigorous psychological evaluations when reviewing applications is important. Rigorous training will also be provided to astronauts going to Mars.

To avoid homesickness, video conferences will be arranged weekly between astronauts and their loved ones. Psychological support from professionals will also be readily available. Due to communication delays on Mars, messages can take up to 20 minutes to reach their recipients, making live conversations with mission control and personnel tedious.(viii) Thus, it is of vital importance to choose resilient members to go on this expedition.

In addition, addressing boredom is important. Entertainment plays a crucial role in reducing the negative impacts of extended space travel. Reading books, watching movies, and listening to music are the best ways to keep astronauts engaged. If additional space is present, bringing VR headsets is also an option, for it allows astronauts to temporarily escape reality. Mission control will send downloaded ebooks, videos, or audio files to entertain the crew. Video games are also an option, as long as they don't hinder productivity. These activities also provide a sense of normalcy despite the vastness of space travel toward Mars. By employing all these measures, we can mitigate the potential negative effects of the mission and ensure the well-being of the Marsonauts.

MARSONAUTS' ROUTINE AND EXERCISE

In space, it is important to be able to stick to a routine and get work done. This allows the mission to produce satisfactory results, making the hefty investment worthwhile. Here is a rough schedule of what an astronaut's daily life might look like (Figure 13). These schedules will vary due to personal preferences and work requirements, but the general structure allows astronauts to complete a plethora of scientific investigations while providing sufficient exercise, leisure, and rest. As for a precise monthly schedule for M.A.R.T.I.A.N. Mission's scientific research and objective fulfillment: it can only be prepared based on the results of the precursor + cargo mission's outcome and discoveries.

It is important to balance an astronaut's work with adequate exercise, rest, and recreation. Thus, astronauts going on the mission to Mars are required to sleep eight hours a day. Astronauts going to Mars are expected to work approximately 9 hours a day (this number may vary based on the task of the astronaut.) Two hours will be dedicated daily to exercise. In addition to physical exercise, the crew will be required to intake 10mg of alendronate (Fosamax) every day. Alendronate is a form of bisphosphonate, a medication that is commonly used to treat osteoporosis. Though bone mass loss in space is ten times as fast as that of osteoporosis, intaking medication will help slow down the process. In a workout, astronauts might follow a routine similar to 1) Pulse raiser (e.g., Advanced Resistive Exercise Device) 2) Dynamic stretches (e.g., Arm circles, lunges with a twist, forward leg swing) 3) Cardiovascular workout (e.g., Running) 4) Resistance exercise (e.g., Therabands) 5) Flexibility workouts (e.g., Pilates, yoga, stretching routine) 6) Static stretches (e.g., shoulder stretch, butterfly stretch, toe touch). The mission will rely on Therabands (resistance bands) to provide astronauts with sufficient exercise. Due to this mission's weight margins, heavier cardiovascular equipment will most likely be brought as well.

COST, WEIGHT, AND FUNDING

Though a manned mission to Mars will be deemed a revolutionary breakthrough, the costs are extremely high. Previous space missions have cost hundreds of billions of dollars. In context, NASA's budget is at 25.4-billion-dollar budget in fiscal year 2023. The rough estimate for M.A.R.T.I.A.N. Mission's payload cost is 6.1 billion dollars, excluding launch vehicles. Funding from multiple organizations is required for the success of this mission, as the first manned mission to Mars should be an international effort. To fund this project, national space agencies such as JAXA, ESU, Roscosmos, CNSA, CSA, and the ISRO will be strongly encouraged to contribute to the cause. Private space agencies such as SpaceX and BlueOrigin will also be invited to aid this project. After the mission, Mars samples will be shared with all space agencies for scientific purposes.

To further encourage funding, this project strongly urges the involvement of non-aerospace companies and the public as well. Donations and sponsors would be greatly appreciated to help reduce the burden of national space agencies. In return for donations, their names will be pasted on the spaceship itself, honoring those who have gone out of their way to help make the mission succeed.

Furthermore, excerpts of an astronaut's daily activities will be recorded. The accumulated clips will be compiled into a documentary by the name of "The Martian Asymptotes". This will help generate more revenue and pay off any pending expenses.

Though the cost of a manned mission is high, the investment is worthwhile. The equipment used on this mission is reusable for an indefinite amount of time, thus helping reduce the prices of future missions to Mars.

Component	Cost (in USD dollars)	Weight (in kg)
Food (hydroponics, aquaponics + algae)	300,000	126
Thermal Regulation System	5,000,000	120
Water Recycling System	100,000,000	700
Subsurface Ice eXtraction Using RedWater (SIXUR)	1,000,000,000	1,000
Exercise equipment (Therabands)	250	0.2
Sanitation Systems	2,000	50
Astronaut Suits	12,000,000	90
Sabatier Process and Electrolysis Machine (SPEM) + Back-up electrolysis machine	1,500,000	4,005
Drones (Battleships A-D)	400,000	160
Scientific Instrumentation	1,980,000,000	765
Collector	200,000,000	500
Finder-Catcher	300,000,000	600

Component	Cost (in USD dollars)	Weight (in kg)
Exploration Vehicle on Mars (EVOM)	2,000,000,000	5,000
Packed food	100,000	1,200
Made in Mars Lander (MIML)	500,000,000	8,000
MIM Power Supply (1 Kilopower unit + Solar panels)	20,450,000	2,300
80 Wash Laundry Machine	670	40
Nitrogen Supply	20,000	2,500
Oxygen Supply	1,200	400
Hydrogen Supply	1,600	100
Clothing	12,000	120
Total:	6,119,767,720	27,778

Tentative factors: If cybernetics and humanoid technology are available in 2031, our weight margin allows them to be included in the mission, along with any other technological advancements we may want to test in 2031.

CONCLUSION

The M.A.R.T.I.A.N. Mission stands as a transformative milestone in human space exploration, presenting a rigorously designed and well-articulated plan for the first manned mission to Mars. The objectives outlined in this report encompass a broad spectrum of scientific pursuits, ranging from the search for past and present life on Mars, the exploration of its geological history and geographic features, to detailed climatological and meteorological observations. These objectives serve as guiding beacons, shedding light on the intricate interplay of Mars' geophysical processes and providing valuable insights into the possibility of habitability on the planet. With a precise timeline for its two-phased launch, commencing in 2029 and 2031, M.A.R.T.I.A.N. Mission exemplifies a strategic approach to human space exploration, bolstered by meticulous planning, engineering expertise, and a commitment to the safety and well-being of the Marsonauts. Our multifaceted scientific objectives, engineering innovations, and human-oriented plans combine to make a cohesive, feasible, and inspiring mission that can bring forth an interplanetary revolution.

WORKS CITED

1. "3D Knit BioSuit™ – Self-Assembly Lab." *Self-Assembly Lab*, selfassemblylab.mit.edu/3d-knit-biosuit.
2. "80wash Washing Machine." *Indiamart.com*, www.indiamart.com/

proddetail/80wash-washing-machine-2851355232430.html. "Air Temperature and Humidity Inside the ISS." *Space Exploration Stack Exchange*, space.stackexchange.com/questions/2539/air-temperature-and-humidity-inside-the iss.

3. Aquaponics, Go G. "What is Aquaponics and How Does It Work?" *Go Green Aquaponics*, 28 Feb. 2022, gogreenaquaponics.com/blogs/news/what-is-aquaponics and-how-does-it-work.

4. ATA. "3D Knit BioSuit." *Specialty Fabrics Review*, 20 Dec. 2022, specialtyfabricsreview.com/2023/01/01/3d-knit-biosuit/.

5. Atkinson, Nancy. "Better Tires to Drive on Mars." *Universe Today*, 13 May 2020, www.universetoday.com/146047/better-tires-to-drive-on-mars/.

6. Belobrajdic, Blaze, et al. "Planetary Extravehicular Activity (EVA) Risk Mitigation Strategies for Long-duration Space Missions." *Nature*, 12 May 2021, www.nature.com/articles/s41526-021-00144-w.

7. "Boldly Go! NASA's New Space Toilet." *NASA*, 2 Aug. 2019, www.nasa.gov/feature/boldly-go-nasa-s-new-space-toilet-offers-more-comfort improved-efficiency-for-deep-space/.

8. "Breathing Easy on the Space Station." *Science Mission Directorate | Science*, 12 2000, science.nasa.gov/science-news/science-at-nasa/2000/ast13nov_1. "Clearing the Air in Space." *NASA*, 2 Nov. 2016, www.nasa.gov/mission_pages/station/research/long_duration_sorbent_testbed/. "Curiosity Finds Hydrogen-Rich Area of Mars Subsurface." *NASA*, 17 Aug. 2015, www.nasa.gov/jpl/msl/pia19809/curiosity-finds-hydrogen-rich-area-of-mars subsurface/.

9. Donna Viola, et al. "Arcadia Planita: Acheron Fossae and Erebus Montes." *NASA*, www.nasa.gov/sites/default/files/atoms/files/viola_arcadiaplanitia_final_tagged.pdf. "ECLSS." *NASA*, 11 Sept. 2017, www.nasa.gov/centers/marshall/history/eclss.html. "Electrolysis in Reduced Gravitational Environments: Current Research Perspectives and Future Applications." *ResearchGate | Find and Share Research*, www.researchgate.net/figure/Oxygen-production-on-the-International-Space-Station ISS-a-Design-of-a-PEM_fig1_366008373.

10. Emspak, Jesse. "Metal Tires for Mars: 'Shape Memory' Could Help Rovers Roll." *Space.com*, 8 Jan. 2018, www.space.com/39305-metal-tires-for-mars-rovers.html. "ESA." *ESA–Robotic Exploration of Mars*, exploration.esa.int/web/mars/-/48523- trace-gas-orbiter-instruments?fbodylongid=2187.

11. "First Rock Dating Experiment Performed on Mars." *California Institute of Technology*, www.caltech.edu/about/news/first-rock-dating-experiment-performed mars-41496.

12. "Getting to the Hellas Impact Structure." *Planetary Science Institute*, 12 June 2014, www.psi.edu/epo/explorecraters/hellastour.htm.

13. Ghosh, Joydeep. "Oxygen Definition, Facts, Symbol, Discovery, Property, Uses." *Chemistry Learner*, 8 Apr. 2023, www.chemistrylearner.com/oxygen.html#cost-of oxygen.

14. Gifford, Sheyna. "Heavenly Hygiene: How Do Astronauts Shower In Space?" *Now. Powered by Northrop Grumman*, 3 Dec. 2022, now.northropgrumman.com/heavenly hygiene-how-do-astronauts-shower-in-space/.

15. "Hellas Planitia." *NASA*, 5 June 2015, www.nasa.gov/multimedia/imagegallery/image_feature_1659.html. "How Much Did the Apollo Program Cost?" *The Planetary Society*, 11 June 2019, www.planetary.org/space-policy/cost-of-apollo.
16. "How the Mars Exploration Rovers Work." *HowStuffWorks*, 9 Jan. 2004, science.howstuffworks.com/mars-rover.htm#pt4.
17. "How to Chart the Price of a Trip to Mars." *Quartz*, 9 May 2018, qz.com/1273644/heres-how-nasa-and-spacex-chart-the-price-of-a-trip-to-mars. Ikhlas Sabouni, Ph.D., et al. "Mars Habitat." *SpaceArchitect.org*, spacearchitect.org/pubs/NASA-CR-189985.pdf.
18. Julie Mitchell, Philip Christensen. "Equatorial Opportunities for Humans on Mars." *NASA*, www.nasa.gov/sites/default/files/atoms/files/mitchell_landingsite_final.pdf. "Just Like Home." *NASA*, www.nasa.gov/audience/foreducators/k4/features/F_Just_Like_Home.html.
19. "L+6, L+7: First Weekend in Space is over | Outpost 42." *Outpost 42*, outpost42.esa.int/blog/diario-di-bordo/single/16-17-first-weekend-in-space-is-over/. "Liquid Nitrogen Spray Could Clean Up Stubborn Moon Dust." *WSU Insider*, 28 Feb. 2023, news.wsu.edu/press-release/2023/02/28/liquid-nitrogen-spray-could-clean-up stubborn-moon-dust/.
20. "Liquid Nitrogen Spray to Clean Spacesuits." *Institut International Du Froid (IIF)*, 27 Mar. 2023, iifiir.org/en/news/liquid-nitrogen-spray-to-clean-spacesuits. "LPI Science Labs and Equipment." *Lunar and Planetary Institute*, www.lpi.usra.edu/science/science-labs-equipment/.

21. "Map of Mars with Major Regions Labeled." *The Planetary Society*, 25 Oct. 2013, www.planetary.org/space-images/map-mars-major-features.
22. "Mars Trek." trek.nasa.gov/mars/#v=0.1&x=-179.20898103211338&y=32.16796814995267&z=6&p=urn%3Aogc%3Adef%3Acrs %3AEPS-G%3A%3A104905&d=&locale=&b=mars&e=-186.2402309009554%2C28.866576609972903%2C172.17773116327118%2C35.469359689932446&s-fz=&w=.Mars.nasa.gov. "ChemCam | Instruments – NASA Mars Exploration." *NASA Mars Exploration*, mars.nasa.gov/msl/spacecraft/instruments/chemcam/.

———. "Communications with Earth." *NASA Mars Exploration*, mars.nasa.gov/mars2020/mission/communications/.

———. "MEDA." *NASA Mars Exploration*, mars.nasa.gov/mars2020/spacecraft/instruments/meda/.

———. "MOXIE for Scientists–NASA." *NASA Mars Exploration*, mars.nasa.gov/mars2020/spacecraft/instruments/moxie/for-scientists/.

———. "MOXIE." *NASA Mars Exploration*, mars.nasa.gov/mars2020/spacecraft/instruments/moxie/.

———. "Mastcam-Z." *NASA Mars Exploration*, mars.nasa.gov/mars2020/spacecraft/instruments/mastcam-z/.

———. "Odyssey Finds Water Ice in Abundance Under Mars' Surface – NASA Mars Exploration." *NASA Mars Exploration*, 28 May 2002, mars.nasa.gov/news/247/odyssey-finds-water-ice-in-abundance-under-mars-surface/.

———. "SHARAD." *NASA Mars Exploration*, mars.nasa.gov/mro/mission/instruments/sharad/.

———. "Summary | Science – NASA Mars Exploration." *NASA Mars Exploration*, mars.nasa.gov/msl/mission/science/summary/.mars.nasa.gov. "Hohmann Transfer Orbit – NASA Mars Exploration." *NASA Mars Exploration*, mars.nasa.gov/resources/6042/hohmann-transfer-orbit/. "Martian Rock-dating Technique Could Point to Signs of Life in Space." *UQ News*, www.uq.edu.au/news/article/2013/12/martian-rock-dating-technique-could-point signs-of-life-space.

23. "MMGIS." *AMMOS:*, ammos.nasa.gov/marswatermaps/?mission=MWR. "NASA Ames Web-based Trajectory Generation Tool." *NASA*, 7 Apr. 2023, trajbrowser.arc.nasa.gov/index.php.

24. "NASA, International Partners Assess Mission to Map Ice on Mars." *NASA*, 3 Feb. 2021, www.nasa.gov/feature/nasa-international-partners-assess-mission-to-map-ice on-mars-guide-science-priorities/.

25. "NASA's FY 2023 Budget." *The Planetary Society*, 28 Mar. 2022, www.planetary.org/space-policy/nasas-fy-2023-budget.

26. "NASA's Treasure Map for Water Ice on Mars." *NASA*, 10 Dec. 2019, www.nasa.gov/feature/jpl/nasas-treasure-map-for-water-ice-on-mars. National Aeronautics and Space Administration. "Environmental Control and Life Support System (ECLSS)." *NASA*, www.nasa.gov/sites/default/files/atoms/files/g 281237_eclss_0.pdf.

    ———. "Environmental Control and Life Support System (ECLSS)." *NASA*, www.nasa.gov/sites/default/files/atoms/files/g-281237_eclss_0.pdf.

    ———. "Mars Science Laboratory/Curiosity." *NASA Mars Exploration*, mars.nasa.gov/msl/news/pdfs/MSL_Fact_Sheet.pdf.

27. "New Brine Processor Increases Water Recycling on the Station." *NASA*, 24 Feb. 2021, www.nasa.gov/feature/new-brine-processor-increases-water-recycling-on-international-space-station.
28. Newman, Dava. "Building the Future Spacesuit." *NASA*, www.nasa.gov/pdf/617047main_45s_building_future_spacesuit.pdf. News Direct. "Mars Manned Mission: MIT Professor Developing Cheaper, More Practical Space Suit." *YouTube*, 1 Oct. 2012, youtu.be/ExH_YEE4DCs.
29. "NO DETERGENT, 80 SECONDS SPIN: A NEARLY WATERLESS WASHING MACHINE." *YOURSTORY*, July 2022, yourstory.com/2022/07/80wash-no-detergent half-cup-water-chandigarh-startup-waterless-washing-machine.
30. "Noachian, Hesperian, and Amazonian, Oh My! --Mars' Geologic Time Scale." *The Planetary Society*, 25 Oct. 2013, www.planetary.org/articles/10251246-noachian hesperian-amazonian.
31. O, Tokumaru. "Prevention of Decompression Sickness During Extravehicular Activity in Space: a Review." *PubMed*, "Other Instruments." *SEIS / Mars InSight*, 28 Oct. 2016, www.seis insight.eu/en/public-2/the-insight-mission/other-instruments.
32. "Planetary Names: Mons, montes: Erebus Montes on Mars." *Planetary Names*, planetarynames.wr.usgs.gov/Feature/1821.
33. "PRODUCT DESIGN Winner / Manned Mars Rover / Montgomery Design International, Inc. / Gregg Montgomery." *International Design Awards™*, www.idesignawards.com/winners-old/zoom.php?eid=9-7458-14. Real Engineering. "How NASA

Reinvented The Wheel—Shape Memory Alloys." *YouTube*, www.youtube.com/watch?v=2lv6Vs12jLc.

34. Rishitosh K. Sinha, Dwijesh Ray. "Extensive glaciation in the Erebus Montes region of Mars." *ScienceDirect*, Oct. 2021, www.sciencedirect.com/science/article/abs/pii/S0019103521002293.

35. Robinson, Brock. "What Are Hydroponic Systems and How Do They Work?" *Fresh Water Systems*, 6 Sept. 2019, www.freshwatersystems.com/blogs/blog/what-are hydroponic-system.

36. "Sample Fetching Rover—Lightweight Rover Concepts for Mars Sample Return." *HTML REDIRECT*, robotics.estec.esa.int/ASTRA/Astra2011/Presentations/Session%206A/01.Allouis.pdf.

37. "Shrink-wrapping Spacesuits." *MIT News | Massachusetts Institute of Technology*, news.mit.edu/2014/second-skin-spacesuits-0918.

38. "A Step Toward Mars." *NASA*, 3 Feb. 2021, www.nasa.gov/chapea/about/. "Subsurface Water Ice Mapping on Mars." *Subsurface Water Ice Mapping*, swim.psi.edu/.

39. "SWIM consistency map of Arcadia Planitia." *ResearchGate | Find and Share Research*, www.researchgate.net/figure/SWIM-consistency-map-of-Arcadia-Planitia The-Extent-and-depth-of-icy-units-are_fig1_350020561.

40. "SWIM Project Maps Potential Sources of Mars Water." *Planetary Science Institute*, 6 Mar. 2019, www.psi.edu/news/marsswim.

41. Tech, Jason M. "Mars-made Rocket Fuel Could Get Astronauts Back to Earth." *Futurity*, 27 Oct. 2021, www.futurity.org/mars-rocket-fuel-space-travel-2647692/. Than Putzig, et al. "Subsurface Water Ice Mapping

(SWIM) in the Northern Hemisphere of Mars." *Subsurface Water Ice Mapping*, 6 Mar. 2019,

42. swim.psi.edu/resources/media/presentations/SWIM_HLS2_Hangout_Mar_2019_Slid es.pdf.

43. Tibbits, Skylar. "Dava Newman Presents 3D Knit BioSuit™ at 2022 MARS Conference – MIT Media Lab." *MIT Media Lab*, www.media.mit.edu/posts/dava newman-presents-3d-knit-biosuit-at-mars-conference/.

44. "Water in Space." *European Space Agency*, www.esa.int/Science_Exploration/Human_and_Robotic_Exploration/International_S pace_Station/Water_in_space.

45. "World's first high performance airless tire made from space-age materials @ NASA." *SEC.gov*, www.sec.gov/Archives/edgar/data/1854861/000167025421000673/document_2.pdf.

[i] We assume that the necessary travel vehicles will be available and lightly touch on the launch process. [ii] A brief overview of each section's contents can be seen in the **Table of Contents**

[iii] Space companies are certainly planning manned missions to Mars, but many focus on developing a lunar base first, or accomplishing other space feats first. Creating advanced propulsion systems or spending significant time on other space missions is not how humans went to the moon, and it is not how we will get to Mars. We need a realistic plan and we need to focus on it first, and that is what M.A.R.T.I.A.N. Mission is. [iv] 0.7 kg food per meal per person, 2.1 kg per day per person, 8.4 kg per day for 4 people, 117.6 kg lasts 14 days for 4 people/28 days for 2 people

[v] 5L water per day per person, 20L per day for 4 people, 280L lasts 14 days for 4 people/28 days for 2 people [vi] 0.84 kg oxygen required per day per person, 3.36 kg per day for 4 people, 47.04 kg lasts 14 days for 4 people/28 days for 2 people

[vii] We will be bringing a hydrogen supply from Earth (which will not contribute much to the weight much as hydrogen is extremely lightweight) for SPEM, which will pump hydrogen when the current supply is low (like when the crew first sets up SPEM and if the hydrogen generated is not sufficient, which is unlikely). The hydrogen generated in

the electrolysis chamber will also be redirected back into the Sabatier Process chamber.[viii] A 20-minute delay is written based on the technological advancements as of July 2023.

MOSES I

ALEXANDER WANG

ANDRE LINTNER-CALVO

ANGELA DE LABRA

ANKITH TIRUMALA

KAL'EL VNSACHOFF

I. ABSTRACT

The following design report presents a comprehensive plan for a human Mars surface mission that prioritizes scientific exploration while considering engineering challenges, human operational factors, and cost limitations. The mission aims to maximize scientific objectives such as geological studies, climatology, paleontology, astrobiology, and resource exploitation. The proposed mission duration is 1.5 Earth years (18 months), with a crew of six Marsonauts and is set to launch on September 19, 2033. This report covers the design of the habitat, surface vehicles, satellites, scientific instruments, power system, crew composition, mission location, rations, exploration plan, and dispute resolution strategies. A compromise between optimizing different design features has been considered to reach the best possible overall design.

II. INTRODUCTION

This mission proposal outlines an ambitious endeavor to deploy GPS satellites in orbit around Mars while simultaneously establishing a subterranean base within a carefully selected crater on the Martian surface. The primary objectives of this mission are to enhance navigation and communication capabilities for future missions, and provide a sustainable, safe, and secure, semi-permanent habitat for future human exploration and scientific research.

The human Mars surface mission aims to expand our understanding of the Red Planet through scientific exploration. This report outlines the key considerations in three major aspects: Science, Engineering, and Human Operations. Each team member will present their respective portion of the design, providing a comprehensive and integrated plan.

June-Month 1	July-Month 2	August-Month 3	September-Month 4	October-Month 5	November-Month 6
Rovers arrive on the surface of Mars melt regolith and 3D-print the habitat	Astronauts arrive and settle in a 3D-printed habitat. Astronauts establish agriculture on Mars	Astronauts will further improve power systems	Astronauts use rovers to collect sample and travel around	Scientific objectives regarding geological studies	Scientific objectives regarding climatological studies
December-Month 7	**January-Month 8**	**February-Month 9**	**March-Month 10**	**April-Month 11**	**May-Month 12**
Scientific objectives regarding astrobiological studies	Scientific objectives regarding paleontological studies	Scientific objectives regarding biomarkers	Astronauts will further explore areas in Mars	Astronauts will look for signs of life	Policy and law Making will begin
June-Month 13	**July-Month 14**	**August-Month 15**	**September-Month 16**	**October-Month 17**	**November-Month 18**
Data from Astronauts Health will be used for new medicine	Further data of the conditions in Mars will be used to create better rovers	Astronauts will install further equipment for more civilizations to come	Astronauts will receive new technology to implement in Mars	Astronauts will start preparing everything to leave	Mission Moses I is over

Mission Timeline

III. LANDING SITE

For this mission, we have decided to land in the Eberswalde region in the southern hemisphere. We have chosen this location because it is likely a former delta or lakebed, meaning there is a good chance to find aquatic features or potential fossils. The crater contains an extremely well-preserved fluvial distributary network in a potential deltaic setting. These factors will help astronauts landing there in their search for past and present life on Mars. In addition, the probability of frozen water under the surface will help the astronauts with water needs. The water could also be split into Hydrogen and Oxygen, which could become fuel for the station.

SCIENTIFIC INTEREST

The Eberswalde crater is home to numerous post-aquatic landforms, including an inverted relief plateau which was likely a former site of riverine outflow sedimentation, potentially producing numerous aquatic clays. Additionally, numerous areas of the crater exist which could have potentially been host to prehistoric Martian life forms, which may have been preserved over time as fossils due to the sedimentation in the area. Crew members will be able to conduct numerous scientific experiments and collect samples of diverse materials for the duration of the mission. Eberswalde is overall a data-rich area of Mars with the potential for numerous scientific discoveries, which the mission will be able to fully exploit throughout its duration for maximized productivity.

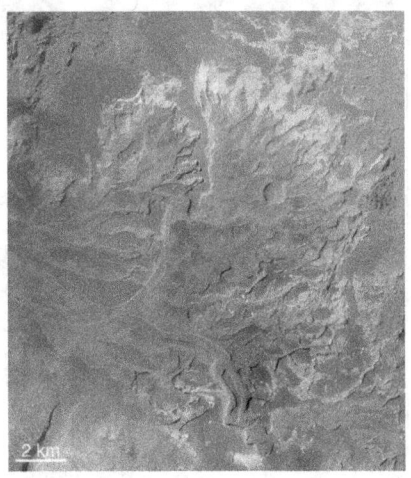

Figure 1: The Eberswalde Delta

To reduce the risk of potential damage to the mission vehicles or crew, a safe landing zone free of dangerous slopes or rocky debris is required. Thanks to imagery and measurements from the Mars Express mission, we now know that Eberswalde is one of the flattest regions on Mars's southern hemisphere, with average slopes of less than 20 degrees. The crater itself consists of a wide, flat, and crucially clear floor, surrounded by the crater walls. This allows for a wide margin of error during the descent to the surface, reducing the stress on the astronauts and increasing the safety margins. Additionally, the clear surface allows for increased mobility during surface excursions, as the risk of potential injury or damage to equipment from surface debris will be heavily reduced. In case of dust storms, the crater itself contains numerous smaller craters within which can potentially be used for emergency shelters if transit back to base is infeasible.

RESOURCE AVAILABILITY

Location is potentially rich in precious metals and aquatic clays due to potential prior sedimentation from flowing water. These resources are useful not only for potential ISRU (In-Situ Resource Utilization), but could also provide valuable scientific insights into past geology and climate conditions. Crater additionally holds water ice deposits for use in

ISWP (In-situ water production), alleviating the need for water brought from Earth, reducing mission weight and cost. Additionally, Crater receives ample sunlight for power and warmth with standard day and night lengths (12 hours 20 minutes), with few obstructions or landforms to block aforementioned sunlight.

MISSION OBJECTIVES

The Moses I mission seeks to accomplish a number of ambitious tasks on Mars with the goal of setting up the foundations for a greater human presence on Mars, as well as furthering our understanding of the solar system and the planets at the same time.

ENGINEERING AND FOUNDATIONAL OBJECTIVES

In-situ Resource Gathering: Identify and gather potential resources local to Mars, such as water, minerals, and precious metals to support human colonization efforts.

Establish First Base: Establish the first semi-permanent outpost on Mars. Specifically a habitat that can support terrestrial life such as humans and plants. Includes several modules or rooms that serve different functions, such as, a greenhouse, communication center, and laboratory.

Begin Mars GPS System: Deploy the first four GPS satellites in orbit around Mars. These satellites will also function as weather satellites, allowing us to gather insight on Mars's climatology.

Automation: The Moses I mission aims to utilize rovers and other autonomous machines and vehicles to gather resources and aid the crew members in their work and studies.

IV. SCIENTIFIC OBJECTIVES (SCIENTIFIC STUDIES ON MARS)

Astro Geological Studies of Mars: Conduct detailed geological studies to understand the planet's past geological processes, identify rock formations, and determine the history of Martian geology.

Climatological Studies of Mars: Investigate the Martian climate, weather patterns, and atmospheric conditions to improve our understanding of the planet's past and potential habitability.

Astrobiological Studies of Mars: Investigate the potential for present life on Mars by studying the presence of microbial life, biosignatures, and habitable environments.

Paleontological Studies of Mars: Explore the possibility of past life on Mars by searching for signs of fossils, microorganisms, or organic compounds in the Martian sands.

Biomarkers: Experiments to observe how human bodies react to living on Mars. Essentially measuring each individual crew member's health parameters as they continue to live on Mars as to assess Mars's effect on the human body.

V. ENGINEERING AND RESOURCE GATHERING
HABITAT DESIGN AND LAYOUT

1. The base will incorporate essential facilities such as a laboratory, communication center, entertainment module, sleeping quarters, a greenhouse for crop cultivation, and a sensory deprivation module for relaxation. It will also feature entrances designed to keep space suits outside while allowing easy access for the crew members.
2. Base Overview: The Mars base will be constructed using modular components that can be transported and assembled on-site. The layout will consist of interconnected modules, providing various functionalities to meet the crew's needs during their mission.
3. Laboratory Module: The laboratory module will be a vital part of the base, equipped with state-of-the-art scientific instruments and workstations. It will support various research activities, including geology, biology, chemistry, and atmospheric studies. The laboratory will be designed with proper safety measures to handle hazardous materials and ensure the crew's well-being.

4. Communication Center: The communication center will serve as the primary hub for all data transmissions to and from Earth. It will be equipped with high-gain antennas for efficient communication with mission control and other interplanetary spacecraft. The center will also house advanced communication equipment to relay signals across vast distances.
5. Entertainment Module: The entertainment module is crucial for maintaining the crew's mental well-being during extended stays on Mars. It will include recreational facilities such as a common area for socializing, a gym for exercise, virtual reality rooms for immersive experiences, and a small library with books and multimedia content.
6. Sleeping Quarters: The sleeping quarters will provide individual private cabins for each crew member. Each cabin will have a comfortable bed, storage space, personal workspace, and access to a communication terminal. Design considerations will prioritize ergonomic layouts to ensure restful sleep and maintain psychological well-being.
7. Greenhouse for Crop Cultivation: The greenhouse module will support sustainable living on Mars by enabling the cultivation of crops for food and oxygen generation (See page # for Agriculture and Greenhouse specifics). The greenhouse comes with a mobile automatic watering system mounted in the ceiling of the greenhouse. The greenhouse will also serve as a recreational space for the crew, fostering a connection to nature in the barren Martian environment.
8. Sensory Deprivation Module: The sensory deprivation module will be a peaceful and quiet space designed to allow crew members to relax, meditate, and reduce stress. It will be equipped with comfortable seating or lying areas, soft lighting, and soundproofing to block out external noises.

This module will contribute to the crew's mental health and help mitigate the challenges of isolation and confinement.
9. Entrance and Airlock Design: The base's entrance will feature an airlock system to maintain pressure and temperature integrity while preventing dust and contaminants from entering the living areas. Crew members can enter through an opening that connects . They will leave their space suits in designated storage areas within the airlock, and after passing through a decontamination procedure, they can access the interior of the base.
10. Safety and Redundancy: The entire base will be designed with redundancy in mind, including backup power systems, communication links, and life support systems. Safety protocols and emergency procedures will be thoroughly established, and crew training will emphasize handling critical situations.

MGPS/WEATHER SATELLITES DESIGN

1. The primary purpose of the satellites is to serve as GPS satellites for Mars, providing accurate positioning and navigation capabilities for future manned and unmanned missions on the planet. Additionally, the satellites will be equipped with weather monitoring instruments to study and analyze the weather patterns of Mars, enhancing our understanding of the Martian climate.

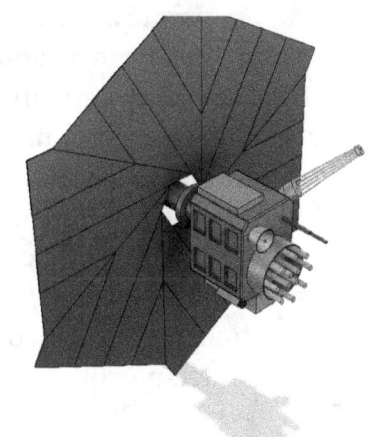

Figure 1: Deployed MGPS Satellite

2. Satellite Specifications: The satellites will be designed to meet the following specifications:
   a. Dimensions: When an undeployed satellite is compact and lightweight to facilitate launch and minimize operational costs.
      i. Undeployed (Solar Panel Folded): Width: 2ft/Length: 4ft/Height: 3ft
      ii. Deployed (Solar Panel UnFolded): Width: 2ft/Length: 5ft/Height: 20ft (see Fig. n)
   b. Power Source: The satellite will be equipped with solar panels to harness solar energy, ensuring continuous operation and recharging the onboard batteries. Sunlight is far more depleted near Mars due to its distance from the sun, these solar panels will have to have a larger width span than an Earth-orbiting satellite and still be compact while the satellite is undeployed. Considering these factors, these solar panels have been designed in a complex arrangement of folding points and angles with geometry resembling that of an origami. This origami-like geometry allows it to unfold from a tight 2ft by 2ft space into a huge solar panel sheet spanning 20ft.
   c. Communication: The satellite will utilize high-gain antennas for efficient communication with Earth and any future Mars missions.
   d. GPS System: The GPS system will be based on a constellation of satellites, providing accurate position and navigation data to surface missions and spacecraft in Martian orbit.
   e. Weather Monitoring Instruments: The weather monitoring suite will consist of the following instruments:
      i. Atmospheric Sensors: To measure pressure, temperature, humidity, and composition of the Martian atmosphere.

       ii. Radiation Detectors: To monitor solar and cosmic radiation levels on the planet's surface.
       iii. Dust and Particle Analyzer: To study dust storms, particles, and their impact on the Martian climate.
       iv. Imaging Sensors: To capture images of Martian clouds, dust devils, and other atmospheric phenomena.
       v. Thermal Infrared Sensor: To monitor temperature variations across different regions.
   f. Data Processing and Storage: The satellite will be equipped with onboard processing and storage capabilities to manage data efficiently before transmitting it to Earth.
   g. Radiation Protection: Adequate shielding will be provided to protect sensitive instruments from the harsh Martian radiation environment.

3. Satellite Orbits and Coverage: The GPS satellites will be deployed in suitable orbits to provide optimal coverage for the entire Martian surface. The satellite's orbit for weather monitoring will be selected to ensure comprehensive observations of different latitudinal and longitudinal regions of Mars.
4. Data Transmission: The satellite will use high-frequency communication bands to transmit GPS and weather data to Earth-based stations and any future Mars missions equipped with compatible receivers.
5. Operational Considerations: The satellite's operations will be managed by a ground control team on Earth, responsible for coordinating its activities, maintaining its orbit, and ensuring smooth data transmission.
6. Benefits: The dual-function satellite will significantly enhance our ability to explore Mars by providing accurate GPS navigation for rovers and astronauts, thereby reducing the risk of mission failures. Additionally, the weather

monitoring capabilities will deepen our understanding of Martian climate patterns, which is crucial for planning long-term manned missions and studying the potential habitability of Mars.

D. POWER SUPPLY

Power is the key to survival on Mars. The crew members need it to stay warm, cook food, and even breathe. Mars is a very harsh environment, with freezing, cold nights and intense dust storms. Designing a reliable power system to accommodate all of this will be of utmost importance. However, Mars is extremely energy-poor. Using solar panels to create solar energy seems like a solution, but on Mars, solar power is only 43% as efficient as it is on Earth due to its 141.6 million miles distance from the sun. Nevertheless, even this depleted sunlight is usually obscured by enormous Martian dust storms for days on end. Our base could still use solar power, but that alone would most likely not be sufficient.

Wind power and geothermal energy are also unfeasible alternatives since there is barely an atmosphere on Mars, and internally, Mars is much too cold. Therefore, nuclear power might be the only option alongside solar power for a more abundant amount of energy. Mars, albeit radioactive, does not harbor easily accessible and convenient radioactive elements. For this reason, nuclear fuel, along with the reactors, would have to be shipped from Earth to Mars. Kilopower reactors would probably be the best types of reactors to use to generate energy for our Mars base.

Kilopower reactors that are being developed and reiterated by a joint venture between NASA and the Department of Energy and use Stirling engines to work might be the solution. Kilopower reactors were designed with planetary colonization in mind and built to enable long-duration stays on planetary surfaces. One Kilopower reactor can produce up to ten kilowatts of electricity which is enough to power an entire household (NASA Space Technology Mission Directorate). An alloy of 7% molybdenum and 93% uranium-235 fuels the reactor. The reactor core is a solid cast alloy structure of enriched uranium. A uranium core has the benefit of avoiding uncertainty in the supply of other radioisotopes, such as plutonium. The core is surrounded by a beryllium oxide reflector, which allows the chain reaction to continue, prevents neutrons from escaping the reactor core, and reduces the emissions of gamma radiation that could impair on-board electronics. (Fig. 5.i) There is no need for a complex control system because the reactor uses nuclear physics to self-regulate the fission reactions. Heat produced by nuclear fission that takes place within the reactor is delivered to free-piston Stirling engines/converters through passive heat pipes filled with liquid sodium. The Stirling engines/converters produce reciprocating motion to drive a linear electric generator. Once the Kilopower reactors are shipped to Mars, they would then be deployed in our chosen power zone by removing a neutron-absorbing boron rod located in the reactor to allow the nuclear chain reaction to begin (Kilopower: A Gateway to Abundant Power for Exploration). (Fig. 5.ii)

Solar panels would also be set up, ideally, in a place within our chosen power zone that receives the most sunlight. Also, the number of solar panels needed to help power our base would be tremendous. Nearly seven football fields worth of solar panels might be needed in order for the energy needs to be sufficiently met. The solar panels could also utilize sensory technology to locate where the sun is in the sky to stay within the sun's direction in order to allow for more efficient solar energy gathering (Mars Society).

AGRICULTURE AND WATER OBTAINMENT

Previous research has concluded that the soil of Mars could and has supported plant life. Scans show the soil contains Oxygen, Nitrogen, Potassium, Phosphorus and other nutrients essential to plant life, which came to Mars from the numerous meteorite impacts in the past and present. The atmosphere also contains over 92% of CO_2, which is significantly more compared to the 0.04% on Earth. However, the high UV radiation levels and the -90°C temperature on Mars would be extremely harmful to plants. The soil is also highly alkaline 1,2. To counter this harsh environment, we would build a greenhouse with walls made of glass and coated with a silica aerogel to serve as significant insulation due to its UV blocking and heat insulation properties. We will also bring around 2340 kg (2.58 tons) of soil from Earth. The ideal soil we would use to grow the plants in the greenhouse would have an ideal composition of approximately 45% minerals (like sand, clay, silt), 5% organic (plant and animal) matter, 25% air and 25% water. It would be crumbly, relatively dark in color, and teeming with microorganisms and earthworms to help break down the soil, and a pH value between 6.5 and 7.5 3. This soil would be perfect for plants like Soybeans, Spinach, Mushrooms, and Wheat. In addition, we would bring Spirulina and Seaweed, which would be placed in an artificial lake. These plants have necessary nutrients like vitamin B12 or have healing properties, something our astronauts would need to survive on Mars 4,5,6. These plants would be harvested in as little as 3 weeks (for the mushrooms) to as long as 20 weeks (soybeans and wheat). Over a one and a half year period, we will be able to harvest over 376,355.1443123 kg of food, just from the greenhouse plants alone. One of our astronauts would focus solely on caring for the plants and researching how they thrive on Mars. We would bring approximately 100 of each species of seed, which would weigh a little over 1.68055 kg and plant them in our greenhouse.

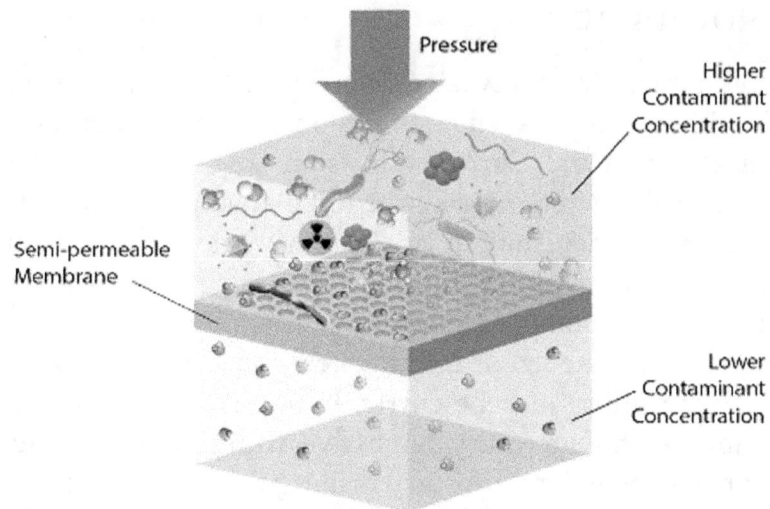

Figure 2. Reverse Osmosis Diagram

We would water the plants in the greenhouse by extracting water from the ice under the surface, purifying it through Reverse Osmosis, which removes 90-99 % of contaminants in water. Since some plants like Seaweed and Spirulina need water to survive, we will make a lake that has salt water in it. To make sure nothing is wasted, we will collect the human waste and purify it, composting the feces and purifying the gray water (dirty water) through a purification system. The system comprises a series of treatment units, beginning with an anaerobic digester, followed by a trickling filter, constructed wetland, and then a disinfection and purification unit. It is intended that the system will attach via appropriate plumbing to the exterior of our camp. The system is designed to be modular and transportable7.

ASTROBIOLOGY

Past missions to Mars revealed that the surface is totally sterilized, without any evidence of life on the surface. However, the results from the Curiosity mission suggested that if we drill at least six meters deep in the red planet, we may find life. This depth was determined by Curiosity scientists to ensure avoiding the effect of UV radiation on living organisms that may be thriving under the surface of Mars. Achieving such a depth utilizing the current drilling techniques (rotary or rotary percussive drilling) may be currently impossible due to their limitations. Although rotary percussive drilling showed a much higher performance than rotary drilling alone, it has thus far been limited to a drilling depth of a few centimeters. Therefore, a new drilling technique capable of reaching a greater depth than past missions, and higher rate of penetration, is critical for the success of future missions searching for life on Mars. This new drilling system would utilize a modified version of Nasa's proposed "Borebots". Our custom bore bots would make use of a rotary ultrasonic drill, which would allow for even greater efficiency. With these, we intend to study Mars's rock history and search for traces of past surface water.

ISWP (In-situ water production), alleviating the need for water brought from Earth, reducing mission weight and cost. Additionally, Crater receives ample sunlight for power and warmth with standard day and night lengths (12 hours 20 minutes), with few obstructions or landforms to block aforementioned sunlight.

MGPS SATELLITE

Part two of the mission entails the deployment of four MGPS (Martian Global Positioning System) satellites into orbit around Mars. These satellites are meant to fulfill a number of purposes.

Firstly, they will not only facilitate navigation on the Martian surface but also begin the formation of a larger GPS system on Mars, one like that of Earth. Additionally, these MGPS Satellites will serve as a useful tool for gathering data on Mar's climatology. With these satellites, the Moses I mission will be able to track the wind and weather patterns on Mars.

OXYGEN OBTAINMENT

Since there is no available oxygen on Mars, astronauts going there will need a reliable source of it. We will obtain it through a device that was designed for the Perseverance rover called MOXIE (Mars OXygen ISRU Experiment), which converts CO_2 back into O_2, in a process similar to plant photosynthesis. ISWP (In-situ water production), alleviating the need for water brought from Earth, reducing mission weight and cost. Additionally, Crater receives ample sunlight for power and warmth with standard day and night lengths (12 hours 20 minutes), with few obstructions or landforms to block aforementioned sunlight.

PALEONTOLOGY

Recent studies have suggested that there may have been life thriving on Mars. However, low temperatures, intense radiation, and low levels of surface water significantly reduce the chances of life on Mars today. Because of this, scientists have started to look at Mars's fossil record, specifically researching rocks from around 3.0–4.0 million years ago, during the Noachian and Hesperian periods of Martian history. Rocks from these periods of Mars history have been a recommended target for fossils by many scientists. Because of this, one of the primary objectives of NASA's Mars 2020 rover is to collect a variety of drilled rock samples from biological promising environments, so that the samples may be sent to Earth for a closer analysis. The ESA (European Space Agency)-Roscosmos ExoMars 2020 will be also equipped with technologies like the ones on Curiosity, which uses two stabilizers and one center drill to drill a hole and collect the sample. The rover then sends the sample to its lab, where it uses instruments to analyze the sample for methane, a gas commonly produced by life forms on Earth. Understanding how, why, and where life may have thrived on Mars will significantly enhance the performance of the astronauts' studies on Mars and may be an invaluable resource when choosing landing sites, sampling strategies, and how we might restore Mars back 8,9.

VI. HUMAN OPERATIONS

MEET THE CREW

For our mission we will have 6 astronauts going to space. The astronauts will have 2 years of training at the Johnson Space Center to get ready for the mission. They will be allowed to bring T-shirts in order to make them feel more comfortable. They will also bring their NASA logo uniform to wear in the mission Moses I.

CHRIS HADFIELD
Commander & Mechanical engineer

Biography

He received a bachelor's degree in mechanical engineering with honors from Royal Military College. Received a Master of Science in aviation systems at the University of Tennessee. He was chief of robotics for the NASA Astronaut Office at the Johnson Space Center. Hadfield was a commander of the NEEMO 14 mission. He has been on 3 flights: STS-74, STS-100, and ISS. " He addressed technical and safety issues for Shuttle Operations Development, contributed to the development of the glass shuttle cockpit, and supported shuttle launches at the Kennedy Space Center " (2004). He also mentioned in an interview that if there was a one-way mission to Mars, he would be honored to be one of the first astronauts on Mars.

Chris Hadfield will be the commander of the Moses I mission. He will be a great addition to the team due to his experience being in spacecraft and doing spacewalks. He will lead the mission and help with the first establishment on Mars. He has experience with fixing equipment, therefore he can repair damaged equipment due to the harsh environment of Mars.

We included a retired Canadian astronaut for the possibility of him joining our Mars mission. However, we also included another commander incase Chris Hadfield decided not to join our Mars mission.

ANDREW J. FEUSTEL
Commander & Geophysicist

Biography
He received a Bachelor of Science in Solid Earth Sciences from Purdue University. He also received a Master of Science Geophysics from Purdue University. He received a Ph.D. in Geological Sciences in Seismology from Queen's University. He has spaceflight experience through STS-125 Atlantis, STS-134, and Expedition 55/56. Feustel was the commander of the ISS. Feustel participated outside the space station  on three spacewalks to perform maintenance. Throughout his career, he has been a spacewalker 9 times totalling around 62 hours.

Andrew J. Feustel will be the commander of the Moses I mission. He will be a great addition to the team due to his experience being in spacecraft and doing spacewalks. He will lead the mission and help with the first establishment on Mars. He has experience with geology in seismology, therefore he could study the seismology on Mars.

JESSICA WATKINS
Geologist & Environmental Science

Biography
She has a Bachelor of Science in geological and environmental sciences from Stanford University. She also has a Doctorate in geology from UCLA. She conducted research on mechanisms of large landslides on Mars through orbital image and spectral data analysis, geological mapping for her Ph.D. research. She was a science team collaborator for NASA's Mars Curiosity rover. She also has spaceflight experience (2023).

Jessica Watkins will be the geologist of the Moses I mission. She has multiple degrees in geology and has focused on Mars. She has tested Mars rock physical properties. She has also researched the Gale crater on Mars. Due to her extensive knowledge on Mars, Watkins will be able to conduct thoroughly detailed geological investigations.

KATHLEEN RUBINS
Biochemistry & Microbiology

Biography

She became the first person to sequence DNA in space. She has a Bachelor of Science in Molecular Biology from the University of California. She also received a Ph.D. in Cancer Biology from Stanford University Medical School Biochemistry, Microbiology, and Immunology Department. She has worked on new medical treatments by investigating different types of viruses. She has also worked on heart research and microbiology in space through Expedition 63 and 64 (2021).

Kathleen Rubins will be the microbiologist of the Moses I mission. She has extensive research in space microbiology and has made groundbreaking discoveries in the medical department. She will be able to aid in the search for life on Mars. If harmful microorganisms are discovered, she will be able to work on medical treatments to prevent them harming the human body.

MICHAEL MASSIMINO
Industrial & Mechanical engineer

Biography
He received a bachelor's degree in industrial engineering from Columbia University. In graduate school he received a master's mechanical engineering and technology policy from MIT. He also received a Degree of Mechanical engineering and Ph.D. Mechanical engineering. He has spaceflight experience by working on the Hubble Space Telescope on the STS-109 Columbia and STS-125 Atlantis (2014).

Michael Massimino will be the mechanical and industrial engineer of the Moses I mission. He will improve and implement systems. He will handle technical aspects required for general maintenance and repairs. His degree in Technology and Public policy will help with implementing future laws, rules, and guidelines on technology usage on Mars. As a mechanical engineer, he will work on the Mars Ascent vehicle.

KJELL N. LINDGREN
Aerospace & Emergency Medicine

Biography

He received a Bachelor of Science degree in biology from the U.S. Air Force Academy. He received a Master of Science degree in cardiovascular physiology from Colorado State University. He received a Doctorate of Medicine from the University of Colorado. He has spaceflight experience through Expedition 44 and 45. He installed a thermal blanket on the Alpha-Magnetic Spectrometer and external cables (2023).

Kjell N. Lindgren will be the doctor for the Moses I mission. In case one of his teammates falls ill, Lindgren will be able to use his knowledge to help his coworker feel better. He is board certified in emergency medicine which will be very helpful if an accident occurs. He also has extensive research on Martian dust so he will help with dust storms.

G. REID WISEMAN
Computer & Systems Engineer

Biography
He received a Bachelor of Science degree in Computer and Systems Engineering from the Rensselaer Polytechnic Institute. He received a Master of Science degree in Systems Engineering from John Hopkins University. He also received a Certificate of Space Systems from the US Naval Postgraduate School. He has spaceflight experience through his participation in Expedition 40 and 41. He will be the commander of NASA's Artemis II mission (2023).

G. Reid Wiseman will be the computer science and software engineer for the Moses I mission. He will handle digital repairs and communications. He will work on the 3D printing module and computing systems to communicate with the base on Earth. He will also work on the Mars rover in case there is a wiring problem.

Local Martian Time	Activity
6:00 am. - 7:00 am.	Morning Wake Up & Preparation
7:00 am. - 8:00 am.	Breakfast
8:00 am. - 9:00 am.	Scientific objective task 1
9:00 am. - 10:00 am.	Scientific objective task 2
10:00 am. - 12:30 pm.	Exercise
12:30 pm. - 1:00 pm.	Cleaning And Maintenance
1:00 pm. - 2:00 pm.	Lunch
2:00 pm. - 3:00 pm.	Scientific objective task 3
3:00 pm. - 6:00 pm.	Scientific objective task 4
6:00 pm. - 7:00 pm.	Dinner
7:00 pm. - 9:30 pm.	Unstructured Free Time
9:30 pm. - 6:00 am.	Sleep

Figure 3: Astronaut Schedule

VII. SCHEDULE, HEALTH, AND COST
SCHEDULE

Subject to change due to the addition of spacewalks and other scientific tasks that are required. Could also include repairing equipment that has been damaged due to weather or environmental conditions. Since there are 6 astronauts, there will be a 3 hour delay between their wake up time. For example, one astronaut will wake up at 6:00 am, the next astronaut at 9:00 am, etc. This will allow for an astronaut to be awake during another astronaut's sleep time incase of an emergency during the night. This will also allow for all astronauts to get the same amount of sleep and perform the same amount of objectives during day and night. Astronauts will also get Sundays and some Saturdays off unless NASA control wants astronauts to perform scientific objectives those days.

After conducting thorough research into the activities of astronauts on the ISS, we concluded that the routine of an astronaut included brushing teeth, 3 meals per day, showers, scientific objectives, exercise, and free time. NASA uses Greenwich Mean Time to create schedules due to the fact that the ISS orbits the Earth every 90 min: 45 min in light, 45 min in darkness. Since Moses I is a mission that will land on Mars with daylight and nighttime, we will be using Martian time. According to NASA, " an astronaut's workday is from approximately 6 a.m. to 9:30 p.m...2.5 hours of physical exercise" (2009). We used this model to build our Martian schedule, Figure 3. The scientific objectives in Figure 3 can vary from laboratory work to working outside the habitat collecting samples.

HEALTH—EXERCISING EQUIPMENT

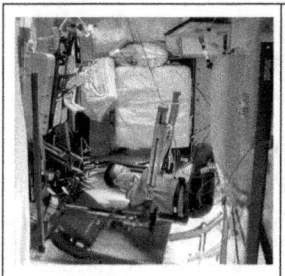  

Figure 4. ARED
Advanced Resistive Exercise Device

Figure 5. CEVIS
Cycle Ergometer with Vibration Isolation System

Figure 6. COLBERT
Combined Operational Load Bearing External Resistance Treadmill

MEDICINE

Exercise is extremely important due to the human muscles and bones deteriorating in space due to microgravity. By exercising, astronauts can maintain their muscle tone and fitness. The exercising equipment includes resistivity, cycling, and running on a treadmill. As seen in Figure 4, astronauts do weights through ARED which uses vacuum cylinders with a flywheel system to simulate weights with gravity. This helps astronauts maintain their bone mass and muscle strength. Astronauts also use cycling, Figure 5, through CEVIS to maintain their leg muscles strong. The CEVIS bicycle is fastened to the ground and has a seatbelt to help the astronauts from floating away. Astronauts use a treadmill, Figure 6, to maintain endurance and collect data on the effects of their muscle and bone for scientists to use. Besides taking some of this equipment from Earth, we can use resources on Mars such as carbon fiber parts that can be fabricated on Mars to make exercising equipment. Unfortunately microgravity does not help the human body. Astronauts will need osteoporosis medicine to help keep bone strength. Astronauts might need nausea medicine since their brains will be disoriented causing them to feel sick. Due to microgravity there is fluid pressure in astronauts faces. To relieve the fluids, astronauts use steroids or nasal spray, Figure 6. There are many complications with astronaut health in microgravity but our mission Moses I will send all of the necessary medical equipment to keep the astronauts healthy. In order to make the life of an astronaut more comfortable, astronauts will be allowed to take 10 pounds or approximately 4.5 kg of safe objects to bring to the habitat. Objects can include a

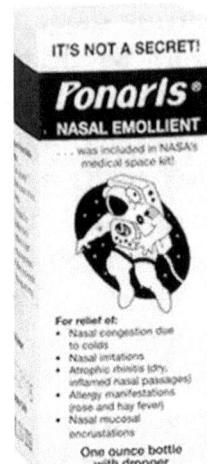

Figure 6. Ponaris Nasal Emollient

photo book, decorations, plushies, etc. This will help better the mental health of the astronauts onboard. To further help adjust the astronauts to their temporary home, there will be an entertainment room with many board games such as chess, checkers, Life, Monopoly, etc. These board games will be adjusted to not float into space by the use of velcro or glue.

NASA is currently working on how to make astronauts feel more comfortable in space to be able to extend human time on extraterrestrial bodies. NASA is going to test astronaut health through CIPHER. Astronauts will have scans to measure bone and joint density. They will also collect blood and urine samples. Scientists will use this type of data in order to improve the health data of astronauts. Astronauts will also complete cognitive tests and undergo MRI. Scientists will use the data in order to see if space affects the brain and thought process. Scientists also want to ensure that astronauts' cardiovascular health is good. Therefore astronauts have to complete CT, ultrasound, MRI, measure heart rate, and blood pressure. Lastly, scientists will measure astronauts' vision, level of dizziness, and body movements. (NASA, 2023) These tests will help monitor the health of the crew members in order to ensure they are healthy to perform their tasks on Mars.

NECESSITIES

Some basic necessities that astronauts will need to take with them are a toothbrush, toothpaste, shampoo/conditioner/body wash, skin care, and deodorant. For women, period products will be necessary for women on board. Some of the more common options include pads, tampons, and birth control. In our mission Moses I, there will be 2 women crew members. On average women require 30 pads or tampons per month. There are 12 months per 1 Earth year. In total there are 18 months for 1.5 Earth years. 18*30 =540 pads or tampons for one woman crew member. Total amount of period products for women is 540*2= 1,080 period products. We will include 2,000 period products in case they have a heavier flow or want to feel more comfortable. A female astronaut could also choose to use a birth control pill everyday which is approximately 548 days or 548 pills. For 2 women it would be 548*2=1,096 pills. Each astronaut should have 9 toothbrushes and toothpastes. Each astronaut should have 5 deodorants. 30 shower and skin care products for each astronaut.

Item	Weight in kg	Total Weight in kg
Toothbrush	0.025	9 *0.025=0.225 kg
Toothpaste	0.125	9 * 0.125=1.125 kg
Deodorant	0.2	5*0.2 = 1 kg
Shampoo/Conditioner/Body Wash	0.5	30*0.5=15 kg
Skin Care	0.5	30*0.5 = 15 kg
Period pad	0.005	2000*0.005=10.0 kg
Period tampon	0.001	2000*0.001=2.00 kg
Birth control pill	0.0005	1096 * 0.0005 =0.548 kg

Base necessities for all astronauts:
Approximate total:15+15+1+0.225 + 1.125 =32.35 kg

OPTION A:
- Pads: 10.0 kg
- Approximate total:32.35 +10.0=42.35 kg

OPTION B:
- Tampons: 2.00 kg
- Approximate total:32.35 +2.00=34.35 kg

OPTION C:
- Birth control pills: 0.548 kg
- Approximate total: 32.35 + 0.548 = 32.9 kg

The 2 women astronauts can choose different options. For example, one can choose a pad and the other one a tampon. They can also decide to use different products throughout the year. We understand that there can be many different options but the total weight will remain approximately between 32.9 kg and 42.35 kg.

EMERGENCY HEALTH PERFORMANCE

These are some of the more common types of emergencies in Space and Earth. Since our launch date is somewhat far, we will continue to learn more about human health on current and upcoming missions. This list can be revised if better technology is presented or new potential emergencies are discovered in space.

Our mission will consist of using agriculture on Mars. With agriculture alone on Mars we will have approximately 376,355 kg of vegetables which include Soybeans, Spinach, Mushrooms, Wheat etc. After doing calculations on food consumption Figure 7, we will have more than enough food to feed all of the crew. Food needed is 5,662.2 kg < Food supply is 376, 355 kg. Unfortunately a balanced meal not only includes vegetables and grains but dairy, protein, and fruits. According to Figure 8, 30 % grains, 30 % vegetables, 20 % fruits, 20 % protein, and a small portion of dairy products. Since we will be able to grow grains and vegetables on Mars we will only need 20 % fruits, 20 % protein, and a small portion of dairy products from Earth. 5,662.2 kg * 40% = 2,264.9 kg. We will take approximately 3,000 kg of food consisting of protein, fruits, grains, and a backup of vegetables and grains. The nutrition value says that astronauts should consume 3,000 calories. To cover all of the calories for one astronaut in one day, the astronaut must eat 700 calories of grains, 400 calories of vegetables, 700 calories of fruits, 900 calories of protein, and 300 calories of dairy. They can add one snack of their choice and a few condiments to their food.

Problem/Emergency	Solution/What to Do
Potential fracture (Very rare to occur)	Compact ultrasonographic devices for detecting fractures. Restraining devices to provide traction and heal the bone. Splints are used since they have versatility and are well tolerated.
Organ failure/problem (such as the heart)	Can perform surgery in space. It has been done before.
Arrhythmias	Use vitamin C and E. Usage of radiofrequency ablation. Heart surgery.
Renal colic	Lithotripsy can be used to remove kidney stones. The protocol is to inject lidocaine 120 mg in 100 mL normal saline intravenously over 10 minutes for pain management.
Venous thrombosis	Anticoagulants/Blood thinners. Enoxaparin is used to prevent blood clots.
Massive hemorrhage	Tranexamic acid to prevent bleeding, usually used in women for menstrual cycles. Transfusion of blood products.
Heart attack	Surgery to open a blocked surgery. Clot-busting and artery-opening medication can stop a heart attack.
Stroke	The treatment is to use tissue plasminogen activator which breaks up the blood clots that block blood flow to the brain.

Water: (Water-Human Consumption)
3.7 liter per day for men

$$4\ men * \frac{3.7\ liter}{day} * \frac{365\ days}{1\ year} * \frac{1.5\ years}{Mission\ to\ Mars} = 8103\ liters$$

2.7 liter per day for women

$$2\ women * \frac{2.7\ liter}{day} * \frac{365\ days}{1\ year} * \frac{1.5\ years}{Mission\ to\ Mars} = 2956.5\ liters$$

8103 + 2956. 5 = 11059.5 liters in total
11059.5 liters = 11,059.5 kg

Food: (Stephanie Watson)
3.8 pounds per astronaut per day

$$6\ astronauts * \frac{3.8\ lb}{day} * \frac{365\ days}{1\ year} * \frac{1.5\ years}{Mission\ to\ Mars} = 12483\ lbs$$

12483 lbs = 5,662.2 kg

Figure 7. Food and Water supply

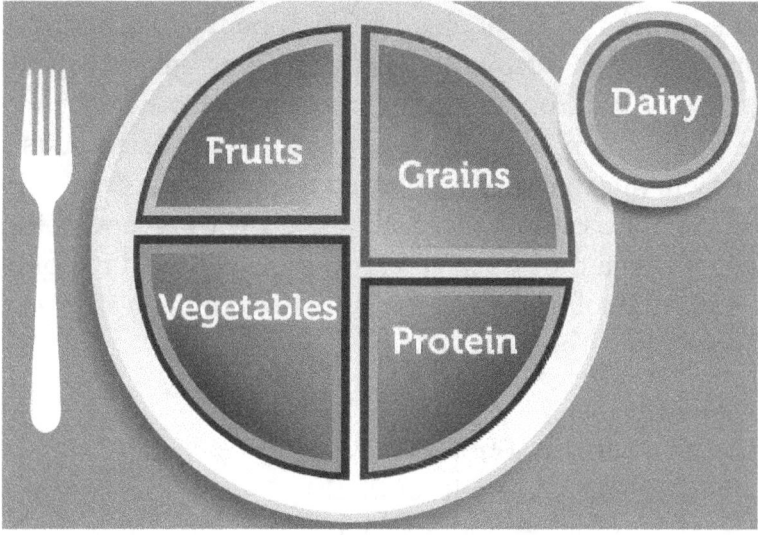

Figure 8. MyPlate

MyPlate Category	What 100 Calories of Food covers
Vegetables	1 Lettuce, 3 Radishes, 14 Spinach, and 25 Mushrooms, 5 Broccoli, 4 Carrots
Fruits	100 Blueberries, 1 Apple, 1 Banana, 20 Cherries, 2 Watermelon cup, 30 Grapes
Grains	½ small slice of bread, ½ roll, ⅓ potato
Proteins	18.7 g Freeze-dried shrimp cocktail, 18.8 g Chicken Breast, 16.7 g Salmon
Dairy	1 oz Cheese, 4.6 g Dry milk
Condiments	Sriracha Sauce, Mustard
Snack	Chocolate, Jerky, Pudding cups,

Figure 9: Favorite Foods for crew members

DISPUTES

Disputes will be solved by following the Space Treaty for arguments about colonization on Mars. They will not be heavily enforced since there will only be 6 astronauts. In order to solve internal disputes, astronauts must remain calm and not resort to violence. All astronauts should respect each other and should express their opinions with reasoning. In case astronauts face an obstacle they had not accounted for, astronauts will call the Earth control base in order to come up with a good solution. If astronauts cannot contact Earth, they will need to come up with potential solutions and use good reasoning for what choice they come up with.

Final Weight:
- Cost : ~ $50,140,000,000
- Tax (+29%) : ~ $14,540,600,000
- Total Cost: ~ $64,680,600,000

WORKS CITED

1. Gary Jordan, Can Plants Grow in Mars Soil?, https://www.nasa.gov/feature/can-plants-grow-with-mars-soil, 2017, Aug
2. R. M. Candanosa, Growing Green on the Red Planet, ChemMatters, 2017, APRIL/MAY, 5-7.
3. Nanette Londeree, Garden Good Guys—Soil, UC Marin Master Gardeners, https://ucanr.edu/sites/MarinMG/files/116762.pdf
4. Danielle Schlehahn, Alyssa Boudreau, Braden Barber, Braden Kowalchuk, Brette Langman, Jason Worobec, Can a Greenhouse Be Established on Mars?, University of Saskatchewan Undergraduate Research Journal, 2017, Volume 4, Issue 1, 1-13.
5. A. Soleimani Dorcheh, M.H. Abbasi, Silica Aerogel; Synthesis, Properties and Characterization, Journal of Materials Processing Technology, 2008, 199, 1-3, 10-26.
6. Silke Grosshagauer, Klaus Kraemer, and Veronika Somoza, The True Value of Spirulina, Journal of Agricultural and Food Chemistry, 2020.
7. D. Blersch, E. Biermann, D. Calahan, J. Ives-Halperin, M. Jacobson, P. Kangas, A Proposed Design for Wastewater Treatment and Recycling at the Flashline Mars Arctic Research Station Utilizing Living Machine Technology, Mars Society Life Support Technical Task Force, Maryland Subgroup, University of Maryland, College Park, MD, 2000.
8. McMahon S, Bosak T, Grotzinger JP, Milliken RE, Summons RE, Daye M, Newman SA, Fraeman A, Williford KH, Briggs DEG. A Field Guide to Finding Fossils on Mars. J Geophys Res Planets. 2018 May;123(5):1012-1040. doi: 10.1029/2017JE005478.

Epub 2018 May 24. PMID: 30034979; PMCID: PMC6049883.

9. Farmer, J. D., and Des Marais, D. J. (1999), Exploring for a record of ancient Martian life, J. Geophys. Res., 104(E11), 26977– 26995, doi:10.1029/1998JE000540.

10. Rossman P. Irwin, Kevin W. Lewis, Alan D. Howard, John A. Grant, Paleohydrology of Eberswalde crater, Mars, Geomorphology, Volume 240, 2015, Pages 83-101, ISSN, 0169-555X, https://doi.org/10.1016/j.geomorph.2014.10.012.Hadfield bio current–NASA. (2004). Retrieved July 10, 2023, from https://www.nasa.gov/pdf/64090main_ffs_bio_hadfield.pdf

11. Jessica Watkins Astronaut Biography. (2023). Retrieved July 10, 2023, from https://www.nasa.gov/sites/default/files/atoms/files/watkins-j.pdfKathleen Rubins Astronaut Biography. (2021). Retrieved July 10, 2023, from https://www.nasa.gov/sites/default/files/atoms/files/rubins-k.pdfMichael Massimino Astronaut Biography. (2014). Retrieved July 10, 2023, from https://www.nasa.gov/sites/default/files/atoms/files/massimino_michael_bio.pdfKjell N. Lindgren Astronaut Biography. (2023). Retrieved July 10, 2023, from https://www.nasa.gov/sites/default/files/atoms/files/lindgren-kn.pdf

12. G.Reid Wiseman Astronaut Biography. (2023). Retrieved July 10, 2023, from https://www.nasa.gov/sites/default/files/atoms/files/wiseman.pdf

13. Lewis, Kevin W., and Oded Aharonson. "Stratigraphic Analysis of the Distributary Fan in Eberswalde Crater Using Stereo Imagery." JGR: Planets, vol. 111, no. E6, Jan. 2006, https://doi.org/10.1029/2005je002558. Accessed 18 July 2023.

14. Andrew J. Feustel Astronaut Biography. (2018). Retrieved July 10, 2023, from https://www.nasa.gov/sites/default/files/atoms/files/feustel-aj_0.pdf
15. https://www.jpl.nasa.gov. "Curiosity Tests a New Way to Drill on Mars." NASA Jet Propulsion Laboratory (JPL), 28 Feb. 2018, www.jpl.nasa.gov/news/curiosity-tests-a-new-way-to-drill-on-mars. Accessed 18 July 2023.published, Space com Staff. "Curiosity Rover's Chemistry Lab Takes 1st First Taste of Mars Soil." Space.com, 14 Nov. 2012, www.space.com/18466-mars-rover-curiosity-soil-sample-sam-instrument.html.
16. "GeoHack–Eberswalde (Crater)." Geohack.toolforge.org, geohack.toolforge.org/geohack.php?pagename=Eberswalde_(crater)¶ms=24_S_33_W_globe:mars_type:landmark. Accessed 18 July 2023.
17. Irwin, Rossman P., et al. "Paleohydrology of Eberswalde Crater, Mars." Geomorphology, vol. 240, no. 240, July 2015, pp. 83–101, https://doi.org/10.1016/j.geomorph.2014.10.012. Accessed 24 Nov. 2022.
18. NASA. "In Depth | Mars." NASA Solar System Exploration, solarsystem.nasa.gov/planets/mars/in-depth/#:~:text=The%20 temperature%20 on%20 Mars%20 can.
19. Sharp, Tim, and Jonathan Gordon. "What Is the Temperature of Mars?" Space.com, 30 Nov. 2017, www.space.com/16907-what-is-the-temperature-of-mars.html.
20. Smith, Michael D., et al. "The Climatology of Carbon Monoxide and Water Vapor on Mars as Observed by CRISM and Modeled by the GEM-Mars General Circulation Model." Icarus, vol. 301, no. 301, Feb.

21. "Top 5 Highest Oxygen-Producing Indoor Plants—FNP." Ferns N Petals, www.fnp.com/article/top-5-highest-oxygen-producing-indoor-plants.

22. dutta, moumita. "86 Space Exploration Quotes for All Budding Astronauts." Kidadl.com, 17 Apr. 2023, kidadl.com/quotes/space-exploration-quotes-for-all-budding-astronauts.

23. https://www.howstuffworks.com/about-stephanie-watson.htm. "How Space Food Works." HowStuffWorks, 19 Feb. 2008, science.howstuffworks.com/space-food3.htm#:~:text=The%20space%20shuttle%20carries%20about. Accessed 20 July 2023.

24. Mars, Kelli. "Experiments to Unlock How Human Bodies React to Long Space Journeys." NASA, 7 Dec. 2022, www.nasa.gov/feature/experiments-to-unlock-how-human-bodies-react-to-long-space-journeys.

25. NASA. "Mars Oxygen In-Situ Resource Utilization Experiment (MOXIE)." 172.31.1.192, 2020, mars.nasa.gov/mars2020/spacecraft/instruments/moxie/.

(Preceding entry, continued:)
2018, pp. 117–31, https://doi.org/10.1016/j.icarus.2017.09.027.

EXPLORING THE RED PLANET
A PIONEERING MISSION TO MARS

MENNA MOHAMED HASSAN

ZICA STEFAN

GHEORGHE DAVID CRISTIAN

SCAFARU GEORGE EDUARD

Hassan, Stefan, Cristian, Eduard

INTRODUCTION

Mars, the enigmatic neighbor of Earth, has captivated the imagination of scientists and space enthusiasts for decades. As technological advancements and our understanding of the cosmos continue to progress, the possibility of embarking on a manned mission to Mars has transitioned from a distant dream to a tangible reality. This report delves into a groundbreaking interplanetary expedition—a mission to Mars, with a comprehensive focus on its scientific objectives — the reason why we are planning the exploration mission, structural design challenges and mission operations.

The purpose of this report is to give a theoretical proposal for what an actual human mission to Mars may look like, under some constraints and limitations, to create a model for future endeavors to making the first big leap on Mars for human-kind.

SCIENTIFIC OBJECTIVES

The primary impetus behind the mission to Mars is to unlock the secrets of this celestial body and gain crucial insights into the planet's past, present, and potential future. Scientific curiosity drives us to explore the geological history of Mars, decipher its atmospheric composition, and investigate the possibility of past or present life.

Our proposal consists of 4 fields of study that may unlock further knowledge about the Martian surface:

PALEONTOLOGY, ASTROBIOLOGY, GEOLOGY AND TOPOLOGY.

Paleontology is the study of past life through certain structures in sedimentary rock that indicate the existence of species of plants, animals and microbes. For our purposes, we will

Exploring the Red Planet

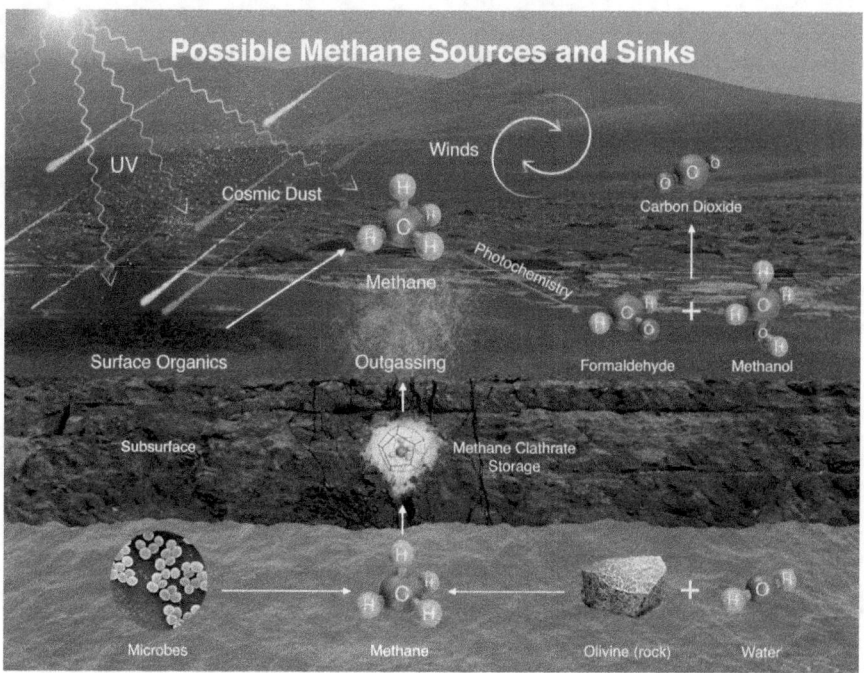

NASA/JPL-Caltech/SAM-GSFC/Univ. of Michigan

be studying rock and clay formations around the compound, specifically Noachian-Hesperian Fe-bearing clay-rich fluvio-lacustrine siliciclastic deposits[1], especially those enriched in silica since they have the best chance of containing fossilized structures of microbes and other microbiological activity. Whether Mars could sustain or not life in its past is out of the question. There is clear geological evidence for warmer, wetter intervals in the past that could have supported life at or near the surface, but our experiments could prove whether or not life on Mars actually existed.

Astrobiology will be the main focus of this mission. We will be studying the soil and regolith for presence of life currently on Mars. We will look at structure, metabolic functions, reproduction, structure[3], whether or not life on Mars is similar to ours or completely different, whether we are direct descendants of it and most importantly whether or not it exists. For this purpose, we have inside the habitat a Microbiology lab fitted with everything that is required for study of this field. We also have the ambition to study the effects of regolith as a soil substitute[2]. We will be studying the growth of plants like peas, soybeans, beans, sprouts and different ferns and mushroom inoculums, generally plants that have a less than 6 months growth period, in the prepared soil samples that will be sterilized and not to see the effects of both the Martian microbiology on Earth's plants and the effectiveness of regolith soil for food production in future missions. This study will provide a lot of useful information for future settlers about growth with limited resources under microgravity.

An artist's conception of a portable Martian greenhouse—NASA

Stimson sandstone formation in Gale Crater on Mars—NASA/Caltech-JPL/MSSS

Geology will provide insights into the chemical makeup of Mars rocks: if there was tectonic activity in the past, we should be seeing evidence of that in the rock (TSC)[4], if there were rivers in a certain region, we should be seeing chemistry and structures that indicate river beds[5], if there are mineral deposits in a certain area we should be seeing a higher concentration of that specific mineral or element in the soil. We will study possible "resource tiles" on Mars, which means more sustainability for future missions. For this purpose, we will give pathfinders handheld mass-spectrometers and other equipment to quickly evaluate on site or bring it to base for more in-depth analyses.

Our final field of study is Topology, for which we provide a unique solution to a mapping problem: LIDAR. We plan on using a light detection and ranging laser scanner fitted on the vehicle to create a database for topographic mapping of regions using mesh renderings of visited places. This should be able to map different relief and surface phenomena. This could also create an interactive map of the actual mission and provide the world with a realistic rendering of what Mars actually looks like.

INFRASTRUCTURE

Surviving and thriving on an alien planet like Mars present unprecedented challenges. To ensure the safety and well-being of the astronauts, state-of-the-art life support systems will be central to the mission's success. These systems will be responsible for providing: breathable air, potable water, sustenance and ensure mission safety and smooth conduct throughout the astronauts' stay on the Martian surface.

We developed some systems that use existing technology to achieve these goals.

LIFE SUPPORT SYSTEMS

One of the main concerns in the deployment of human life on the surface of Mars is the issue of providing adequate shelter for Marstronauts that is easily deployable, with minimal damage to any components, can be moved once it lands and most importantly can provide a safe environment for any settlers during rest or inactive periods. This should provide life support systems that provide oxygen in a pressurized atmosphere

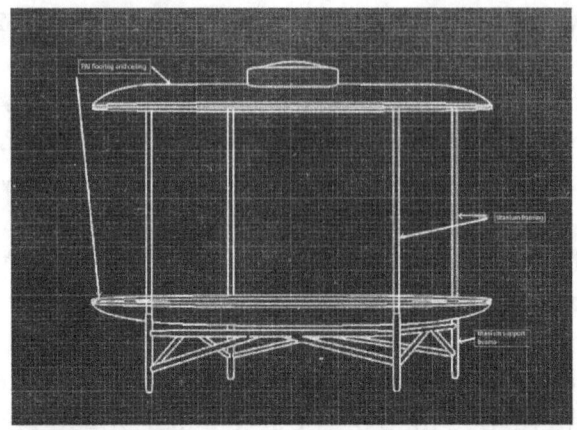

Concept art created in 2019–NASA

that can keep the concentration of O2 at 21%, electricity for all of the apparatus and electrical components that the settlers will be using while inside the compound and access to water for cleaning and other uses and it must also yield enough space for the scientific equipment, furniture and personal belongings.

For our design we decided that modular shelter would be the best approach, since you can theoretically infinitely expand your base in case of project expansion. This also allows flexibility if certain components get damaged while landing.

The design consists of a main operational base that must be constructed on site along with four pieces of tubing that interlock with each other that make up the habitat's accommodation and storage of the crew. The main base is made up of a titanium frame made out of 6 cm wide tubing with metal suspension systems for contact. This framing will be already assembled when it lands on the planet using thrusters and parachutes so as to keep the orientation of the shelter. The entire titanium support structure will be around 310 kilograms in weight.

The flooring and ceiling are made out of Polyamide-imide (PAI)[6] composites reinforced with titanium tubing that can sustain the weight of 4 people along with all the apparatus necessary (around 7 – 9 tons under Martian gravity) for the mission's success. They are hollow components lined with perpendicularly placed crossed corrugations that prevent deformation under stress. They have a face lined with high friction rubber for grip inside the habitat, and have the underside covered with the walls of the inflatable part of the habitat. The floor and ceiling of the habitat will weigh around 780 kilograms considering that the construction of the structures is mostly hollow.

The body of the pod is made out of a Vectran[7] (fiber made out of LCP) woven tarp that inflates to a cylinder of about 2.3 meters in height and 5 meters in diameter (total usable volume of 43kl out of which we estimate about 39kl will be atmosphere after placing the equipment inside the pod) that will be attached to the flooring and ceiling prior to the deployment. It has fabric pockets through which go 4 titanium support tubes, not unlike a tent design, to maintain the habitats shape. The Vectran sheet will have holes for installing the 2 air-locking doors that enable the expansion of the habitat. The entire weight for the walls will be around 1 ton.

The Vectran case will be lined with flexible aerogel-fiber glass sheets for thermic insulation and every habitat will be covered in a tarp made out of lining of Hydrogenated boron nitride nanotubes (hydrogenated BNNT's[8]) that extends to the ground as a means of protecting equipment under the habitat from dust and radiation. Hydrogenated BNNT's are our way of

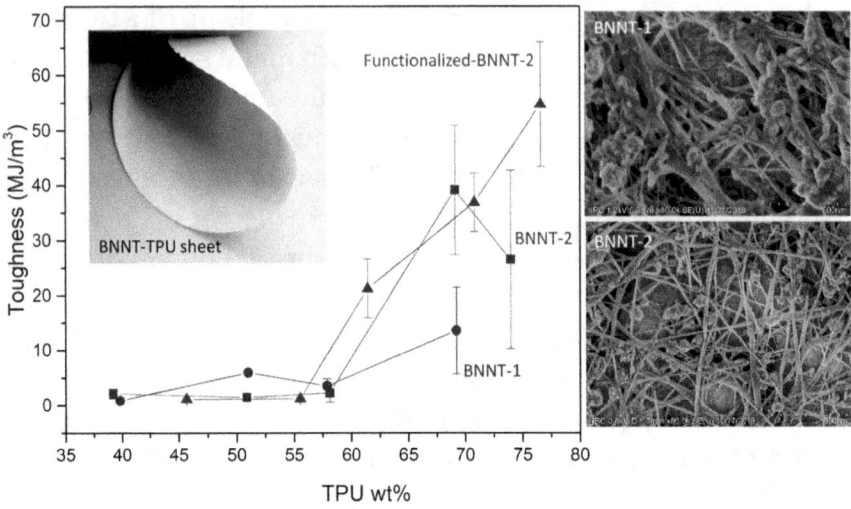

protection our crew from cosmic and solar radiation on the surface of mars.

The pod is fitted with an Aluminum tube about 1 meter in diameter in the center of the habitat to create the airlock. This will be installed on site, along with the vent, air compressor and habitat door needed to make the habitat enterable (with minimal loss of atmosphere). Ladders will be screwed outside the habitat and placed on this "hallway" for convenience. This device weighs about 190 kilograms without taking into consideration the compressor needed for achieving vacuum. From our estimations we would need less than 10-12 CFM (160-200 liters per minute) to create a vacuum similar to the atmosphere of Mars inside this chamber in less than 2 hours and also inflate the habitat at the beginning of the mission. A typical vacuum pump in that range is 500 – 550 Watts and weighs around 34 kilograms.

Under the pod there will be enough space to install the air filtering system tubing, battery, water pump and tank, air compressor for release, dehumidifier for recycling of water and storage for equipment that is not dust or air composition

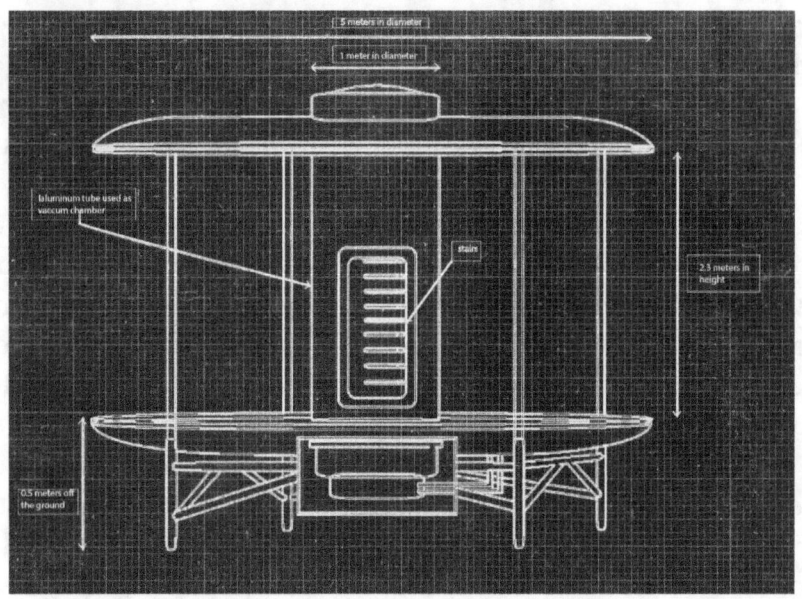

ESA developed Berthing Docking Mechanism—ESA

sensitive. The flooring will already have a section of piping for easier access. Wiring will also be installed through the flooring. The entire volume will be inflated through the compressors with 80% Nitrogen and 20% Oxygen pressurized at 1.2 atmospheres to account for loss of gasses ejected by the vacuum chamber at the start and return of a "Mars Walk".

The modules will also be made out of Vectran, each having two endings and 4 meters of length. Each ending is made out of titanium tubing, in the form of two connected eccentric circles that give the corridor it's horizontal cylinder shape. There will be 4 such tubes, one with an intersection for accommodation of 3 entry points. The smaller titanium frame will play the role of door and air-lock. Each door and small frame are about 1.5 meters in height/ diameter, with the bigger framing being 2.30 meters in diameter (for all 4 pods ~ 40kl or 36-32 kl of atmosphere once the equipment and furniture has been placed). The larger frame will also have triangular flat supports on the underside to keep the modules upright. This design is very similar to Bigelow's expandable activity module, but it has more components that make it more suitable for planet surface activity, so our weight estimations for one module is around 1600 kilograms, including the pressurized doors, flooring, tubing (water and air), electronics (radiators, lights and other devices) and PAI caps. The airtight seal will have the same design as the one from the ISS[9]. Every tube will have an "empty" side from which they will attach to an already pressurized environment and a "full" side, fitted with an airtight door for fitting more modules or a plastic stopping cap that will serve as a wall for the end of the habitat. Each tube will be inflated from the main habitat's air compressor by opening the door once the seal between the module and the pressurized environment will have been tested. Flooring for these modules and ladders to accommodate for the height difference, along with any tubing and furniture will be first brought in from outside in the main pod and installed into each module.

Every auxiliary structure, ration, tool and habitat module will be dropped in with landing balloons and parachutes. The only thruster assisted landing equipment will be for the main habitat support frame and the landing pod.

ACCOMMODATION

Considering that our crewmembers will have to spend 6 months on the Red Planet far from the civil domain of their homeworld, their loved ones and the comfort of a decent shower, we will need to ensure the fact that they will have the necessary appliances to survive in a clean and safe environment.

For that we have to provide necessary furniture, spaces and equipment for: cleaning, heating, eating, sleeping and communicating. Exercising equipment will be provided: one resistance

 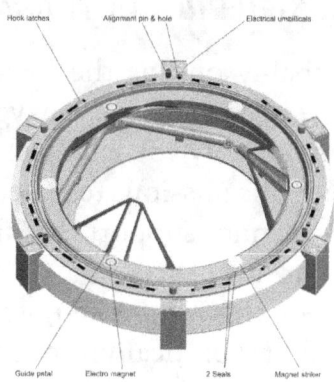

band squat machine and one resistance band treadmill with adjustable resistances to account for muscle and bone density loss.

Two of the modules will be furbished into apartments, accommodated with lightweight bunk beds, a nightstand, a desk with shelves, floor lights and toilet, with a common shower cabin fitted into the main pod. Every water reliant appliance will be connected to the water filtering system that will filter out waste and compost it, turn it into feed for the algae purifier or eject it into a collection tank for waste disposal.

Heating will be achieved through electric radiators that will be found among the landed materials. Lockers for suits with electromagnets to eject Martian dust will be placed in the main pod. Tables and chairs will also be available inside the habitat for eating.

Communication will be made through high gain antennas[6] located outside the habitat in extension of the support poles of the main pod for Earth-Mars communication. We will also have a communications server inside the habitat, wired through the satellites currently orbiting mars for relatively high speed, long-distance chat and vocal communication between crewmembers.

OXYGEN PRODUCTION AND AIR FILTRATION

Probably one of the most important habitation systems we have to develop is the oxygen production system. Without oxygen not only you cannot send out pathfinders for scouting and scientific missions to collect data about the Martian surface you also cannot support any kind of habitation system for humans to survive.

For this we looked at one possible source of oxygen that could theoretically produce oxygen indefinitely with minimal assistance: algae. The photosynthetic process can be used in two ways, for air filtration of the habitat (closed loop) and oxygen production for use outside the habitat.

The Air filtration system is made out of 2 parts: the bioreactor necessary to convert the buildup of CO_2 inside the habitat and a system of pressurized ventricular-like segregated pipes with vents that establish the flow of air through the bioreactor and inside the habitat, similar to what the circulatory system looks like in animals.

The pipes in this instance are separated into 2 kinds: pipes that flow to the bioreactor and pipes that draw the oxygenated air back into the habitat. They are the veins and arteries of the system. They are linked to 2 air compressors similar to the one inside the vacuum chamber (6-8 CFM for adequate flow, 400 Watts) for each flow direction. The air goes through a series of tubing arms fitted with one-way watertight valves that have holes in them for air distribution through the tank of the bioreactor. After the air leaves the tank, it enters the second set of pipes that release it into the compound.

The bioreactor, which acts as the lungs of the system is an acrylic pressurized water tank that yields about 4000 liters of water (that will house at landing around 400 liters) with 4 liters of Walne Medium[10] for support of growth of 1 gram of biomass per 1 liter of treated water in microgravity conditions. This should suffice for 4 Marstronauts living and exercising inside the compound. The Algae that we will use is Chlorella Vulgaris, along with redundancy in form of inoculum of N. muscorum and A. plantesis in case of culture failure. Inside the tank there will also be cold LEDs to provide enough light for the culture to photosynthesize. In the circular economy of the algae tank the only replenishing services the algae needs is CO_2, heat and light, with the possibility of enriching the medium with fertilizer made with regolith[11] and human waste.

The oxygen producing system will have many similarities with the air filtration system, but there will be a direct feed of atmospheric CO_2 in the system that will be converted into Oxygen. Unfortunately, concentrations of CO_2 are deadly for plants in the upper 1% or 10 000 ppmv, so the second bioreactor needs a cycling stable atmosphere. The process for extracting oxygen will be the same as in industrial use: with fractional distillation[12].

The algae will have a similar atmosphere to that of the inside of the habitat that will liquify periodically and be inserted back into the bioreactor with a small percentage of the oxygen being removed to fill oxygen tanks that will be used for outside missions. For each mission there will be about 4 15 liter oxygen tanks for a 3 hour round trip per Marstronaut, which the algae may produce in 0.5 – 1 days.

The air inside the bioreactor needs to be filtered of biomass, and then dried and depleted of CO_2 for preventing ice or dry ice forming inside the distiller. The fractional distiller will be insulated and heated with a precise electric heater for the separation of gases. The remaining Nitrogen and Oxygen along with the water vapor that has been dehumidified will be reinserted into the tank, while the CO_2 will be ejected outside the habitat.

Both of the reactors will be located in the "garden" modular pod for protection from the elements and ease of cleaning, since the mass of algae will need to be periodically reduced so as to not kill the remaining algae in the tank from overpopulation and decomposition. The excess algae will be used for compost and fertilizer for nitrogen fixing plants inside the garden in the regolith fertilizer experiments.

THE MARTIAN SUIT

A Mars suit, also known as a Mars space suit, is specifically designed for conducting extravehicular activities (EVAs) on the surface of the planet Mars. Unlike suits intended for spacewalks in the near vacuum of low Earth orbit, Mars suits prioritize mobility and durability against abrasion. Mars has a surface gravity that is approximately 37.8% of Earth's, about 2.3 times that of the Moon. This lower gravity presents a significant concern for the weight of the suit, while the absence of a vacuum reduces certain thermal requirements.

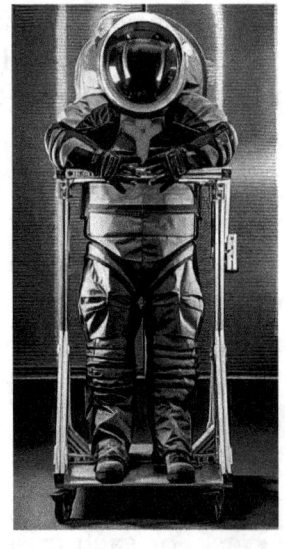

NASA Z-2 spacesuit prototype-NASA

When worn on the Martian surface, these suits must address the unique atmospheric conditions of Mars. The Martian atmosphere has a pressure ranging from about 0.6 to 1 kilopascal (0.087 to 0.145 psi). Consequently, the suits need to provide sufficient oxygen for the astronaut, considering that the Martian air primarily consists of carbon dioxide. Additionally, the Martian atmosphere is significantly thinner than Earth's atmosphere at sea level. The suit must also contend with the extreme temperatures of the Martian surface, ranging from -88 to -128 degrees Celsius.

Radiation exposure is a big concern, particularly during solar flare events that can cause a rapid increase in the amount of radiation in a short period of time. Therefore, Mars suits must incorporate measures to mitigate the harmful effects of radiation on astronauts during their surface operations.

The NASA Z-2 suit, a Mars suit design from the 2010s, incorporated electroluminescent patches to facilitate crew members' identification of one another. To assess its performance, the Z-2 suit underwent three types of tests: vacuum chamber tests, tests conducted in NASA's Neutral Buoyancy Laboratory (a facility simulating zero gravity), and tests in a rocky desert environment. These evaluations were part of the larger Z series space suit development.

In the context of Mars suit development, the Mars 2020 Perseverance rover carried out a materials test called the SHERLOC experiment[13]. This experiment included a test target featuring materials used in space suits. Its objective was to measure how these materials react to the Martian environment. Six materials were selected for testing: Orthofabric[14], Teflon, nGimat-coated Teflon, Dacron, Vectran, and Polycarbonate. The results of this test will aid in the selection of optimal materials for future Mars space suits[15].

NASA subjected potential Mars suit materials to Mars-equivalent ultraviolet (UV) radiation for 2500 hours and subsequently examined the effects on the materials. This testing aimed to address concerns about how the suits' materials respond to chemically reactive Mars dust and prolonged exposure to ultraviolet light, considering the expected duration and usage of the suits.

In designing Mars surface extravehicular activity (EVA) suits, one researcher drew inspiration from Medieval armor suits. Some proposed features for Mars suits include a Heads-up display projected onto the visor, integrated communications equipment, life support systems, and a voice-recognition assistant.

The Biosuit[16] is a form-fitting mechanical counterpressure suit that applies pressure through the structure and elasticity of the material, as opposed to prior space suits that rely on pressurized gas. This unique design eliminates the need for gas pressure, which can make traditional suits rigid when inflated, resembling a balloon.

The Aoudo[17] suit, developed by the Austrian Space Forum, serves as a simulator for planetary surface activities. While it ventilates with ambient air, it incorporates various features to simulate a space suit. Additionally, it facilitates the testing and advancement of technologies like a heads-up display integrated into the helmet.

The AX-5[18] suit, part of a series of hard suits developed at NASA Ames, contrasts with the current soft or hybrid suits. The latter utilize a lower-pressure pure oxygen atmosphere, requiring individuals going on extravehicular activities (EVA) to pre-breathe oxygen to prevent decompression sickness. In contrast, a hard suit can employ a high-pressure atmosphere, eliminating the need for pre-breathing, while still maintaining maneuverability compared to a high-pressure soft suit.

A simulated Mars suit was employed during the HI-SEAS Earth-based[19] spaceflight analog tests conducted in Hawaii, USA during the 2010s.

The design of Mars suits has also been utilized as a subject for technology education, allowing students to explore and learn about the intricacies of space suit technology and design.

ENVIRONMENTAL DESIGN REQUIREMENTS

The most critical factors for immediate survivability and comfort on the Martian surface are to provide: sufficient pressure to prevent the boiling of body fluids; supply of oxygen and removal of carbon dioxide and water vapor for breathing; temperature control; and protection from cosmic radiation.

The atmospheric pressure on Mars exhibits variations based on elevation and seasons; however, it is insufficient to sustain life without the aid of a pressure suit. The lowest pressure that the human body can endure, known as the Armstrong limit, is equivalent to the pressure at which water boils (vaporizes) at the average temperature of a human body, approximately 6.3 kilopascals (0.91 psi). In contrast, the average surface pressure on Mars measures only about one-tenth of this value, at 0.61 kilopascals (0.088 psi). The highest pressure on Mars, found at the lowest surface elevation in the Hellas Basin, reaches 1.24 kilopascals (0.180 psi), roughly twice the average pressure. Throughout the Martian year, which spans about two Earth years, there is a seasonal variation caused by the sequential freezing and sublimation of carbon dioxide (which constitutes 95.9% of the atmosphere), resulting in a global fluctuation of approximately 0.2 kilopascals (0.029 psi) in atmospheric pressure.

However, it is important to note that the Martian atmosphere contains only 0.13-0.14% oxygen, significantly lower than the 20.9% found in Earth's atmosphere. As a result, breathing the Martian atmosphere is impossible for nearly all organisms, necessitating the provision of oxygen at a pressure exceeding the Armstrong limit.

A thin layer of gold on the visor plastic bubble of current space helmets, shields the face from harmful parts of the Sun's spectrum. Visor designs, in general, have a design goal of allowing the astronaut to see, but block ultraviolet and heat, besides the pressure requirements.

It has been detected that ultraviolet light does reach the surface of Mars. Martian carbon dioxide tends to block ultraviolet light of wavelengths shorter than about 190 nm, however above that there is less blocking depending on the amount of dust and Rayleigh scattering. Significant amounts of UVB and UVC light are noted to reach the surface of Mars.

Another consideration is what would happen if astronauts somehow breathe in Mars dust. The health effect of Mars dust is a concern, based on known information about it which includes that it may be abrasive and/or reactive. Studies have been done with quartz dust and also compared it to lunar dust exposure. An Apollo 17 astronaut complained of hay fever like symptoms after his Moon walk. The lunar dust was known to cling to the space suits and be taken in with the astronauts when they came into the Apollo Lunar Module.

WATER EXTRACTION

Water ice in the form of debris covered glaciers or ice sheets that could be up to hundreds of meters thick has been discovered and mapped in the mid latitude of Mars. This presents a unique opportunity for in situ resource utilization (ISRU) of water, where the location could be favorable for a future human base. Under NASA funding, Honeybee Robotics developed and demonstrated water extraction from subsurface ice with a Technology Readiness Level (TRL) 5 RedWater system in a Mars-simulated environment that utilizes 2 proven terrestrial technologies: coiled tubing (CT) and the Rodriguez well (a.k.a. RodWell)[20].

The performance of the system was evaluated in terms of drilling with pneumatic cuttings clearing, melting a well, and extracting the water from the well to a tank at the surface. The storage of the water will be made with a pressurized water tank that can hold 1000 liters of water.

They will find water sources through the GPS systems provided by satelites orbiting Mars, with predetermined paths of conduct installed on their machines.

After the extraction of water for 8 days of about 6000-10000 liters of water to place inside the habitat for showers and air

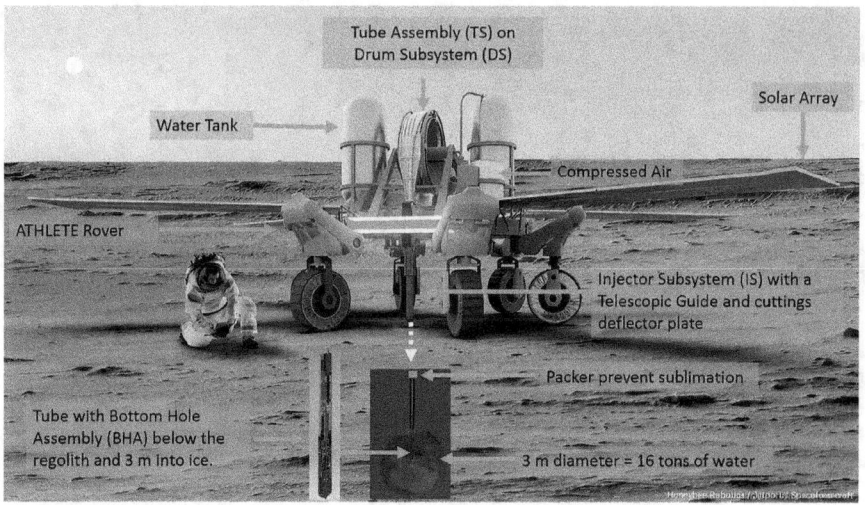

RedWater with all the subsystems—Ninth International Conference on Mars 2019

filtration. Afterwards, the crew will periodically bring in more water until they have enough to live comfortably. This process will take 15-20 days total. The habitat will house a storage tank that yields about 4000 liters of circulating water that will be continuously filtered from the air and urine of the crewmates with a filtration system similar to that of the ISS.

THE MARTIAN VEHICLE

As we are aware, Mars has about half the surface area of Earth, therefore it is necessary to have a reliable vehicle for safe travel across the planet. Our designed vehicle, inspired by the futuristic Mars rover at Kennedy Space Centre Visitor Complex, is specifically engineered to withstand the planet's radiation and harsh soil conditions.

The vehicle's frame is constructed using titanium, chosen for its exceptional corrosion resistance and high

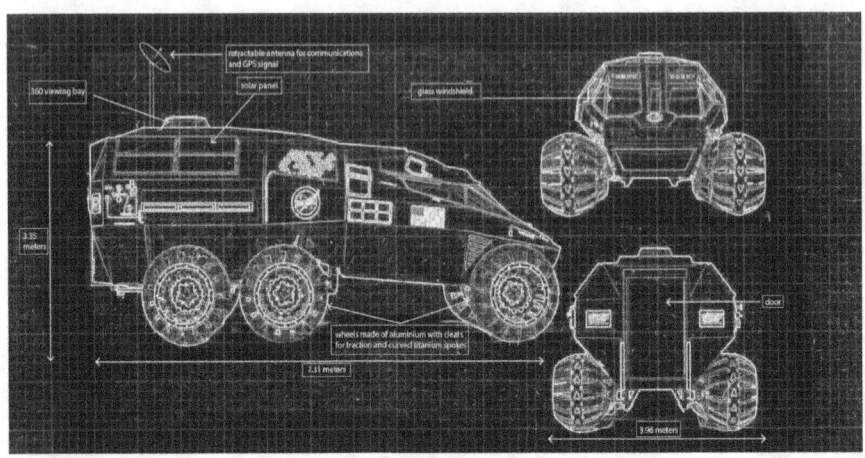

The Mars rover concept vehicle — NASA

strength-to-density ratio, surpassing that of any other metallic element. Its dimensions are as follows: height of 3.35 meters, length of 7.31 meters, and width of 3.96 meters. In addition to the vehicle, there will be an antenna for local and Earth communication, as well as for GPS signal reception, enabling safer and better-organized navigation across the Martian desert.

The wheels play a crucial role in traversing Mars' surface. Since regular tires cannot be used, we have opted for aluminum wheels similar to those used on previous Mars rovers, employing the same mechanism. To withstand the terrain, the vehicle will feature king shock off-road suspensions, akin to those found in large off-road trucks. Since solar power is abundant on the Martian surface due to its thin atmosphere and large exposure to sunlight, equipping rovers with solar panels to charge electric batteries ensures a continuous and sustainable power supply for extended missions. There will be 10 solar panels on the car: 8 on the sides and 2 on top of it.

Another key consideration in this endeavor is the choice of propulsion systems for the transportation vehicle. While traditional internal combustion engines have been the go-to option

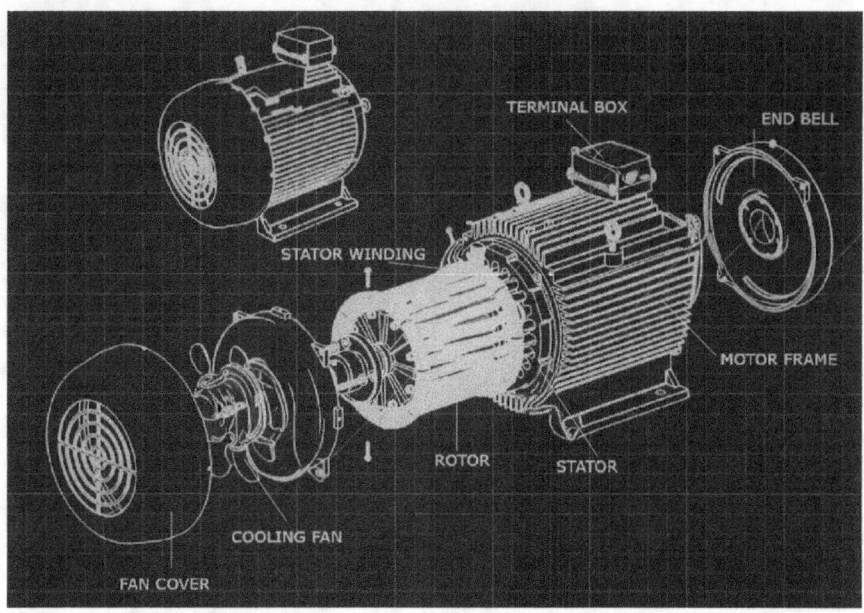

for Earth-based vehicles, the unique challenges and conditions of Mars make electric engines a compelling choice.

Mars is a harsh environment with limited resources, particularly when it comes to energy. Relying on conventional internal combustion engines would necessitate carrying substantial amounts of fuel from Earth, adding considerable mass and cost to the mission. In contrast, electric engines offer unparalleled energy efficiency and the ability to harness power from renewable sources available on the red planet.

The electric motor[21] will be our saving grace, since methane as a fuel source is verry costly energy-wise to produce.

These engines will be positioned with one near the first set of wheels and another at the rear. Given the vehicle's high energy requirements, it will be powered by four lithium-ion batteries, placed between the two motor bays. The batteries have a nominal capacity of 100 kWh, comprising 7,920 cells, with 95 kWh of usable energy. Their total weight amounts to approximately

360 kilograms. Additionally, the car will be equipped with three solar panels: two on the sides and one on top, ensuring a steady supply of power.

Its maximum speed range is 30 km/h and inside of it we will have stored 6 tubes of oxygen, every tube lasting for 45 minutes each. This means that the overall area we can explore is around 3000 km² over the whole mission. The entire car will weigh about 2.5 tons.

COMMUNICATION

Effective communication on Mars is vital for the success of human missions and maintaining connections with Earth. Establishing reliable communication links between Mars and Earth requires powerful and efficient systems. International space agencies, including NASA with its Deep Space Network (DSN)[22], employ strategically located antennas for transmitting and receiving signals from spacecraft and rovers on Mars.

Various methods, such as radio waves or laser communications[23], facilitate communication between Mars and Earth. Radio waves are commonly used due to their ability to penetrate the Martian atmosphere, while laser communications offer potential for higher data transfer rates.

Due to the varying distance between Mars and Earth caused by their orbital positions, communication experiences time delay. Known as round-trip light time, this delay can even reach 20 minutes. Mission operators and astronauts must account for this delay, anticipating longer response times.

Ground-based mission control centers serve as command hubs for Mars missions. They coordinate and monitor activities of astronauts, rovers, and mission assets on Mars. Real-time communication with the crew is facilitated, providing guidance, support, and troubleshooting assistance.

Martian crew members require communication systems within habitats or during extravehicular activities. Wireless devices, intercoms, and specialized communication systems integrated into Mars suits enable connectivity among the crew.

Future Mars missions may employ IP networks akin to the internet for efficient communication between habitats, rovers, and mission components. This enables data sharing, collaboration, and remote operations.

POWER GENERATION

For Power generation we will use solar panels. They are relatively cheap, easy to transport and to setup. For our requirements we estimate that the air compression systems, water circulation and filtration systems and heating we will spend about 100 -120 kWh per day. For our vehicle which will run for only 2-3 hours per day for an average of 60 km per day which is 12 kWh per day. The extra accommodation, including lights which may run constantly adds up to 40–58 kWh per day. Suit electric components which will also run for 2-3 hours per day will consume 20 kWh daily.

Using these estimations, we can infer that our system will average 172–210 kWh per day. That amount of energy spending can be covered by a system of 55 solar panels (1.76 tons) with a rating of 500 W that produce energy for 12 hours per day. To create redundancy, we will need a power storage system in the form of an industrial Lithium battery[24] that, for a rating of 215 kW, weighs about 2 tons.

LANDING GEAR

Even though we talked about other technical details about the habitat and equipment, now comes the most iconic moment of the mission that marks it's beginning: the Landing.

After a 7-month trip towards the red planet the 2 spacecraft landing units will enter low Mars orbit. One of them will house the framing of the main habitat that will also serve as the landing pod for the Marstronauts and the air supply for the first 8 days of expeditions. It will have a heat shielding unit that will cover the assembled unit (without pressurization) so as to not damage the walls of the inflatable. The crewmates will be wearing their suits with full function active for preparing the habitat as soon as they land. The habitat will have a thruster attached to it that will slow down the pod, along with the parachute, to almost a full stop. The weight of propellant (hydrogen) using the rocket equation[25] after taking into account the stopping power of the parachute is about 5 tons of fuel.

The second spacecraft that houses the rest of the equipment, along with the atmosphere inside the habitat and the 600 liters of water necessary for the beginning of the mission inside and outside of the hull of our vehicle along with the modular pods will be landed using balloons made out of Vectran (commonly used) to reduce impact damage and also weight by eliminating the need for thrusters.

SCIENTIFIC INSTRUMENT

As one of the goals of our Mission to Mars is to learn more about Mars' environment, so, various research will be done for studying the soil and its components. Hence, we will need research tools like bucket augers to hold the Mars regolith. Then, we can use scout mini autonomous mobile base to transport the samples. After that, the samples will be analyzed in the lab by using the laboratory instruments such as microscopes. Consequently, the observations/ results collected during the analysis will be saved on laptops. In addition to using Tech devices for research, we will use an infrared thermometer to measure the daily body's temperature for Marsnauts. Moreover, we will leverage the locations on Mars which have high temperatures by using the sun rays to produce electricity. This will be achieved by using solar panels to collect the rays then, the electric current will flow to the charge controller which sends it to the battery to either save it, use it as DC power or use it as AC power.

HUMAN OPERATIONS

Our project depends on the operational skills, planning and work that our crew can output. They need tight schedules to increase efficiency of the mission, outstanding qualifications and experience for field operations and system management, emergency procedures in case of unexpected outcomes and recreational and entertainment systems in place to combat boredom, fatigue and home-sickness.

Considering the requirements we have planned the following events and schedules for our pathfinders to have every possible advantage in succeeding and surviving in the Martian environment.

CREW

The mission will have four crew members. The four Marsnauts have experience in most of the STEM fields which will enable them to leverage their skills in doing their tasks during the Mars mission.

The crew members consist of a systems engineer, electronics/ mechanical/ aerospace engineer, doctor/ surgeon, and an ecologist. The Systems Engineer will design, construct and test aircraft, spacecraft, missiles, satellites and equipment. In addition, the Systems Engineer will be responsible for making sure that all of the subsystems in a spacecraft work together so that the spacecraft meets its objectives. The Electronics/ Mechanical/ Aerospace Engineer will have three responsibilities. First, monitoring the Technological equipment in the spaceship. Second, making quick and long-term decisions in case any device encountered an unexpected damage. Third, checking the spaceship system with the systems engineer. The Doctor/ Surgeon must have advanced experience in Physical and Psychological health and how living on Mars impacts the human body. The Doctor/ Surgeon will have five tasks. First, checking the crew members' health daily. Second, saving crew members health data. Third, giving advice for crew members on what missions they can or cannot do based on their current health condition. Fourth, offering medicines and first aid if needed. Fifth, conducting Biomedical/ Biology research. The Ecologist will have four responsibilities. First, planting crops. Second, monitoring the food amount daily consumption by the crew members. Third, conduct research about Mars soil and see how it can be used for planting. Fourth, exploring locations on Mars that may have evidence of past life.

There is no commander. Each crew member is responsible for their own tasks. This will give the Astronauts a strong feeling of leadership and responsibility which will lead to outstanding work. However, if the crew encountered any problems/ conflicts, the systems engineer can offer advice and help.

LANDING LOCATION

The mission will be done in Mawrth Vallis[26], located at 22.3°N, 343.5°E. The reason for choosing this location is due to its abundance of Fe/Mg-smectites, which can be located and studied, with deposits mapped and entered into the database. In addition, we will study clay deposits, which are common in this region, for finding evidence of metabolic activity indicative of organic life or fossilization of past life present on the Red Planet. Finally, the Mawrth Vallis is located near Chryse Planitia which is known for having subsurface ice that can be harvested using the mining techniques developed by Honeybee Robotics.

LANDING SEQUENCE

After landing, but before the installment of life support systems, the cremates will leave the lander through the airlock on top of the habitat. They will place the ladder previously attached to the floor outside the habitat to retrieve all of the equipment and the externals of the habitat from the vehicle. They will place anything essential for the habitat inside the main pod and proceed to the next step.

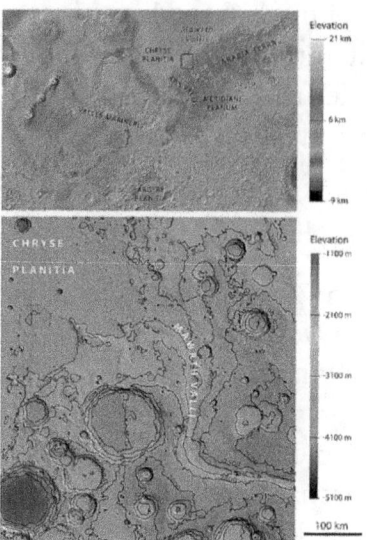

Localization of the Mawrth Vallis region on the MOLA topography

Then, they will install the solar panels and battery into the wiring installed in the flooring of the pods. This will provide the unit with enough power to fuel the necessary systems and devices.

For the next step, the crew will install the life support systems to the now functional habitat, inflating the main pod and placing the tubes into the main habitat through the airlocks placed along the walls. They will furbish the newly placed pods with the air filtration system, the biomass, 400 liters of water, 4 liters (total of 404 kilograms) of Walne medium to start the culturing and 200 liters of water for water rationing (200 kilograms), flooring, plant pots, accommodate with beds and racks for devices and equipment and furbishing the microbiology lab in the intersection side of the modular pods.

After these stages are complete, the next step for our pathfinders is to find water and start the RedWater process for drilling, after which they will melt the water, purify it and place it into the system of plumbing inside the habitat and completing the 8000 liters of medium they need for the oxygen production system.

SCHEDULE

The first priority of the crew after landing is finding water and harvesting it in an alert and consistent manner for the next 10 days. Water is a precious commodity on Mars, and obtaining a sustainable supply is vital for survival and continued exploration. Additionally, astronauts will undergo emergency preparedness drills to equip them with the necessary skills and knowledge to handle unforeseen challenges that may arise during their stay on the red planet.

From the third day onward, the mission will adopt a well-structured 6-month routine, which will strike a balance between work, research, and relaxation. This daily schedule will serve as the framework for the astronauts' activities, ensuring maximum efficiency and mental well-being.

The 6 months routine is as follows:

- **7:30–Waking Up:**
  Astronauts will begin their day at 8:00, allowing ample time for rest and recovery. A good night's sleep is essential for their physical and mental health, especially in the demanding Martian environment.
- **8:30–Shower:**
  Maintaining personal hygiene is crucial for the well-being of the astronauts and the overall cleanliness of the habitat. Regular showers will help them feel refreshed and ready to tackle the day's challenges (in order to conserve water, we will have 2 people in the crew shower one day and the other 2 the next day and so on)

- **9:00 – Breakfast:**
  A nutritious breakfast will provide the necessary energy and sustenance for the day's activities.
- **10:00 – System Check:**
  Ensuring that all equipment and systems are functioning correctly is paramount for a successful mission. Regular checks will identify and address any issues promptly, preventing potential setbacks.
- **11:00 – Research Activities:**
  The morning will be dedicated to various research tasks:
  a. **Planet Exploration via Vehicle:** Astronauts will explore the Martian terrain using vehicles, allowing them to cover more ground efficiently and collect valuable data. (to be noted, before and after an expedition we will have a maintenance check up to see if our exploration gear is unharmed and ready to use again in the next trip; the trip is going to be performed by 2 people, while the other 2 will be doing other research from the base-laboratory.)
  b. **Biological Research for Plant Growth and Microbial Life:** Studying the growth of plants on Mars will provide crucial insights into the planet's potential for sustaining life and future colonization efforts.
  c. **Clay Extraction for Paleontology Studying:** The examination of Martian clay can offer essential clues about the planet's past, potentially unveiling its geological history.
- **14:00 – Free Time:**
  Allocating leisure time allows astronauts to unwind, socialize, and pursue personal interests, promoting a healthy work-life balance.
- **15:00 – Communication with Earth Headquarters:**
  Regular check-ins with Earth headquarters will maintain a connection with our home planet, providing

updates on progress and offering emotional support to the team.
- **17:00–Exercise:**
  Physical fitness is crucial for astronauts, especially in the low-gravity environment of Mars. Regular exercise will help maintain their health and prevent muscle atrophy.
- **18:30–Continued Research:**
  Evening hours will be dedicated to further plant research and unloading samples collected by rovers, maximizing the use of daylight for outdoor tasks.
- **20:30–Dinner:**
  A well-prepared and nourishing dinner will fuel the astronauts for the next day's activities and encourage camaraderie during shared meals.
- **21:30–Sleep:**
  A restful night's sleep is vital for the astronauts' mental and physical well-being. Sufficient rest prepares them for the challenges of the following day.

EMERGENCY PLANS

The importance of an emergency plan is quantified by the importance of the failure of the system that said plan needs to prevent. For our purposes there are 2 situations that need immediate addressing when anomalies appear. The first such problem appears in the oxygen filtration system.

Unlike the filtration of water or electrical components that can be easily soldered or replaced/ repaired, bioactive systems cannot be easily replaced, especially when the culturing of such organisms is so slow and tedious. So, after one of the algae cultures showed signs of dying off and everything has been tried by the microbiologist to save that culture with no results, the team will enter the Oxygen Emergency plan.

The plan consists of saving as much biomass as possible from the dying algae and saving it for compost in specialized tanks, with some remaining species in isolated medium tanks for refurbishing. Then the functions of the first tank will be passed along to the second tank, with all exploration missions being interrupted until the recalibration of the ecosystem. A new redundant strain of algae will be introduced into the bioactive tank after recalibration to start culturing after which it will be monitored for the next 6 days. This process will happen every time the algae die off with possibility to recirculate algae until a mutation occurs in one of them to let them survive in the tank's conditions.

The second emergency situation is malfunction of vehicle in exploration mission. Human resource is invaluable and irreplaceable, so we need to conserve it as much as possible. When two pathfinders find themselves lost in the wilderness of Mars they will have use of many systems to repair the vehicle, including a secondary power-source located at the back of the vehicle. The crew is instructed to leave all samples and equipment on site and to mark their GPS with their location so they can get the most of the battery and return home, retrieving it the next day.

CONCLUSION

In conclusion, this mission models what a trip to Mars could look like under the specified constraints. The total mass of the inventory is in the range of 27 to 31 tons of material, including air supply, landing gear, habitats, furniture, accommodation, power supply, life support systems, transportation, rations, radio equipment and human crew along with other redundant systems necessary for emergency. This model is by no means perfect and completely accurate regarding the engineering and present technologies, but it is scientifically sound and feasible in the next 3 to 5 years. We are proposing this as a reference for future planning of missions and we believe it to be valuable at least as inspiration to future pathfinders trying to achieve the improbable for the future of mankind.

We recommend the use of inflatable habitation systems since they are cheap and easy to set up on the Red Planet. They offer plenty of protection from the elements and are ideal for an on-the-go base. We also recommend the use of bioreactors as a source of oxygen since they only use metabolic functions to produce the essence of surface life for little electric energy.

The mission to Mars represents a pivotal moment in the annals of human history, where our species embarks on a daring odyssey to explore and potentially inhabit another planet. Throughout this report, we have delved into the scientific objectives, life support systems, and mission goals that will drive this extraordinary interplanetary endeavor. As we conclude, it becomes evident that this ambitious mission is not merely an exploration of the Red Planet but a transformative journey that holds profound implications for the future of humanity and our place in the cosmos.

REFERENCES:

1. A Field Guide to Finding Fossils on Mars – National Library of Medicine
2. "Cyanobacteria as Candidates to Support Mars Colonization: Growth and Biofertilization Potential Using Mars Regolith as a Resource" – Frontiers in Microbiology
3. "Mars Curiosity Rover Sees a Strong Carbon Signature in a Bed of Rocks – Could Indicate Biological Activity"–SciTechDaily

4. "The impact of tectonic stress chemistry on mineralization processes: A review" – ScienceDirect
5. "Scientists analysing Martian mudstones reveal chemistry of ancient lake in study" – Imperial College London
6. "What is PAI?"–Curbell Plastics
7. "Vectran"–Wikipedia
8. "Real Martians: How to Protect Astronauts from Space Radiation on Mars"–NASA
9. "Sealed with Care – A Q&A" -NASA
10. "Walne Medium"–Biocyclopedia
11. "Cyanobacteria as Candidates to Support Mars Colonization: Growth and Biofertilization Potential Using Mars Regolith as a Resource" – Frontiers in Microbiology
12. "Air Separation Process"–SIADMacchineImpianti
13. "Scanning Habitable Environments with Raman and Luminescence for Organics and Chemicals"–Wikipedia
14. "Mars Suit"–Wikipedia
15. ibid.
16. ibid.
17. ibid.
18. ibid.
19. "HI-SEAS"–Wikipedia
20. "RedWater: Water Mining System for Mars" – Mary Anne Liebert
21. "Electric Motor"–Tech Vision
22. "What is the Deep Space Network?"–NASA
23. "Laser communication in space"–Wikipedia

24. "What Kind of Battery is Used for Solar Panels?" – We Recycle Power
25. "Tsiolkovsky rocket equation"–Wikipedia
26. "Phyllosilicates in the Mawrth Vallis region of Mars"–AGU
27. https://www.pushan.in/solar-electricity.php
28. https://www.industry.gov.au/australian-space-discovery-centre/pathways-career-space/space-systems-engineer#:~:text=Space%20systems%20engineers%20design%2C%20construct,the%20spacecraft%20meets%20its%20objectives

MISSION TO MARS 2023
"HEXA-HIVE"

FARES SABBAGH

ABDALLAH DARWESH

MUHAMMED AL MUHAIMED

LOBABA KABALAN

ANAS SHAHIN

AHMAD SADEK ALBASATNEH

ABSTRACT

The Hexa-Hive mission is a planned to stay on mars for around 1.5 years and aims to study the possibility of future life on Mars. This complete project takes in account all of the factors for this mission's success. Since icy water is proved to exist within mars, we chose a landing site in which water is about 1 meter deep underground.

Using a drilling system that was studied thoroughly, we should be able to secure one of the most important life dependencies for our habitat. The habitat has a shape of a flower with a hexagonal central chamber. This design, as well as the ExoMars Program, inspired the name of the project: A mix of hexa, standing for the hexagonal chamber and that rhymes with Exo, and hive, which is both hexagonal, and symbolizes team-work and cooperation.

Upon landing, the closed-flower-shaped habitat will start to automatically deploy its aluminum foundations (i.e. petals). For the atmosphere inside the habitat, we will be using multiple MOXIE devices to provide us with Oxygen and will bring tanks from Earth for Nitrogen. Those two gases will first be mixed and then released into the habitat to synthesize an earth-like internal atmosphere.When it comes power generation, we'll generate the needed electricity from solar panels and Kilopower reactor. In addition, our mission's Marsonautes will have a balanced food diet that consists of MRE-like meals, as well as freshly-grown food. The Deep Space Network communication system will be used for the mission to ensure continuous communication with the Earth. The physical and mental health of the astronauts on board are a priority for us. Our advanced health and entertainment systems will help ensure that the astronauts will stay in a pristine condition throughout the entire trip.

SCIENCE

2.1 LAUNCH AND RETURN

For the Launch, we will be departing form Earth in Jun-26-2035. The time it will take to reach Mars will be around 208 days. Mars arrival will be on Jan-20-2036. We chose this specific launch date because of its optimal distance and time it need to go to and from Mars. The total stay on Mars will be for 1.49 years, and the Mars departure Jul 17-2037. The mission will end on Jan-25-2038. The total mission duration will be 2.58 years and This wil be the most optimal launch window in the next 15 years according to our research.[18]

2.2 LANDING

To reach the deep layers of the Martian surface, that are not easily reachable with current technologies, we looked for already dug sites, craters!

And because our priority for a human mission is water we decided to search in northern latitudes that are above 40 where

Figure 2.1: Water depth map in Mars

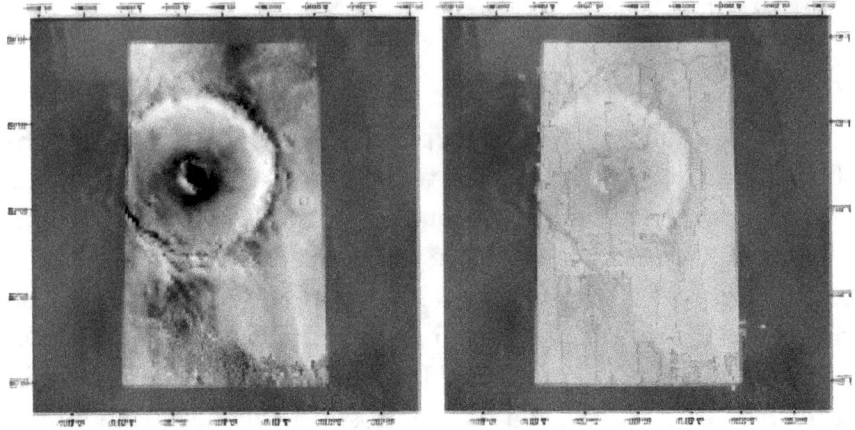

Figure 2: Milankovic Crater

subsurface water is confirmed to exist, and according to last orbital surveys, the shallowest region for subsurface water is somewhere between 200 and 280 longitudes.

The outlined box in Figure 2.1 represents the ideal region to send astronauts for them to be able to dig up water ice from the Martian surface.[25]

Using Caltech's Murray Lab 3D Map of Mars[4] we searched for possible suitable craters to land and after measuring he diameter of nearly each one we find that Milankovic (see Figure 2.2), at exactly the following coordinates: (-147.153047, 54.068565). It is suitable for our explorations that will, according to NASA, the mission will be limited to 100km[43], and since according to the IAU it has a diam eter of 113.51 and is stretched between 55.42 Northernmost Latitude and 53.51 Southernmost Latitude and from 215.08 Easternmost Longitude and 211.78 Westernmost Longitude.[19] It's floor is flat in some regions and covered with dunes, and also has clefts and holes which will be of a great geological importance, not to mention that this region is located in a minor impact possibility region, and the cherry on top is that residing in a crater can provide protection to some degree against strong Marian storms due to the occurring of turbulent flaw when winds face a hole. It has a temperature range of 17C in the day, and can go as low as -40C at night.[32]

2.3 SCIENTIFIC MISSION

During this mission, the crew will have different objectives to work and do research on, including but not limited to exploring the possibility of life on the Martian surface, be it in the past, present, or the future. This will be accomplished by using different instruments and sensors to detect if there is any sign of past or present life in the subterranean water or the regolith of the planet.

We will also be studying the effects of the Martian environment of humans and different animals, like ants and mice; how will they react to different gravity? will their behavior change after a while? what psychological effects will it have on them long-term? Finding a way to make a Mars Colony is also an important factor in our mission; what infrastructure will it need? how long will it take? what things should we bear in mind while searching for these answers?

Another thing we will be looking into is the geological structure of the planet. From what it is formed? why has it changed so much over the years? what could happen in the not so near future? and these questions can help us better understand the history of mars and will help in learning new ways to conquer the planet and make it our own.

For researching all of this, we have brought will us plenty of instruments that will help us check for each and every thing needed to be able to accomplish this mission and learning the most about this red planet.

2.4 AGRICULTURE

2.4.1 Method

Our favorable method of agriculture is a hydroponic system. Hydroponics produce crops 50% faster than traditional agricultural methods. The system will be fully automated so that minimal monitoring would be required. NASA plant physiologist Dr. Ray Wheeler believes that all the resources necessary for hydroponic farming can be either recycled from those initially used on the journey to Mars, acquired on the surface of the planet, or made on site, a process known as In-Situ Resource Utilization (ISRU). A major source of recycled materials would be wastewater and urine collected and processed by the Environmental Control and Life Support System found aboard all spacecraft. Other required nutrients, like iron, can be found in the soil and on the surface of Mars[41]. The briny ice water located in subsurface pockets also contain nutrients that can be harvested, like calcium[40]. However, we will mainly depend on recycling or already-in-use water.

We will use aerogel to artificially create a solid-state greenhouse effect. Our inflatable dorms will be covered with a 2-3 cm-thick layer of silica aerogel. This will allow for the transmittance of sufficient visible light and raising the temperature beneath it perma nently to above the point of melting water, while also being opaque to UV radiation.[45]

2.4.2 Crops to consider

Leafy plants are the more efficient to grow as they can be harvested more often and incorporated into more types of food. We will rely on fast-growing, nutrient-dense plants, or plants that take a little longer yet have edible leaves (like onions). Another excellent choice is potatoes, which, when given an equivalent amount of light, may produce twice as much food as seed crops. Chosen plants should also have the benefit of

Mission to Mars 2023: "Hexa-Hive"

Crop	Growth Period	Nutrients	Calories per 100g
Potato	8 to 12 weeks	Carbohydrates, Vit. C, Vit. B6, Fiber, Protein, Magnesium, Potassium, Calcium	104
Kale	5 to 6 weeks	Carbohydrates, Protein, Fiber, Fat, Potassium, Calcium	50
Spinach	4 to 6 weeks	Vit. A, Vit. C, Vit. K, Folate, Iron, Potassium	23
Lentils	6 to 8 weeks	Protein, Fiber, Fat, Potassium, Iron, Magnesium, Vit. B6, Carbohydrates	353
Onions	9 to 12 weeks	Fiber, Protein, Vit. C, Vit. B6, Potassium	40
Sweet Potato	8 to 12 weeks	Carbohydrates, Fiber, Vit. A, Vit. C, Vit. B6, Protein, Iron, magnesium	86
Tomato	6 to 8 weeks	Carbohydrates, Protein, Potassium	19
Bok Choy	5 to 6 weeks	Carbohydrates, Protein, Vit. K, Vit. A, Vit. C, Folate	13

Table 2.1: Suggested Crops

having the majority of the plant being edible. Spices and nutrition supplements will be brought from earth as fresh food would be cooked before being consumed.

Food will be grown in such a way that it can be picked on-demand. For example, assuming that a meal that contains spinach requires 3 heads, we will plant 45 heads that can be harvested 15 times (the 15 times rule is something we'll follow with all plants). This will enable us to have all of our planted crops continuously. An area of a squared meter of plant-able space is enough to grow around 60 plants. Using this formula, we'll need up to 6 square meters of plant-able area. With all the equipment needed for the hydroponics system to work, we will around 25 squared meters for the system to fully function.

2.4.3 MREs

Processed food (similar to MREs) will be consumed during the 1.5 years spent on mars.. This processed food will just need to be heated at most and will be eaten directly from the bag. Those MREs (Meals Ready to-Eat) will be somewhat similar to those of Earth's, but will be modified to be suitable to Marsonauts.

An MRE packs 1,200 calories into a lightweight package that can withstand a 100-foot airdrop and has a minimum shelf life of three and a half years at 27C. We will have dehydrated food that will need water to re-hydrate and provide a nutritious and tasty meal (similar to instant noodles), MREs weighs around 700 grams.[23] The food pack age will be made out of clear, aluminum oxide-coated plastic laminate.[22] Each would weigh approximately 1kg after it had been modified. It has dimentions of approximately 20x16x5 cm A full-year's supply with 3 meals per day will weigh about 4 metric tonnes. Processed food used by NASA, called the "Safe Haven Food", could also be used as a backup, since it can supply the crew with at least 2000 calories a day, and has at least 2 years or shelf life, hence there should be no issues with that.[9]

There will be a weekly food menu that will repeat each week with the possibility to change once per every 2 months. During the first 6 weeks where almost no greens have grown fully, dependence will be fully on processed food. This means they will consume 3 MREs per day (the same will go for emergencies). After fresh food has grown, Marsonauts will have 2 MREs alongside freshly-made food. Fresh food will be incorporated in the daily diet starting week 4, and the weekly food program will be set on week 5 and will get in effect on week 6 and it will be re-evaluated bimonthly.

ENGINEERING

3.1 HABITAT

As the name suggests our habitat's cen tric chamber is shaped as a hexagonal of 8 meters in diameter and 3 meters high, that is a solid structure made from stain less steel frame and 5mm thick aluminum alloy called since it is lightweight.[2] It has five inflatable chambers that will ex pand into their final size after landing on the Martian surface. (We also accounted for the relative high pressure applied on the chambers walls and thus made it a bit spherical). It has an internal volume of $675 m^3$.

3.1.1 Materials

For astronauts in deep space and on the surface of Mars there are two main compo nents of the radi ation environment: solar particle events (SPEs) and galactic cosmic rays (GCRs). [39] hydrogen, with its charge-to-mass ratio of 1, is the optimal material for slowing incoming ionizing particles. [26] All the protection layer we will be using will be as follows:

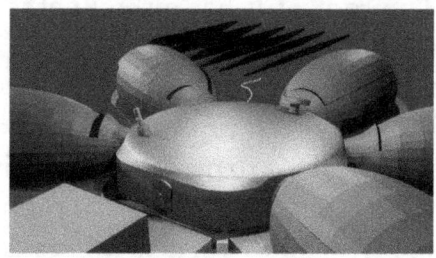

Figure 3.1: Habitat Design

1. BNNTs, enriched with hydrogen (H-BNNT): Of particular interest is the H 10BNNT material is its pliability. Taking advantage of this allows it to be applicable to fabric space-suits as well as inflatable shelters and articulating robotics. [1]
2. PE Thin Film: Is a multi-purpose as the fabrication method imbues it with directional thermal conductance. Given the stringent mass restrictions for any space application.

3. Carbon Nano-Tubes (CNTs): Provides the capability of introducing active elements into fabrics with benefits over traditional metal wires or strips because of their improved mechanical properties, low density, making them a lightweight option, and better resistance to flex fatigue.[42]
4. Aerogel: they have a thermal conductivity of 0.020.44 W/mK and a density of 0.25 g/cm^3.

The main hexagonal structure of the habitat will have an approximate weight of 10 tons and may cost upwards of 13 billion dollars.

3.1.2 Layout

The roof of it has a thickness 5cm to store the needed water for hydroponic planting, general use, and drinking. Which in total, will store 2075 liters of water. Water is recycled using the same techniques used in the ISS. The reason for the water placement is to protect the habitat from radiation, and protect mars from any human contamination. Inside this chamber is the hydroponic hall with it's transparent walls has an are of $30 m^2$. Moving away from the center, one of the Habitat walls has the airlock (so called mud room), it is the main entrance to the habitat with two doors, it is 3m tall, 1.5m wide and 2m high, each of the other hexagonal sides has a door that leads to an inflatable chamber which is 5m height, 8m tall, and 4m wide.

One contains the crew's room, another inflatable chamber will function as a command and system control center, it will have all computers and technologies needed to stay in contact with earth and to monitor and control life supporting systems of the habitat at real time, it will also host the solar batteries (note: each side section has it's life supporting systems (water, gases, electric network) separated from the centric chamber and controlled from the command center so that in case of any hazardous problem occurred in any chamber it does not affect the other chambers.

Another chamber will house the lab, which will contain biological and geological analyzing tools and machines. The last chamber will house the gym room and a salon.

3.2 POWER SYSTEMS

To power the habitat and all its equipment, we will use a two part system for generating the required electricity. NASA did a study back in 2016 about the power needs of a potential Mars habitat, and as their research suggests, it has a peak power need of $15kW$, which the combination of the fission and solar systems can handle that load easily.[27]

First, as the main source of power generation, we will use one of NASA's Kilopower RTGs, with a weight of 1.8 tonnes. It will be able to generate a maximum of $10kW$ continuously.[30] And the best thing is, it is relatively cheap, costing under 20M per system.[31]

As a secondary power generation system, and as a storage medium, we will use a solar array consisting of Rocketlab's IMM-α space solar cells[13], as they are very lightweight (Solar cell mass of $49mg/cm^2$, $77mg/cm^2$ with a $3mm$ cover glass), flexible, and have an efficiency of 32%, while it seems low, as the technology progresses further, the efficiency of similar technologies may reach upwards of 40 43% in the coming years. while no cost estimate has been given by the manufacturer, we did estimate that the whole system would cost upwards of 10M. We will be using a system that has an area of $90m^2$, with a spare of $15m^2$, which will weight about $82kg$ for the panels, an additional $100kg$ for the mounting, and around $20kg$ for wiring. They will be able to produce around $15kW$ if the conditions are right, which is not always the case, so a more reasonable $10kW$ is expected.

Solar panels have a couple of downsides however, they require cleaning every time a sand storm occurs, they don't work during the day, their power outputs drop around 50% during the Martian winter, and they need some kind of storage system to store the excess power they produce during the day.

For the storage of the excess electricity generated either by the solar panels or the RTGs, we will be using a battery pack consisting of 1188 of NanoGraf's INR-18650-M38A Li-ion cylindrical cells in a 33S36P configuration, costing roughly 25 each (estimated price), with a capacity of around $3.8Ah$ and a nominal voltage of $3.55V$ with a weight of 50g per cell[17], we used these cells specifically for their excellent specific weight (Minimum: $777Wh/L$) and the fact that they can handle the rough working conditions of Mars. It will need to be kept inside the habitat as the thermal conditions on the surface of Mars won't allow the batteries to work correctly. This battery pack will have a capacity of $16kWh$ and an over-estimated weight of $100kg$, it can be charged from 0 to 100% during the day just by using the solar panels. They will act as a secondary power source when the output of the Kilopower reactor isn't enough, or there is a problem with it. There will be a special system designed to handle the load in a way where it will use power from the Kilopower system first, then the solar array, then will resort to the batteries.

So the total weight for the power system should equal around $2160kg$ with some overhead just in case.

3.3 AIR

3.3.1 Oxygen Supply
We will use NASA's Mars Oxygen In-Situ Resource Utilization Experiment (MOXIE) for oxygen generation inside the habitat. It is a small, lightweight oxygen generating device that creates

it from the carbon dioxide in the air using an electrolyzer. that weighs 17.1kg and costs 43M.[29]

It can produce up to 10 grams of oxygen per hour, which is equivalent to about 0.4 moles of oxygen. To calculate the number of MOXIE devices needed for an astronaut to breathe for one day, we need to consider the oxygen consumption rate of the astronaut. On average, an adult at rest consumes about 0.25 to 0.35 moles of oxygen per hour.[35] Assuming a consumption rate of 0.3 moles of oxygen per hour, we can calculate the number of MOXIE devices required:

Number of MOXIE devices = O_2 consumption rate / MOXIE O_2 production rate Number of MOXIE devices = 0.3 / 0.4 = 0.75 devices.

Therefore, to meet the oxygen needs of an astronaut for one day, approximately 0.75 MOXIE devices would be needed. And Because our crew consists of 4 people in total, we will be using 3 MOXIE devices to obtain the required amount of oxygen needed. And will also bring 2 spares just in case of these devices breaks, or for generating Oxygen for the oxygen tanks on the suits or the rover.

The weight of this whole system is $86kg$. 3 MOXIE Devices working 24/7 will draw approximately $900W$ in total, which is a worst-case scenario. The output of these devices can be adjusted based on the oxygen needs of the crew -if they are not in the habitat, sleeping, or depending on the oxygen consumption

3.3.2 Earth-Like Atmosphere

As breathing in pure Oxygen is lethal in high concentrations, we will use a system simi lar to NASA's ECLSS (Environmental Control and Life Support System)[28], which will maintain a fixed ratio of Oxygen and Nitrogen in the air, where the oxygen concentration level is 21% and the rest is Nitrogen, and the pressure will stay at 1atm. We will bring with us 305kg Nitrogen to fill the habitat with and 93kg of Oxygen. We will bring with us an extra 30kg of Nitrogen in case of a failure or an emergency, or the small air lost while opening and closing the airlock.

The ECLSS also has a Air Revitalization System that is dedicated to cleaning the cir culating air, this involves removing trace contaminants produced by electronics, plastics and human off-gassing, including carbon dioxide exhaled by the crew during normal res piration.

3.4 WATER

3.4.1 Consumption

The average human drinks around 3.2 to 3.5 liters per day. while this number might change according to their wight, sport schedule and physical activity during the whole day, it is a good estimate for our usage. The Marsonaut excretes around 1.8 liters, and since 95% of urine is water, and NASA has recovered 98% of it in the ISS by using the ECLSS, 93% from total urine will be recovered. This amounts for around 1.68L per day from each Marsonaut. This means that the Marsonaut's daily net consumption of water is around 1.33L.

The entire crew's daily water need will be about 12.8-14.8L with a daily net consumption of 5.304L per day. The hydroponic system requires around 7 liters of water per m^2 of plantable area. Our system has an area of $6m^2$ of plantable area, so we'll need 42L of water for the first fill. The plants also absorb around 12.2L of water but will excrete around 6.1L back to the system. This means that around 6.1L of irrigation water to be added to the system every day.

3.4.2 Collection

On another note, we will also be using the Sabatier reaction, also known as the Sabatier process or Sabatier reaction cycle, which is a chemical reaction that involves the reaction of carbon dioxide (CO2) and hydrogen (H2) to produce methane

(CH4) and water (H2O). The general equation for the Sabatier reaction is:

$$CO2 + 4H2; = CH4 + 2H2O$$

In this reaction, carbon dioxide and hydrogen gas are combined in the presence of a catalyst, usually a metal catalyst such as Nickel (Ni), Ruthenium (Ru), or Cobalt (Co). The reaction is usually carried out at high temperatures (around 300-400C) and moderate pressures, usually in a range of 20-30 bar (2-3 Mpa). Methane, a valuable fuel for rockets and vehicles, has a wide range of uses, including as a fuel for heating, cooking, and electricity generation, etc... The Sabatier reaction is exothermic, meaning it releases energy as heat during the process. The catalyst helps lower the activation energy required for the reaction to occur, increasing the reaction rate, and improving the overall efficiency of the process.

So, by bringing with us a 1.5 tons of hydrogen, we can expect an output of around 6.75 tons of water, which will be more than enough for the whole mission, without relying on underground water and the equipment needed to safely extract, purify and store it.[6]

3.5 VEHICLES

3.5.1 Manned-Rover
We will use NASA's new Mars rover concept. The Mars rover concept vehicle operates on an electric motor, powered by solar panels and a 700-volt battery. The rover separates in the middle with the front area designed for scouting, and is equipped with a radio and navigation provided by the Global Positioning System. The back section serves as a full laboratory which can disconnect for autonomous research.

The Mars concept rover is 8.6m long, 4.2m wide, 3.4m tall and weighs an estimated 2270kg–about the size of a pickup truck. This rover concept vehicle could move as fast as 96 to 112 km/h, but is designed to travel between 16 to 24 km/h during exploration. It has six 1.3-meter-tall, 0.7-inch-wide wheels designed to accommodate the soil, dunes and rocks of Mars.[36] The rover will have a place for the helicopter that can be placed in -like a dome-. The diameter of the circle of the dome will be 1.2m.

Our exploration journeys will last for 3 days at most, so we will take water for the two astronauts in these 3 day, so, 18 liters, which weigh 18kg.We will use6 M-60 cylinder Oxygen tanks that also last for more than 3 days, and have an empty weight of 60kg, we will use the other 2 MOXIE devices to fill them up onve we arrive at Mars.[3] The rover will be improved upon to be able to handle the increased wight and new instruments. It will also have a special mechanism to connect with drill.

According to our mission objectives, the instruments we are going to provide the rover with are:

1. Cameras: MastCam (Mast Camera): to take color images and videos. MAHLI (Mars Hand Lens Imager): it's close-up images reveal the minerals and textures in rock surfaces. MARDI (Mars Descent Imager): to take color shots of the terrain below the rover.
2. Spectrometers: APXS (Alpha Particle X-Ray Spectrometer). When it is placed right next to a rock or soil surface, it uses two kinds of radiation to measure the amounts and types of chemical elements that are present. ChemCam's (Chemistry and Camera) laser, camera and spectrograph work together to identify the chemical and mineral composition of rocks and soils. CheMin (Chemical and Mineralogy), performs chemical analysis of powdered rock samples to identify the types and amounts of different minerals that

are present. SAM (Sample Analysis at Mars) is made up of three different instruments that search for and measure organic chem icals and light elements that are important ingredients potentially associated with life.
3. Radiation Detectors: RAD (Radiation Assessment Detector), helps to prepare for future human exploration of Mars. RAD measures the type and amount of harmful radiation that reaches the Martian surface from the sun and space sources. DAN (Dynamic Albedo Of Neutrons), looks for telltale changes in the way neutrons released from Martian soil that indicate liquid or frozen water exists underground.
4. Environmental Sensors: REMS (Rover Environmental Monitoring Station), and it contains all the weather instruments needed to provide daily and seasonal reports on meteorological conditions around the rover.
5. Atmospheric Sensors: MEDLI (Mars Science Laboratory Entry Descent and Landing Instrument) measured the heating and atmospheric pressure changes that occurred during the descent to help determine the effects on different parts of the spacecraft.[15]

3.5.2 Helicopter

We will use the Ingenuity drone, it has a weight of 1.8kg, 0.5m high, and has a solar array on top of the rotor system that charges six lithium-ion batteries, the solar array charges batteries every one to two Martian day. there are two cameras on Ingenuity: One color with a horizon-facing view for terrain images and one black-and-white for navigation.[34] The purpose of it: To study Mars' climate, To take pictures of Mars' surface, To help determine water locations, To help study geological formations.

It can reach altitudes as high as 18m[16], and has a maximum speed of 19 km/h.[14]

3.6 SUIT

We will be using the Q Suit that will have different parts and technologies from more than one suit to make sure that we have the best performance for Mars' conditions. Each suit wil weigh around 50kg.

3.6.1 Body

The body of the suit will be made out of different layers in order to protect the Marsonauts from external factors, which include:[37]

1. Outer Layer: This needs to be highly protective and resistant to the harsh Mar tian conditions and environment. So, for this layer we will use a mixture of three materials which are Orthofabric-Teflon/Nomex/Kevlar and that will provide a per fect protection against temperature and radiation.
2. Insulation Layer: Because of the extremely low temperature, we need to keep astronauts warm throughout their exploration. For this layer we will use Aerogel and Aluminized Mylar. and the light weight of this materials will provide excellent thermal insulation.
3. Pressure Layer: As mars has a thin atmosphere, we will need to provide a higher internal pressure to let the Marstronauts breathe comfortably. We will use Polyurethane coated fabrics—like Nylon and Polyester-.

The suit will also house different systems and technologies that will make them safer and more reliable. A Life Support System; which will provide oxygen and remove carbon diox ide. We will use the same system of the Z2 spacesuit. A Liquid Cooling and Ventilation Garment (LCVG); we will use the LCVG of xEMU. It will have spandex/water/ethyl vinyl acetate.

Cooling is required therefore water is circulated through the LCVG tubing to remove excess body heat.[33]

3.6.2 Accessories
1. Helmet: It will be isolated from the body, and we will use a SpaceX's helmet[12] and add some technologies like an AR (Augmented Reality) view. We will be using the same materials of the body in addition to fiberglass.
2. Gloves: Since each SpaceX suit is tailor-made, our best option is to use SpaceX's gloves. They should be flexible to let the astronaut's hands and fingers move easily.[11]
3. Miscellaneous: Each suit will be equipped with a smart watch with certain tech nologies to measure the astronaut's vital capabilities (blood pressure, remaining oxygen in the tank, the temperature inside and outside the suit, the pressure inside the suit...).

HUMAN OPERATIONS

4.1 CREW

For our mission to Mars, there will be four Marsonauts with different specialties.

4.1.1 Skills

1. IT Engineer: Studies everything related to the manufacturing, construction, preparation, and maintenance of all vehicles, is also responsible for all technol ogy support services, they require the ability to think quickly and solve problems under pressure. They should be familiar with all the equipment onboard the habitat and the various instruments and the right ways to fix each of them.
2. Astrobiologist/Botanist: Collects and analyzes all the information and knowl edge that helps to better understand

the chance of discovery life on Mars, they also carry out scientific experiments to obtain the largest amount of confirmed infor mation and knowledge. He is also responsible for maintaining the health and good growth of cultivated plants and for how to increase the amount of production to provide food for the astronauts.
3. Doctor (MD)/Therapist: Takes care of the astronauts' health and makes sure everything is under control, and prevent or control the exposure of an astronaut to threats to their health. A part of his mission is to also take care of the mental health of his crewmates, support their morale, and keep them away from frustration and depression.
4. Geologist/Astrophysicist: Measures and interprets data to establish or confirm scientific theories and laws. Studies the structure of the plant, the rocks that make it up, and the processes that occur on it over time. which will help in undercovering new scientific theories.

The Commander of this mission will be the Doctor, because they will have the best knowledge on how to solve problems that may arise in between the crew members, and because they are a psychologist, they will have a good understanding on how the human brain works and will be the best member to handle difficult situation and making the optimal decisions.

4.1.2 Schedule

The crew should be able to handle the extreme stress and home-sickness that they will suffer, due to them being away from home for a long time. In Table 4.1, we made a suggested time schedule for the crew members, but this is rather flexible and can be changed on the fly depending on what is important.

Throughout the mission, there will be tasks that the team will need to do, like conducting research, and bi-weekly rover exploration and data collection expeditions.

4.1.3 Training
For our crew, they will undergo intense training around 6 months before the mission launch date.

Task	Duration
Breakfast	30 minutes
Morning workout	90 minutes
Lunch	30 minutes
Break/Nap time	30 minutes
Chores/Work	240 minutes
Dinner	30 minutes
Entertainment/Free time	120 minutes
Miscellaneous	150 minutes
Sleep	510 minutes

Table 4.1: Time Schedule

Marsonauts onboard will also need at least 1.5 hours of workouts, and will have time for themselves.

4.2 COMMUNICATION

4.2.1 Deep Space Network
For the communication with earth we chose to communicate via the DSN system (Deep Space Network), which is NASA's international array of giant radio antennas that sup ports interplanetary spacecraft missions, plus a few that orbit Earth. The DSN also provides radar and radio astronomy observations that improve our understanding of the solar system and the larger universe.

It consist of The deep-space communications facilities placed approximately 120 degrees apart around the Earth: at

Goldstone, in California's Mojave Desert; near Madrid, Spain; and near Canberra, Australia. This strategic placement permits constant observation of spacecraft as the Earth rotates on its own axis.[5]

4.2.2 Data Rate

The data rate direct-to-Earth varies from about 500 bits per second to 32,000 bits per second (roughly half as fast as a standard home modem). The data rate to the Mars Re connaissance Orbiter is selected automatically and continuously during communications and can be as high as 2 million bits per second. The data rate to the Odyssey orbiter is a selectable 128,000 or 256,000 bits per second (4-8 times faster than a home modem). An orbiter passes over the antenna and is in the vicinity of the sky to communicate with the antenna for about eight minutes at a time, per sol. In that time, between 100 and 250 megabits of data can be transmitted to an orbiter. That same 250 megabits would take up to 20 hours to transmit direct to Earth! The antenna can only transmit direct to-Earth for a few hours a day due to power limitations or conflicts with other planned activities, even though Earth may be in view much longer.

It generally takes about 5 to 20 minutes for a radio signal to travel the distance be tween Mars and Earth, depending on planet positions. Using orbiters to relay messages is beneficial because they are much closer to Perseverance than the DSN antennas on Earth.

4.2.3 Frequency Bands

The antenna communicates with the orbiters and the DSN through radio waves. They communicate with each other through X-band, which are radio waves at a much higher frequency than radio waves used for FM stations.

The radio waves to and from the antenna are sent through the orbiters using UHF (Ultra High Frequency–typically around 400 Megahertz) antennas, which are close-range antennas that are like walkie-talkies compared to the long range of low-gain and high-gain antennas. All three orbiters active at Mars – NASA's Mars Odyssey and Mars Reconnaissance Orbiter and the European Space Agency's Mars Express – were at positions where they could receive transmissions from the Mars Science Laboratory spacecraft.

4.3 SAFETY

4.3.1 Physical Factors

Radiation Effects:
Exposure of radiation on Earth has been observed to increase the risk of cancer and degenerative diseases, such as heart disease and cataracts. Health risks for astronauts from radiation exposure in space are mainly driven by long-term impacts.

Different Gravity Fields Effects:
Transitioning from one gravity field to another is trickier than it sounds. It affects spatial orientation, head-eye and hand-eye coordination, balance, and locomotion, with some crew members experiencing space motion sickness. When shifting from weightlessness to gravity, astronauts may experience post-flight orthostatic intolerance where they are unable to maintain their blood pressure when standing up, which can lead to lightheadedness and fainting.

NASA has learned that without Earth's gravity affecting the human body, weight bearing bones lose on average 1% to 1.5% of mineral density per month during spaceflight. After returning to Earth, bone loss might not be completely corrected by rehabilitation; however, their risk for fracture is not higher without the proper diet and exercise routine.

4.3.2 Psychological Factors

Isolation and Confinement:

The Marsonauts will live in an isolated and confined environment, with only a few other people. Additionally, crews will likely be international and multi-cultural, making cross-cultural sensitivity and team dynamics paramount to mission success. their internal biological clocks, or circadian rhythm, might also be altered by factors like different day and night cycles, a small and noisy environment, the stress of prolonged isolation and confinement, and a 37-minute extended day on Mars. It is important to prepare for the fatigue astronauts may experience during mission, given that there will be times with heavy workloads and shifting schedules. To prevent crew boredom.[44]

Cognitive Effects:

Anxiety symptoms have been reported and linked to negative interpersonal inter actions, as well. Indeed, the heterogeneity of the space crew in terms of size, ethnic background, languages and roles may result in tension and communication issues among the crew members, which is vital to the success of the mission. Prolonged isolation from loved ones and routine on Earth also pose a risk for the mental well being of Marsonauts. This may relate to reduced stimulation, or feeling unable to assist with family emergencies back on Earth. Evidence from space analogues would also suggest that such factors may be responsible for a wide range of symptoms, including fatigue, altered circadian rhythms, sleep disturbance and neurocognitive impairments.[38]

4.3.3 Treatment and Supplements

For the Radiation Effects:

The habitat and the suit that the Marsonauts are going to have a radiation shielding system; so their bodies will be protected from these radiation doses. In addition to the Potassium iodide (KI) salt doses that are effective in the protection from thyroid cancer (which may be caused by the radiation),[24] in this case each mar sonaut will take 130 mg-KI dosages per day.[21]

For the Difference in the Gravity Fields:
We will use three exercising machines:1- Treadmill Walking Running Machine with two bonds and a belt to be stuck to the ground; it weighs 23kg, price 267 and consume 800 Watts power.[10] 2- EVOLVE–Red Spin Bike Exercise Bike it also will be provided with bones and a belt Weight 11kg, price 155 and it is battery powered (2 AA batteries required).[20] 3- ROCKY which is an ultra-compact, lightweight exercise device that meets the exercise and medical requirements needed it weigh approximately 10kg.[8]

To Minimize Long Term Psychological Effects: VR devices for each Mar sonaut will be used to offer a better experience for family communication and an earth environment simulation room to give a psychological relief. We will also bring with us anti-depression medication, specifically Serotonin and Norepinephrine Re uptake Inhibitors (SNRIs), because of minimal side effects, and it good treatment efficiency.[7]

NASA scientists are using devices, such as actigraphy, that help assess and improve sleep and alertness by recording how much people move and how much ambient light is around them. New lighting, spurred by the development of Light-Emitting Diode (LED) technology, is used on the space station to help align astronaut's circadian rhythms and to improve sleep, alertness, and performance.

4.4 ENTERTAINMENT

To keep the morale high and help the crew with their mental heath, and help them not get bored all the time and lose motivation and drive to keep going, we have set aside 2 hours daily for their personal needs and entertainment purposes.

We will provide them with all sorts of thing that will keep them entertained, like having a VR setup, gaming computers, a small library, chess or any tabletop game that they will want to bring with them and fun daily challenges that crew members can take on that will be chosen by random each morning.

Each crew member also has a 250kg of mass for them to bring their personal belongings that aren't included in the original mission equipment. They can bring games, souvenirs, or anything that will make them happy and help boost the morale of the whole team.

COST

Our main source of funding for this mission will be taking sponsors for this mission. They will have their brand on shirts and around the main hall of the habitat. They will also be talked about in official press conferences and this will be a huge advertisement deal for any brand or company willing to pay up the the hefty price for the first manned-mission to Mars.

We could also receive funding from organizations around the world willing to help in order to test their equipment, conduct specialized research or just brig stuff to and from Mars!

Name	Count	Wt (Kg)	Price (Mil USD)
Habitat	1	10000	13000
General Equipment N/A	1000	10	
Suit	5	250	500
Rover	1	2330	3000

Name	Count	Wt (Kg)	Price (Mil USD)
Helicopter	1	2	80
Power System 1	2160	31	
Oxygen System 5	514	215	
Water System 1		1600	0.01
Saftey Equipment N/A	44	0.01	
MREs	4760	4760	0.1
Clothes	273	1200	0.1
Personal Belongings N/A	1000	N/A	
Total	26016	16836.	22

Table 5.1: Prices and Weights

REFERENCES

1. Advanced thermal, radiation, and dust protection for spacesuits and space systems. https://ttu-ir.tdl.org/handle/2346/86463.
2. Aluminium alloys in space applications: A short report. https://www.akademiabaru.com/submit/index.php/araset/article/view/1956.
3. Aluminum oxygen cylinder size m-60—cga540 valve & carry handle. https://www.liveactionsafety.com/aluminum-oxygen-cylinder-size-m-60-cga540-valve-carry-handle/.
4. Caltech's murray lab 3d map of mars. https://murray-lab.caltech.edu/CTX/V01/SceneView/MurrayLabCTXmosaic.html.

5. Communications with earth – mission. https://mars.nasa.gov/msl/mission/ communications.
6. Compact, lightweight adsorber and sabatier reactor for co2 capture and reduction for consumable and propellant production. https://ntrs.nasa.gov/citations/20120015003.
7. Depression medicines. https://www.fda.gov/consumers/free-publications-women/depression-medicines.
8. Exercise device for orion to pack powerful punch.
9. Food for space flight. http://www.nasa.gov/audience/forstudents/ postsecondary/features/F_Food_for_Space_Flight.html.
10. Goplus 2 in 1 folding treadmill, 2.25hp superfit under desk electric treadmill, installation-free with blue tooth speaker, remote control, app control and led display, walking jogging for home office.
11. How spacex mastered space suits. https://primalnebula.com/ how-spacex-mastered-space-suits/.
12. How spacex's sleek spacesuit changes astronaut fashion from the space shuttle era. https://www.space.com/spacex-crew-dragon-spacesuits-explained.html.
13. Imm-alpha space solar cell. https://www.rocketlabusa.com/assets/Uploads/ RL-SolAero-Data-Sheet-IMM-Alpha.pdf.
14. Ingenuity mars helicopter's record-breaking flight. https://mars.nasa.gov/ resources/26770/ingenuity-mars-helicopters-record-breaking-flight.
15. Mars curiosity rover instruments. https://mars.nasa.gov/msl/spacecraft/ instruments/summary.
16. Mars helicopter–nasa. https://mars.nasa.gov/technology/helicopter/.

17. Nanograf 18650-ng38. https://www.nanograf.com/18650.
18. Nasa ames research center trajectory browser. https://trajbrowser.arc.nasa. gov/index.php.
19. Planetary names. https://planetarynames.wr.usgs.gov/Feature/3893.
20. Pooboo magnetic exercise bike stationary, indoor cycling bike with built-in bluetooth sensor compatible with exercise bike apps& ipad mount, comfortable seat and slant board, silent belt drive, 350lbs weight capacity.
21. Potassium iodide (ki) and radiation emergencies: Fact sheet. https://www.health. ny.gov/environmental/radiological/potassium_iodide/fact_sheet.htm.
22. Space food packaging: A review of its past, present and future materials and tech nologies. https://onlinelibrary.wiley.com/doi/10.1002/pts.2752.
23. The Science Behind Feeding a Mission to Mars -insidescience.org. https://www. insidescience.org/news/science-behind-feeding-mission-mars.
24. Thyroid cancer risk factors — risk factors for thyroid cancer. https: //www.cancer.org/cancer/types/thyroid-cancer/causes-risks-prevention/ risk-factors.html.
25. A water ice map for mars. https://www.jpl.nasa.gov/images/ pia23514-a-water-ice-map-for-mars.
26. Space radiation cancer risk projections and uncertainties–2010. https://ntrs. nasa.gov/citations/20130001648, Jul 2010.
27. Surface power for mars. https://ntrs.nasa.gov/citations/20160014032/, Jul 2016.
28. Environmental control and life support system (eclss) fact sheet. https://www. nasa.gov/sites/default/files/atoms/files/g-281237_eclss_0.pdf, Jul 2017.

29. Nasa's 2020 mars project report. https://oig.nasa.gov/docs/IG-17-009.pdf, Jan 2017.
30. Nasa's kilopower reactor development and the path to higher power missions. https: //ntrs.nasa.gov/citations/20170002010/, Jul 2017.
31. Kilopower press conference. https://www.nasa.gov/sites/default/files/ atoms/files/kilopower_media_event_charts_16x9_final.pdf, Feb 2018.
32. Gis analysis of promising landing sites for manned flight to mars. https://www.e3s-conferences.org/articles/e3sconf/abs/2019/64/e3sconf_ catpid18_02004/e3sconf_catpid18_02004.html, Jul 2019.
33. Nasa advanced space suit pressure garment system status and development priorities 2022. https://ntrs.nasa.gov/citations/20220009207, Jul 2022.
34. Ingenuity landing press kit – quick facts. http://www.jpl.nasa.gov/news/press_ kits/ingenuity/landing/quick_facts/, Jul 2023.
35. Mars oxygen in-situ resource utilization experiment (moxie)–nasa. https://mars. nasa.gov/mars2020/spacecraft/instruments/moxie/, Jul 2023.
36. Mars rover helps visitor complex kick off new exhibit. http://www.nasa.gov/ feature/mars-rover-to-help-visitor-complex-kick-off-new-exhibit, Jul 2023.
37. and. The space shuttle extravehicular mobility unit (emu). http://www.nasa.gov/ stem-ed-resources/sfs-extravehicular-mobility-unit.html.
38. Alessandro Arone, Tea Ivaldi, Elisabetta Parra, Walter Flamini, Donatella Marazziti, and Konstantin Loganovsky. The burden of space exploration on the mental health of astronauts: A narrative review. *Clinical Neuropsychiatry*, 18(5):237–246, November 2021.

39. Francis A. Cucinotta and Marco Durante. Physical basis of radiation protection in space travel. 83(4):1245–1281, Dec 2011.
40. Erik Fischer, Germ´an M. Mart´ınez, Harvey M. Elliott, and Nilton O. Renn´o. Ex perimental evidence for the formation of liquid saline water on mars. *Geophysical Research Letters*, 41(13):4456–4462, July 2014.
41. Linda Herridge. Nasa plant researchers explore question of deep-space food crops. http://www.nasa.gov/feature/nasa-plant-researchers-explore-question-of-deep-space-food-crops, Feb 2016.
42. Kavya K. Manyapu, Pablo De Leon, Leora Peltz, James R. Gaier, and Deborah Waters. Proof of concept demonstration of novel technologies for lunar spacesuit dust mitigation. *Acta Astronautica*, 137:472–481, 2017.
43. NASA. Nasa seeks ideas for where on mars the next giant leap will take place. http://www.nasa.gov/journeytomars/mars-exploration-zones.
44. NASA. What happens to the human body in space? http://www.nasa.gov/hrp/ bodyinspace.
45. R. Wordsworth, L. Kerber, and C. Cockell. Enabling martian habitability with silica aerogel via the solid-state greenhouse effect. *Nature Astronomy*, 3(10):898–903, July 2019.

www.ingramcontent.com/pod-product-compliance
Lightning Source LLC
LaVergne TN
LVHW010146070526
838199LV00062B/4274